THE CLASS STRUCTURE OF
THE ADVANCED SOCIETIES

D0358222

THE CLASS STRUCTURE OF
THE ADVANCED SOCIETIES

Anthony Giddens

Fellow of King's College and
Lecturer in Sociology,
University of Cambridge

HUTCHINSON
London Melbourne Sydney Auckland Johannesburg

Hutchinson Education

An imprint of Century Hutchinson Ltd

62–65 Chandos Place, London, WC2N 4NW

Century Hutchinson Publishing Group (Australia) Pty Ltd
16–22 Church Street, Hawthorn, Melbourne, Victoria 3122

Century Hutchinson Group (NZ) Ltd
32–34 View Road, PO Box 40–086, Glenfield, Auckland 10

Century Hutchinson Group (SA) (Pty) Ltd
PO Box 337, Bergvlei 2012, South Africa

First published 1973
Reprinted 1974, 1977, 1978
Second edition 1981
Reprinted 1983, 1986

Printed and bound in Great Britain by
Anchor Brendon Ltd, Tiptree, Essex

British Library Cataloguing in Publication Data
Giddens, Anthony
   The class structure of the advanced societies. –
   2nd ed.
   1. Social classes
   I. Title
   301.44′09172′2   HT609

ISBN 0 09 141891 7 paper

CONTENTS

PREFACE

The preface to a book is always composed last of all, and is normally the place where the author, surveying the results of his labours, tells the reader about the volume he would have written if only he had been able to overcome the manifest inadequacies of the work now in front of him. I shall not try to elicit sympathy in this way, and rather than seeking to apologise for the failings of this work (of which I am certainly conscious), I shall merely indicate some of the objectives I initially set out to accomplish, in the hope that this will help the reader to pick his way through the text as painlessly as possible. Anyone who has the temerity to write about the theory of social class is immediately plunged into controversy by the very way he approaches his subject—by the materials he chooses to discuss and by what he ignores, for no study in this field can refer to more than a small selection from the almost unending literature which exists on the topic. I should therefore perhaps begin by underlining the obvious: that this book is firmly grounded in the European tradition of class theory. What I have tried to do, in a sense, is to use concepts drawn from this tradition in order to turn it back against itself, and thereby to work out a new framework for the analysis of what I think remain the central problem-areas of sociology. I have quite deliberately made little allusion to the large body of writings by American authors dealing with 'stratification'—even where they employ the term 'class'. It will become apparent to those who read on that my concerns are for the most part quite different from theirs.

For some while, as it is presented in the works of non-Marxist sociologists at least, the concept of class seems to have become enveloped with a sort of atmosphere of seedy decay. Although they are unwilling or unable to abandon the notion altogether, many such writers are dissatisfied with it as an instrument of sociological analysis, and feel that, like Victorian architecture, whatever appeal it might once have had has disappeared with the passing of the era which created it. Without at all wishing to push the architectural analogy any further, I should emphasise that I believe this dis-illusionment with the concept of class to be one which rests on false premises; if the concept cannot accomplish all that is asked of it today, the reason is that those who first brought the notion to the forefront of social theory—including Marx—have placed demands upon it which it could not possibly bear, not that it has been made obsolete by the social changes which have intervened since the nineteenth century. The observation is frequently made that, as so much effort has been expended since Marx to reformulate the concept of class, any further endeavour along these lines is inevitably destined only to increase the confusion which already exists in its use. When, however, I began a systematic analysis of the literature of fairly recent origin upon the theory of class structure, I was struck by its very sparseness—not in terms of its numerical strength, but in terms of its analytical penetration. Confusion and ambiguity in the use of the term 'class' are abundantly evident; but distinctive and considered attempts to revise the *theory* of class upon a broad scale are few indeed. I have chosen to discuss only three such attempts in detail: those involved in the writings of Dahrendorf, Aron and Ossowski. The choice is admittedly a somewhat arbitrary one, and I have treated their ideas as representative of much of the theoretical literature in the field—although Ossowski's *Class Structure in the Social Consciousness* to some extent stands apart from the works of the others as a more novel enterprise. With the exception of Max Weber, whose writings constitute one of the main points of reference of the whole book, I have avoided direct discussion of the works of earlier generations of critics of Marx. I have also expressly refrained from entering into any lengthy analyses of the Marxist literature on social class, apart from Marx's work itself. This is not because I think that this literature has made no substantial contributions to class theory. While I do in fact consider that most Marxist writing has made pitifully few contributions of this sort, the works of some recent Marxist authors seem to me both significant and valuable. If I have not discussed these in detail, it is because my disagreements with them are built into the major propositions which I have developed, and these emerge clearly enough at the various stages of my argument.

The chapters in the book separate into five main parts, although

of course the same themes run through all of them. Chapters 1–4 are
preparatory in character, and cover specific aspects of existing
theories of class structure. Rather than merging Chapters 3 and 4,
as I was originally inclined to do, I have offered in the first of these a
brief, unvarnished account of the ideas of the three relatively recent
'Marx-critics' mentioned above, reserving an evaluation of these for
the subsequent chapter. Thus the reader who is already familiar
with the writings of these authors can skip Chapter 3 altogether
without in any way losing the thread of the discussion. In Chapters
5, 6 and 7, I set out a new analysis of class theory, moving on in
succeeding chapters to apply some of the concepts established
therein, first to the capitalist and then to the state socialist societies.
Finally, two summary chapters bring together the main conclusions
which I wish to draw from what went before.

I should like to thank Percy Cohen, Geoffrey Hawthorn, David
Lockwood, Gavin Mackenzie and Gian Poggi, all of whom made
extremely perceptive and useful comments upon an initial draft of
the manuscript. I owe a lot to various conversations over the past
two years with Geoffrey Ingham, Michael Mann, Ali Rattansi, and
Philip Stanworth. I also wish to express my gratitude to Bogdan
Szajkowski, for help with the translations from Polish and Russian;
to Ronald Dore, for advice on Japanese source materials; and to
Lesley Bower for many kinds of administrative assistance.

A.G.

Cambridge

INTRODUCTION

We are told that modern sociology is in a condition of crisis. Such a view has been expounded at considerable length by Gouldner, concerning academic or 'Western' sociology, and with more economy by Birnbaum, writing of contemporary Marxist social thought.[1] Now sociologists are chronically subject to self-doubt and we might ask whether there is indeed anything unusual about the present situation of controversy or sociological *accidie*. The answer, I think, is that there is. The 'crisis'—a trite and unsatisfactory term in itself—in contemporary sociology is symptomatic of the fact that we stand at an important phase of transition in social theory. In broad outline, the origins of the current situation are not at all difficult to discern. Two, connected, sets of factors are involved. One is to be found in the events which, in the past few years, have disrupted the pattern of 'consensus politics' in the capitalist societies: the increase in strike levels in certain countries, the struggles in France in 1968, and the eruption of student protest movements. To these may be added the conflicts which have arisen within the socialist world, culminating in the Soviet invasion of Czechoslovakia. The second factor is the manifest poverty of the dominant forms of theory in sociology in accounting for these events. In academic sociology, structural-functionalism and its main interpretative support, theories of 'the end of ideology', appear blank and barren in the face of a new upsurge of social and political conflict in the West. But Marxism, especially as transmuted into the official ideology of state socialism, seems equally inept when confronted with the events of the recent past.

We may note four main responses, on the level of theory, to these

1. Superior figures refer to bibliographical references and notes, pp. 295–316.

circumstances: each represents an attempt to depart from the premises involved in structural-functionalism, but each also has a tie with Marxist thought. The first seeks either to replace, or to complement, structural-functionalism with 'conflict theory' (referred to by Dahrendorf as 'coercion theory'). This approach actually has its origins in the middle 1950s, and originated purely as an intellectual critique of structural-functionalism: but it has received some considerable impetus to its popularity in the last decade. In the hands of Dahrendorf, Lockwood and Rex, it was formulated as a response to what these authors perceived to be unacceptable assumptions built into structural-functionalism, as represented in the works of Talcott Parsons. According to this standpoint, Parsons' writings give an unsatisfactory account of the origins of social 'order', because they fail to grapple with the significance of oppositions of interest generated by sectional divisions within society as a whole: 'integration theory' ('consensus' or 'value theory') needs to be complemented or interlaced with 'conflict theory', such as may be derived from aspects of Marx's work.[2] The difficulties inherent in this sort of standpoint are many, and I shall not discuss them here. It must suffice to point out that those who have advocated it share major points in common with the type of theoretical position which they set out to attack. 'Conflict theory', I think, is the other side of the structural-functionalist coin, and is characterised by most of the same limitations.

A second mode of approach is one which has sometimes been closely linked with 'conflict theory', but which is in substance quite distinct from it. This is the view which seeks to contrast 'conservative' with 'radical' sociology. The point of departure here is ideological rather than sociological; since, as it is argued, most academic sociology, and in particular structural-functional theory, is tied to a 'conservative' ideological standpoint, its biases and weaknesses can be exposed by a sociological perspective informed by a 'radical' position. This approach faces severe epistemological problems, since it is not at all clear where 'radical sociology' stands in relation to its subject-matter. Marxism has always encountered epistemological difficulties in seeking to sustain the claim to be both an empirically verified body of theory and a moral guide to political action: hence its ever-present tendency to dissolve into straightforward positivism, or alternatively into ethical relativism—a tendency most vividly illustrated in the clash between Kautsky and Bernstein. But the difficulties raised by the conception of 'conservative' versus 'radical' sociology are even more pronounced, since the implication is that there is not, as in Marxism, one supposedly scientifically validated interpretation of social reality, but that there are two competing ideological ones.[3]

It is the recognition of such problems which has helped to prompt a third response to the current travails of sociology, which finds the remedy in a narcissistic application of the sociology of knowledge.[4] Like the attempt to construct a 'radical sociology', this constitutes a protest against the proposition, considered by most critics to be intrinsic to structural-functionalism, that social theory and sociological research are 'neutral' in respect of the social phenomena they set out to interpret or explain. Undoubtedly it is valuable and fruitful (as I shall further emphasise below) to examine the history of social thought in terms of the social and political contexts which have generated the principal traditions or modes of social theory. But it needs no special perspicacity to see the *petitio principii* involved in the notion that such an exercise can in itself produce a new theoretical framework for sociology; the transmutation of sociology into the sociology of knowledge is a logically impossible endeavour.

Finally, the relatively sudden demise of structural-functionalism has stimulated a resurgence of a crude voluntarism, linked to what I would call a retreat from institutional analysis.[5] The leading forms of social theory, it is asserted, have treated man as *homo sociologicus*, the creature rather than the creator of society, as a passive recipient of social influences rather than as an active, willing agent who injects meaning into an otherwise featureless moral universe. If the charge is in some degree warranted, the inferences which are drawn from it—that the most vital aspects of social existence are those relating to the triviata of 'everyday life', whereby the individual shapes his phenomenal experience of social reality—easily rationalise a withdrawal from basic issues involved in the study of macro-structural social forms and social processes. In so far as this is the case, we simply abandon the problems which have always been the major stimulus to the sociological imagination. Something of a similar observation can be made about the emphases contained in the works of certain recent Marxist writers. The contemporary revival of Marxist scholarship in the West, and the rehabilitation of such authors as Lukács and Korsch, who in an earlier generation questioned the determinism of 'official' Marxism, has had many welcome consequences. In conjunction with the belated assimilation of the significance of Marx's early writings for the interpretation of *Capital* and other later works, it has given us a full appreciation of both the symmetry and the subtlety of Marx's thought. But it has also produced a form of 'Marxism' which, relying almost wholly upon ideas selectively drawn from Marx's youthful works, has

introduced a voluntarism which is as one-sided and defective as that
advocated in some contemporary streams of academic social
theory.[6]

I do not believe that any of these four critical responses to
structural-functionalism supplies what is most needed at the present
juncture—however important their contributions may be to other
basic problems in sociology. The origins of the intellectual limitations
of structural-functionalism, I think, have to be traced much further
back than is ordinarily assumed.[7] Two general views of the main
phases in the evolution of social thought in the nineteenth and early
twentieth centuries can be distinguished, one associated with
academic sociology, the other with Marxism. Each sees a major
watershed, a 'great divide' in this evolution.[8] The most common
standpoint adopted by the former is that stated, with great technical
sophistication, in Parsons' *The Structure of Social Action*, and much
more crudely by many subsequent writers. The 'great divide' in the
history of social thought, according to this conception, occurs in the
works of those authors—notably Durkheim and Max Weber—
whose most characteristic ideas were elaborated in the period
1890–1920. More specifically, these thinkers, so it is presumed,
broke away from the ideologically inspired, speculative philosophy
of history which distinguished the writings of their predecessors:
sociology became established as an empirically grounded, scientifically rigorous field of study, on a par with already established professional disciplines. Those who have taken this standpoint have
generally ignored, as Parsons did in his path-breaking work, the
social and political events which formed the environment in which
writers such as Durkheim and Weber elaborated their contributions
to sociology.[9] The watershed in the progress of social thought is
treated as an intellectual advance created by the logical and empirical
analysis of the basic parameters of sociological method.

The orthodox Marxist interpretation—again, advanced with
greater or lesser degrees of subtlety—is inevitably quite different,
and does tend to look to the social background in which the writings
of the 1890–1920 generation were produced, in assessing their
significance. According to this viewpoint, of course, the watershed
which divides ideology and philosophy from science in man's understanding of his society is to be found in the work of Marx. The
writings of the so-called 'founders' of modern sociology are taken to
represent a bourgeois rejoinder to Marx: in social terms, an intellectual defence of capitalism in the face of the threat posed by the
growth of revolutionary Marxist parties at the turn of the century.
Far from being the first contributions to a newly scientific sociology,

the works of Durkheim, Weber and their contemporaries constitute
a retrenchment of bourgeois ideology.

I do not wish to discuss here the relative merits of these competing
views, but merely to point out their implications for the identification
of the tasks with which contemporary social theory should be concerned. Those who have accepted the position most common in
academic sociology, derived from or comparable to that set out by
Parsons, have essentially severed social theory from the concerns
which originally (that is to say, throughout the nineteenth and early
twentieth centuries, not only in the 1890–1920 period) inspired all
of the most prominent social thinkers—the nature of the transformation which destroyed 'traditional' society and created a new
'modern' order. Parsons' discussion of Pareto, Durkheim and
Weber in *The Structure of Social Action*, for example, almost completely obliterates this overriding concern, by interpreting their
work as an immanent statement of an emerging universal framework
of sociological method and theory. The creation of an abstract
'general theory' is, then, construed as the basic goal to be striven for
in sociology. How far such an objective is feasible is not at issue;
what is important is that the whole weight of emphasis has become
directed away from the analysis of development. It has become
implicitly accepted that the fundamental characteristics of 'traditional'
(that is, 'pre-industrial') society and of 'modern' society are *known*.
Thus, if a place is allowed for the study of 'development', it is in
examining the processes whereby a given society makes the movement from one type to the other. And this is what 'development'
now *means* in sociological discourse. 'Underdeveloped' countries are
contrasted to 'developed' ones, as though social change stops when
a society becomes industrialised—whereas industrial societies
unquestionably introduce a rate of social change previously unparalleled in history.

At first sight, it would appear as though this could not be so with
Marxism: for Marx always placed emphasis above all upon the
unfolding of human potentialities through social development, and
upon history as the key to the understanding of man's life in society.
But Marxism has become blinkered by its own conception of the
'great divide'. For it is only those who have sought to attack the
official orthodoxy who have really tried to treat Marxism as a
method, rather than as an established and incontrovertible set of
propositions about class society in general, and about capitalism in
particular. Confronted with the plain fact that the processes of
change within capitalism since Marx's lifetime have not universally
produced an ever-gathering momentum towards revolutionary

change, the response of Marxism has been to look for the explanation of this outside of capitalist society itself—by reference to the theory of imperialism. If the transcendence of the capitalist order has not been achieved, it is not because of factors intrinsic to the development of capitalism since the nineteenth century, but is a result of the transference of class conflict to the relationship between the capitalist societies and the 'underdeveloped' world; through the exploitation of the non-industrialised countries, the effects of class exploitation within capitalist society have been blunted or deflected. Whatever the elements of validity in such a view, its effects have again been, as in academic sociology, to focus attention almost wholly upon liberation struggles in 'Third World' countries. The consequence is that, at least until very recently, there has been an almost complete sterility in orthodox Marxist interpretations of the development of capitalism over the seventy years of this century. Marxism is even less equipped to deal adequately with the development of those societies in which it itself reigns as the chief principle of political legitimation.

The dominant trends within academic sociology, and the general cast of Marxist social thought, therefore, have each acted to close off any significant progress in our understanding of the problems which stimulated the first great contributions to modern social theory. If sociology is in a period of transition, it is because the main orientation of social theory over the past three decades has not given us adequate means to undertake the analysis of these problems. Bland assertions of the 'end of ideology', coupled with ill-considered use of the blanket term 'industrial society', have passed for concrete analysis in academic sociology, particularly in the United States. Orthodox Marxism, on the other hand, is like the blind man who insists that he has not lost his sight, even while blundering into the furniture and unable to make sense of his surroundings.

The crisis of sociology is also a crisis of socialism, in its two major forms, Marxism and social democracy. While I shall not discuss the merits of these, in any direct sense, as forms of political philosophy, I believe that the analyses given in this book are of immediate relevance to their claims as normative guides to political action. It is also as well to emphasise that this work is in no sense to be seen as an overall interpretation of the development of the advanced societies; nor does it attempt a sustained analysis of the modern state. As an investigation of the problem of class structure, it examines only certain aspects of these phenomena, and draws upon a long tradition of studies of class theory in order to do so. Some of the propositions I shall set out to establish are conventional and already broadly accepted, both by those of a non-Marxist persuasion and by Marxists; other assertions which the book contains will certainly be regarded as heretical by either or both schools of thought.

I make no bones about declaring that new departures are needed in contemporary social theory and yet seeking to inquire into what is a long-standing problem in sociology—one might say, *the* problem in sociology:[10] the question of classes and class conflict. The logic of such a procedure is surely self-evident. But I might stress that this book should not be regarded as the latest in a well-populated line of attempts to 'refute' Marx by showing how inappropriate his ideas are to an industrial order which has progressed far beyond nineteenth-century capitalism. I do believe however that, in a fundamental sense, in the industrialised third of the world, we live in a society which is both 'post-Marxist' and 'post-bourgeois', although not in a society which is 'post-capitalist', let alone 'post-industrial'.

In order to facilitate the reading of what is sometimes a closely textured work, I shall mention here some of the main theorems proposed in the book.

1. Problems of class theory, and of the interpretation of the development of the advanced societies, have in the past been obfuscated by oversimplified comparisons between 'traditional' and 'modern society' (or whatever synonyms might be employed for these terms). Such comparisons, which are very deeply engrained in the history of sociology from the nineteenth century onwards, have normally been expressed as abstract typologies—'feudalism' versus 'capitalism', *Gemeinschaft* versus *Gesellschaft*, 'mechanical' versus 'organic solidarity', etc. To clarify: what has been at fault has not been the creation of these typologies, which is perfectly legitimate and necessary, but their *application* as interpretative models. Two assumptions, usually latent rather than explicitly stated, have guided their application: (a) that the characteristic nature of any given society is primarily governed by its level of technological or economic development; (b) that consequently the most economically developed society (however that be defined), at any given point of time, presents other societies with an image of their future in the present.

2. Each of these propositions must be *rejected*, in the form stated above. That they have prejudiced the progress of class theory is illustrated above all in the striking, and oft-remarked, contrast between the treatment of the notion of class by American and European sociologists. The first have been notably suspicious of the utility of the concept, have identified it with 'stratification', or not infrequently have bluntly denied its usefulness in contemporary

sociology in any form whatsoever;[11] the latter have tended to regard it as essential to their analyses. This reflects, I shall argue, real and quite profound differences between the past development of the United States and the European societies. While these differences have often been pointed to, their real significance for class theory, and for the interpretation of the development of the capitalist societies, has been lost—precisely because of the assumptions noted above. For from these it has been deduced that, either the European societies constitute the 'type case' (Marx), and that consequently the social structure of the United States will veer towards them in the future; or, much more common nowadays, that the United States, as the technologically most sophisticated society in the world today, provides the 'type case', towards which the former societies will move.

3. Rather than speaking of the 'existence' or 'non-existence' of classes, we should speak of types and levels of what I shall call *class structuration*. The factors which influence levels of class structuration are not to be traced to economic or technological complexity alone, or even primarily, and *cannot be directly inferred from the designation 'class society'*. Capitalism, for reasons which I shall expand upon below, is intrinsically a class society, and this is true of the United States as it is of other societies; but this does not invalidate the fact that levels of class structuration in the latter country have been, and are likely to continue to be in the forseeable future, more weakly defined than in most other capitalist countries.

4. Differences in the development of the capitalist (and state socialist) societies are not simply to be understood, as has often been implied in the past, as a result of the influence of divergent 'cultural values'; there are persistent differences in socio-economic *infrastructure* which can be distinguished, but which are concealed behind the use of the general label 'industrial society' as it has been applied in recent sociology. It is not the major purpose of this book to identify and to attempt to classify these in any exhaustive fashion —although this must be one of the urgent tasks facing a revitalised comparative sociology. Rather, I shall concentrate upon a limited number of societies as a source of empirical reference in order to illustrate my case. In discussing the capitalist countries, I shall refer mainly to materials relating to the United States, Britain, France and Japan; in analysing state socialist society, I shall draw primarily upon materials concerning the Soviet Union, Poland, Czechoslovakia and Yugoslavia. The case of France is particularly instructive since, just as many academic sociologists have discerned in the United States an emergent future for other societies, many Marxists have looked to France—since 1968—in a similar way. The events of May

1968 in France have again revived a faith in the potential of the working class to lead the revolutionary cataclysm which will signal the end of capitalist society. The reality is more prosaic: that there are specific factors which have shaped the development of French society and which separate it (together with Italy) from the majority of other capitalist countries; it is, in a sense, at an opposite extreme from the United States. It is not surprising that France and Italy should have been the source of the most stimulating and original currents in recent Marxist thought; it is, equally, not surprising that some of the ideas produced by these writers (e.g., that of the revolutionary 'new working class') appear something less than illuminating when applied directly, for example, to the United States.

To point to the existence of chronic differences in infrastructure between societies is *not* to accord a necessary and universal causal primacy to infrastructural factors themselves. On the contrary, I shall argue that specifically political influences, which both condition and express such differences, must be allocated a primary role in interpreting the formation and development of class structures.

5. This leads to a criticism of so-called 'convergence theory', as involving the conception that the differences between the capitalist and state socialist societies are becoming diminished, which is distinct from those which are ordinarily offered. Certainly 'convergence theory' is misleading or erroneous because it conforms to the two assumptions about social development which I have already referred to, and rejected. But, equally important, I would argue, the debate has been cast in an empirical frame of reference which obscures the ramifications of the issues involved. Most of the contributions to the controversy have made comparisons between the United States on the one hand, and the Soviet Union on the other; but this is, in some ways—and with complicating factors deriving from the extent of the political domination of these countries over others—to compare the *least typical* cases of each generic type of society.

6. 'Convergence theory' now appears rather old-fashioned and clumsy, and has been abandoned, at least in the naïve ways in which it was presented a decade ago, by many of its erstwhile supporters. But it has been supplemented by new—or newly elaborated—forms of technocratic theory, in particular the theory of 'post-industrial society'. I shall argue that these must in turn be severely censured, whether they are employed in reference to capitalist society, to state socialist society, or both. If Daniel Bell is advanced capitalism's most persuasive advertising man, Herbert Marcuse is the author of its most successful publicity stunt! Technocratic theory and the

idea of what Roszak calls the 'counter-culture' are two faces of the
updated thesis of the 'end of ideology'.

7. In this book I advance a somewhat heretical view, not perhaps
of capitalism as such—i.e., as a principle of economic organisation—
but of *capitalist society*. Marx followed orthodox political economy
in identifying the heyday of capitalist society with the early nineteenth-century British capitalist economy. I believe this to be at
best misleading, and at worst false. But virtually everyone has
accepted such a view, which carries the logical implication that any
movement towards state 'intervention' in economic life and, as many
non-Marxist writers have suggested, the acceptance of the legitimacy
of collective bargaining in industry and the enfranchisement of the
working class, represent some sort of partial supersession of capitalist
society. The opposite is the case; capitalist society only becomes
fully developed when these processes occur—although the question
of the role of the state is a complicated one because, as Polanyi has
pointed out, the 'free market' was something of a fiction even in
nineteenth-century Britain, let alone other countries where the state
played a self-consciously active role in fostering industrial capitalism.

8. State socialism is not appropriately regarded as the transcendence of capitalist society, but is nevertheless distinctly different, as a
form of 'industrial society', from the latter. The contrast between
capitalist and state socialist society is the living manifestation of
what I shall refer to as the 'paradox of socialism': a dilemma
resulting from two constituent elements in socialist theory, a clash
between the principle of the regulation of production according to
human need, and the principle of the elimination or reduction of the
exploitative domination of man over man. This is, if one likes, a
modern expression of the classical dilemma of freedom versus
equality, but manifest in a very specific form.

MARX'S THEORY OF CLASSES

It is Saint-Simon, rather than Comte, who is most properly regarded as the father of sociology, in spite of the fact that the latter author gave the new discipline its name. Saint-Simon's ideas have a double line of filiation, leading on the one hand to the positivism of Comte, and from there, through Durkheim, to modern theories of 'industrial society'; and on the other to the analysis and critique of 'capitalism' as formulated by Marx and subsequent generations of Marxists.[1] Saint-Simon was not a systematic thinker. His writings are chaotic and, not infrequently, self-contradictory. But he did draw together the elements of a coherent theory of social classes, placed within the framework of an interpretation of the development of Europe from the Classical era up to the age of modern industrialism. Society, according to Saint-Simon, passes through stages of growth, maturity and decline; each successive type of society contains the 'germ of its own destruction', which is generated by its own internal development. The contemporary age, he believed, is one in which class conflict is rife, because it is an era of transition: decayed feudalism is not yet fully destroyed, and the newly emergent industrial society is only partially formed. Saint-Simon identified the material source of the new society in the development of the free urban communes toward the end of the feudal period; these established an urban 'citizenry', independent of the feudal aristocracy. This urban bourgeoisie formed the nucleus of the new class of *industriels*, deriving their claims to power from their ownership of movable property created in manufacture.

Saint-Simon's use of '*industriel*', like his use of the notion of 'class' generally, was far from being completely consistent. On some occasions, he spoke of industrialists as a definite sub-grouping of society, a class distinct from the *proletaires*. More characteristically, however, he treated the *industriels* as the totality of those involved in industrial production, contrasting them with those 'parasitic' elements still caught up within the remnants of the feudal order. The class of *industriels* thus comprises every individual 'who works to produce or to put at the disposal of the different members of society one or several means of satisfying their needs or their physical tastes . . .'[2] It is in this latter sense that Saint-Simon spoke of the industrialist class as eventually destined to become the 'only class' in society. In industrial society, the coercive domination of a minority over the majority, which has characterised previous societal forms, will be superseded by an order which is freely accepted by all of its members. The advent of the industrial society transfers the human drive to power from the subjugation of men to the subjugation of nature. Hence the 'one-class' society is a 'classless' society—although by no means an egalitarian one in terms of the differential distribution of rewards. In industrial society, the 'administration' of things will replace of the 'government' of men: the state, as an instrument of class domination, will disappear.

It is obvious that many of the principal elements of Marx's conceptions of classes and class conflict are found in Saint-Simon. But if Marx owed much to Saint-Simon, he also drew heavily upon other theoretical traditions—including above all, of course, classical German philosophy and the orthodox political economy of Smith and Ricardo—and the general standpoint which he fashioned is an immensely more compelling synthesis than that developed by his predecessor. No major idea in social thought is ever the product of a single mind; rather, the great thinker gives concrete expression to conceptions which are becoming formed within the intellectual climate of his time. In most of Marx's writings, as in those of Saint-Simon, the concept of class is freely employed without the provision of a formal definition. Not until near the end of his life did Marx feel it necessary to offer a formal discussion of the attributes of class; and the famous fragment on 'the classes', which appears at the end of the third volume of *Capital*, breaks off at just that point at which it would appear that he was about to offer a concise statement of the nature of the concept. It is evident that this is one of the factors which has helped to further complicate the already difficult issues involved in the debate over the 'interpretation' of Marx's works in this respect: the formal characteristics of Marx's concept of class have to be inferred from the variety of writings in which he analysed class relationships in specific contexts.

In common with that of Saint-Simon, Marx's theory of class was worked out as part of an attempt to grapple with the nature of the changes which had dramatically transformed the traditional social structures of Europe. But what was for Saint-Simon (as for Durkheim) a temporary period of 'crisis' in the transition between feudalism and industrial society, became in Marx's writings a major element in a threefold movement of feudalism–capitalism–socialism. To be sure, capitalism for Marx is, in an important sense, a transitory 'stage' which occupies the interim period between feudalism and the more stable, classless society of the future. But it is not merely a phase of 'disorder' attendant upon the painful process of the replacement of feudalism by industrialism; it is a genuinely new form of society, with its own characteristic structure and its own internal dynamic. Marx was not a critic of 'industrialism', but of 'capitalist-industrialism'. Capitalism has to be faced and analysed in its own terms. Class conflict is not, as it was for the French positivists, an indication of the 'maladjustment of functions' in the emergence of industrial society, but expresses the very innermost character of capitalism. The difference here is a fundamental one. For in the first view, class conflict is a phenomenon which will disappear largely of its own accord once the last vestiges of feudalism have dropped away. Consequently, in the works of the most sophisticated representative of this stream of thought, Durkheim, the study of classes only occupies a relatively minor role. Marx was in accord with the theorists of 'industrial society' that the advent of industrialism makes manifest the enormous wealth which can be generated by human productive activity: but the 'contradictory' character of capitalism, which ultimately derives from its class structure, allows for only a limited realisation of the potential creative powers (both 'material' and 'cultural') which industrial production makes possible.

Wherever the conception of 'industrial society', in one guise or another, has gained the ascendant in sociology, concern with classes tends to fade into the background, as irrelevant to the immanent order. This was already the case with Saint-Simon: the issue of 'class', and especially 'class conflict', turns primarily upon the struggle between the 'non-productive' elements of a dying feudalism and the productive 'industrial class', the single 'class' of industrial society. The new society is to be a differentiated one, in terms of the distribution of material rewards; but the relationships between the various groupings in the division of labour will be essentially compatible, since access to occupational positions will be determined not by inherited social privilege, but by talent and capacity. Whatever the subsequent importance of the conception of 'industrial

society' in sociology—and that, of course, is very considerable—
this tradition of social thought has made rather few significant
contributions to the theory of classes.[3]

1. FUNDAMENTALS OF MARX'S MODEL

According to Marx's theory, class society is the product of a determinate sequence of historical changes. The most primitive forms of
human society are not class systems. In 'tribal' societies—or, in
Engels' term, 'primitive communism'—there is only a very low
division of labour, and such property as exists is owned in common
by the members of the community. The expansion of the division of
labour, together with the increased level of wealth which this
generates, is accompanied by the growth of private property; this
involves the creation of a surplus product which is appropriated
by a minority of non-producers who consequently stand in an
exploitative relation *vis-à-vis* the majority of producers. Expressed
in the terminology of Marx's early writings, alienation from nature,
which characterises the situation of primitive man, yields place to
an increasing mastery of the material world, whereby man both
'humanises himself' and develops his culture; but the increasing
dissolution of the alienation of man and nature is attained only at
the price of the formation of exploitative class relationships—at
the price of an increase in human self-alienation.

Marx was not always careful to emphasise the differences between
capitalism and prior forms of class system which have preceded it in
history. While it is the case that all (written) history 'is the history
of class struggles',[4] this most definitely does not mean that what
constitutes a 'class' is identical in each type of class society (although,
of course, every class shares certain formal properties which define
it as such), or that the process of the development of class conflict
everywhere takes the same course. Marx's rebuke to those of his
followers who had assumed the latter is instructive in this respect.
Several of the factors which characterised the origins of the capitalist
mode of production in Western Europe in the post-medieval period
existed previously in Ancient Rome, including the formation of a
merchant/manufacturing class and the development of money
markets. But because of other elements in the composition of Roman
society, including particularly the existence of slavery, the class
struggles in Rome took a form which resulted, not in the generation
of a 'new and higher form of society', but in the disintegration of
the social fabric.[5]

The diverse forms and outcomes of class conflict in history

explain the different possibilities generated by the supersession of
one type of society by another. When capitalism replaces feudalism,
this is because a new class system, based upon manufacture and
centred in the towns, has created a sort of enclave within feudal
society which eventually comes to predominate over the agrarian-
based structure of feudal domination. The result, however, is a new
system of class domination, because this sequence of revolutionary
change is based upon the partial replacement of one type of property
in the means of production (land) by another (capital)—a process
which, of course, entails major changes in technique.[6] While capitalism, like feudalism, carries 'the germ of its own destruction' within
itself, and while this self-negating tendency is also expressed in the
shape of overt class struggles, their underlying character is quite
different from those involved in the decline of feudalism. Class
conflict in capitalism does not represent the struggle of two competing forms of technique, but stems instead from the incompatibility of an existing productive technique (industrial manufacture)
with other aspects of the 'mode of production'—namely, the organisation of the capitalist market. The access of a new class to power
does not involve the ascendancy of a new form of private property,
but instead creates the conditions under which private property
is abolished. The proletariat here is the equivalent of Saint-Simon's
'industriels': because it becomes the 'only class' in society, its
hegemony signals the disappearance of all classes.

The problem of Marx's usage of the term 'class' is complicated, given the fact that he does not provide a formal definition
of the concept. In approaching this matter, it is valuable to make a
distinction between three sets of factors which complicate discussion
of the Marxian conception of class—factors which have not been
satisfactorily separated in the long-standing controversy over the
issue. The first of these refers simply to the question of terminology—
the variability in Marx's use of the word 'class' itself. The second
concerns the fact that there are two conceptual constructions which
may be discerned in Marx's writings as regards the notion of class:
an abstract or 'pure' model of class domination, which applies to all
types of class system; and more concrete descriptions of the specific
characteristics of classes in particular societies. The third concerns
Marx's analysis of classes in capitalism, the case which overwhelmingly occupied his interests: just as there are in Marx 'pure' models
of class, so there are 'pure' and 'concrete' models of the structure
of capitalism and the process of capitalist development.[7]

The terminological issue, of course, is the least significant of the
three sets of questions here. The fact of the matter is that Marx's

terminology is careless. While he normally uses the term 'class' (*Klasse*), he also uses words such as 'stratum' and 'estate' (*Stand*) as if they were interchangeable with it. Moreover, he applies the word 'class' to various groups which, in theoretical terms, are obviously only parts or sectors of 'classes' properly speaking: thus he speaks of intellectuals as the 'ideological classes', of the *Lumpenproletariat* as the 'dangerous class', of bankers and money-lenders as the 'class of parasites', and so on.[8] What matters, however, is how far this terminological looseness conceals conceptual ambiguities or confusions.

The principal elements of Marx's 'abstract model' of class domination are actually not difficult to reconstruct from the generality of his writings. This model is a dichotomous one. In each type of class society, there are two fundamental classes. Property relations constitute the axis of this dichotomous system: a minority of 'non-producers', who control the means of production, are able to use this position of control to extract from the majority of 'producers' the surplus product which is the source of their livelihood. 'Class' is thus defined in terms of the relationship of groupings of individuals to the means of production. This is integrally connected with the division of labour, because a relatively developed division of labour is necessary for the creation of the surplus product without which classes cannot exist. But, as Marx makes clear in his unfinished discussion at the end of the third volume of *Capital*, 'class' is not to be identified with source of income in the division of labour: this would yield an almost endless plurality of classes. Moreover, classes are never, in Marx's sense, income groupings. Modes of consumption, according to Marx, are primarily determined by relations of production. Hence his critique of those varieties of socialism which are directed towards securing some kind of 'distributive justice' in society—which seek, for example, the equalisation of incomes: such forms of socialism are based on false premises, because they neglect the essential fact that distribution is ultimately governed by the system of production. This is why it is possible for two individuals to have identical incomes, and even the same occupations, and yet belong to different classes; as might be the case, for example, with two bricklayers, one of whom owns his own business, while the other works as the employee of a large firm.

It is an axiom of Marx's abstract model of classes that economic domination is tied to political domination. Control of the means of production yields political control. Hence the dichotomous division of classes is a division of both property and power: to trace the lines of economic exploitation in a society is to discover the key to the understanding of the relations of super- and subordination which apply within that society. Thus classes express a relation not only between 'exploiters and exploited', but between 'oppressors and oppressed'. Class relations necessarily are inherently unstable: but a dominant class seeks to stabilise its position by advancing (not usually, of course, in a consciously directed fashion) a legitimating ideology, which 'rationalises' its position of economic and political domination and 'explains' to the subordinate class why it should accept its subordination. This is the connotation of the much quoted assertion that

The ideas of the ruling class are in every epoch the ruling ideas: i.e., the class which is the ruling *material* force of society, is at the same time its ruling *intellectual* force. The class which has the means of material production at its disposal, has control at the same time over the means of mental production, so that thereby, generally speaking, the ideas of those who lack the means of mental production are subject to it.[9]

In the abstract model, classes are conceived to be founded upon relations of mutual *dependence* and *conflict*. 'Dependence' here means more than the sheer material dependence which is presupposed by the division of labour between the classes. In Marx's conception, classes in the dichotomous system are placed in a situation of reciprocity such that *neither class can escape from the relationship without thereby losing its identity as a distinct 'class'*. It is this theorem, heavily influenced by the Hegelian dialectic, which binds the theory of classes to the transformation of types of society. Classes, according to Marx, express the fundamental identity of society: when a class succeeds in, for example, elevating itself from a position of subordination to one of domination, it consequently effects an overall reorganisation of the social structure. In the dichotomous system, classes are not, of course, 'dependent' upon each other in the sense of being collaborating groups on a level of equality; their reciprocity is an asymmetrical one, since it rests upon the extraction of surplus value by one class from the other. While each class 'needs' the other—given the continued existence of the society in unchanged form—their interests are at the same time mutually exclusive, and form the basis for the potential outbreak of open struggles. Class 'conflict' refers, first of all, to the opposition of interests presupposed by the exploitative relation integral to the dichotomous class relationship: classes are thus 'conflict groups'. This is, however, a point at which Marx's terminology is again variable. Whereas in his normal usage a 'class' represents any grouping which shares the same relationship to the means of production, regardless of whether the individuals involved become conscious of, and act upon, their common interests, he occasionally indicates that such a grouping can be properly called a 'class' only when shared interests do generate communal consciousness and action. But there is not really any significant conceptual ambiguity here. On the contrary, by this verbal emphasis, Marx seeks to stress the fact that class only becomes an important social agency when it assumes a directly political character, when it is a focus for communal action. Only under certain conditions does a class 'in itself' become a class 'for itself'.

Most of the problematic elements in Marx's theory of classes stem from the application of this abstract model to specific, historical forms of society—that is to say, they turn upon the nature of the connections between the 'abstract' and 'concrete' models of class. The first question to consider in this respect is the relationship between the dichotomous class system, presupposed by the abstract model, and the plurality of classes which, as Marx admits, exist in all historical forms of (class) society. Although Marx nowhere provides an explicit discussion of this matter, there is no serious source of difficulty here. Each historical type of society (Ancient society, feudalism and capitalism) is structured around a dichotomous division in respect of property relations (represented most simply in each case as a division between patrician and plebeian, lord and vassal, capitalist and wage-labourer). But while this dichotomous division is the main 'axis' of the social structure, this simple class relation is complicated by the existence of three other sorts of grouping, two of which are 'classes' in a straightforward sense, while the third is a marginal case in this respect. These are: (1) 'Transitional classes' which are in the process of formation within a society based upon a class system which is becoming 'obsolete': this is the case with the rise of the bourgeoisie and 'free' urban proletariat within feudalism. (2) 'Transitional classes' which, on the contrary, represent elements of a superseded set of relations of production that linger on within a new form of society—as is found in the capitalist societies of nineteenth-century Europe, where the 'feudal classes' remain of definite significance within the social structure. Each of the first two examples results from the application of two dichotomous schemes to a single form of historical society. They represent, as it were, the fact that radical social change is not accomplished overnight, but constitutes an extended process of development, such that there is a massive overlap between types of dichotomous class system. (3) The third category includes two principal historical examples: the slaves of the Ancient world, and the independent peasantry of the medieval and post-medieval period. These are 'quasi-class groupings', in the sense that they may be said to share certain common economic interests; but each of them, for different reasons, stands on the margin of the dominant set of class relationships within the societies of which they form part. To these three categories, we may add a fourth 'complicating factor' of the abstract dichotomous system: (4) Sectors or sub-divisions of classes. Classes are not homogeneous entities as regards the social relations to which they give rise: Marx recognises various sorts of differentiations within classes.

It should be noted that none of these categories involves sacrificing the abstract conception of the dichotomous class system: but they do make possible the recognition of the existence of 'middle classes', which in some sense intervene between the dominant and the subordinate class. 'Middle classes' are either of a transitional type, or they are segments of the major classes. Thus the bourgeoisie are a 'middle class' in feudalism, prior to their ascent to power; while the petty bourgeoisie, the small property-owners, whose interests are partly divergent from those of large-scale capital, form what Marx sometimes explicitly refers to as the 'middle class' in capitalism. If the terminology is again somewhat confusing, the underlying ideas are clear enough.

The position is less clear with another important problem bearing upon the relationship between the 'abstract' and 'concrete' models of class: that of the significance of the development of markets for the analysis of class relationships. While manufacture for exchange on a market, together with the formation of a money economy, are phenomena which occur in Ancient Rome, these are of greatest significance in relation to the transformation of feudalism in later European history. There can be no doubt that these phenomena, in conjunction with the expansion in the division of labour to which they give rise, serve to bring about important differences between the character assumed by class relationships in capitalism as compared to those which pertain in feudalism. The main features which serve to differentiate classes in these two forms of society may be reconstructed from various of Marx's writings, but he himself does not seem to have fully explored the implications of his views on the issue—a fact which is perhaps largely to be attributed to his relative lack of interest in the displacement of feudalism by capitalism, as compared to the anticipated transcendence of capitalism by socialism. Terminological discrepancies at this point probably do indicate conceptual ambiguity. Thus, whereas on most occasions Marx

speaks of 'feudal classes', at other times he expresses the view that
'the emergence of class is itself a product of the bourgeoisie';[10] and
he writes, for example, speaking of the decline of feudalism, 'Die
Bourgeoisie ist schon, weil sie eine Klasse, nicht mehr ein *Stand*
ist, dazu gezwungen, sich national, nicht mehr lokal zu organisieren
und ihrem Durchschnittsinteresse eine allgemeine Form zu geben.'[11]*
In the latter vein, Marx contrasts 'class' with 'estate', holding that
'class' only comes into being with the formation of markets and
with the emergence of a national economy. Which of these is the
genuine thread of Marx's thought?

The answer is both. In other words, while feudalism is founded
upon a class system, which conforms to the 'abstract model' of
classes, there are nevertheless major contrasts between feudal
and capitalist classes examined on a concrete level. Feudalism, like
capitalism, is built upon a dichotomous class relation, centring in
this instance upon ownership of landed property. But this class
structure also differs in basic aspects from that created by the advent
of the capitalist market. The class structure of feudalism is mediated
through the personalised ties of fealty which are sanctioned legally
in the differentiation between estates. These are not purely 'economic'
relationships; in the estate structure, economic and political factors
are fused. It is, moreover, a system based primarily upon the small-
scale, local community: production is primarily geared to the known
needs of the community. The spread of capitalism, however, inexor-
ably destroys both feudal bonds and fealty and the relatively
'self-contained' character of the local community. Capitalism
stimulates the growth of national and international markets: in the
capitalist division of labour, the independent character of local
regions becomes undercut, and society becomes welded into a
single system of interdependent producers. This leads to a separation
of the 'economic' and the 'political': class relationships, governed
by the contractual ties entered into by capital and wage-labour
on the open market, thereby become purely 'economic' relationships
in a very definite sense. The same process gives rise to the differentiated structure of the capitalist state: 'Through the emancipation
of private property from the community, the state has become a
separate entity, beside and outside civil society; but it is nothing
more than the form of organisation which the bourgeoisie necessarily
adopt both for internal and external purposes, for the mutual
guarantee of their property and interests.'[12]

* 'By the mere fact that it is a class and no longer an *estate*, the bourgeoisie
is forced to organise itself no longer locally, but nationally, and to give a general
form to its mean average interest.' (Marx and Engels, *The German Ideology*).

In order to further explore the characteristics of classes in capitalism, it is necessary to examine Marx's theory of capitalist development in some detail.

2. CAPITALISM AND CAPITALIST DEVELOPMENT

Marx's abstract or 'pure' model of capitalism is set out principally in the first volume of *Capital*. There he compares his mode of procedure to that of a physicist who observes the phenomena which he wishes to analyse 'in their most typical form and most free from disturbing influence'. Hence he takes the case of Britain as his primary point of reference: for Britain is the 'classic ground' of capitalism.[13] But while the British development supplies the grounding of his analysis, he attempts to use this to establish an abstract treatment of the generic principles of the capitalist mode of production, by 'disregarding' all those specific, historical factors which 'hide the play' of the 'inner mechanism' of capitalism.

Marx's abstract model of capitalism begins from a difficult problem of economic theory—one which, so it seemed to him, was completely concealed by the theory of orthodox political economy. This is the problem of the origin of surplus value. Given the fact that the essence of capitalism is expressed in the class relation between capital and wage-labour, whereby the working class must sell its labour to the former group in exchange for the means of their livelihood, it follows from the assumptions of Marx's abstract model of classes that this relation must rest upon the appropriation of surplus value by the capitalist class. In prior forms of class system, the exploitative motive of class relationships is easy to discern: a definite amount of produce is handed over, for example, from a vassal to his lord. But capitalism, as is emphasised by orthodox political economy, has 'freed' men from subjection to such unjust exchanges. In the capitalist market, the derivation of surplus value is not to be traced to the direct extraction of produce, either through force or through customary appropriation, from wage-labour: labour is 'bought and sold at its value' on the market, like any other commodity.

In solving this 'riddle' of capitalist production, Marx effects a neat connection between certain essential characteristics of the class situation of the wage-labourer and the structural demands of the capitalist market. Capitalism presupposes what Marx calls a separation between 'the personal and the class individual'.[14] The 'freeing' of men from the obligations inherent in feudalism has created a new type of class dependence, in which the 'economic' character of the worker is severed or alienated from his character as an integral human being. In capitalism, labour is treated on a par with any other commodity, as a product to be bought and sold on the market. But what the worker sells, in fact, is his labour-*power*, an economic capacity, which can be quantified and assessed in terms of a monetary standard in common with the material products of his labour. Surplus value is explained by reference to the fact that, as the labour-power of the worker is a commodity, its 'cost of production' can be calculated just like any other commodity. This is constituted by the cost of providing the worker with sufficient returns to 'produce and reproduce himself': the differential between this and the total value created by the worker is the source of surplus value.

The creation of labour as 'pure exchange-value' is thus integral to the operation of capitalism. This in turn presupposes the separa-tion of 'economic' from 'political' man. Capitalism depends upon the 'negative reciprocity' of economy and polity: the domination of the bourgeoisie as a class is secured by *political freedoms* which (1) free the market from political influence or control, by setting up an opposition between egoistic self-seeking (the pursuit of profit) in the economic sphere, and the 'universal participation' offered in the sphere of politics; (2) allow men therefore to dispose of them-selves on the market as 'free' agents (as compared to the situation in feudalism, in which men are bound by obligations which cut across market considerations). The capitalist state is thus not only an agency which coordinates and enforces the contracts upon which capitalism depends: the very existence of the state and politics (in Marx's sense) is predicated upon the innermost conditions of capitalist production.

The relationship of capital and wage-labour as set out above, then, involves the creation of a free competitive market in both capital and labour. In *Capital*, Marx sets himself the task of estab-lishing the 'laws' which cause this system to modify itself from within, and eventually to prepare the conditions for its transcendence by socialism. There are, in the abstract model, two processes of particular importance here: (1) the incipient socialisation of market forces, shown particularly in the growth of joint-stock companies— 'capitalism without the capitalist', and (2) the polarisation of the classes, capital and wage-labour. These are related rather than wholly separate processes, since both are created by the 'inner logic' of the trend of development of the capitalist system. The significance of the first, of course, is fundamental, because it implies a transform-ation of the very principles upon which capitalism is based. Capitalism is founded above all upon the individualistic pursuit of profit in the free market, whereby production is tied to capital investment. The capitalist market is 'anarchic' in the sense that there is no social organisation mediating between production and consumption. In the feudal community—as in any traditional economy—production is geared to the known needs of the locality. But this tie is broken through with the arrival of the far more extensive and complex system of commodity exchanges which constitutes the capitalist market. According to Marx, it is the dislocation between production and consumption which provides the background to the occurrence of the crises which are endemic to capitalism. In capitalism, for the first time in human history, a considerable volume of over-production is possible—'overproduction', that is, not necessarily in terms of actual needs, but in terms of the capability of consumers to purchase the goods in question.

The occurrence of crises, and the business failures which these provoke, provide a major impetus towards the concentration and centralisation of capital, as expressed, on the one hand, in the growth of large firms at the expense of smaller enterprises, and on the other, in the emergence of state banks, finance houses, etc. The significance of the joint-stock company is that it provides open demonstration of the fact that modern industry can function without the direct intervention of private property. The joint-stock company thus, as 'the ultimate development of capitalist production', brings about 'the abolition of the capitalist mode of production within the capitalist mode of production itself.'[15] This is not 'social-ism', because the joint-stock company still functions within the overall framework of the capitalist market; but it nevertheless represents the emergence of a set of relations of production quite distinct from those which characterise the original structure of capitalism.

As a result of its own workings, therefore, capitalism transforms itself 'from within'. It is thus poised for the movement to a new type of social and economic order: but this can only be actualised by the revolutionary action of the working class. In the abstract model of capitalism, the development of the revolutionary potential of the working class is linked to three aspects of the polarisation of classes: (a) the disappearance of those classes and segments of classes which 'complicate' the main dichotomous class system of capital and wage-labour; (b) the progressive elimination of diversified sectors within the working class itself; (c) the growing disparity between the material wealth of capital and wage-labour (*Verelendung*: often rendered by the fittingly ugly term 'emiseration'). The first of these is in a sense already assumed by the abstract model, at least as regards the 'transitional classes' which remain as a residue of feudalism. These are destroyed by the coming to maturity of capitalism, which voraciously swallows up all remaining outposts of the traditional form of society. But the advance of capitalism also leads to the elimination of the 'sub-class' of the petty bourgeoisie, who 'sink into the proletariat'. The increasing internal homogeneity of the working class is assumed by Marx to derive primarily from the trend towards mechanisation stimulated by the constant drive towards technological change which is generated by capitalism. The main phenomenon here is the disappearance of skilled labour; the task of the skilled worker is taken over by the machine, and all labour becomes reduced to single, repetitive operations.

Marx's views upon the third of these sets of factors—the so-called 'emiseration thesis'—are notoriously difficult to evaluate. Did Marx believe that it is the tendency of capitalism to cause an absolute deterioration in the material living standards of wage-labour, or did he hold that capitalism creates a *relative* disparity between the returns according to labour and those occurring to capital? Apparently contradictory statements can fairly readily be found in Marx. Thus in *Capital* he speaks bluntly of the 'accumulation of wealth generated at one pole' of capitalist society, as compared to the 'accumulation of misery' at the other 'pole'.[16] In 'Wage Labour and Capital', on the other hand, he appears to envisage this contrast as a relative matter:

A house may be large or small; as long as the surrounding houses are equally small it satisfies all social demands for a dwelling. But let a palace arise beside the little house, and it shrinks from a little house to a hut. The little house shows now that its owner has only very slight or no demands to make; and however high it may shoot up in the course of civilisation, if the neighbouring palace grows to an equal or even greater extent, the occupant of the relatively small house will feel more and more uncomfortable, dissatisfied and cramped within its four walls.[17]

In fact, the confusion over this issue derives less from Marx's own writings than from those of some of his subsequent interpreters, who have not distinguished adequately between Marx's treatment of the 'price of labour' and his analysis of the 'relative surplus population'—the 'reserve army' of chronically unemployed workers. It is clear from the presuppositions of Marx's general economic theory of capitalism that, while there may be fluctuations in the earnings of labour, these earnings can never deviate too far from the standard which is set by the theorem that labour is bought and sold 'at its value': the wages of labour cannot rise above the conditions which provide for the basic subsistence of the worker. The expansion of the 'reserve army' is connected to this, since this pool of unemployed labour constitutes a permanent resource which employers can use to depress rises in returns accruing to labour in times of economic prosperity. It is the reserve army which represents the main focus of the absolute poverty and deprivation created by capitalism.

The distinction is important because, according to Marx, it is not the chronically destitute who form the source of the impetus to the revolutionary action of the working class. On the contrary, the most poverty-stricken elements in society tend to be reactionary in attitude, and are open to manipulation by conservative interests. The worsening of the relative position of the bulk of the working class, on the other hand, together with the aspects of 'polarisation' discussed previously, provide the combination of circumstances which promote the development of the class consciousness of the proletariat. However, other factors, themselves endemic to the capitalist mode of production, facilitate the creation of class consciousness. These include the concentration of the working class in the urban areas, and the creation of large-scale productive units, which give men a ready perception of their common position[18]—a perception which is also clarified by the sudden deprivations experienced in the periodic crises to which capitalism is subject. But 'class consciousness' is only significant when it takes on an organised and, more specifically, a political form. The very character of bourgeois democracy, with its sharply delineated sphere of the 'political', makes possible forms of union and party organisation which can advance the revolutionary claims of the working class.

It is mistaken to treat the principles established in Marx's abstract model of capitalist development, as is so often done, as 'predictions' about the proximate future of historical capitalist societies. The 'laws' which Marx speaks of as 'working with iron necessity towards inevitable results' represent tendential properties which are built into the innermost functioning of the capitalist mode of production; but these 'laws' are, in his words, 'like all other laws, modified in [their] working by many circumstances'.[19] In other words, a theoretical understanding of the structural properties of the capitalist market must be complemented by historical studies of the specific characteristics of particular societies. This includes Britain, upon which the abstract model is based; but many of Marx's more historical writings concern the cases of Germany and France.

The initial source of Marx's views, of course, is to be traced to his early assessment of the 'retardation' of German social development. Germany experienced what was, in a sense, the first 'revolution' of modern times—the Reformation—but this was a revolution confined to the sphere of ideas, and thereby prepared the way for what Marx saw as the characteristic German tendency to dislocate the realm of the spiritual from that of the material. The cultural achievements of Germany, contrasting radically with its low level of political and economic advancement, bore witness to this. Under the influence of the Young Hegelians, Marx sought to resolve this contradiction through rational criticism, in the manner of David Strauss and Bruno Bauer. But the events which forced him into exile in Britain also helped to demonstrate the necessity of studying the 'inner dynamics' of capitalism—and these were most developed in that latter country. Whereas in Britain, as in France, the bourgeoisie had already come to be in the ascendant, in Germany, in the early part of the nineteenth century, it 'had just begun its contest with feudal absolutism'. Hence the first task, in Germany, was the fostering of a bourgeois society, so as to effect the displacement of the 'absolute government', with its 'following of parsons, professors, country squires and officials'.[20] The contrasts between this situation and the conditions pertaining in Britain and France gave rise to quite different forms of capitalist state. Marx's various discussions of these conditions, on the historical level, contain two partly separable notions about the sorts of circumstances which can generate the revolutionary transformation of capitalism.

One appears in his writings, in slightly different forms, near the beginning and near the end of his career. This is the thesis that the exposure of a socially backward country to the influence of advanced industrial technology may create an explosive conjunction of events, producing a very transient 'bourgeois stage' of society, which is then rapidly followed by a socialist revolution. Such a course of events is precisely what Marx anticipated in Germany in 1848. But a similar potentially explosive conjunction of circumstances reappeared decades later, in Russia—although in this instance Marx seems to have thought that, provided that a Russian revolution was the signal for the occurrence of socialist revolutions in the industrially developed countries of Western Europe, it could be possible, because of the continuing existence of communal property in the *mir*, for Russia to proceed directly to a successful socialist revolution without the intervention of a 'bourgeois stage'. However this may be, in the case of both Germany and Russia it is not the internal contradictions of capitalism which generate the impetus to revolutionary change, but rather the contradictions brought into being by a relatively sudden confrontation of the 'traditional' and the 'modern'. Given the occurrence of the process of revolutionary change in the more 'backward' country, this stimulates the spread of the revolution to the more advanced societies, whose influence can then react back upon the former.

The second version of a theory of revolutionary change is that which follows directly from the abstract model of capitalist development elaborated in *Capital*. Here, for reasons already indicated previously—that is to say, the massing of the proletariat in urban areas, the creation of homogeneous conditions of labour, etc.— the circumstances promoting revolution are stimulated, not by the clash between the old and the new, but by the internal maturation of capitalism *itself*.

Why, then, was it France, rather than Britain, which occupied Marx's attention during much of his career, as the probable locus of the revolutionary conflagration? The answer given by Marx is clear, if not wholly convincing in the light of the abstract analysis in *Capital*.

In Britain, Marx points out, the revolutionary process which led to the decline of the feudal order was at a relatively distant point in history, and brought about the evolution of a 'compromise' political system within which the expansion of industrialism had been accommodated. France, by contrast, had experienced the cataclysmic bourgeois revolution of 1789, and was the original source of the political theory of socialism. In France, the recent occurrence of the bourgeois revolution meant that the society was still split into different fragments, such that the role of the 'transitional' classes was particularly important. Hence the position of the bourgeoisie was, from the beginning, fraught with peculiar difficulties, and the process of capitalist expansion worked its effects upon a proletariat already sensitised to the possibilities of revolutionary politics. The character of class relations in France, at least in the first three-quarters of the nineteenth century, expressed itself as a kind of balance, in which executive power devolved into the hands of Louis Napoleon. These factors therefore created a socio-political system of a fragile character; as Engels wrote in 1891, 'Thanks to the economic and political development of France since 1789, Paris has been placed for the last fifty years in such a position that no revolution could break out there without assuming a proletarian character . . .'[21]

Engels' statement could now be revised to include the past one hundred and thirty years. In subsequent chapters, I shall return to a discussion of the development of the economic and political structure of France; but I shall argue that the explanation of the nature and course of that development, while it must begin from the very historical factors which Marx looked to, involves breaking with some of the most fundamental of his more general ideas.

THE WEBERIAN CRITIQUE

For the most significant developments in the theory of classes since Marx, we have to look to those forms of social thought whose authors, while being directly influenced by Marx's ideas, have attempted at the same time to criticise or to reformulate them. This tendency has been strongest, for a combination of historical and intellectual reasons, in German sociology, where a series of attempts have been made to provide a fruitful critique of Marx—beginning with Max Weber, and continuing through such authors as Geiger, Renner and Dahrendorf.[1] Weber's critique of Marx here has been of particular importance. But, especially in the English-speaking world, the real import of Weber's analysis has frequently been misrepresented. The customary procedure has been to contrast Weber's discussion of 'Class, status and party', a fragment of *Economy and Society*, with the conception of class supposedly taken by Marx, to the detriment of the latter. Marx, so it is argued, treated 'class' as a purely economic phenomenon and, moreover, regarded class conflicts as in some way the 'inevitable' outcome of clashes of material interest. He failed to realise, according to this argument, that the divisions of economic interest which create classes do not necessarily correspond to sentiments of communal identity which constitute differential 'status'. Thus, status, which depends upon subjective evaluation, is a separate 'dimension of stratification' from class, and the two may vary independently. There is yet a third dimension, so the argument continues, which Weber recognised as an independently variable factor in 'stratification', but which Marx treated as directly contingent upon class interests. This is the factor of 'power'.[2]

Evaluation of the validity of this interpretation is difficult because there is no doubt that Weber himself accepted it—or certain elements of it. What is often portrayed in the secondary literature as a critique of 'Marx's conception of class' actually takes a stilted and impoverished form of crude Marxism as its main target of attack. But this sort of determinist Marxism was already current in Germany in Weber's lifetime, and since Weber himself set out to question this determinism, the true lines of similarity and difference between his and Marx's analysis of classes are difficult to disentangle.[3] The most adequate way of approaching this issue is to follow a similar scheme of discussion to that which has been employed in the first chapter. As in Marx, we find in Weber's writings treatments of 'classes' and 'capitalist development' as abstract conceptions; and these can be partly separated from his specifically historical discussions of the characteristics of particular European societies.[4]

1. CLASS AND STATUS GROUPS

In the two versions of 'Class, status and party' which have been embodied in *Economy and Society*,[5] Weber provides what is missing in Marx: an explicit discussion of the concept of class. There are two principal respects in which this analysis differs from Marx's 'abstract model' of classes. One is that which is familiar from most secondary accounts—the differentiation of 'class' from 'status' and 'party'. The second, however, as will be argued below, is equally important: this is that, although Weber employs for some purposes a dichotomous model which in certain general respects resembles that of Marx, his viewpoint strongly emphasises a *pluralistic conception of classes*. Thus Weber's distinction between 'ownership classes' (*Besitzklassen*) and 'acquisition classes' (*Erwerbsklassen*) is based upon a fusion of two criteria: 'on the one hand . . . the kind of property that is usable for returns; and, on the other hand . . . the kind of services that can be offered on the market', thus producing a complex typology. The sorts of property which may be used to obtain market returns, although dividing generally into two types— creating ownership (*rentier*) and acquisition (entrepreneurial) classes —are highly variable, and may produce many differential interests within dominant classes:

Ownership of dwellings; workshops; warehouses; stores; agriculturally usable land in large or small-holdings—a quantitative difference with possibly qualitative consequences; ownership of mines; cattle; men (slaves); disposition over mobile instruments of production, or capital goods of all sorts, especially money or objects that can easily be exchanged for money; disposition over products of one's own labour or of others' labour differing according to their various distances from consumability; disposition over transferable monopolies of any kind— all these distinctions differentiate the class situations of the propertied . . .[6]

But the class situations of the propertyless are also differentiated, in relation both to the types and the degree of 'monopolisation' of 'marketable skills' which they possess. Consequently, there are various types of 'middle class' which stand between the 'positively privileged' classes (the propertied) and the 'negatively privileged' classes (those who possess neither property nor marketable skills). While these groupings are all nominally propertyless, those who possess skills which have a definite 'market value' are certainly in a different class situation from those who have nothing to offer but their (unskilled) labour. In acquisition classes—i.e., those associated particularly with the rise of modern capitalism—educational qualifications take on a particular significance in this respect; but the monopolisation of trade skills by manual workers is also important.

Weber insists that a clear-cut distinction must be made between class 'in itself' and class 'for itself': 'class', in his terminology, always refers to market interests, which exist independently of whether men are aware of them. Class is thus an 'objective' characteristic influencing the life-chances of men. But only under certain conditions do those sharing a common class situation become conscious of, and act upon, their mutual economic interests. In making this emphasis, Weber undoubtedly intends to separate his position from that adopted by many Marxists, involving what he calls a 'pseudo-scientific operation' whereby the link between class and class consciousness is treated as direct and immediate.[7] Such a consideration evidently also underlies the emphasis which Weber places upon 'status groups' (*Stände*) as contrasted to classes. The contrast between class and status group, however, is not, as often seems to be assumed, merely, nor perhaps even primarily, a distinction between subjective and objective aspects of differentiation. While class is founded upon differentials of economic interest in market relationships, Weber nowhere denies that, under certain given circumstances, a class may be a subjectively aware 'community'. The importance of status groups—which are normally 'communities' in this sense—derives from the fact that they are built upon criteria of grouping other than those stemming from market situation. The contrast between classes and status groups is sometimes portrayed by Weber as one between the objective and the subjective; but it is also one between production and consumption. Whereas class expresses relationships involved in production, status groups express those involved in consumption, in the form of specific 'styles of life'.

Status affiliations may cut across the relationships generated in the market, since membership of a status group usually carries with it various sorts of monopolistic privileges. Nonetheless, classes and status groups tend in many cases to be closely linked, through property: possession of property is both a major determinant of class situation and also provides the basis for following a definite 'style of life'. The point of Weber's analysis is not that class and status constitute two 'dimensions of stratification', but that classes and status communities represent two possible, and competing, modes of group formation in relation to the distribution of power in society. Power is *not*, for Weber, a 'third dimension' in some sense comparable to the first two. He is quite explicit about saying that classes, status groups and parties are all 'phenomena of the distribution of power'.[8] The theorem informing Weber's position here is his insistence that power is not to be assimilated to economic domination—again, of course, a standpoint taken in deliberate contrast to that of Marx. The party, oriented towards the acquisition or maintenance of political leadership, represents, like the class and the status group, a major focus of social organisation relevant to the distribution of power in a society. It is, however, only characteristic of the modern rational state.

Weber's abstract discussions of the concepts of class, status group and party, while providing the sort of concise conceptual analysis which is missing in Marx, are nevertheless unfinished expositions, and hardly serve to do more than offer a minimal introduction to the complex problems explored in his historical writings. In these latter writings, Weber details various forms of complicated interconnection between different sorts of class relationships, and between class relationships and status group affiliations. In the history of the European societies, there has been an overall shift in the character of predominant types of class relationship and class conflict. Thus in Ancient Rome, class conflicts derived primarily from antagonisms established in the credit market, whereby peasants and artisans came to be in debt-bondage to urban financiers.[9] This tended to cede place, in the Middle Ages, to class struggles originating in the commodity market and involving battles over the prices of the necessities of life. With the rise of modern capitalism, however, relationships established in the labour market become of central significance. It is evident that for Weber, as for Marx, the advent of capitalism dramatically changes the character of the general connections between classes and society. The emergence of the labour contract as the predominant type of class relationship is tied to the phenomenon of the expansion of economic life, and the formation of a national economy, which is so characteristic of modern capitalism. In most forms of society prior to modern capitalism, even in those in which there is a considerable development of manufacture and commerce, status groups play a more important role in the social structure than classes. By creating various sorts of restriction upon enterprise, or by enforcing the monopolisation of market privileges by traditionally established groups, status affiliations have in fact, as is shown in Weber's studies of the Eastern civilisations, directly inhibited the formation of modern capitalist production.

2. CONCEPTION OF CAPITALISM

Apart from the brief exposition in the set of lectures published under the title of *General Economic History*, there is no general statement in Weber's works of an 'abstract model' of modern capitalism and capitalist development comparable to that set out by Marx in *Capital*. But such a model can be formulated by inference from Weber's writings. The prominence which has been given to *The Protestant Ethic* has tended to obscure some of the main presuppositions of Weber's analysis, and also has helped to direct attention away from certain of the most significant divergences between this analysis and that of Marx, moving the emphasis instead to a sterile debate over the 'role of ideas' in history. Weber accepts a substantial part of the Marxian treatment of the conditions underlying the emergence of modern capitalism in post-feudal Europe. These conditions include the rise of an urban manufacturing class (Weber shows in some detail, however, that the *political autonomy* of the urban communes is a phenomenon which has a deeply engrained historical significance in Western Europe) whose transformation into fully fledged capitalistic entrepreneurs presupposes the formation of a mass of nominally 'free' wage-labourers expropriated from their means of production, who consequently must sell their labour on the market in order to gain a livelihood.

Two main features of Weber's 'abstract model' of modern capitalist development separate his views decisively, however, from those of Marx. The first of these is to be found in his analysis of 'expropriation'. For Weber, the 'expropriation' of the worker is not confined to the industrial sphere: this is only one element in a much more extensive process of 'expropriation' which is found in all the major institutional sectors of society. The expropriation of the worker from control of his means of production is paralleled in the state by the separation of the official from control of the 'means of administration', and in the army by the separation of the soldier from control of the 'instruments of war'. The second factor is Weber's treatment of 'rationality'. Whereas for Marx there is an essential distinction between the 'rationality of technique' and the 'rationality of domination' (in capitalism objectification and alienation tend to become assimilated, but these will be separated with the transcendence of capitalism by socialism), for Weber these are inevitably tied together within the general process of rationalisation entailed by the spread of the modern capitalist order.[10] The rationality of the modern capitalistic enterprise, in Weber's view, is perhaps the single most important factor which distinguishes the modern type from more traditional economic forms. Hence modern capitalism is inseparable from systematised cost accounting, whereby the enterprise is maintained on a stable and continuous level of operation.

These two features of modern capitalism are linked, however, through Weber's interpretation of the association between modern capitalism and bureaucratisation. The spread of bureaucracy both entails the 'expropriation of the worker'—in Weber's sense—and involves the application of rationality to the organisation of human conduct. Hence it is primarily with reference to the concept of bureaucratisation that Weber integrates the 'rationality of technique' and the 'rationality of domination'. The class relationship between capital and wage-labour, although a major component of the formation of modern capitalism, does not reveal the most fundamental characteristics in terms of which bourgeois society differs from the traditional order. For Weber, the trend towards the expansion of bureaucratisation expresses the integral character of the modern epoch: the rationalisation of human conduct creates a systematised and hierarchical division of labour which is not directly dependent upon the capitalist class structure. Thus while Weber's analysis follows that of Marx in recognising, rather than a twofold division between feudalism and 'industrial society', a threefold classification of feudalism–capitalism–socialism, the effect of his position is definitely to foreclose the possibility of any radical reorganisation of capitalism. In other words, the transcendence of capitalism by socialism, which Weber certainly recognised as a probable future occurrence, extends and completes the trends already characteristic of capitalism rather than creating a wholly new form of social organisation. At the risk of some oversimplification it can be said that, whereas Marx's abstract model of capitalist development proceeds from the 'economic' to the 'political', Weber's model is derived from the opposite process of reasoning, using the 'political' as a framework for understanding the 'economic'.[11] 'The rise of the modern nation-state, with its body of bureaucratic officials, whose conduct is oriented to impersonal norms of procedure rather than to the traditionally established codes associated with patrimonialism, serves as a paradigm case for Weber's analysis of bureaucratisation in general. The rational state, Weber stresses, is by no means merely an 'effect' of the formation of modern capitalism, but precedes its emergence, and helps to promote its development.

It is not clear how far Weber, on the abstract level, accepted the analysis of the process of the economic transformation of the capitalist economy set out by Marx in *Capital*. Certainly Weber believed that a fully socialised system would face certain definite economic problems which are not met with in capitalism.[12] What is clear is that he rejected Marx's analysis of the 'contradictions' in the capitalist *class structure*—especially in the oversimplified form in which this analysis was represented by some of the leading Marxist theoreticians of his time. According to Weber, the expansion of modern capitalism does not lead to the pauperisation of the worker, either in an absolute or a relative sense; from the beginnings of the capitalist era, the material position of the working class has been generally superior to that of rural labour. Nor does the process of capitalist development create an increasingly polarised class structure involving two internally homogeneous classes. On the contrary, the tendency is towards a diversified system of class relationships. The complexity of market relationships generated by the capitalist division of labour creates a variety of different, but overlapping, economic interests—as is suggested in Weber's formulation of *Erwerbsklassen*. Weber's model of classes, involving the possibility of important levels of class differentiation *within* the category of the 'propertyless' is of particular significance here. In so far as certain groupings of manual workers, through their unions, combine to monopolise, or even only partially control, access to the possession of certain marketable skills, they serve to introduce cleavages of class interest at the lower levels of the class structure. Perhaps even more important, the spread of bureaucratisation stimulates a progressive growth in the proportion of non-manual workers in the labour market—workers in occupations where recruitment is governed by the possession of various levels of educational qualification. This creates an expanding 'white-collar' grouping, whose class situation differs substantially from that of those in manual occupations.

In his conceptual discussion of class, besides distinguishing the purely economic *Besitzklassen* and *Erwerbsklassen*, Weber also refers to what he calls 'social classes'. A social class, in Weber's sense, is formed of a cluster of class situations which are linked together by virtue of the fact that they involve common mobility chances, either within the career of individuals or across the generations. Thus while a worker may fairly readily move from an unskilled to a semi-skilled manual occupation, and the son of an unskilled worker may become a semi-skilled or perhaps a skilled worker, the chances of either intra- or inter-generational mobility into non-manual occupations are much less. While the conception of the 'social class' remains relatively undeveloped in Weber's writings, it is of particular interest in relation to his model of capitalist development. As Weber himself points out, the notion of 'social class' comes much closer to that of 'status group' than does the conception of purely economic class (although, as with economic class situation, individuals who are in the same social class are not necessarily conscious of the fact). The notion of social class is important because it introduces a unifying theme into the diversity of cross-cutting class relationships which may stem from Weber's identification of 'class situation' with 'market position'. If the latter is applied strictly, it is possible to distinguish an almost endless multiplicity of class situations. But a 'social class' exists only when these class situations cluster together in such a way as to create a common nexus of social interchange between individuals. In capitalism, Weber distinguishes four main social class groupings: the manual working class; the petty bourgeoisie; propertyless white-collar workers: 'technicians, various kinds of white-collar employees, civil servants—possibly with considerable social differences depending on the cost of their training'; and those 'privileged through property and education'.[13] Of these social class groupings, the most significant are the working class, the propertyless 'middle class' and the propertied 'upper class'. Weber agrees with Marx that the category of small property-owners (*Kleinbürgertum*) tends to become progressively more restricted with the increasing maturity of capitalism. The result of this process, however, is not normally that they 'sink into the proletariat', but that they become absorbed into the expanding category of skilled manual or non-manual salaried workers.

To emphasise, therefore, that Weber's 'abstract model' of classes is a pluralistic one is not to hold that he failed to recognise unifying ties between the numerous combinations of class interests made possible by his conception of 'class situation'. But there is no doubt that his viewpoint drastically amends important elements of Marx's picture of the typical trend of development of the capitalist class structure. Even Weber's simplified ('social class') model of capitalism diverges significantly from the Marxian conception, in treating the propertyless 'middle class' as the category which tends to expand most with the advance of capitalism. Moreover, the social classes do not necessarily constitute 'communities', and they may be fragmented by interest divisions deriving from differentials in market position; and finally, as Weber shows in his historical writings, the relationship between class structure and the political sphere is a contingent one.

Most of Weber's detailed writings on the specific forms of capitalism of his day concentrate upon the case of Germany—a country in which the confrontation between a 'feudal' agrarian system and an emergent industrial capitalism was felt much more sharply than in most of the other Western European countries. Like Marx before him, Weber was acutely conscious of the differences separating German social development from that of both Britain and France. Like Marx, Weber frequently used these countries as a point of reference with which to contrast the 'backwardness' of Germany; but Weber's assessment of the significance of Germany's transition to modernism differs considerably from that of his predecessor—and whereas Marx's views were, by and large, established prior to the unification of the country under Prussian hegemony, Weber's writings take their point of departure from the social and political residue of the formation of the integral German nation-state.

The rise (and fall!) of Bismarck appeared to Weber as the prime example of the independent significance of the 'political' as compared to the 'economic'. The political unification of the country was accomplished, not through the leadership of the more economically advanced, 'bourgeois' German states, but as a result of Bismarckian power politics, deriving a main source of support from the *Junker* landlords of East Prussia. Subsequently, Germany became, in a very rapid space of time, a fully industrialised state without becoming a 'bourgeois society'. According to Weber's analysis, this situation was largely a result of the political vacuum left by the very successes of Bismarck's policy after he himself had lost power. Bismarck had systematically weakened the liberals, retarded the political education of the working class by forcing the Social Democrats outside the constitutional framework of government, and generally had left the country with a dearth of capable political leadership. Thus, in Weber's eyes, it was futile to suppose—as did the more 'vulgar' Marxists of the time—that the advance of industrialism would inevitably produce the accession of the bourgeoisie to power. On the contrary, Weber's political writings from the turn of the century onwards constantly revert to the theme of the continuing subordination of bourgeois elements to the traditionally established elite groups.

In this context, Weber saw the expectations of certain of the leaders of the Social Democratic party, that the further evolution of capitalism in Germany would lead in the near future to a 'breakdown' or calamitous economic crisis, culminating in a process of revolutionary change, as wholly futile. In his view, the immediate future of the working class was necessarily bound to that of the bourgeoisie. Not, as Marx had hoped some half a century earlier, that a bourgeois revolution would be rapidly followed by a proletarian one: according to Weber the working class could only secure some real progress in both its economic and political fortunes within the framework of a bourgeois order. The occurrence of a socialist revolution, as Weber made clear in his writings during the Revolution of 1918–19, could only lead to the establishment of an ossified bureaucratic state.[14] For Weber, the hopes of Marxists that the existing state bureaucracy could be 'smashed' or otherwise radically transformed by the means of political revolution were completely misplaced. It is one of the essential characteristics of bureaucracy, as Weber argues in his more general writings, that it is 'escape-proof': the attempt to transform an existing bureaucratic administration only serves ultimately to increase its hold.

3. MARX AND WEBER

Much of Max Weber's sociology may be said to constitute an attack upon the Marxian generalisation that class struggles form the main dynamic process in the development of society. This theorem is questioned by Weber, on a theoretical level, in two main respects: first that, by seeing the 'political' as secondary and derivative, it greatly exaggerates the significance of 'economic' relationships within the infrastructure of social organisation; second, that it fails to recognise the part played in history by status affiliations, created as bases of group formation through processes which are not directly dependent upon class relationships. While most secondary writers—and, to some extent, Weber himself, especially in so far as he set out to question 'vulgar Marxism'—have taken the second of these points to be the most important, it is the first, especially in regard to the theory of capitalist development, which is the more significant.

Weber himself accepted that it is 'class situation' rather than 'status situation' which is 'by far the predominant factor' in the system of relationships generated by modern capitalism.[15] He recognised that modern capitalism is a 'class society' in two senses: that it vastly extends the range of market operations beyond that characteristic of prior forms of society; and that it is a system based upon the relationship between capital and 'free' wage-labour. But his interpretation differs from that of Marx in relation to the connection between these aspects. The most essential element of (modern) capitalism is not its class character; the decisive 'break' which separates capitalism from the preceding traditional order is the rationalised character of the capitalist productive enterprise, a phenomenon which remains integral to any form of socialism which may supersede capitalist society. The formation of the class relationship between capital and wage-labour, which certainly presupposes the expropriation of the worker from direct control of his means of production, becomes symptomatic of a much broader process, rather than being the central feature of the new form of society which replaces feudalism.

Marx's writings on the nature of the relationship between the state and society contain a definite ambiguity. On the one hand, the theorem is advanced that the state is nothing more than the vehicle whereby the interests of the dominant class are realised: the state is merely an agency of class domination. On the other hand, many of Marx's comments upon the capitalist state show an awareness of the administrative significance of the state as the 'supervisor' of the operations of capitalist production. The ambiguity is not as marked as may initially appear, since it is clear that Marx wishes to argue that the very administrative functions of the capitalist state, by ensuring the operation of the contractual obligations upon which the free market in labour depends, are of key importance to the maintenance of the class relationship of capital and wage-labour; the state provides a cohering framework for the class structure inherent in the capitalist mode of production. But nevertheless there is an important difference, which is nowhere coherently analysed by Marx, between the conception (1) that the state is, in a direct sense, the *instrument* of class domination, and hence that most of its organisational characteristics are contingent upon the capitalist system of class relationships, and (2) that the state is a coordinating agency which is responsible for the overall administrative operations of the society *within* which a relationship of class domination pertains in the 'separated' economic sphere. The theory of bureaucracy has a focal importance in this respect, and much of the special significance of Weber's use of a 'political' rather than an 'economic' paradigm is illuminated by comparison of his views with those of Marx on this matter.

In his various writings on bureaucracy, Marx undoubtedly places most weight upon the first of these conceptions. The bureaucratic state is portrayed as a 'parasitic' growth upon society, an expression of the class domination of the bourgeoisie, and destined therefore to disappear when class society is transcended. This is why, indeed, there is in Marx nothing more than a fairly rudimentary theory of bureaucracy, derived from a simple 'inversion' of Hegel's conception of the state bureaucracy as the 'universal class'. Whereas Hegel argued that the bureaucracy represents the general interests of the community, as against the egoistic interests of those in civil society, Marx holds that the bureaucratic state is a focused manifestation of the sectional interests of the dominant class. It follows that the 'bureaucratic problem' is resolved as one element of the disappearance of classes, and demands no special analysis. Weber's standpoint, on the other hand, places the overwhelming emphasis upon the second conception mentioned above: the bureaucratic state offers a paradigm of the typical form of social organisation called into play by the emergence of capitalism. The class relationships which pertain in capitalism are not the determining factor in this: the administrative form exemplified in the bureaucratic state constitutes the necessary framework of 'rationalised' economic enterprise. Weber does not deny that the operation of the capitalist market, if left to function in an 'unfettered' manner, acts to favour the material fortunes of capital; but the transformation of this situation, through the abolition of private property in the means of production, cannot provide the means for the total transformation of society envisaged by Marx.

3

SOME LATER THEORIES

1. DAHRENDORF: CLASSES IN POST-CAPITALIST SOCIETY

Dahrendorf's theory of class and class conflict, as described particularly in his *Class and Class Conflict in Industrial Society*, treats themes previously developed by Geiger and others, but elaborates upon them in a different way. While he couches his ideas in terms of a 'positive critique' of Marx, he eventually reaches a theoretical position which departs very substantially from the one established by that thinker.[1] Like Geiger (and, of course, Weber before him), Dahrendorf offers two related sets of criticisms of Marx, concerning supposed conceptual weaknesses in Marx's notions of 'classes' and 'class conflict' on the one hand, and in his (abstract) model of capitalist development on the other.

According to Dahrendorf, Marx's works are based upon an illegitimate fusion of 'sociological' and 'philosophical' elements. We must draw a strict separation between those of Marx's propositions which are, in Dahrendorf's terms, 'empirical and falsifiable' and those which belong to a 'philosophy of history'. Propositions such as 'class conflict generates social change' are of the first type, while statements such as 'capitalist society is the final class society in history', or 'socialism leads to a complete realisation of human freedom' are not capable of either verification or falsification by reference to documented fact.[2] The task of the sociologist is to sift out those of Marx's ideas which can be embodied within an empirically verifiable theory of classes.

In Dahrendorf's view, the conjunction of 'sociological' and 'philosophical' elements in Marx's writings serves to mask a fundamental weakness in the connection which he makes between classes and private property. 'Property' can be conceived of in two ways:

in a broad sense, as *control* of the means of production, regardless of the specific manner in which that control is exercised; or, more narrowly, as the legally recognised right of ownership. 'Property' is not *what* is owned, but refers to the rights relating to the object. In the broad sense of property, these rights are defined in a generalised manner, and hence it can be said that property is a 'special case of authority'. In this sense, the manager of an industrial enterprise in a society in which private ownership of capital has been abolished, in so far as he has directive *control* of the enterprise, may be said to exercise 'property rights'. In the narrower meaning, by contrast, authority is a 'special case of property': i.e., the authority structure of the enterprise is dependent upon 'who owns the means of production' in the legal sense. According to Dahrendorf, Marx's analysis of classes and private property turns upon the latter, 'narrow' definition of 'property'. The existence of classes and, correspondingly, the disappearance of classes in socialist society, in Marx's formulations, are tied to social conditions in which legal title to property ownership is in the hands of a minority of individuals. In a society in which legal ownership of property by private individuals is abolished, there can—by definition—be no classes.

It is only because Marx employs the narrow conception of property that he is able to integrate, in an apparently plausible way, the 'sociological' with the 'philosophical' aspects of his theory:

By asserting the dependence of classes on relations of domination and subjection, and the dependence of these relations on the possession of or exclusion from effective private capital, he makes on the one hand empirically private property, on the other hand philosophically social classes, the central factor of his analysis. One can retrace step by step the thought process to which Marx has succumbed at this point. It is not the thought process of the empirical scientist who seeks only piecemeal knowledge and expects only piecemeal progress, but that of the system builder who suddenly finds that everything fits! For if private property disappears (empirical hypothesis), then there are no longer classes (trick of definition)! If there are no longer any classes, there is no alienation (speculative postulate). The realm of liberty is realised on earth (philosophical idea).[3]

The confusions inherent in this reasoning disqualify Marx's conception of classes, in unmodified form, as a viable scheme for analysing the class structure of modern societies. This is demonstrated further by the inadequacy of Marx's analysis in the face of the changes which have affected capitalism since the close of the nineteenth century. 'Capitalism', as Marx knew it, has become transformed: not through a process of revolution, however, and not in the direction which he anticipated. Here Dahrendorf introduces the conception of 'industrial society', of which capitalism is only one sub-type. Capitalism is that form of industrial society which is distinguished by the coincidence of the legal ownership of private property, in the hands of the entrepreneur, and actual *control* of the means of production. In this type of society, the two senses of 'property' overlap with one another—which explains Marx's failure to distinguish between them on the theoretical level. The modern form of society no longer preserves this characteristic, and is thus quite different from capitalism as Marx knew it: while it is still an 'industrial society', it is also a 'post-capitalist' society.

Dahrendorf details the following changes as being the most significant in the transformation of capitalism: (1) The decomposition of capital. Although, in the third volume of *Capital*, Marx discussed the growth of joint-stock companies, and the 'functional irrelevance of the capitalist', he failed to discern their true significance. In Dahrendorf's view, this has to be understood as a process of role differentiation, whereby the blanket category of 'capitalist' has become separated into the two categories of 'shareholder' and 'manager'. This process does not represent an enclave of socialism within capitalism; rather, it constitutes a progressive separation between the two forms of 'property' which were temporarily united in capitalist society. The authority of the managerial executive does not rest upon legal property rights. Since the interests of managers are not wholly convergent with those of shareholders, it follows that the real outcome of the development of joint-stock companies is the fragmentation of the unitary 'capitalist class'. (2) The decomposition of labour. Marx held that the mechanisation entailed by the growing maturity of capitalist production leads to the elimination of skilled labour, and thus to the increasing internal homogeneity of the working class. In fact, this has not occurred. On the contrary, the trend has been towards the maintenance, and even the expansion, of skilled labour; and the 'semi-skilled' category has intruded between the skilled and the unskilled. Far from becoming increasingly homogeneous, the working class has become more diversified: the differences in skill-level serve as a basis for divisions of interest which cut across the unity of the class as a whole. Thus the internal differentiation at the lower levels of post-capitalist society complements that which occurs in the upper echelons with the decomposition of the capitalist class.

(3) The growth of the 'new middle class'. The expansion of administrative or non-manual occupations is again a phenomenon unanticipated by Marx. But while the decomposition of capital and wage-labour is a consequence of social changes which have disaggregated these previously coherent classes, 'the "new middle class" was born decomposed'.[4] The so-called new middle class, according to Dahrendorf, is not in fact a distinct class at all, but consists of two parts: those workers who are part of an administrative chain of authority ('bureaucrats'), and those who occupy positions outside such hierarchies (such as shop assistants). The bureaucrat, whether high-placed or lowly, shares in the exercise of authority, and thus his position is directly linked to that of the dominant groups in society; those workers in the second type of situation, on the other hand, are closer to the position of manual workers. But these two sectors of the 'new middle class' therefore add to the diversification in the structure of post-capitalist society already implied by the twin processes of the decomposition of the capitalist and the working class.

(4) The increase in rates of social mobility, which Dahrendorf regards as one of the principal characteristics of industrial society. The effects of widespread inter- and intra-generational mobility are twofold. First, these act to diminish the boundaries between classes, and thus to corrode any rigid barriers which might otherwise grow up between them. Secondly, the existence of high rates of social mobility serves to 'translate' group conflict into individual competition.[5] Group antagonisms—class conflicts—become dissolved into a competitive struggle between individuals for valued positions within the occupational system. (5) The achievement of 'citizenship rights', as embodied in universal suffrage and welfare legislation, for the mass of the population. These are not simply formal privileges, but have had real effects in undercutting the extremes of political and economic disparity found in nineteenth-century capitalism. The Marxian anticipation of a polarisation between the economic fortunes of capital and wage-labour is again quite at variance with the actual trend of development: 'by institutionalising certain citizenship rights, post-capitalist society has developed a type of social structure that excludes both "absolute" and many milder forms of privilege and deprivation'.[6] (6) The 'institutionalisation of class conflict', in the form of recognised procedures of industrial arbitration. The recognition of the right to strike, together with the existence of mutually accepted methods of resolving differences, has had the effect of confining conflicts to the sphere of industry itself, preventing them from ramifying into class conflicts.

These changes can only be adequately understood by abandoning an orthodox Marxian standpoint. Nonetheless, Dahrendorf argues, certain elements of Marx's conception must also be retained. The most important of these concerns Marx's emphasis that every (class) society incorporates conflicts which create a pressure towards internal change: there is an inherent connection between conflict and change. Secondly, Marx rightly assumes that social conflict must be understood in terms of a two-party model: a theory of class conflict must be founded upon recognition that, in any situation of antagonism, the struggle devolves upon two primary classes. While there may be coalitions, there are always two main positions in a conflict situation. But having accepted these formal properties of Marx's model, Dahrendorf explicitly repudiates most of the substantive content of the Marxian view. Marx's conception of class, as both a 'sociological' and 'philosophical' notion, is tied to his fusion of the two senses of 'property'. If the 'sociological' part of this conjunction has any validity, it is limited to nineteenth-century European capitalism. For the purpose of his theory of history, Marx universalises a particular—the connection between private property (narrow sense) and authoritative control (broad sense) which existed in the nineteenth century. A more adequate theory of class and class conflict, Dahrendorf suggests, must reverse this relation. That is to say, rather than class being defined in terms of ownership of private property (narrowly conceived), the tie between private property and authority, given such prominence by Marx, should be seen as a special case of a much broader relationship between class and authority. Marx's 'private property' should be seen as only a specific instance of authoritative rights of control more generally. 'Class', therefore, should be defined in terms of authority relationships: rather than ownership versus non-ownership of property, class should be taken to refer to *possession of, or exclusion from, authority*:

in every social organisation some positions are entrusted with a right to exercise control over other positions in order to ensure effective coercion ... in other words ... there is a differential distribution of power and authority ... this differential distribution of authority invariably becomes the determining factor of systematic social conflicts of a type that is germane to class conflicts in the traditional (Marxian) sense of the term. The structural origin of such group conflicts must be sought in the arrangement of social roles endowed with expectations of domination and subjection.[7]

'Authority', following Weber, is defined as the legitimate right to issue commands to others: 'domination' represents the possession of these rights, while 'subjection' is exclusion from them. Within 'imperatively coordinated associations'—i.e., groups which possess a definite authority structure (e.g., the state, an industrial enterprise)— possession of, and exclusion from, authority generates opposing interests. These interests may not be perceived by those involved: a 'quasi-group', in Dahrendorf's terminology, is any collectivity whose members share latent interests, but who do not organise to further them. Where a collectivity does organise itself for this purpose, it becomes an 'interest group'.

The utility of this *schema*, in Dahrendorf's view, is not limited in its application to post-capitalist societies: it can also be used to cover the characteristics of the class structure of capitalism as described, in different terms, by Marx. Thus the development of nineteenth-century capitalist enterprise may be said to have stimu- lated the emergence of two quasi-groups, capital and labour. The specific character of capitalist society, however, derived from the fact that industrial and political conflict were 'superimposed' upon one another. The conflict between capital and labour was not confined to industry, but extended to the political sphere, since political authority was largely conterminous with economic domina- tion. As a result of this superimposition of interest divisions, class conflict became particularly intensive as organised interest groups began to form to represent the divergent claims of capital and wage- labour. But the very appearance of these interest groups, and the concrete changes which they have helped to bring into being, have undermined the possibility of the revolutionary upheaval foreseen by Marx.[8]

According to Dahrendorf's conceptual scheme, it follows that 'post-capitalist' society is necessarily a class society. But, no less obviously, its class system is very different from that of capitalism. The most far-reaching of the various changes in terms of which Dahrendorf seeks to distinguish 'capitalism' from 'post-capitalism' is the institutional separation of industrial and political conflict— a phenomenon which derives from the connected processes of the establishment of collective bargaining in industry and the attainment of universal franchise in the political sphere. This is manifest in the fact that the occurrence of industrial conflict, in the main, has no direct repercussions upon political action. According to Dahren- dorf, 'the notion of a workers' party has lost its political meaning'.[9] There is no integral connection between trade unions and 'labour' parties in the Western countries: those links which still exist are merely the residue of tradition. The same is true at the higher levels. The position of authority occupied by the manager in the enter-

prise yields no direct political influence: the latter is allocated independently of relationships pertaining in the industrial sphere.

2. ARON: INDUSTRIAL SOCIETY

Rather than being directed solely to a critique of Marx, Aron's
various writings on the development of 'industrial society' are
focused upon a comparative assessment of Marx and Tocqueville.[10]
In common with Saint-Simon, of course, Tocqueville saw occurring
in the newly emerging social order of post-feudal Europe, not the
establishment of a new set of conflicting classes, but the development of tendencies towards democratisation and levelling. How far
does the subsequent movement of society since the nineteenth
century bear out the vision of Marx, in tending towards the polarisation of classes and the growing intensity of class conflict? Alternatively,
how far has Tocqueville's anticipation of a growth in social differentiation, accompanied by the progressive impetus towards the
eradication of inequalities, been realised?

These questions cannot be answered, Aron stresses, without
taking account of the fact that there have been two 'paths' of
social development in the modern world—one confined to the internal evolution of capitalism itself, and the other, although not
originating within the advanced capitalist societies, claiming to
represent the supersession of capitalism. The contrasts between these
two forms of society, capitalist and socialist, cannot be understood,
however, without recognising that they also share certain important
elements in common as types of industrial society. The simplest
abstract definition of 'industrial society' involves three principal
characteristics: where the vast majority of the labour force is concentrated in the secondary and tertiary sectors; where there exists
a constant impulsion, in contrast to the relatively static character
of traditional societies, to expand productivity; and, consequently,
where there is a rapid rate of technological innovation.[11] If this
elementary definition of industrial society be adopted, Aron argues,
it follows that certain formulae in Marx's analysis of capitalism apply also to the contemporary socialist or 'Soviet-type'
societies:

Marx considered that one of the main characteristics of capitalism was
the accumulation of capital. We know today, from factual evidence,
that this is a characteristic of all industrial societies to the degree to
which, obsessed by the anxiety to heighten production, they are obliged
to invest a growing volume of capital in machinery. In the same way,

Marx considered that the worker was exploited because he did not receive, in the form of wages, the whole of the value produced by his labour. But, whatever the regime, this is obviously necessary, since a proportion of the value that is created must be reinvested. . . . In both societies (capitalist and socialist), certain individuals are privileged: that is to say, they have higher incomes than those of workers at the bottom of the hierarchy. The phenomenon of capital accumulation or 'exploitation' is common to both types of industrial society, and not characteristic of one type in contrast to the other.[12]

This 'exploitation' of the worker occurs within societies committed to ideals of democratic egalitarianism. All contemporary industrial societies proclaim the rule of the 'common man'; but at the same time as they do so, they generate inequalities which contradict their professed ideals. But this 'contradiction' is closer to that which might be envisaged following certain of the ideas of Tocqueville than those deriving from Marx.

Like Dahrendorf, Aron distinguishes two aspects of Marx's theory of classes: 'factual propositions' and 'philosophical propositions' which are intertwined in Marx's writings. Only the factual assertions—e.g., 'the material and moral suffering of the working class becomes worsened, and as a consequence of this worsening the workers become more revolutionary'[13]—can be examined in relation to empirically observable developments which have occurred in society since Marx's time, and are necessarily of a different order to statements which express a metaphysical philosophy of history. This distinction is directly relevant to Marx's concept of class, for there are, according to Aron, two definitions of 'class' in Marx. The first is that which treats 'class' as referring to the place of a grouping of individuals within the process of production, a conceptualisation which might be acceptable to a sociologist who is not of a Marxist persuasion. The second, however, ties the notion of class to (unrealisable) goals, such as that the 'domination of man by man' can be transcended with the supersession of capitalism by socialism—conceptions which are not acceptable unless one embraces Marx's theory *in toto*. It is the conjunction of these two elements in Marx's writing, Aron emphasises, which helps to explain the continuing fascination of social thinkers with the notion of class. But this is, in turn, bound up with the attraction exerted by Marxism itself—a phenomenon which Aron explains in 'Tocquevillean' terms. Modern societies, in so far as they are 'democratic', are exposed to the 'contradiction' between their declared faith that all men are equal and the manifest political and economic inequalities which exist within them. 'The industrial democracies proclaim the equality of individuals, in work and in the realm of politics. Now the fact is that there is great inequality in incomes and in modes of life.'[14] The constant tension between the ideal and the reality, and the vision of a society in which this is dissolved—through the revolutionary action of a deprived class—explains the passionate commitment which Marxism can stimulate.

It follows that, for Aron, while Marx's ideas express certain of the aspirations generated by this inherent tension within industrial society, they do not provide a satisfactory analysis of its sources— even if we neglect Marx's 'philosophy of history', and confine ourselves to his 'factual propositions' about classes and class conflict. Marx's theory of class, Aron suggests, drew heavily upon observations which relate primarily to the proletariat, the 'class *par excellence*'. In nineteenth-century Europe, during the early phases of industrialisation, the proletariat, excluded from political power, working and living in uniformly degrading circumstances, appeared as the type-case of an oppressed class. But no other class conforms to this degree to the criteria of distinctiveness which Marx sought to apply. The 'bourgeoisie', for example, has never been such a clearly identifiable grouping, if it is defined as including everyone above the (not clearly demarcated) category of 'small property owner'. According to Aron, any theory of class must come to terms with the indefinite character of social reality *itself*: 'classes' are rarely such distinct and clearly identifiable groupings as was the nineteenth-century proletariat. The ambiguity of conceptual discussions of class since Marx reflects an actual condition in reality. This 'uncertainty in social reality', Aron argues, must 'be the point of departure of any enquiry into social classes'.[15] Social thinkers in the Western societies have been obsessed with the problems of class, but have been incapable of reaching acceptable definitions of the phenomenon. The paradox is resolved in terms of the preceding analysis: industrial societies (of both types, capitalist and socialist) continually generate inequalities, whilst at the same time removing many of the forms of manifest discrimination that characterised previous types of society which were not influenced by democratic ideas. Legally prescribed relationships of inequality, for example, such as existed in the medieval estates, have been abolished; the hierarchical structures of industrial societies are more fluid and less clearly delineated. Moreover, these structures are of a complicated kind, involving a multiplicity of phenomena.

Under what conditions, therefore, Aron asks, can we speak of the existence of distinguishable classes? There are three sets of circumstances in which we may *not* do so: (1) Where the main principle of hierarchical differentiation is not economic, but religious or racial. (2) Where the fate or the 'life-chances' of the individual do not depend primarily upon the group to which he belôngs within society, but exclusively upon himself: in other words, where something close to full equality of opportunity prevails. (3) Where the socio-economic conditions of everyone are fundamentally similar. None of these three sets of circumstances obtains within the industrial societies, and consequently 'it is not illegitimate to speak of social classes, socio-economic categories (*ensembles*) defined by a plurality of criteria and constituting more or less real groups, within the total society'.[16] The equivocation 'more or less real' is deliberate. If classes were, as Marx implied, clearly defined groupings, normally producing a consciousness of class unity, there would be no problem. But of the four major classes which are often recognised by sociologists as existing within capitalist societies, there is none which takes a clear-cut form. The 'bourgeoisie' is 'not a coherent unity'; the 'middle class' (or, as is frequently said, 'middle *classes*') constitutes 'a kind of hold-all' in which individuals are placed if they cannot be put into any of the other classes; the 'peasantry' is sometimes described as a single class, and on other occasions is treated as composed of two classes in relation to the ownership of property (farm owners and agricultural workers). Even the working class, which approximates most closely to the notion of a distinguishable and unified class group, is far from being a homogeneous entity, as measured either by socio-economic criteria or by political affiliation.

Marx was correct, Aron agrees, in believing that classes only become important agencies in history to the degree that they manifest a unified group consciousness, expressed particularly in the context of a struggle with other classes. While the working class may be characterised by shared objective and subjective traits, it does not manifest, in modern capitalist societies, the form of class consciousness necessary to provide the impulsion towards effecting a fundamental change in society. The role of 'class messianism', as set out in Marxism, has been a paradoxical one. It has undoubtedly played a major part in recent history, and thus in one sense has been endorsed by social developments since Marx's time; but it has been invalidated at the same time, because those who have adopted it, according to the theory, should not have done so. The influence of Marxism, as an organising political catechism, has been in inverse relation to capitalist development. On the whole, the working class has been less revolutionary the more advanced the capitalist forces of production. Marxism has become an influence promoting the industrialisation process in the less developed countries, rather than expressing the demands of mature capitalist society. The 'socialist' countries are those which have followed a different route to industrial society than that taken by the countries of Western Europe.

The development of industrial society, Aron argues, should be understood in terms of a distinction between 'stages of economic growth' and 'modes of industrialisation'. At each stage of economic growth we find the emergence of different forms of 'contradiction' which can be resolved according to divergent modes of social and political control. In the initial phase of industrialisation, for example, it is necessary to promote rapid capital accumulation and investment, which can only be accomplished by some form of authoritative regime that restricts consumption on the part of the mass of the population. The 'contradiction' here is that the advance of (future) prosperity depends upon the self-abnegation of the present generation. The form which this took in the early development of capitalism in Western Europe, however, differs considerably from that which, legitimised within the framework of Marxist socialism, it assumed in the Soviet Union.

In a developed industrial society, whether 'capitalist' or 'socialist', the need for the authoritative or forced imposition of self-denial upon the population diminishes. But the 'Tocquevillean dilemma' assumes a burgeoning importance: the new 'contradiction' is between the democratic demand for 'levelling' and the continuing existence of inequalities.

3. OSSOWSKI: IMAGES AND CONCEPTS OF CLASS

Ossowski's *Class Structure in the Social Consciousness* attempts a general examination of the criteria which have been used, both in popular thought and in more systematic sociological analysis, to identify forms of 'class' (and forms of 'classlessness').[17] The language of 'class', Ossowski points out, is permeated with spatial metaphor, representing society in terms of a 'vertical' order of divisions or 'layers' piled upon one another. But this vertical representation has assumed a variety of types, and it is the objective of Ossowski's work to analyse these.

The simplest type is the 'dichotomic' conception of class structure. The conception of a polar division between two main classes in society, Ossowski shows, is one which constantly appears in history. There are three principal modes in which this representation occurs,

corresponding to the sorts of privilege according to which advantages
are distributed: (1) The 'rulers and the ruled': a division of power or
authority, centred upon a separation between those who command
and those who obey (Dahrendorf's conception of 'class', of course,
falls into this category). (2) The 'rich and the poor': an economic
differentiation, dividing those who own wealth or property from
those who do not. (3) Those 'for whom others labour' and those who
are the 'labouring class': a separation emphasising the *exploitation*
of one group by another. These three modes of representing a
dichotomous class division are not, of course, mutually exclusive,
although where they are found together one of them tends to be
treated as dominant and as determining the others. Most socialist
thinkers of the nineteenth and twentieth centuries, according to
Ossowski, have regarded the third category ('exploitation') as being
conditional upon one or other of the first two, and consequently
have looked to the abolition of the former as the medium for the
elimination of exploitative class relationships. But there have been
important exceptions to this, among whom may be placed Saint-
Simon. Since Saint-Simon's 'working class' includes all the 'real
producers', industrialists as well as propertyless wage-labourers,
his 'classless society' is quite compatible with major differentials in
power and wealth.[18]

The existence of 'middle classes' is sometimes recognised in
dichotomic schemes, but these are always seen as secondary groupings which are appendages of one or other of the two major class
groups. What Ossowski calls 'schemes of gradation', the second
main type of representation of class structure, differ from dichotomous conceptions in that a middle class (or classes) is often regarded
as the most basic class, the position of other classes being determined
in relation to it. In dichotomic forms of class imagery, moreover,
each class is defined in terms of its dependence upon the other. In
gradation schemes, on the other hand, the relationship between
classes is one of ordering rather than dependence: this sort of conception is normally applied in a descriptive rather than an explanatory manner. Ossowski distinguishes two types of gradation scheme:
the 'simple' and the 'synthetic'. In the former, a representation of
class structure is made according to a single criterion, such as income. This was the case, for example, with the original Roman
census categories: under the Republic, citizens were divided into
six income classes. Synthetic schemes involve a similar rank ordering
of classes, but apply a combination of criteria to effect the ranking.
This is the typical conception of social class, Ossowski suggests,
adopted by most contemporary American sociologists. Thus War-

ner's studies, for instance, set up a synthetic gradation scheme yielding six major classes in American society.[19]

The third principal form of class imagery Ossowski calls the 'functional scheme'. Here society is seen as being divided into functionally interrelated groupings in the division of labour. This conception usually recognises a plurality of classes; rather than being perceived as antagonistic groups, as tends to be the case in dichotomic representations, or as a set of ranked divisions as in gradation schemes, classes are considered to be interdependent and cooperative agencies. Certain contemporary sociological interpretations of class systems are of this kind: for example, those which identify a set of functionally interdependent classes such as 'managers', 'clerical workers', 'skilled workers', etc.—or, on a more ideological level, Stalin's conception of 'non-antagonistic classes' in the Soviet Union. Such classes are not measured in terms of uniform gradations on a scale: a given class differs from a second in respects which are distinct from those by which the second class differs from a third.

The significance of Marx's theory of classes is that it ties together strands drawn from each of the three modes of representation of class structure within a single, coherent theory: 'the writings of Marx form some sort of immense lens which concentrates the rays coming from different directions, and which is sensitive both to the heritage of past generations and to the creative resources of modern science.'[20] Marx's writings integrate the inherent revolutionary appeal of the dichotomic scheme with a systematic analysis of other properties of class relationships as these existed in the contemporary European societies of his time. The dichotomous conception, according to Ossowski, is most prominent in Marx's more propagandist writings, in which he sought to stimulate the development of a revolutionary consciousness. In his more scholarly writings, however, he was forced to blunt the clarity of the dichotomic perspective by introducing 'intermediate' classes, and managed to arrive at a descriptive assessment of class relationships in historical societies. Thus while, according to Ossowski, Marx's works embody each of the three main ways of representing class structure—the dichotomic, gradation and functional schemes—these are conceived in a new way, in terms of the intersection of two or more dichotomous class divisions.[21]

In Marx's writings, of course, the class societies of the present are counterposed to the classless order of the future. The concept of 'classlessness' in fact, Ossowski points out, has as long a history as that of 'class'. Just as images of class have differed, so have notions of classlessness. In the modern world, however, there are two versions of classlessness which are particularly important as political ideologies. One of these simply involves a stress upon a functional scheme as against any competing modes of interpreting class relationships. Unlike the dichotomic and gradation schemes, which stress the asymmetry of class divisions, the functional conception involves the idea that classes are mutually supportive. Concentration upon functional connections, therefore (as in the notion of 'non-antagonistic classes'), can serve as a means of reducing the apparent significance of class divisions—not by lessening inequalities of wealth or power, but by emphasising the cooperative nature of classes. This conception differs radically from Marx's version of 'classlessness', since the latter presupposes a much more profound dissolution of class relationships. But it is a development of the functional interpretation of classlessness which has actually come to predomina⁺e in modern political ideology—and not only in the Western societies, committed to liberal democratic ideals, but also the socialist countries, nominally committed to Marx's classless society.

The American image of 'non-egalitarian classlessness', according to Ossowski, is formed primarily around the notion of equality of opportunity: everyone, regardless of origins, is presumed to have the same chance, if he possesses the appropriate capacities, of reaching the highest levels in the occupational system. The structure of Soviet society, as portrayed in Marxist orthodoxy, might appear to be quite different from this. In fact, there are very close similarities:

The socialist principle 'to each according to his needs' is in harmony with the tenets of the American creed, which holds that each man is the master of his fate, and that a man's status is fixed by an order of merit. The socialist principle allows of the conclusion that there are unlimited opportunities for social advancement and social demotion; this is similar to the American concept of 'vertical social mobility'. The arguments directed against *uravnilovka* [equalisation of wages] coincide with the arguments put forward on the other side of the Atlantic by those who justify the necessity for economic equalities in a democratic society.[22]

The main difference between the two ideological standpoints, Ossowski suggests, is that, according to the socialist view, 'non-egalitarian classlessness' is only a temporary phase. Nevertheless, while the ultimate objective is different, the distinction here is not a radical one. For, according to socialist theory, the transition to 'egalitarian classlessness' is to be a progressive, not a revolutionary, process—and liberal democracy also envisages a continual advance towards the further realisation of the principle of equality of opportunity.

The conception of 'non-egalitarian classlessness', in common with any sort of functional scheme, tends to appeal to those who wish to defend an existing social order. Dichotomic representations, on the other hand, often have a revolutionary connotation, since they tend to perceive class relationships as antagonistic in character. Gradation schemes, being primarily descriptive, are more neutral than either of the other two. The fact that these three types of imagery reappear throughout history, and are to be traced in both ideological thought as well as in the more systematic conceptions of modern sociology, Ossowski stresses, demonstrates the ubiquity of the social interests which generate them. This does not mean, however, that the formulations of sociology can be directly equated with popular images of class structure. Rather, the older conceptions form the background against which concern with class as a sociological concept came to dominate social thought from the turn of the nineteenth century onwards. Marx's theory, in particular, drew upon deeply engrained themes in the European cultural heritage, and connected the revolutionary appeal of the dichotomic conception to a concrete analysis of the class relationships in nineteenth-century capitalism.

But like Dahrendorf and others, Ossowski sees the relevance of Marx's conception of class as largely limited to a form of society (i.e., 'early capitalism') in which economic power was the mainspring of social and political organisation. This type of society, as Marx anticipated, proved to be a transitory one. The social changes which have occurred since the nineteenth century, however, while they have partly been shaped by Marx's ideas, have departed from the line of development he foresaw. Socialism, in one sense, has diverged from capitalism, because it has not sprung, as Marx believed it must do, from the latter; but, in another sense, the two forms of society, capitalism and socialism, have evolved in a similar direction. The Marxian conception, in its 'classical' formulation, can today be no more usefully applied to the analysis of the class structure of the Western societies, which have moved far away from a situation in which private property 'rules', than it can be to those societies in which private property has been formally abolished:

In situations where the political authorities can overtly and effectively change the class structure; where the privileges that are most essential for social status, including that of a higher share in the national income, are conferred by a decision of the political authorities; where a large part or even the majority of the population is included in a stratification of the type to be found in a bureaucratic hierarchy—the nineteenth-century concept of class becomes more or less an anachronism, and class conflicts give way to other forms of social antagonism.[23]

4

MARX'S CRITICS: A CRITIQUE

1. THE RECENT CRITICS

'For the past eighty years', as Bottomore has remarked, Marx's theory of class 'has been the object of unrelenting criticism. . . '[1] The work of recent authors such as Dahrendorf, Aron and Ossowski is thus in a sense only the tip of the iceberg. Few of the ideas set out in their writings touch upon matters which do not have a long history in the critical literature, stretching back to Weber's generation of 'Marx-critics'. On the other hand, much of this literature is repetitive, and the contributions of the above three writers may be regarded as embodying most of the significant points of critical attack upon Marx's ideas which have been developed since Weber. As I have emphasised earlier in this book, there are two related issues in the writings of those concerned with Marx's analysis of classes and class conflict: one bears upon the validity of Marx's interpretation of the development or trend of evolution of capitalism, and the other upon more abstract conceptual criticisms of his notion of class. Since these are necessarily closely connected, it is neither desirable nor possible to sever them completely. But the problem of capitalist development does pose special difficulties, which will be confronted in a later chapter; the discussion in this chapter will be focused primarily upon conceptual criticisms of Marx.

Marx's theory of class, as each of the three authors stress, was formulated in the context of a conception of political *Praxis*. It is obvious that Marx's writings cannot be treated as a purely academic exercise in social interpretation: not only were they conceived with a practical end in view, but they have subsequently exerted a tremendous political and ideological influence in society. These factors, according to Marx's critics, both hamper the accurate exposition of his ideas themselves, since revolutionary exhortation mingles with reasoned analysis, and obscure the question of the validity of his theory, because that theory has itself become a 'social fact'. The situation is worsened, as Dahrendorf accentuates strongly, by the heavy overlay of 'philosophical' elements which made it possible for Marx to integrate his more concrete discussions of class with his theory of the transcendence of capitalism by socialism. It is interesting to note, however, that these very factors have often been seen, by those sympathetic to Marx, as a major source of *defence* of his theory. It is argued that the principal strength of Marx's standpoint, which separates it from 'academic social science', is its fusion of theory and practice. Marxism, it is held, is a *method* rather than a fixed set of generalisations and findings. Consequently, the 'validity' or otherwise of Marx's ideas has to be judged in terms of their success in *Praxis*.[2] The 'philosophical' aspects of Marx's theory of class are, from this perspective, a necessary part of its character as both analysis and critique of capitalism.

The problems raised by these issues relate to the general question of the proper nature of sociological theory, and its relationship to political practice, and thus concern matters which go beyond the scope of this book. They are relevant here only in so far as they bear immediately upon difficulties in the interpretation of Marx's conceptions of class and class conflict. The point is that both views, the critical and the sympathetic, tend to underestimate the importance of what Dahrendorf calls the 'sociological'—as opposed to the 'philosophical'—elements in Marx's thought. If Marx was more than just a social scientist, he was still more of a social scientist than many of either his critics or his followers have given him credit for.

Dahrendorf's discussion, in particular, is unconvincing. According to him, the 'philosophical' elements in Marx's writings constantly intrude upon the 'sociological' generalisations so as to render the latter 'either meaningless or false'. An example which Dahrendorf quotes is Marx's belief 'that all social conflicts and all structure changes can be explained in terms of antagonisms of class', a generalisation which 'is as impermissible as it is untenable'.[3] But this is hardly an adequate representation of Marx's views. Certainly Marx's writings contain sweeping assertions, especially in his more propagandist works (notably *The Communist Manifesto*), such as the statement that 'all past history is the history of class struggles', but it is quite obvious that such propositions cannot be treated in isolation from his more detailed discussions. Moreover, he frequently and expressly rejected that interpretation of his views which sees them as advancing a distinctive philosophy of history: philosophy must be replaced by a 'real, positive science' of social development, a science whose results 'by no means provide a recipe or scheme, as does philosophy, for neatly trimming the epochs of history'.[4] Rather than separating, as Dahrendorf attempts to do, 'philosophical' and 'sociological' elements in Marx's thought, it is more appropriate to distinguish, as has been suggested earlier, Marx's 'abstract model' of class from his 'concrete' analyses of class relationships. If this is a distinction which is in a certain sense imposed on Marx, it is less arbitrary than that utilised by Dahrendorf. In these terms, those aspects of Marx's ideas which Dahrendorf chooses as the main focus of critical attack appear in a new light. Marx clearly did not hold that 'all social conflicts can be explained in terms of class antagonisms', if this is taken to mean that there have been no other forms of significant group struggles in history. Nor did he hold that the class conflicts which have occurred over the course of the history of the Western European societies have been identical in content.[5]

According to Dahrendorf, the weakness in Marx's formulations is particularly manifest in the latter's treatment of the relationship between class and private property. By failing to isolate the two senses of the term 'property', Marx was able to effect a—spurious—connection between his theory of class relationships and his philosophy of history. But this is again a most questionable interpretation. If Marx was unaware of the distinction between the two senses of 'property', how could he have worked out his analysis of the significance of the joint-stock company within modern capitalism—an analysis which Dahrendorf actually discusses in some detail? For the importance of the development of the joint-stock company, as Marx seeks to show, is that it creates a division between the (legal) property-owner and effective control of the enterprise. The joint-stock company shows precisely that these two senses of 'property' are not to be confused. Although, in discussing class relationships, Marx does not make a terminological distinction between 'ownership' (narrow sense of 'property') and 'control' (broad sense of 'property'), it is hardly convincing to hold that he was unaware of it. It is surely evident that, in contrasting the 'class character' of capitalism with the 'classlessness' of socialism, Marx did not consider, as Dahrendorf asserts, that this is a transition which can occur simply through the legal abolition of private property. The separation between legal title to private property and actual control of the capitalist enterprise in the joint-stock company exemplifies major processes of change which have taken place within capitalism, whereby the 'classical' form of 'anarchic' competition within the unfettered market is displaced by an incipient socialisation of market relations. Socialism involves the actualisation of these incipient processes within capitalism: the legal abolition of private property, enacted through the revolutionary action of the working class, is only *possible* because of the set of changes which have already helped to transform capitalism from within.

While it is held to be based upon a reformulation of Marx's theory of class, Dahrendorf's approach actually owes little of a concrete nature to Marx's formulations. What Dahrendorf preserves of Marx's conception really amounts to two considerations—both of them primarily formal in character: the acceptance of a dichotomous, 'conflict' model of classes, and the emphasis that it should be the task of a theory of class to provide an explanatory account of social change. But the substance of Dahrendorf's concept of class is, quite obviously, very different from that taken by Marx;[6] and its effect is to rob the notion of whatever there was that was distinctive in the traditional usage of the term by the latter author. For the notion of class, in the writings of Marx, as well as those of virtually all who have been influenced by him, above all concerns the analysis of interconnections between economy and society, between economic relationships and social relationships. Dahrendorf's concept, transmuting the notion of 'class division' into that of 'authority division', has no intrinsic affinity with such problems whatsoever.

It nevertheless could be argued, of course, that it helps to illuminate these by allowing us to examine them in a fashion which is not possible using the traditionally established concepts. But there are at least three objections which can be made that cast doubt upon the usefulness of Dahrendorf's scheme. In the first place, it is difficult to accept that authority divisions can be readily analysed in terms of a dichotomous division between a 'dominant' and a 'subordinate' group: those who 'hold' or 'share in' authority as contrasted with those who do not. While under certain circumstances this may apply, more often it is the case that a system of authority—as is specified in Weber's treatment of bureaucratic organisations—involves a graded hierarchy of relationships. Conflicts between groups *within* the hierarchy may be more important than those between those who 'have' authority and those who have not; and it is, to say the least, a rather forced interpretation which includes the most humble clerical worker in the government bureaucracy within the 'ruling class'. Secondly, there is no reason to assume, even granted that authority may be usefully treated as a dichotomous division, that the exercise of authority presupposes a (latent) opposition of interest between those in authority and those who are subject to that authority. In Marx's theory, there is a definite structure of relationships, involving the creation and appropriation of surplus value, which generates a necessary opposition of interest between classes. But this is lacking in Dahrendorf's conception. How far a given division of authority presupposes a conflict of interest cannot be settled *en gros*, but depends upon both the mode of organisation of that authority (e.g., how far those subject to authority voluntarily accept their situation, what mechanisms of representation and sanction they possess *vis-à-vis* the 'holders' of authority, etc.) and the nature of the objectives which the institution in question is set up to realise.

Thirdly, Dahrendorf's view logically implies the recognition of an indeterminate plurality of classes. A 'dominant' and 'subordinate' class can be identified in any 'imperatively coordinated association': i.e., any organisation having some kind of determinate distribution of authority. Thus classes may exist in cricket clubs as much as in industrial enterprises. Dahrendorf, of course, recognises that this is so, and thus restricts his discussion to 'the two great associations of the state and the industrial enterprise'.[7] But this obviously presumes some criterion whereby such organisations are recognised as more 'significant' for class analysis than others; and this in turn takes us back to certain elements in the more traditional concepts of class which Dahrendorf originally claimed to have abandoned.[8] In Marx's writings such criteria are established by the general theoretical framework within which the concept of class is employed: namely, that which analyses the fundamental role of economic relationships in conditioning the rest of the social and political structure.

Finally, Dahrendorf's approach completely eliminates the possibility of a 'classless' society. This is a trivial statement in itself, given his conception of class, since it must be conceded that definite patterns of authority are necessary in any conceivable kind of large-scale society. The important thing is that Dahrendorf's view directs attention away from the contrast between 'class' and 'classlessness' as conceived in Marxian theory. Whatever defects there may be in Marx's treatment of these matters, Dahrendorf's approach does not provide us with an adequate means of dealing with them. Indeed, Dahrendorf might be accused of escaping from the issues involved by the same sort of terminological speciousness of which he accuses Marx: 'for while private property may disappear (empirical hypothesis), this can have no possible bearing upon the existence or disappearance of classes (trick of definition)'! In attempting to reformulate the concept of class, Dahrendorf throws out the baby with the bath-water. While we cannot be content with the concept of class used by Marx, if we are to analyse satisfactorily the sort of problems which were at the centre of his preoccupations, we do not make any significant theoretical gains by substituting 'authority' for 'class'. We already possess in sociology a reasonably adequate conceptual framework with which to analyse systems of authority, and there is little purpose served in confusing this with the terminology of 'class'.[9]

Ossowski's work is more genuinely original and, while it is not primarily an attempt to 'revise' the Marxian concept of class, it maintains a concern with a factor integral to Marx's writings: the phenomenon of 'class consciousness'—although Ossowski is interested less in consciousness of 'class unity' than in cognitive images of the class structure. But these are linked, he points out, in definite ways: thus the 'dichotomic scheme', if it penetrates and becomes part of public ideology, tends to stimulate and reinforce an awareness of class solidarity on the part of a proto-revolutionary class.[10]

But Ossowski attaches the dichotomic scheme too closely to its social function as revolutionary propaganda. He stresses that dichotomic conceptions of class tend to involve the presumption of conflict of interest, and hence are associated with a revolutionary questioning of the existing order. But this is not by any means always the case, either in popular imagery, or in more academic sociological discussions of class. Dichotomous imagery often forms part of representations of class relationships which are tied to a 'conservative' standpoint, and which may represent the two classes in question as in harmony rather than conflict. Such is frequently found in images which are fostered in aristocratic forms of government, stressing the natural and legitimate capacity of a certain minority to lead.[11] In the realm of sociological analysis, 'conservative' dichotomic schemes appear (and within a framework of conflict analysis) in the writings of the 'elite theorists' Pareto and Mosca. Moreover, even in Marx the propagandist connotation of the two-class conception is less marked than Ossowski implies. While it may be accepted that the dichotomous portrayal of class relationships in Marx's more specifically political writings does carry a pronounced, and deliberately evoked, emotional appeal, it is important to emphasise, as has been shown in a previous chapter, that the two-class scheme is primarily an abstract analytical model which guides Marx's thinking throughout his works. According to Ossowski, with 'Marx the revolutionary, the dichotomic conception of social structure is dominant', whereas 'Marx the theorist' tends to rely upon the 'gradation' and 'functional' schemes.[12] But this is misleading, if not completely incorrect; the two-class scheme, which is directly tied to the theory of surplus value, is the necessary basis of the theoretical structure elaborated in *Capital*.

Nor is it clear why Ossowski interprets his 'functional scheme'— three or more classes in a division of labour—as entailing a conception of harmony between the classes. Certainly it is readily possible to point to images of class structure which have this emphasis, such as the quoted example of Stalin's 'non-antagonistic classes', but the implication does not appear to be a necessary one. Where three or more classes are represented as composing the class structure, it may still be recognised that there are endemic conflicts between them. To be sure, it may be held that the classes in question will tend to form 'coalitions' in circumstances of overt conflict; but such 'coalitions' may be transitory or shifting in character, and not subsumable under a dichotomous class model. Representations of this sort are common in the writings of sociologists: in, for example, analyses of the so-called caste structure of the South in the United States.[13]

Moreover, concepts of class which employ multiple criteria do not, as Ossowski seems to assume, necessarily conform to his descriptive 'gradation scheme'. This is the case, for instance, with Weber's categories of class differentiation. If these fit anywhere in Ossowski's classification of images of class, they approximate most closely to the functional scheme. But Weber's identification of 'class position' allows the recognition of various possible bases of class formation. There may be a multiplicity of differing 'classes' in terms of aggregates of individuals sharing common market positions; the most significant combinations of these may be elucidated in the contrast between *Besitzklassen* and *Erwerbsklassen*; and a further classification may be developed using Weber's conception of 'social class'. All of these diverse 'classes' are, however, founded in the division of labour; they are not (like Warner's 'classes') examples of Ossowski's gradation scheme.[14]

However useful or apposite Ossowski's classification of forms of class imagery may be in illuminating representations of class in popular ideology, it is not very helpful in identifying the main lines of difference between the ways in which the concept has been used in sociology. While Ossowski is undoubtedly right in pointing to the mutual influence of popular ideology and sociological thought, the relationship between these remains ambiguous in his analysis, and it is misleading to merge the two, as he tends to do. Thus while the 'dichotomic scheme', as he presents it, may be frequently linked to some sort of revolutionary intent, as is apparent in Marxism, there are numerous uses of this scheme which do not carry this implication—nor a clearly 'conservative' one either. It is not only in Marx that a dichotomous model of class is reconciled with the recognition of the existence of several classes in any empirical society. Thus Weber's *Besitzklassen* and *Erwerbsklassen* embody a dichotomous division based, following that of Marx, upon ownership and exclusion from ownership of property in the means of production; and Dahrendorf's two-class model, when applied to the analysis of any given society, identifies numerous 'classes'.

Although Ossowski holds that the Marxian concept of class, applicable to nineteenth-century capitalism, has lost much of its relevance today, he provides little indication of what should replace it, or how it might be modified for application to the contemporary world. In the end he appears to opt for an extreme nominalism: 'it is possible to apply the majority, if not all, of the schemes we have been considering to almost every class society. Different conceptual categories correspond to different problems.'[15] This is hardly satisfactory.

The problem of nominalism, that is, of the 'reality' of the classes postulated by sociologists, is at the forefront of Aron's concerns in his discussion of 'industrial society'. In fact, in comparing the Marxian use of the term 'class' with that typically employed in American sociology—as, for example, in Warner's writings—Aron labels the former 'realist' and the latter 'nominalist'. According to the first standpoint, Aron points out, class is an historical reality, defined both in terms of its existence as a 'fact in material reality' and a consciousness of unity on the part of individuals who are its members. The other view, by contrast, is 'nominalist' because, since 'class' is treated as equivalent to 'stratification', it is not recognised as constituting a 'real totality', but is seen as an aggregate of individuals, who are differentiated from one another in terms of various kinds of social and psychological criteria.[16] Rather than reviving old debates about whether class is a 'real phenomenon' or a 'creation of the observer',[17] Aron opts for the view that it is reality itself which is 'equivocal': classes are rarely—if ever—the 'self-conscious actors' of Marx's theory.

This rests, however, upon an evident oversimplification of Marx's position. It is surely clear that 'class consciousness' can take, and has taken, various forms; and far from being the 'prototypical' shape of class consciousness, the experience of the proletariat is unique. According to Marx, the revolutionary action of the working class represents the first and only time in history that the vast mass

of the population constitutes a class 'for itself'. The prior exam
of revolutionary change—the rise of the bourgeoisie in post-medieval
society—involved only segments of the subordinate class; and was
quite different in character from the (optative) process of development
of a class-conscious proletariat. The 'class consciousness' of the
bourgeoisie, moreover, did not take the form of an awareness of
collective solidarity but, on the contrary, was expressed as a diffusely
felt need to escape from the constraints of feudalism, manifest
in the struggle for the 'freedom of the individual'.

The usefulness of the concept of class would certainly be sharply
limited if it were confined to the sort of conception which Aron
takes as his polemical foil in evaluating the Marxian standpoint.
While it is arguable that certain later Marxists have come close to
having adopted such a view,[18] it cuts across the main thrust of Marx's
writings. The proletariat is not so much, as Aron puts it, the 'class
par excellence', as the 'class to end all classes'. In this respect the
contrast which Ossowski draws between the 'dichotomic' and
'gradation' schemes is nearer to the truth than Aron's opposition of
'realist' and 'nominalist' standpoints: whereas for those writing in
the Marxian tradition, 'class' is treated as an explanatory concept,
the identification of 'class' and 'stratification' normally implies
that it is being used in a descriptive fashion. In Aron's discussion,
it is never clear how far the notion of class is to be attributed with
explanatory significance.

The 'choice' between the two approaches to the problem of class
avoids what is perhaps the major issue stemming from Marx's
writings: the nature of 'class society' and its possible transcendence.
The point about Marx's analysis of capitalism is that it is a form of
economy and society which is constructed *in terms* of a class relation.
But by beginning with a conception of industrial society, Aron
really prejudges the issues raised by the Marxian standpoint.[19]
A 'class society' for Aron is either one distinguished by the continuing prevalence of inequalities in income, prestige, style of life,
on the one hand, or by the existence of unified, 'historically acting'
class groups on the other. In the first sense, it is fairly obvious that
any modern society, either extant or realistically conceivable,
must necessarily be a class society. In the second sense, no society is:
the proletariat is the one distinguishable 'class' which really fits
the case, and then only at intermittent periods. Neither of these are
exhaustive of the range of possibilities implied in the Marxian
analysis of class domination.

Aron makes little contribution towards reconceptualising the
notion of class and in the end appears to identify 'class' directly

although agreeing that 'strata' are not merely
stical aggregates, but constitute 'psycho-social
n societies are 'class societies' insofar as they are
nd stratified, and in so far as such stratification
sive and self-conscious groups: 'classes do exist more
long as social stratification exists (and it appears to
e from industrial society), an interpretation in terms of
classe.   always be possible'.[20] But we must resist the tendency
to identify 'class' and 'stratification', and the view that class is a
particular 'type' of stratification. This usage, like Dahrendorf's
identification of class and authority,[21] inevitably entails the conclusion that all societies are 'class societies', and obscures some of
the main problems raised by Marx's work.

2. MAX WEBER

Of all the attempts which have been made to revise the concept of
class since Marx, that developed by Weber has, deservedly, enjoyed
most currency. Unlike the view offered by Dahrendorf, Weber's
approach shares much more than a formal similarity with that
established by Marx, since Weber accepts that ' "Property" and
"lack of property" are . . . the basic categories of all class situation'.[22] Indeed, it is easy to exaggerate the degree to which
Weber's view departs from that of Marx, especially since, in broad-
ening the concept of 'market situation', Weber's argument could
be expressed by saying that marketable skills constitute a form of
'property' which the individual is able to dispose of to secure a
given economic return.

One major difficulty with Weber's conception, however, is the
same as that faced by Dahrendorf: that is to say, it implies the
recognition of an indefinitely extensive number of 'classes'. A 'class'
refers to any aggregate of individuals who share a common market
situation, in terms of goods or capabilities which they possess. But
the range of 'goods and capabilities' possessed by individuals is
highly variable, and one could push this view to its *reductio ad
absurdum* by supposing that every individual brings a slightly
different combination of possessions or skills to the market, and
hence there are as many 'classes' as there are concrete individuals
participating in market relationships. In practice, of course, it is
only the more glaring differences between market situations of
individuals which are likely to be worth terming 'class differentials'.
But even then we are likely to be left with a very large number of
'classes'—as there are, indeed, included within Weber's classification

of *Besitzklassen* and *Erwerbsklassen*. While it might be useful for some purposes to resort to such a complicated scheme, in the main it is likely to be too unwieldy to be capable of general application, and in fact Weber appears to make no use of it at all in his empirical writings.

When Weber uses the term 'class' in the main body of his writings, he normally appears to employ it in two senses: (1) In a straightforward Marxian sense, as where he talks of the 'bourgeoisie', 'peasantry', 'working class', etc. (2) To refer to what, in his conceptual discussion of the matter in *Economy and Society*, he calls 'social class'. The relationship between these two connotations of 'class', however, is obscure, since Weber's analysis of the concept of 'social class' is exceedingly cursory. Moreover, the definition of the latter concept seems in part to cut across the initial formulation of 'class' as an aggregate of common market situations. Since the notion of 'social class' only appears in the second, later, discussion of classes and status groups, the conclusion to be drawn is that Weber came to see the inadequacies of the earlier version. But as the later formulation to some extent abandons the position that class refers solely to economic interests in the market, it tends to blur the clear dividing-line which Weber originally sought to establish, between class situation and the social groupings and forms of action which may develop among those who share common positions in the market.

Weber undoubtedly set out his concept of 'class position' in order sharply to differentiate his standpoint from the Marxian one—and particularly from certain variants of Marxism which were current in his own time:

To treat 'class' conceptually as having the same value as 'community' leads to distortion. That men in the same class situation regularly react in mass actions to such tangible situations as economic ones in the direction of those interests that are most adequate to their average number is an important and after all simple fact for the understanding of historical events. Above all, this fact must not lead to that kind of pseudo-scientific operation with the concepts of 'class' and 'class interests' so frequently found these days, and which has found its most classic expression in the statement of a talented author, that the individual may be in error concerning his interests but that the 'class' is 'infallible' about its interests.[23]

But in his desire to stress the contingent character of class consciousness and class action, Weber provides little systematic indication of the conditions under which class relationships *do* generate an awareness of mutual identity of interest or a propensity to active organisation on the basis of class interests—beyond saying that these are 'linked to general cultural traditions'.[24] If he had developed further the notion of 'social class', he might perhaps have been able to establish a more satisfactory analysis of the factors which influence how far class becomes a 'subjective' phenomenon.

The gaps in Weber's discussion at this point are perhaps due in part to his tendency to confuse two elements in the distinction between 'classes' and 'status groups'. One factor in his stress upon the significance of conceptually separating the latter from the former is undoubtedly again his wish to differentiate the concept of 'class' from subjective awareness of solidarity. Now the existence of a 'status group', depending upon some sort of social evaluation of some men by others, presupposes such subjective awareness. One pole of the distinction between 'classes' and 'status groups' thus centres upon the contrast between the 'objective' and the 'subjective': 'class' is a phenomenon which operates independently of the individual's perception of his situation, since it is given in the structure of the market; 'status', on the other hand, is founded in consciousness of group affiliation and differentiation. But classes and status groups are also distinguished in virtue of the fact that the first are created in the sphere of production, the second in the sphere of consumption.[25] Both points clearly bear directly upon the Marxian interpretation of the role of classes in social development; but the second is probably more fundamental, because it follows from it that, in so far as status groups play a major part in any given society, relationships formed in the process of production—always central in Marx—are correspondingly reduced in significance.

The distinction between these two aspects of Weber's discussion of status groups is important, because one directs attention to 'status awareness' as a form of consciousness of social differentiation separable from that generated by class position, while the other stresses the importance of forms of group structure which originate outside the economic order. While these two may overlap, they are very definitely not the same. Thus the feudal estates, founded upon discriminations established in law, belong to the latter category, and are obviously in various respects very different from the forms of consciousness of differential prestige, honour, etc., which may exist in capitalist society. The use of a single concept (*Stand*) to embrace both of these sets of phenomena confuses as much as it illuminates. While status group relationships, as Weber analyses them, may refer to 'feudal' elements which persist within capitalism (as in the case of aspects of the style of life of the *Junkers*), these are distinguishable from, say, the 'status consciousness' of the 'artist' or 'professor' as compared to that of the 'industrialist'.[26]

3. CONCLUSION

It has not been my purpose, in criticising Marx's critics, to hold
that their work may be dismissed out of hand, and I shall make
use of certain of their ideas in my subsequent analysis of the theory
of class structure. But I do wish to assert that their writings, as
they stand, do not contain an acceptable formulation of such a
theory; nor do they offer a satisfactory appraisal, for the reasons
which I have discussed, of the weaknesses in the Marxian standpoint.
It is to this latter task I now turn.

5

THE MARXIAN STANDPOINT REASSESSED

1. CLASS AND THE DIVISION OF LABOUR

The origins of concern with 'class' and with 'class society', of course, are to be traced to the 'great transformation' in the European societies: the decline and final disintegration of feudalism, and its replacement by a new social and economic order. Marx developed his conception of class in the belief that the liberation of men from the constraints of feudalism had delivered them up to new forms of bondage—no longer, however, founded in a God-given, natural order of domination and subordination, but created by the exigencies of the 'free' capitalist market. In Europe, there was not one, but several 'feudalisms'; but within the divergences which existed both at the height of the system and in the 'post-feudal' period,[1] it is possible to discern a common institutional structure which contrasts dramatically with the form of economy and society which superseded it.

(1) In feudalism, there was an 'authoritative allocation of work'. According to the medieval principle *Unusquisque maneat in ea vocatione in qua dignoscitur vocatus*, every man should carry out dutifully the tasks involved in that vocation, and that vocation only, to which he has been assigned in the divinely sanctioned hierarchy of occupations. With the decline of the medieval order, this principle becomes dissolved: 'individuals are free to expend their energies, skills, and goods as they will'.[2]

(2) Closely related to this stood the formulae separating society into the legally differentiated estates: 'it was precisely the hallmark of a member of a particular estate that he could not move out of his own estate and that whatever status he enjoyed, he was rigidly

controlled by the norms applicable to his estate. These norms concerned his very standing within society, concerned any privileges he might have had, including the right of inheritance, of marriage . . .'[3] The abolition of legally sanctioned estate privileges freed men for participation in a competitive labour market.

(3) The feudal economy, based upon the manorial community, mainly involved production for a set of known, local consumer needs. The development of commodity production, with the concomitant expansion of a money economy, substitutes the price mechanism as the link between producers and consumers spatially distant from each other.

(4) Patterns of domination and subordination in feudal society, both on the level of the manorial community and among the higher ranks, were above all of a personalised kind. *Hommage de corps*, the ties of fealty and bondage, constituted the essential foundation of the feudal structure; the society was composed of 'a vast system of personal relationships whose intersecting threads ran from one level of the social structure to another'.[4] Such a system is evidently incompatible with one organised in terms of impersonal market principles, and presupposing formal equality of opportunity.

(5) In the feudal system, 'economic' and 'political' power were fused together. The decline of feudalism was accompanied, and promoted, by an emerging separation of these two institutional spheres, commerce and industry on the one hand, and the state on the other.

(6) Feudalism, primarily agrarian in character, was necessarily bound to the countryside. The emergence of the new social and economic order was contingent upon the growth of the towns, whose existence was predicated upon trade and manufacture. Even as far back as the eleventh century, the term *bourgeois* (burgess, burgher) became applied to designate the town-dweller, recognised to be completely different from the knight, cleric or villein.[5]

While wishing to treat feudalism as a class system, Marx was at the same time heavily influenced by, and sought to emphasise, the depth of these contrasts between feudalism and capitalism; hence his uncertainty in the matter of accepting a clear-cut distinction between 'estate' and 'class'. Weber made such a distinction, but then again confused the issue by assimilating 'estate' and 'status'. The denotation of the concept of class will be discussed in detail below, but at this juncture it is appropriate to indicate that the interests of conceptual clarity are best served by the adoption of a clear differentiation between estate (and 'estate society') and class (and, therefore, 'class society'). Classes thus only come into being when the previously noted characteristics of feudalism are undermined or dissolved. In this way we can establish, in a preliminary manner, certain general parameters governing the application of the class concept. First, classes are *large-scale* groupings. The emergence of classes presupposes a break with the sort of social and economic system, characteristic of feudalism as well as of other types of traditional society, based primarily upon the self-sufficient local community. The decisive factor promoting this transcendence of the local community is the formation of market relationships and a division of labour allowing the production of commodities. Secondly, classes are *aggregates* of individuals rather than social 'groups'. This does not mean that classes cannot give rise to concrete groups which have clearly definable 'boundaries' and which are formed of a common pool of interactions linking members to one another. But whether or not this is so depends upon various additional conditions. Thirdly, the appearance of classes presupposes the dissolution of the personalised ties of fealty or obligation characteristic of feudal society, and their replacement by 'impersonal' relationships of a contractual kind. Finally, classes are nominally 'open': that is to say, class membership is not determined by inherited position guaranteed by custom or law.[6]

In order to proceed further, however, we must examine some of the difficulties presented by Marx's theory of class, in relation to capitalism and *its* anticipated transcendence by socialism.

Marx used the term 'capitalism' in a specific sense. There has been a common tendency among economic historians, both in Marx's time and more recently, to trace capitalism back deep into the Middle Ages[7]—and, often, to identify its existence in prior epochs of history also. In this usage, 'capitalism' is normally equated with the formation of commercial relationships, and money markets, involving trading operations. Marx explicitly rejected this view. Thus he criticised Weber's mentor, Mommsen, for example, on the grounds that the latter finds 'a capitalist mode of production in every monetary economy'.[8] Nor, according to Marx, is it satisfactory merely to hold that capitalism is a system of commodity production. What really distinguishes capitalism as a form of economic system is that labour (power) *itself* becomes a commodity, bought and sold on the market:

The historical conditions of its existence (i.e., the existence of capitalism) are by no means given the mere circulation of money and commodities. It can spring into being only when the owner of the means of production and subsistence meets in the market with the free labourer selling his labour-power. And this one historical condition comprises a world's history. Capital, therefore, announces from its first appearance a new epoch in the process of social production.[9]

The importance of this is that it ties the very definition of capitalism to the existence of a class system linking capital and wage-labour; and this, in turn, according to Marx, creates a whole 'superstructure' of social relationships in 'bourgeois society'. There is quite evidently a difference between the division separating nobility and bourgeoisie in post-feudal society and that separating bourgeoisie and proletariat in capitalism. In the first case, the two groupings in question are not tied to one another in an exploitative relationship founded in the division of labour. The bourgeoisie, as it were, develop within an enclave within the feudal system, but are not an integral part of it. The conflicts which arise between them and the nobility derive from the growing economic and political power of the towns in the face of a weakening feudal economy. Conflict between bourgeoisie and proletariat, on the other hand, originates in the exploitative connection which binds the two classes, and which constitutes the essential core of capitalism as a social and economic system. The difference is a fundamental one, and while it is recognised by Marx, its implications tend to be hidden within the general framework in terms of which he attempts to set out an account of the process of revolutionary change from one type of society to another.

This process involves the expansion of a new set of forces of production within an existing set of relations of production, such that a growing tension is created which eventually culminates in the revolutionary overthrow of the latter.[10] But while, in the transition from feudalism to capitalism, the evolving character of the 'forces of production' involves a series of changes in technique (manufacture and, subsequently, 'machinofacture' in factory production) making for the rise of a new class, this is not the case with the development of socialism out of capitalism. The growth of a new set of 'forces of production' within capitalism refers to the process whereby an incipient socialisation of production threatens to undermine the competitive market upon which the capitalist economy is based. By and large the forms of technique characteristic of capitalism remain under socialism. Marx's writings have often been interpreted as a kind of technological determinism, and while this is hardly a defensible interpretation, it is indicative of an obscurity or weakness in his thought at this point, depending upon three of the major concepts involved in his general 'materialist thesis': the 'means of production' (*Produktionsmittel*), the 'relations of production' (*Produktionsverhältnisse*), and the 'mode of production' (*Produktionsweise*). Marx normally uses the first as equivalent to technique: the technological form in terms of which material production takes place in any given society. The second refers to the social relationships which, as Marx stresses in contradistinction to the political economists, are always presupposed in any sort of productive activity; the third refers to the overall organisation of social and technical relationships involved in a system of production, and thus comprises the first two (cf. *Produktionskräfte*: 'forces of production'). The notion of the relations of production is of primary significance here, since it represents the main conceptual connection whereby, in Marx's writing, technique is related to the overall socio-economic system which is formed by a society. As Marx employs the term, 'relations of production' covers at least three distinguishable sets of socio-economic relationships: (1) Those involved in the operation of any given technique of production. Thus the working of a conveyor belt places men not only in definite relationships with the machine, but also with each other. We may call these *'paratechnical relations'*.[11] (2) Those involved in linkages between productive units: as where goods are exchanged on a market. (3) Those involved in the linkage between production and distribution (consumption).

In his discussions of the types of 'mode of production' which have succeeded each other in history, Marx tends to assimilate all of these sets of relationships; or rather, to give prominence to one or another when it happens to fit with a particular argument he wishes to advance. The famous proposition that 'The hand-mill gives you society with the feudal lord; the steam-mill, society with the industrial capitalist'[12] is an example. Such statements lend an apparent support to the contention that Marx's historical materialism is simply a technological determinism. Even allowing for the fact that it was written in a polemical vein, the proposition is manifestly false; the hand-mill has existed in other systems besides feudalism and the steam-mill, or modern variants of it, will presumably continue to play a part in the technological apparatus in socialist society. The point is that the connection between paratechnical relations and the broader economic relationships involved in any given system of production is a variable one; and the character of the second depends less upon the nature of the first than upon the ways in which relationships are formed by coercion, custom, or law. A similar point may be made about the connections between production and distribution, and the social relationships engendered by these. In his general theoretical writing Marx normally treats patterns of consumption as almost completely dependent upon production; but in other places he recognises the significance of the former as influencing production rather than being shaped by it.[13]

These inadequacies or oversimplifications in Marx's writings derive from two sources. One is of a very general character, and rests upon the premises of his 'materialism'. In 'reversing' Hegel's philosophy, Marx began from the standpoint 'that man must be in a position to live in order to "make history" ', that is, that production is a necessary exigency for the existence of human life, and hence that every society presupposes some form of 'economy'. While this is unobjectionable, it does not follow from this, as Marx proceeds to infer, that 'the nature of individuals [and society] depends upon the material conditions determining their production'.[14] In other words, it is not legitimate to claim that, because men must eat to live, their mode of life is necessarily determined by the manner in which they produce what they eat. Whether or not the latter is the case can only be discovered by the direct sociological and economic analysis of definite forms of society. It is even less valid to hold that the structure characteristic of a given society is controlled by the type of technique employed in production. While the general tenor of Marx's thought clearly runs contrary to any sort of simple technological determinism, the fact that he fails to deal adequately with the relationship between technique and other aspects of the 'relations of production' is indicative of the weaknesses inherent in his treatment of 'infrastructure' and 'superstructure'. It is not my intention here to enter into anything like an overall critique of Marx's conception of historical materialism, but it is worth emphasising that the defects and ambiguities of Marx's view definitely stem in part from a lack of clarity over how far phenomena characteristic of capitalism can be generalised to all types of society. The emergence of the capitalist market vastly expands the degree to which 'industry' influences the general range of human conduct in society. But it is not always evident in Marx which aspects of this are specific to the capitalist mode of production and which are not:[15] hence the already mentioned hesitation over the differentiation between 'estate' and 'class'.

The origins of such insufficiencies in Marx's thought are less important, however, than their consequences for his theory of class. Fundamental here is the problem of the division of labour, a concept which Marx took over from the political economists. In his early writings Marx identifies the growth of the division of labour as the source of human alienation. The division of labour, although creating material wealth, 'fragments' generic human capabilities. Marx did not abandon this view in his mature writings, in which he sought to examine, in a concrete fashion, the social and economic processes underlying what he had previously called, in a diffuse fashion, 'alienation'. The growth of the division of labour, however, 'fragments man' in two principal ways, which are not conceptually distinguished by Marx. In the first place, the division of labour promotes the specialisation of occupational activity—a process which is carried furthest by the growth of mechanised production in capitalism. In this sense, the division of labour 'subordinates man to the machine', limiting the range of the activities of the worker to routine, repetitive operations. The alienative effects of the division of labour, from this aspect, are closely linked to the growth in technological complexity.[16] But the expansion of the division of labour also 'fragments man' by dividing human society into classes. Classes only come into existence when a surplus product is generated, such that a division of labour is possible between those who produce and those who do not; and such that the latter are placed in an exploitative relation *vis-à-vis* the former. The alienative character of the division of labour in this sense is expressed in the fact that, in virtue of the development of a class system, men are forced in substantial degree to cede control over their actions to others.

In socialist society, according to Marx, alienation will be transcended, and the division of labour, in the sense of occupational specialisation, will disappear together with classes. The link between these two processes, of course, is the abolition of private property. The difficulties in Marx's theory at this point are not, however, to be dismissed as the result of a mere 'trick of definition', but derive instead from a failure to reconcile satisfactorily the two aspects of the alienative character of the division of labour, a failure which in turn stems from the uncertain role allocated to technique, as noted above. Occupational specialisation, whereby one man is, for example, a 'welder', while another is a 'plumber' or a 'doctor', is primarily the outcome of technological change. Marx is certainly correct in holding that this is promoted in large degree by the rise of capitalism, which prizes above all the efficient generation of profit; and in this respect the tendency towards occupational differentiation is certainly directly related to the class system. But this is not the same as showing that the transcendence of that class system makes necessary, or even possible, the abolition of the division of labour in the broader sense. For, according to

Marx, the formation of socialism is predicated upon the creation of a material abundance which is established as a potential by the technology developed within the capitalist modes of production, but which cannot be fully realised because of the intrinsic limitations of that mode of production.

It is significant that, in those places in his writings where he offers something more than cryptic allusions to a future society in which the division of labour will be abolished, Marx tends to give prominence to pre-industrial occupations—as in the famous passage describing a society 'which makes it possible for one to do one thing today and another tomorrow, to hunt in the morning, fish in the afternoon, rear cattle in the evening, criticise after dinner, just as I have a mind, without ever becoming hunter, fisherman, shepherd or critic'.[17] In spite of leaning upon a perspective drawn from the pre-industrial era, in his vision of the new social and economic order which is to replace capitalism, Marx certainly does not wish to align himself with the opponents of industrial technology *per se*. But the fact that he was drawn to rely on such analogies is indicative of the unresolved difficulties in his views at this point. When he speaks of the 'abolition' or disappearance of the division of labour, Marx normally uses the Hegelian term *Aufhebung*, which implies 'transcendence' rather than 'eradication' in any simple sense. But the only hints in his writings as to how this 'positive abolition' of the division of labour might come about consist in a few generalisations, commonplace in the nineteenth century, about the tendency of mechanisation to eventually culminate in automated production, whereby 'man relates himself to [the labour] process merely as a supervisor and controller'.[18]

This has a direct relevance to the problem, discussed at length by Dahrendorf, of the authority structure of industry and the state in the socialist society envisaged by Marx. In capitalism, authority relationships in each of these two spheres ultimately rest upon rights inherent in the possession and deployment of capital. In neither case are these rights legitimised, as in feudal society, as the natural rights of a specific minority; their legitimacy derives from newly recognised concepts of freedom and equality. In the sphere of the economy itself, freedom of contracts effectively sanctions the dominance of the owner of capital, since the wage-labourer is forced to deliver himself into the hands of the capitalist by dint of economic necessity. This position of nominal freedom and actual bondage is reinforced and stabilised by the modern state, which recognises 'political' rights of citizenship, but specifically separates these from industry. Thus in Marx's analysis the authority structure of capitalist industry is treated as flowing from the rights, and therefore the powers, of capital as bolstered or sanctioned by the bourgeois state. The problem of the influence of technique upon relationships of domination and subordination *within the industrial enterprise itself* receives little attention. It is, of course, intrinsic to Marx's views that the achievement of a classless society will produce a wholesale reorganisation of industry; but given the absence of a direct discussion of the problem of technique, it remains obscure how this is to be achieved. It is obvious that the arrival of automated production on a grand scale would be compatible with, or demand, new forms of social relationships within industrial organisations, but Marx nowhere discusses such possibilities in any detail. The matter is treated by Engels, who simply argues that a strict division of labour is necessitated by modern technology, and that this in turn will presuppose the same sort of hierarchy of authority in industrial enterprises under socialism as that characteristic of capitalism: 'The automatic machinery of a big factory is much more despotic than the small capitalists who employ workers ever have been. . . . If man, by dint of his knowledge and inventive genius, has subdued the forces of nature, the latter avenge themselves upon him by subjecting him, in so far as he employs them, to a veritable despotism independent of all social organisation.'[19] While it seems clear, from the various partial references to the problem in the *Grundrisse* and elsewhere, that Marx himself did not accept such a view, certainly the difficulties posed are not satisfactorily resolved in his writings.

Marx's reluctance to offer much detail upon the social forms to be characteristic of socialism (apart from the 'transitional stage', which merely universalises relations inherent in capitalism, with the state assuming the role of 'capitalist') also leaves unclear other aspects of the prospective organisation of industry, and indeed of the state itself. For, assuming that Marx believed that, even in the 'higher stage' of communism, industrial organisation would still entail some definite distribution of authority, there are few indications as to how this is to be linked to the 'abolition of political power' which Marx speaks of in discussing the state. It is evident enough that 'abolition of political power' has to be read in a similar sense to 'abolition of the division of labour': it does not imply the simple destruction of the bourgeois state, but its transcendence by a new form of social organisation which synthesises elements already present in the existing structure. The state 'disappears' in the sense that it is 'subordinated to society'. A clear indication of what Marx meant by the latter phrase is given in his discussion of the proposed organisation of the Paris Commune. In the Commune, 'the repressive organs of the old governmental power were to be amputated', by instituting universal suffrage, making officials revocable at short terms, drawing these officials from the mass of the population, and paying them wages equivalent to those of workmen. 'The Commune was therefore to serve as a lever for uprooting the economic foundations upon which rests the existence of classes, and therefore of class-rule. With labour emancipated, every man becomes a working man, and productive labour ceases to be a class attribute'.[20] But there is very little direct discussion in Marx's works of the problem posed for this standpoint by the differential distribution of technical knowledge and skills—the equivalent to the problem of the division of labour seemingly enforced by the technique within the sphere of industry, and the factor given the central place in Weber's analysis of the sources of bureaucratic hierarchy.

In Marx's writings, therefore, the contrast between the 'class character' of capitalism and the 'classlessness' of socialism is a complicated one, involving several overlapping strands; and its complexities are not adequately expressed by the concept of class which Marx adopts in his abstract model, as centring upon ownership versus non-ownership of the means of production. These complexities remain largely concealed in Marx's analysis for two reasons. One is that he took over the notion of class in a relatively unexamined way from the works of prior authors. The other is his refusal to enter into anything other than the most general terms in describing the anticipated 'higher stage' of the classless society. Although Marx's position on this matter undeniably accords with his strictures against 'utopian socialism', it nevertheless serves to reinforce a disinclination to analyse the full implications of the antithesis between 'class society' on the one hand, and 'classlessness' on the other. We may recall Dahrendorf's discussion at this juncture. The point is not that the formal abolition of private property equals classlessness as a 'trick of definition', but that it is only one moment in a complex and protracted process of social and economic change.

2. THE GENESIS OF CLASS CONFLICT

It has already been pointed out that the process of class conflict attendant upon the transcendence of feudalism by capitalism, as Marx conceives of it, differs from that which is generated by the further development of capitalism itself.[21] The struggle between feudal nobility and rising bourgeoisie, in fact, does not appear in the classification of conflicting classes which Marx offers in a summary statement at the opening of *The Communist Manifesto*, which asserts that 'Freeman and slave, patrician and plebeian, lord and serf, guildmaster and journeyman, in a word, oppressor and oppressed, have stood in constant opposition to one another, carried on an uninterrupted, now hidden, now open conflict, a conflict that each time ended, either in a revolutionary reconstitution of society at large, or in the common ruin of the contending classes.'[22] Here the criterion for the identification of class conflict is obviously that of the 'exploitative dependence' of one class upon the other in the dichotomous model; there is a direct conflict of interest having its source in the appropriation of surplus value by a non-productive class. In the case of nobility and bourgeoisie, however, conflict of interest derives from the need of the latter to dissolve the social and economic relationships characteristic of the feudal order, and of the former to maintain them.[23] Thus although the bourgeoisie is in one sense a 'subordinate' class within post-feudal society, in another sense it constitutes a 'dominant' class, in terms of the exploitative relationship in which it stands with wage-labour.

It is clear that, in contrast to the situation in feudal society, the relationship between bourgeoisie and proletariat within capitalism involves *both* of these forms of interest-conflict; but the two are not separated by Marx. The theory of surplus value discloses the exploitative connection between capital and wage-labour, thereby showing that capitalism entails a class system of a sort equivalent to those noted in the passage from *The Communist Manifesto*. But the relationship between these two classes also embodies an incipient, and progressively more marked, 'contradiction' which parallels that between feudal landlord and capitalist—although, as I have previously pointed out, this does not involve a clearly identifiable change in productive technique, as occurs in the transition from feudalism. In the case of capital and wage-labour, the conflict between the 'old' and 'emergent' modes of production hinges upon the opposition between the individualistic pursuit of profit in a competitive market and the socialisation of market relationships, which increasingly intervenes with the growing maturity of capitalism.

Distinguishing these two forms of interest-conflict between the two major classes in capitalism may be important in elucidating the origins and nature of the class consciousness of the proletariat. In general, it would be true to say that one of the weakest, or least clarified, aspects of Marx's writings concerns the relationship between class and class consciousness—between class 'in itself' and class 'for itself'. In the first place, Marx's use of the term 'class consciousness' is quite variable. At least three potentially distinct sets of circumstances are covered by it: where the members of a given class share certain common attitudes and beliefs, regardless of the content of those attitudes and beliefs; where class members are aware of belonging to a particular class, and thereby of sharing common class interests; and where members of a class, or a certain proportion of them, actively organise to pursue such interests.[24] But, more important, Marx gives only a few indications as to the *conditions* governing the development of proletarian class consciousness, in any of these senses. One reason for this, it can be argued, is that, in the prior historical example which Marx looked to— the transition from feudalism to capitalism—the factors involved in the formation of the class consciousness of the rising class were relatively unproblematic. The bourgeoisie came into being in the towns, and derived their position from control of a means of production separate from that of agrarian feudalism; their class consciousness was not expressed in terms of any generalised recognition of their role in history, nor even of an awareness of collective class interests, but rather in terms of a struggle for 'individual rights'. None of the other groupings mentioned by Marx in the above passage as 'oppressor and oppressed', however, either achieved even this level of class consciousness, or played a revolutionary role in history. Thus, for example, while peasant rebellions were not an uncommon phenomenon in feudal and post-feudal Europe, their chiliasm rarely bred a consciousness that the earthly social structure could be changed, and their concrete aims were normally confined to economic goals or to the aspiration to remove certain particular individuals from positions of power.[25]

In spite of the various setbacks to Marx's hopes for the emergence of an actively class-conscious proletariat, notably in Britain, he never seems to have entertained any doubt that such a consciousness would come into being. The conventional explanation of this looks to Marx's supposed 'determinism', holding that, since he believed the socialist revolution to be 'inevitable', and since he saw human consciousness as an 'epiphenomenon' of material change, he saw no need to examine in any detail the social conditions which might promote the class consciousness of the proletariat. But, quite apart from the validity or otherwise of such interpretations, a more specific reason is suggested by the analysis I have developed here. For Marx tended to merge two sets of phenomena: (1) the relationship of exploitation existing between bourgeoisie and proletariat within capitalism (deriving from the fact that whatever is appropriated by one class from the total volume of production is denied to the other); and (2) the revolutionary consciousness (not necessarily the same as the experience of exploitation) which embodies the possibility of a radical transformation of the existing social and economic order. As will be suggested below (Chapter 7), the connection between these two forms of consciousness is much more tenuous than Marx implicitly assumes. While the first is frequent, if not chronic, in class societies, the second is rare; and while the existence of the second form tends to imply the first, the reverse is not at all necessarily the case. Even in Marx's own writings on the prospective development of capitalism, we can quite readily distinguish these two sets of factors in the few remarks he does make about the conditions facilitating the growth of the class consciousness of the proletariat. Thus, on the one hand, he mentions factors such as the increasing relative disparity between the wages of the worker and profit accruing to the capitalist; the fact that the worker, under the stimulus of economic necessity, is more and more reduced to a mere 'appendage of a machine', with the alienative consequences which this has for his enjoyment of work; and the growth of an enormous 'reserve army' of semi-permanently unemployed labour. To the second category belong the increasing 'simplification' of the class structure by the elimination of transitional classes; the massing together of workers in large-scale industrial organisations; the growth of national modes of communication, making possible the formation of centralised unions and workers' political parties; and the general process of secularisation fostered by capitalism, which permits a fully rational understanding of the historical mission of the working class. The point about these latter phenomena is that they express, not the specific consequences of the exploitative nature of the interdependence of wage-labour and capital, but rather the character of the mode of production which, engendered by capitalism itself, will eventually replace it— i.e., a system of socialised production, based upon the rational adjustment of production to need.

3. PRODUCTIVE AND UNPRODUCTIVE LABOUR

Fundamental to Marx's conception of historical materialism is the notion of 'man as the producer'. Man distinguishes himself from the animals as soon as he begins to produce; in the process of production, he both modifies the material world and changes himself—thereby setting into motion a dialectical interchange which underlies all human technological and intellectual culture. The correlate of this general emphasis in the theory of classes is the idea of productive as opposed to unproductive labour, which Marx found a rationale for in the labour theory of value as formulated in classical economic theory. The labour theory of value was originally devised as a prop for the view of the early political economists that the land-owning nobility were a parasitical grouping, profiting from the labour of others—the assumption which Saint-Simon also built into his contrast between feudalism and 'industrial society'. In working out the origin of surplus value in the capitalist economy, Marx sought to turn back the labour theory of value against its own proponents, showing that the new society replacing feudalism was still one divided into those who create value and those who are parasitical upon the value created by the others.

How successful Marx's account of either value or surplus value is in terms of the technical demands of economic theory—in predicting prices, etc.—is neither here nor there. What is important is its implications for the theory of classes. In discussing this, it is necessary to emphasise the essential role of the labour theory of value in Marx's work. Not for nothing has it been said of Marx that he 'was the only Ricardian who ever went through with the labour theory of value'.[26] For even Ricardo himself, particularly towards the end of his career, recognised other factors besides labour as creating value.[27] Marx did not, and while his consistency in this respect allowed him to clarify elements which are confused or obscure in the writings of his predecessors, it gives rise to major difficulties in the analysis of the class structure of capitalism. Productive labour, that is labour which creates value, depends, according to Marx, upon the interplay between nature and human labour-power. Those whose work can be described in these terms create the surplus value off which men in 'unproductive' occupations live; in capitalism, this refers to the working class, who produce the commodities which are bought and sold on the market. The operations of the market, the circulation of commodities or money, whereby commodities are converted into money or vice versa, are intrinsically unproductive. Those whose occupations involve the administration of these operations live off the surplus value created by the labourer.

The result of this, however, is to connect the economic structure of capitalism too closely to that of feudalism, as a system of agrarian production. In a society in which the bulk of the population is employed in agriculture, at a near-subsistence level, it makes some sense to separate that population into a mass of 'producers', and a minority of 'non-producers' who, deriving their existence from surplus value created by the former group, are in an exploitative position in relation to them; and this provides a close approximation to the main axis of the class structure of this type of society. In feudalism, the lord appropriates the surplus product to the peasant, and uses it directly for his own consumption. But this is not at all the same in capitalism, which depends upon a money economy in order to allow exchange of goods in a vast market. Complex processes of 'distribution' are imperative to the latter type of economy, and to the other forms of social organisation which it engenders. While the theory of exploitation developed by Marx in relation to the source of surplus value in capitalism allows him to draw close parallels between the capitalist class system and the system which preceded it in history, it also serves to obscure the significance of the administrative structure of the new society.

Consequently the workers employed in the 'non-productive' occupations, but who are nevertheless propertyless, hold an ambiguous position in Marxian theory. The assertion that Marx was unaware of the growth in the 'white-collar sector' promoted by the expansion of capitalism does not stand up to examination; indeed Marx refers to this grouping directly at various points in his writings. But he was not able to embody any sort of satisfactory treatment of it in his theory. Since workers in administrative occupations are 'non-productive', and depend for their existence upon appropriating a portion of the surplus product of manual labour, it would appear that they effectively form part of the dominant class. But, on the other hand, since they are, with manual workers, separated from control of their means of production, they must sell their labour on the market in order to secure the means of their livelihood. Quite apart from the difficulties which are raised in determining what sort of overt class and political affiliations, according to Marx's theory, these workers might be expected to develop, there are obvious problems here in comparing the 'class society' of capitalism to the 'classless' order of the future. For if the 'exploitative' character of capitalism is given in the extraction of surplus value from productive labour, then the abolition of exploitation in the classless society would apparently imply a return to a situation in which labour reaps the full reward of the value which it has created. But this is manifestly impossible, given the multiplicity of administrative functions entailed in the capitalist mode of production—functions which will become expanded in significance, rather than become diminished, with the advent of a socialised market. *Any* form of society, therefore, which depends upon large-scale production and exchange of goods, must necessarily involve, according to the terms of Marx's economic theory, the extraction of surplus value from the producing majority. Nothing in Marx's works indicates which mechanisms will control the 'rate' of extraction of surplus value in socialist society, and how accumulated value will be distributed. Apart from the few brief statements in the *Critique of the Gotha Programme*, which in any case only deal with the 'transitional stage' from capitalism to socialism, Marx avoids the problem, since it again belongs to those issues which are left to be dealt with only when the 'higher stage' of communism has come into being.

The unsatisfactory character of Marx's view of 'unproductive labour' also helps to explain the relatively undeveloped character of the theory of bureaucracy in his writings. Bureaucracy is an 'independent power' merely to the degree that it represents the interests of one class in its exploitative ascendancy over another; and Marx only discusses bureaucracy in relation to the state and its anticipated transcendence in socialism. Whatever the deficiencies of the Weberian analysis of bureaucracy (some of which, as I shall argue below, can be clarified by comparing this to Marx's view), it serves to direct attention to problems largely ignored by Marx.

4. THE FORM OF CLASS RELATIONSHIPS

In identifying the two major classes in capitalism, Marx simply took over current terminology by using the terms 'bourgeoisie' or 'capitalists' on the one hand, and 'proletariat' or 'working class' on the other. As regards Marx's 'abstract model' of classes, this scheme presents no particular difficulty; the bourgeoisie are those who possess and deploy capital, while the proletariat are the mass of propertyless workers who sell their labour-power to the former grouping. However, on the empirical level, as Marx was well aware, this neat simplicity is not easy to reconcile with the complicated structure of actual forms of society. In each of the leading European societies of Marx's time (not excluding 'revolutionary' France), 'pre-capitalist' groupings, or 'transitional classes', remained of importance at all levels of the social structure; and Marx recognised that, under most circumstances, classes are internally diversified rather than homogeneous entities. But while he discussed these matters at some length in relation to the historical analysis of specific societies, he did not really confront them on a theoretical level.

One issue of some significance here is that of mobility between classes—a phenomenon given much prominence in Saint-Simonian theory. Marx's view was apparently governed by his attitude towards the conception of 'equality of opportunity' as a bourgeois ideology masking the reality of class relationships. On the whole, he seems to have accepted without much question that, if this ideology were at any time anything more than a mere fiction, it was only in the early stages of capitalist development that men of humble origins may have become successful capitalist entrepreneurs— although Marx poured scorn upon the political economists who regarded the combination of 'initiative' and personal frugality shown by such self-made men as both an explanation for and a legitimation of the power of capital. But with the further maturity of capitalism as the dominant mode of production, capital becomes self-reproducing, and the two main classes consequently become largely self-recruiting groupings over the generations. Except for a few comments upon the special case of the United States, where the fluidity of 'interchange between the classes' retards the development of proletarian class consciousness, Marx gave little attention to the possible influence of mobility upon forms of class relationship and class consciousness in employing the received notions of 'bourgeoisie' and 'proletariat'. There is undoubtedly some substance to Aron's complaint about the somewhat indefinite character of classes in Marxian theory. Marx's indiscriminate use of the term 'class' itself allowed him to skate over some of the difficulties involved here: if, for example, the central meaning of 'bourgeoisie' is clear enough—referring to the owners of large-scale capital— Marx also frequently uses the word in a much broader and more ill-defined way, including under it various categories of persons who are assumed to be in some sense in the service of the interests of this more restricted grouping, such as government officials, lawyers, etc. The problem is of more than formal significance. For a crucial theorem in Marx's writings is the subservience of political power to economic power as manifest in ownership of capital. But by shifting his use of 'class' to sometimes include political as well as economic categories, Marx frequently tends to assume what should be demonstrated.

I shall confront these and other problems directly in the two following chapters, moving on in Chapter 8 to undertake a general dis-discussion of capitalist development.

6

RETHINKING THE THEORY OF CLASS (I)

A large part of the chequered history of the concept of class has to be understood in terms of the changing concerns of those who have made use of the notion, concerns which reflect changing directions of emphasis within sociology itself. It hardly needs emphasising that, in Marx's writings, the concept is the focal element in a generalised interpretation of the succession of different types of society in history; and that what is original in Marx's application of it is not to be found so much in any elaboration of the notion itself, but in his attempt to show how the class structure of capitalism generates a new form of classless order. To say simply that Marx used 'class' in an 'explanatory' sense, whereas many later writers have been more interested in using it as a 'descriptive' category, is to gloss over the main point at issue when comparing the Marxian usage with subsequent attempts to amend or reconstruct it within a non-Marxist sociological framework. The essential motive-force in the Marxian endeavour, and the one which gives Marx's thought much of its compelling quality, is to be found in the thesis that the innermost character of capitalism (paralleled, of course, in the analysis of the other, prior, types of society, Ancient and feudal) is revealed by demonstrating the nature of the class relationship between capital and wage-labour. The concept of class, as Marx employed it, has little significance when taken out of the context of that overall scheme; and, as I have indicated in the last chapter, the weaknesses and difficulties associated with the Marxian concept derive primarily from aspects of Marx's theory often regarded as separable from his use of the notion of class as such.

I shall argue that a fruitful reconceptualisation of the notion of class can be achieved by treating these aspects of Marx's writings as a point of departure; but that such a reconceptualisation must also be extended to include the notions of 'class society' and 'class-lessness'. This, in turn, implies a revitalisation of ideas which, while integral to the Marxian conceptual armoury, have been largely abandoned by non-Marxist sociologists.

1. FORMAL PROPERTIES OF THE CLASS CONCEPT

In the previous chapter I have already suggested certain general attributes which should be taken as preliminary characteristics of 'class', namely that a class is a large-scale aggregate of individuals, comprised of impersonally defined relationships, and nominally 'open' in form. At this point we may push further towards a more positive delimitation of the class concept.

One of the confusing aspects of much of the literature upon the theory of class is that, whereas some approaches (e.g. that of Marx) assume the existence of only a limited number of classes in any given type of society, others recognise an indefinite multiplicity of classes. This is reflected in the everyday language of sociology: whereas some writers speak of, for example, the 'working class', others refer to the 'working classes'.[1] It should be clear that the use of a dichotomous conception of class, as an 'abstract model', does not necessarily lead to the recognition of only a restricted number of classes. Whether or not the latter is the case depends upon the nature of the criteria used as the axis of the dichotomy. Since the Marxian conception places the emphasis upon ownership or exclusion from ownership of property in the means of production, it inevitably produces a relatively simple portrayal of empirical class structure, complicated only by the existence of 'transitional classes'. The Weberian analysis is more complex; while Weber's *Besitzklassen* and *Erwerbsklassen* preserve the criterion of ownership of the means of production, the further factor of 'marketable skill' is introduced, thus differen-tiating among the propertyless. Finally, Dahrendorf's use of posses-sion of or exclusion from authority, although intrinsically a simple model, yields a potentially almost infinite number of classes when applied to any existing society.

As Ossowski emphasises, dichotomous class models have normally been used by those who wish to underline the significance of class conflict. But, as I have already pointed out, the connection is not a necessary one; dichotomic schemes can and have been employed by those who wish to accentuate the natural harmony of classes. What links a dichotomic model to a conception of class conflict is that the dichotomic division in question is conceived to involve an opposition of interest between the two classes, which in turn tends to imply the existence of an exploitative relationship between them. whereby one class is able to secure certain returns at the expense of the other. The most important inadequacy of dichotomous interpretations of class structure is that, by their very nature, they make it conceptually difficult to recognise the existence of 'middle' classes. The Marxian scheme copes with the problem of middle classes in two ways (see above, p. 31). One is by treating them as part of a dichotomous class order of a different type. In this sense, the bourgeoisie are a middle class with reference to post-feudal society. But this is in effect to deny that the bourgeoisie is a 'middle' class in the sense of a class intervening between two others in a single system of classes; and, of course, no one has ever suggested calling the proletariat a 'middle' class. The other mode of meeting the difficulty in Marxian theory is that of calling a 'class' what is in fact, by reference to the overall trend of Marx's thought, only a segment of a class. Thus the petty bourgeoisie, if it is to be regarded as a class separable from the *grande* bourgeoisie, is so in virtue of a difference in scale of enterprise owned, not because it is in an exploited position *vis-à-vis* the latter class.

Neither of these solutions is entirely satisfactory, and neither is able to encompass that grouping which has always escaped adequate analysis in Marxist terms; the 'new middle class' in capitalism. If it be granted, however, that abandoning the dichotomous model does not necessarily entail relinquishing the notion of class conflict, then it follows that most of the traditional problems of class analysis developed from within the Marxian standpoint may be tackled in a different framework—together with others either not faced by Marx, or which cannot be readily analysed in his terms. The most obvious alternative in the literature discussed previously is that established by Weber. But, for reasons already given, this is not acceptable as it stands. The various strands in Weber's two formulations of the concept of class are not always definitely worked out (i.e., the connections between the general statement of 'class position' in the earlier account and the typology of *Besitzklassen* and *Erwerbsklassen* in the later discussion). Further he does not specify clearly how the potentially very large variety of differing 'class positions' are to be reduced to a number of classes manageable enough for the explication of major components of social structure and processes of social change,

In clarifying some of these matters we may start from the premise, which is fundamental for both Marx and Weber: that, in capitalism, *the market is intrinsically a structure of power*, in which the possession of certain attributes advantages some groupings of individuals relative to others. While it is a power structure, the market is *not a normatively defined system of authority* in which the distribution of power is, *as such*, sanctioned as legitimate. The rights of property, and of the sale of labour, are rights of the alienation or disposal of *goods* ('commodities' in the Marxian sense), which underpin the system of power, not in spite of, but because of the fact that they are specified in terms of freedom of economic exchange. The operation of market relationships obviously presupposes the existence of normative agreements (ultimately sanctioned by the state) which define the general conditions governing the formation of contractual ties, etc.; but these norms merely specify the boundaries to the framework. The market is thus a system of economic relationships founded upon relative bargaining strengths of different groupings of individuals. The development of capitalism dissolves the differentiation between labour and commodity markets which exists in more rudimentary forms of economy, since labour itself becomes a commodity. This is the basis, of course, of Marx's dichotomous model; those who are propertyless are almost completely powerless in the bargaining encounter as compared to those who own property in the means of production. In accepting that 'property and lack of property are the basic categories of all class situations', Weber adopts the same view, although he then proceeds to suggest further that we may identify other attributes which create class differences among the propertyless.

The deficiency in Weber's reinterpretation of Marx's view is that it is not sufficiently radical. While Weber recognises the unsatisfactory character of the Marxian standpoint, particularly as regards the undifferentiated category of the 'propertyless', he does not pursue the implications of his own conception far enough. Dahrendorf has suggested that we may stand the Marxian concept of property on its head in terms of its relation to authority; the implications of the Weberian analysis, however, are that the conception of property may be 'inverted' or generalised in a different way, which does not sacrifice the economic foundation of the concept of class. 'Property' refers, not to any characteristics of physical objects as such, but to rights which are associated with them, which in turn confer certain capacities upon the 'owner'. In the market, of course, the significance of capital as private property is that it confers certain very definite capacities upon its possessor as compared to those who are 'propertyless'—those who do not own their means of production. But we can readily perceive that, even in the Marxian view, the notion of 'propertylessness' is something of a misnomer. For if 'property' is conceived of as a set of capacities of action with reference to the operations of the market, it is evident that the wage-labourer does possess such capacities. The 'property' of the wage-labourer is the labour-power which he brings for sale in entering into the contractual relation. While this fundamentally disadvantages him in the competitive bargaining situation in relation to the owner of capital, this is not simply a one-way power relationship: the 'property' which the wage-labourer possesses is needed by the employer, and he must pay at least some minimal attention to the demands of the worker—providing a basis for the collective withdrawal of labour as a possible sanction. It would be departing too much from usual terminology to refer to capital and to the labour-power of the worker both as 'property'; and, anyway, the point is rather that 'property' (capital) is a particular case of capacity to determine the bargaining outcome, rather than vice versa. So I shall continue to speak below of 'property' (in the means of production) in a conventional sense, and shall use the term 'market capacity' in an inclusive manner *to refer to all forms of relevant attributes which individuals may bring to the bargaining encounter*.

It is an elementary fact that where ownership of property is concentrated in the hands of a minority and in a society in which the mass of the population are employed in industrial production, the vast majority consequently offer their labour for sale on the market. Because of his general emphasis upon 'productive labour', and because of his expectation that it is in the nature of modern technology to reduce productive operations to a homogeneous skill-level, Marx failed to recognise the potential significance of differentiations of market capacity which do not derive directly from the factor of property ownership. Such differentiations, it seems clear, are contingent upon the scarcity value of what the individual 'owns' and is able to offer on the market. As Weber indicates, possession of recognised 'skills'—including educational qualifications—is the major factor influencing market capacity. Differentiations in market capacity may be used, as various recent authors have indicated, to secure economic returns other than income as such. These include, principally, security of employment, prospects of career advancement, and a range of 'fringe benefits', such as pension rights, etc.[2] In the same way as the capacities which individuals bring to the bargaining process may be regarded as a form of 'property' which they exchange on the market, so these material returns may be regarded as forms of 'good' which are obtained through the sale of labour-power.

In the market structure of competitive capitalism, *all* those who participate in the exchange process are in a certain sense in (interest) conflict with one another for access to scarce returns. Conflict of interest may be created by the existence of many sorts of differential market capacities. Moreover, the possible relationships between property and 'propertyless' forms of market capacity are various. Speculative investment in property may, for example, be one of the specific market advantages used by those in certain occupations (thus directors are often able to use 'inside knowledge' to profit from property deals). Marx himself, of course, recognised the existence of persistent conflicts of interest within property-owning groupings: notably, between financial and industrial sectors of the large bourgeoisie, and between large and petty bourgeoisie.

The difficulty of identifying 'class' with common market capacity has already been alluded to with reference to Weber. While Weber's concept of 'market situation' successfully moves away from some of the rigidities of the Marxian scheme, it tends to imply the recognition of a cumbersome plurality of classes. There would appear to be as many 'classes', and as many 'class conflicts', as there are differing market positions. The problem here, however, is not the recognition of the diversity of the relationships and conflicts created by the capitalist market as such, but that of making the *theoretical transition from such relationships and conflicts to the identification of classes as structured forms*. The unsatisfactory and ill-defined character of the connections between 'class position', the typology of *Besitzklassen* and *Erwerbsklassen*, and 'social classes' in Weber's work has already been mentioned. But the problem is by no means confined to Weber's theoretical scheme. Marx was certainly conscious of the problematic character of the links between class as a latent set of characteristics generated by the capitalist system and class as an historical, dynamic entity, an 'historical actor'. But his contrast between class 'in itself' and class 'for itself' is primarily one distinguishing between class relationships as a cluster of economic connections on the one hand and class consciousness on the other. This emphasis was very much dictated by the nature of Marx's interests, lying as they did above all in understanding and promoting the rise of a revolutionary class consciousness within capitalism. While it would by no means be true to hold that Marx ignored this completely, it can be said that he gave only little attention to the modes in which classes, founded in a set of economic relationships, take on or 'express' themselves in definite social forms.

Nor has the matter been adequately dealt with in the writings of later authors. In fact, one of the leading dilemmas in the theory of class—which figures prominently, for example, in Aron's discussion—is that of identifying the 'reality' of class. Not only has there been some considerable controversy over whether class is a 'real' or 'nominal' category, but many have argued that, since it is difficult or impossible to draw the 'boundaries' between classes with any degree of clarity, we should abandon the notion of class as a useful sociological concept altogether.[3] Only Dahrendorf seems to have attempted to give attention to the problem within the framework of an overall theory of class, and since his identification of class with authority divisions is unacceptable, his analysis does not help greatly.

The major problems in the theory of class, I shall suggest, do not so much concern the nature and application of the class concept itself, as what, for want of a better word, I shall call the *structuration* of class relationships.[4] Most attempts to revise class theory since Marx have sought to accomplish such a revision primarily by refining, modifying, or substituting an altogether different notion for the Marxian concept of class. While it is useful to follow and develop certain of Weber's insights in this respect, the most important blank spots in the theory of class concern the processes whereby 'economic classes' become 'social classes', and whereby in turn the latter are related to other social forms. As Marx was anxious to stress in criticising the premises of political economy, all economic relationships, and any sort of 'economy', presuppose a set of social ties between producers. In arguing for the necessity of conceptualising the structuration of class relationships, I do not in any way wish to question the legitimacy of this insight, but rather to focus upon *the modes in which* 'economic' relationships become translated into 'non-economic' social structures.

One source of terminological ambiguity and conceptual confusion in the usage of the term 'class' is that it has often been employed to refer both to an economic *category* and to a specifiable cluster of social groupings. Thus Weber uses the term in both of these ways, although he seeks terminologically to indicate the difference between 'class' (as a series of 'class positions') and 'social class'. But in order to insist that the study of class and class conflict must concern itself with the interdependence of economy and society, it is not necessary to identify the term 'class' with the divisions and interests generated by the market as such. Consequently, in the remainder of this book, I shall use the term in the sense of Weber's 'social class'—appropriately explicated. While there may be an indefinite multiplicity of cross-cutting interests created by differential market capacities, there are only, in any given society, a limited number of classes.

It will be useful at this juncture to state what class is *not*. First, a class is not a specific 'entity'—that is to say, a bounded social form in the way in which a business firm or a university is—and a class has no publicly sanctioned identity. It is extremely important to stress this, since established linguistic usage often encourages us to apply active verbs to the term 'class'; but the sense in which a class 'acts' in a certain way, or 'perceives' elements in its environment on a par with an individual actor, is highly elliptical, and this sort of verbal usage is to be avoided wherever possible. Similarly, it is perhaps misleading to speak of 'membership' of a class, since this might be held to imply participation in a definite 'group'. This form of expression, however, is difficult to avoid altogether, and I shall not attempt to do so in what follows. Secondly, class has to be distinguished from 'stratum', and class theory from the study of 'stratification' as such. The latter, comprising what Ossowski terms a gradation scheme, involves a criterion or set of criteria in terms of which individuals may be ranked descriptively along a scale. The distinction between class and stratum is again a matter of some significance, and bears directly upon the problem of class 'boundaries'. For the divisions between strata, for analytical purposes, may be drawn very precisely, since they may be set upon a measurement scale—as, for example, with 'income strata'. The divisions between classes are *never* of this sort; nor, moreover, do they lend themselves to easy visualisation, in terms of any ordinal scale of 'higher' and 'lower', as strata do—although, once more, this sort of imagery cannot be escaped altogether. Finally we must distinguish clearly between class and elite. Elite theory, as formulated by Pareto and Mosca, developed in part as a conscious and deliberate repudiation of class analysis. In place of the concept of class relationships, the elite theorists substituted the opposition of 'elite' and 'mass'; and in place of the Marxian juxtaposition of class society and classlessness they substituted the idea of the cyclical replacement of elites *in perpetuo*. Their use of terms such as 'governing class' and 'political class' is in fact confusing and illegitimate. I shall argue below, however, that the concept of elite is not at all incompatible with class theory; on the contrary, stripped of some of the connotations with which it has sometimes been encumbered, the notion is of essential significance.

2. THE STRUCTURATION OF CLASS RELATIONSHIPS

It is useful, initially, to distinguish the *mediate* from the *proximate* structuration of class·relationships. By the former term, I refer to the factors which intervene between the existence of certain given market capacities and the formation of classes as identifiable social groupings, that is to say which operate as 'overall' connecting links between the market on the one hand and structured systems of class relationships on the other. In using the latter phrase, I refer to 'localised' factors which condition or shape class formation. The mediate structuration of class relationships is governed above all by the distribution of mobility chances which pertain within a given society. Mobility has sometimes been treated as if it were in large part separable from the determination of class structure. According to Schumpeter's famous example, classes may be conceived of as like conveyances, which may be constantly carrying different 'passengers' without in any way changing their shape. But, compelling though the analogy is at first sight, it does not stand up to closer examination, especially within the framework I am suggesting here.[5] In general, the greater the degree of 'closure' of mobility chances—both intergenerationally and within the career of the individual—the more this facilitates the formation of identifiable classes. For the effect of closure in terms of intergenerational movement is to provide for the *reproduction* of common life experience over the generations; and this homogenisation of experience is reinforced to the degree to which the individual's movement within the labour market is confined to occupations which generate a similar range of material outcomes. In general we may state that the structuration of classes is facilitated *to the degree to which mobility closure exists in relation to any specified form of market capacity.* There are three sorts of market capacity which can be said to be normally of importance in this respect: ownership of property in the means of production; possession of educational or technical qualifications; and possession of manual labour-power. In so far as it is the case that these tend to be tied to closed patterns of inter- and intragenerational mobility, this yields the foundation of *a basic three-class system* in capitalist society: an 'upper', 'middle', and 'lower' or 'working' class. But as has been indicated previously, it is an intrinsic characteristic of the development of the capitalist market that there exist no legally sanctioned or formally prescribed limitations upon mobility, and hence it must be emphasised that there is certainly never anything even approaching complete closure.

In order to account for the emergence of structured classes, we must look in addition at the proximate sources of structuration.

There are three, related, sources of proximate structuration of class relationships: the division of labour within the productive enterprise; the authority relationships within the enterprise; and the influence of what I shall call 'distributive groupings'. I have already suggested that Marx tended to use the notion of 'division of labour' very broadly, to refer both to market relationships and to the allocation of occupational tasks within the productive organisation. Here I shall use the term only in this second, more specific, sense. In capitalism, the division of labour in the enterprise is in principle governed by the promotion of productive efficiency in relation to the maximisation of profit; but while responding to the same exigencies as the capitalist market in general, the influence of the division of labour must be analytically separated as a distinctive source of structuration (and, as will be discussed later, as a significant influence upon class consciousness). The division of labour, it is clear, may be a basis of the fragmentation as well as the consolidation of class relationships. It furthers the formation of classes to the degree to which it creates homogeneous groupings which cluster along the same lines as those which are fostered by mediate structuration. Within the modern industrial order,[6] the most significant influence upon proximate structuration in the division of labour is undoubtedly that of technique. The effect of industrial technique (more recently, however, modified by the introduction of cybernetic systems of control) is to create a decisive separation between the conditions of labour of manual and non-manual workers. 'Machine-minding', in one form or another, regardless of whether it involves a high level of manual skill, tends to create a working environment quite distinct from that of the administrative employee, and one which normally enforces a high degree of physical separation between the two groupings.[7]

This effect of the division of labour thus overlaps closely with the influence of the mediate structuration of class relationships through the differential apportionment of mobility chances; but it is, in turn, potentially heavily reinforced by the typical authority system in the enterprise. In so far as administrative workers participate in the framing, or merely in the enforcement, of authoritative commands, they tend to be separated from manual workers, who are subject to those commands. But the influence of differential authority is also basic as a reinforcing agent of the structuration of class relationships at the 'upper' levels. Ownership of property, in other words, confers certain fundamental capacities of command, maximised within the 'entrepreneurial' enterprise in its classical form. To the extent to which this serves to underlie a division at 'the top', in the control of the organisation (something which is manifestly influenced, but not at all destroyed, if certain of the suppositions advanced by the advocates of the theory of the separation of 'ownership and control' are correct) it supports the differentiation of the 'upper' from the 'middle' class.

The third source of the proximate structuration of class relationships is that originating in the sphere of consumption rather than production. Now according to the traditional interpretations of class structure, including those of Marx and Weber, 'class' is a phenomenon of production: relationships established in consumption are therefore quite distinct from, and secondary to, those formed in the context of productive activity. There is no reason to deviate from this general emphasis. But without dropping the conception that classes are founded ultimately in the economic structure of the capitalist market, it is still possible to regard consumption patterns as a major influence upon class structuration. Weber's notions of 'status' and 'status group', as I previously pointed out, confuse two separable elements: the formation of groupings in consumption, on the one hand, and the formation of types of social differentiation based upon some sort of non-economic value providing a scale of 'honour' or 'prestige' on the other. While the two may often coincide, they do not necessarily do so, and it seems worthwhile to distinguish them terminologically. Thus I shall call 'distributive groupings' those relationships involving common patterns of the consumption of economic goods, regardless of whether the individuals involved make any type of conscious evaluation of their honour or prestige relative to others; 'status' refers to the existence of such evaluations, and a 'status group' is, then, any set of social relationships which derives its coherence from their application.[8]

In terms of class structuration, distributive groupings are important in so far as they interrelate with the other sets of factors distinguished above in such a way as to reinforce the typical separations between forms of market capacity. The most significant distributive groupings in this respect are those formed through the tendency towards community or neighbourhood segregation. Such a tendency is not normally based only upon differentials in income, but also upon such factors as access to housing mortgages, etc. The creation of distinctive 'working-class neighbourhoods' and 'middle-class neighbourhoods', for example, is naturally promoted if those in manual labour are by and large denied mortgages for house buying, while those in non-manual occupations experience little difficulty in obtaining such loans. Where industry is located outside of the major urban areas, homogeneous 'working-class communities' frequently develop through the dependence of workers upon housing provided by the company.

In summary, to the extent to which the various bases of mediate and proximate class structuration overlap, classes will exist as distinguishable formations. I wish to say—as will emerge in detail in later chapters—that *the combination of the sources of mediate and proximate structuration distinguished here, creating a threefold class structure, is generic to capitalist society.* But the mode in which these elements are merged to form *a specific class system*, in any given society, differs significantly according to variations in economic and political development. It should be evident that structuration is never an all-or-nothing matter. The problem of the existence of distinct class 'boundaries', therefore, is not one which can be settled *in abstracto*: one of the specific aims of class analysis in relation to empirical societies must necessarily be that of determining how strongly, in any given case, the 'class principle' has become established as a mode of structuration. Moreover, the operation of the 'class principle' may also involve the creation of forms of structuration within the major class divisions. One case in point is that which Marx called the 'petty bourgeoisie'. In terms of the preceding analysis, it is quite easy to see why ownership of small property in the means of production might come to be differentiated both from the upper class and from the ('new') middle class. If it is the case that the chances of mobility, either inter- or intragenerationally, from small to large property ownership are slight, this is likely to isolate the small property-owner from membership of the upper class as such. But the fact that he enjoys directive control of an enterprise, however minute, acts to distinguish him from those who are part of a hierarchy of authority in a larger organisation. On the other hand, the income and other economic returns of the petty bourgeois are likely to be similar to the white-collar worker, and hence they may belong to similar distributive groupings. A second potentially important influence upon class formation is to be traced to the factor of skill differential within the general category of manual labour. The manual worker who has undergone apprenticeship, or a comparable period of training, possesses a market capacity which sets him apart from the un-skilled or semi-skilled worker. This case will be discussed in more detail below; it is enough merely to indicate at this point that there are certain factors promoting structuration on the basis of this

differentiation in market capacity (e.g., that the chances of intergenerational mobility from skilled manual to white-collar occupations are considerably higher than they are from unskilled and
semi-skilled manual occupations).

So far I have spoken of structuration in a purely formal way,
as though class could be defined in terms of relationships which
have no 'content'. But this obviously will not do: if classes become
social realities, this must be manifest in the formation of common
patterns of behaviour and attitude. Since Weber's discussion of
classes and status groups, the notion of 'style of life' has normally
come to be identified as solely pertaining to the mode whereby a
status group expresses its claim to distinctiveness. However, in so
far as there is marked convergence of the sources of structuration
mentioned above, classes will also tend to manifest common styles
of life.

An initial distinction can be drawn here between 'class awareness' and 'class consciousness'.[9] We may say that, in so far as class
is a structurated phenomenon, there will tend to exist a common
awareness and acceptance of similar attitudes and beliefs, linked
to a common style of life, among the members of the class. 'Class
awareness', as I use the term here, does *not* involve a recognition
that these attitudes and beliefs signify a particular class affiliation,
or the recognition that there exist other classes, characterised by
different attitudes, beliefs, and styles of life; 'class consciousness',
by contrast, as I shall use the notion, does imply both of these. The
difference between class awareness and class consciousness is a
fundamental one, because class awareness may take the form of
a denial of the existence or reality of classes.[10] Thus the class awareness of the middle class, in so far as it involves beliefs which place a
premium upon individual responsibility and achievement, is of this
order.

Within ethnically and culturally homogeneous societies, the
degree of class structuration will be determined by the interrelation-
ship between the sources of structuration identified previously.
But many, if not the majority, of capitalist societies are not homogeneous in these respects. Traditionally, in class theory, racial or
religious divisions have been regarded as just so many 'obstacles'
to the formation of classes as coherent unities. This may often be so,
where these foster types of structuration which deviate from that
established by the 'class principle' (as typically was the case in the
battles fought by the rearguard of feudalism against the forces
promoting the emergence of capitalism). The idea that ethnic or
cultural divisions serve to dilute or hinder the formation of classes

is also very explicitly built into Weber's separation of (economic) 'class' and 'status group'. But this, in part at least, gains its cogency from the contrast between estate, as a legally constituted category, and class, as an economic category. While it may be agreed, however, that the *bases* of the formation of classes and status groups (in the sense in which I have employed these concepts) are different, nonetheless the tendency to class structuration may receive a considerable impetus *where class coincides with the criteria of status group membership*—in other words, where structuration deriving from economic organisation 'overlaps' with, or, in Dahrendorf's terms, is 'superimposed' upon, that deriving from evaluative categorisations based upon ethnic or cultural differences.[11] Where this is so, status group membership itself becomes a form of market capacity. Such a situation frequently offers the strongest possible source of class structuration, whereby there develop clear-cut differences in attitudes, beliefs and style of life between the classes. Where ethnic differences serve as a 'disqualifying' market capacity, such that those in the category in question are heavily concentrated among the lowest-paid occupations, or are chronically unemployed or semi-employed, we may speak of the existence of an *underclass*.[12]

3. CONTRADICTION AND THE GENESIS OF CLASS CONSCIOUSNESS

In the previous section, a distinction has been made between 'class awareness' and 'class consciousness'. It can be said that, whereas class structuration presupposes the existence of class awareness, the existence of class consciousness is problematic. Class consciousness involves, first of all, the recognition, however vaguely defined, of another class or of other classes: perception of class identity implies cognisance of characteristics which separate the class of which one is a member from another or others. But it is possible to classify various 'levels' of class consciousness.[13] The most undeveloped form of class consciousness is that which simply involves *a conception of class identity and therefore of class differentiation*. This can be distinguished from a level of consciousness which involves a conception of class conflict: *where perception of class unity is linked to a recognition of opposition of interest with another class or classes*. The connection between this and the first level of class consciousness may be expressed, to borrow a Socratic term, as a *maieutic* one; in other words, it is mainly a process of developing and clarifying ideas which are latent in perceptions of class identity and differentiation. This distinction is not the same, however, as that made by Marx between a class 'in itself' and a class 'for itself'. In the first place, the Marxian distinction does not separate class structuration from class consciousness (as I have defined the latter term). But, more important in the context of the discussion here, Marx does not discriminate between class consciousness as perception of conflict of interest, and what I shall designate as the third level of consciousness—namely, *revolutionary class consciousness*. In contrast to conflict consciousness, this involves *a recognition of the possibility of an overall reorganisation in the institutional mediation of power* (see below, pp. 121–2), *and a belief that such a reorganisation can be brought about through class action*. In Marx's writings (although not in those of Lenin) the emergence of revolutionary class consciousness is assumed to be a direct outcome of, if not wholly indistinguishable from, consciousness of conflict of class interest. It will be a fundamental part of my argument here, however, that such is not the case; that the conditions underlying the genesis of revolutionary class consciousness are different from those involved in the formation of 'conflict consciousness'.

In the controversies which have surrounded Marxism since the late nineteenth century, the problem of the 'role of ideas', in relation to Marx's 'materialism', has occupied a prominent position. For, as it might seem, if the factors which govern social change are located in the infrastructure, and if ideas are in some sense merely a 'reflection' of the substratum, then the emergence of class consciousness is itself simply an epiphenomenon of the real process of movement which transforms one type of society into another. Such a position apparently removes man from his own history, and leads to the endemic difficulties faced by orthodox dialectical materialism in recognising the active or voluntaristic character of human conduct. The relatively recent publication of Marx's early writings, and the revitalisation of Marxist scholarship to which this has given rise, has effectively dispelled this interpretation.[14] The conception which is universalised in dialectical materialism is in fact treated by Marx as historically contingent—and, more specifically, as an expression of the reification characteristic of bourgeois thought. It is precisely a recovery of the capacity of the subject to separate reification from objectification which should be regarded (according to Marx) as the premise of the transformation of capitalism. In the Marxian view, then, consciousness is not the 'effect' of human activity in the material world, but constitutes the attribution of meaning which guides conduct, and is inseparable from that conduct.

In general terms, this may be regarded as an adequate theoretical background for the analysis of class consciousness. In accounting for the origins of diverse forms of class awareness and consciousness, there is thus no need to become embroiled in fruitless controversy over the relationship between the (so-called) 'material' and 'ideal', as if these were competing explanations of conduct. Class structuration necessarily expresses itself in terms of action oriented to meanings; Marx's treatment of class consciousness is deficient not because it is 'mechanical', or considers ideas merely as 'epiphenomena', but for other reasons. Class structuration, therefore, always implies either class awareness or class consciousness. The problem, at least as regards the working class in capitalism, is to determine the conditions which facilitate the development of conflict or revolutionary consciousness. It should be made clear that, according to the argument outlined above, this is at the same time a problem of structuration—or rather of the specific *forms* of structuration whereby class consciousness is manifest; any level of class 'consciousness may be manifest in the conduct of all, or the majority, of the members of a class, or only in that of certain sectors or groups within it (trade unions, political parties, etc.).

In analysing the origins of class consciousness it is useful to make a distinction between *conflict* and *contradiction*.[15] Both terms appear in Marx's writings, but he does not make a clear differentiation between them. As a class society, capitalism is built upon a conflict of interest between capital and wage-labour; it is this class opposition, in Marxian theory, which is regarded as the ultimate source of the more particular social and economic 'contradictions' whereby the capitalist mode of production is undermined from within, by the growth of the set of productive forces which constitute incipient socialism. I shall use the term class 'conflict' to refer to an opposition of class interests: 'conflict consciousness' involves recognition of such an interest opposition. The term 'contradiction', however, I shall use to refer to a discrepancy between *an existing and an immanent mode of industrial control*. By 'industrial control', I mean the mediation of control (see below, pp. 121–2) within the enterprise, at any specific level of the authority structure. It will be a basic part of my argument in later chapters that the stability of capitalist society depends upon the maintenance of an insulation of economy and polity, such that questions of industrial organisation appear as 'non-political'. In fact, any threat to the system of industrial control has immediate implications of a political nature. I propose to advance the view in this book that conflict consciousness tends to become revolutionary consciousness only *where class conflict originates in contradiction*; and that, far from there being a necessary correspondence between these and the advancing maturity of capitalist society, as is assumed in Marxian theory, they only coincide under conditions which are distinct from those to which Marx gave most prominence.

We must first of all consider the factors which influence the development of conflict consciousness. In large part, these may be said to concern whatever promotes the *visibility* (transparency) of class structuration. This is the case, for example, with those characteristics of capitalism which Marx mentions as facilitating the emergence of a proletariat 'for itself', such as the 'homogenising' effects of mechanisation upon the labour task, or the significance of the large-scale factory in herding together a mass of workers in a single place. In each of these examples, the conditions of existence of individuals tend to make their common class characteristics readily visible. This is not so with the peasantry, whom Marx, speaking of nineteenth-century France, compares to a 'sack of potatoes': the isolated nature of the working environment of the peasant tends to inhibit the perception that he shares common class interests with others. But other aspects of class structuration, to which Marx gives little attention, may influence, or even decisively effect, visibility.[16] Thus, as Weber pointed out, the manual worker may frequently feel more hostility towards the industrial manager, who issues commands to him and with whom he is in relatively direct contact, than towards the owner of the enterprise, or towards the even more remote banker or financier. Visibility is normally most strongly accentuated where there is a coincidence of class and status group criteria, especially where the latter involves an ethnic differentiation. Conflict consciousness, of course, need not be reciprocal, and indeed such normally is the case with the relationship between working class and middle class in capitalist society. The assertion of class interest on the part of the working class clashes with the typical class awareness of the middle class, whose members tend to perceive the social order in terms of individualistic notions of 'personal achievement' and 'initiative', etc.[17]

Perception of identity of class interests in opposition to another class or classes naturally fosters the development of organisations or agencies devoted to the advancement of those interests. It is to such agencies, of course, that Marx looked to supply the spearhead of the working-class movement. And it cannot be doubted that, in unions and political parties, conflict consciousness may be clarified and made more precise than is normally the case in the more diffuse class consciousness of the rank-and-file worker. These agencies are then in a position to react back upon, and to attempt to direct, the class consciousness of the mass. While the very institutionalisation of agencies, nominally set up to promote certain class interests, may provide a further factor intervening between the member of the class and the actual furthering of his interests, in general terms this is an acceptable interpretation of the processes involved in heightening conflict consciousness. What it does not adequately explain is why such consciousness should take a revolutionary form.

If the most important factor advancing conflict consciousness is *visibility* of class differentials, the most important factor influencing revolutionary consciousness is *relativity of experience* within a given system of production. Revolutionary consciousness, as I have defined it, involves a perception of the existing socio-economic order as 'illegitimate' and a recognition of modes of action which can be taken to reorganise it on a new basis. Such a perception is virtually always foreclosed for the members of chronically underprivileged groupings whose conditions of labour remain stable over time. Its creation implies a framework by reference to which individuals can distance their experience from the here-and-now, the 'given' social reality, and envisage the possibility of one which differs radically from it. The term 'relative deprivation' is inadequate as applied in this context. The experience of deprivation (which is necessarily 'relative', since an individual who feels himself to be deprived must in some sense orient himself to a standard of legitimacy) is simply one element in the picture; feelings of resentment of a diffuse nature only take on a revolutionary character when they are fused with a concrete project, however vaguely formulated, of an alternative order which can be brought into being.

Now in Marxian theory, as I have already indicated, conflict stemming from division of interest in class relationships is conflated with that deriving from contradiction. This helps to explain the origin of what is sometimes regarded as a blind-spot in Marx's conception of the development of the class consciousness of the proletariat in capitalism: that is, why the revolt of the working class should take the form of an orientation towards an *institutional* transcendence of the existing order. The answer, evidently enough, is that the working class are the bearers of a new 'principle' of social and economic organisation whose operation contradicts that regulating the capitalist mode of production. But it is not at all clear how the members of the working class come to perceive that this is so. Marx's analysis at this point tends to revert to referring to the results of the exploitative dependence of wage-labour upon capital and hence to the effects of 'emiseration' as manifest in the relative fixity of wages and the growth of the industrial reserve army. However, as mentioned in Chapter 1, there is also a second Marxian theory of revolution, which looks instead to the clash between a 'backward', agrarian order, and the impact of 'advanced' technique. It is this sort of situation, I wish to say, which actually tends to underlie the formation of revolutionary class consciousness, rather than the former. In such circumstances, the emergence of contradiction is abrupt and marked, and has consequences which affect all aspects of the life of the worker, thus creating what may be regarded as the paradigm case for the (potential) development of revolutionary consciousness in the modern world.

Two things must be noted here. In the first place, the creation of revolutionary class consciousness does not necessarily occur, as Marx assumed, at least in his conception of the emergence of a revolutionary proletariat, out of the *maturity* of capitalism, as a simple heightening of conflict consciousness. Its sources are different, and there is no reason to hold that it is intrinsically linked with the sorts of social condition which act to produce or heighten conflict consciousness—a fact which has important implications, discussed further below. Second, it follows that the sources of revolutionary consciousness will tend to be linked either to those groupings on the fringes of 'incorporation' into a society based upon industrial technique (e.g., peasants whose traditional mode of production has been undermined), or conversely to those involved in the most progressive technical sectors of production.

Much of the literature on these matters, of course, has been primarily concerned with class consciousness as a source of impetus to political action, meaning here the formation of working-class parties with some kind of revolutionary programme. While I shall not in any way sidestep the issues raised in this regard, I do not propose to discuss the phenomena underlying party organisation in detail. I think that Lenin was essentially correct in asserting that 'the working class, solely by its own forces, is able to work out merely trade union consciousness',[18] but that it is mistaken to suppose that this can be transformed into revolutionary consciousness primarily through the medium of active party leadership. There are important elements of truth in Luxemburg's view of the origins of revolutionary consciousness, as compared to that of Lenin. For if we may agree with Lenin that revolutionary consciousness does not arise 'spontaneously' from the mature capitalist production, we may also accept that the factors generating such consciousness among the rank and file concern far more than the nature of political leadership, and have to be looked for in conditions of labour of the working class as such.

7

RETHINKING THE THEORY OF CLASS (II)

1. ELITES AND POWER

As Marx insists, the market structure of capitalism depends upon a definite form of political power, a specific form of the state. In this sense, Poulantzas is quite correct to claim that 'social class is a concept which indicates the effects of a totality of structures, the expression of a mode of production or a social formation in the actions of those who are their carriers: it is a concept which designates the effects of the total structure in the realm of social relationships'.[1] In the abstract, the form of the capitalist state depends upon a separation of the spheres of political and economic hegemony, guaranteed in terms of rights of private property. But, as I have pointed out, apart from his historical studies of 'Bonapartism', Marx gave little attention to the nature of the connections of economic and political power. This again can be expressed as a problem of *mediation*. It is certainly one of the most characteristic emphases of the Marxian perspective that, in capitalism especially (but also, in a general sense, in the prior types of class system), the realm of the 'political' is subordinate to that of the 'economic'. What remains relatively obscure in Marx is the specific form of this dependence, and how it is expressed concretely in the domination of the ruling class.[2] The importance of this, as I have also indicated above, is not confined to the analysis of the social structure of capitalism, but bears directly upon the question of the classless character of socialism. It relates, in addition, to issues brought to the forefront by the critique of the Marxian standpoint advanced by the 'elite theorists' of the turn of the century. The substance of this critique, in the writings of such as Pareto and Mosca, may be expressed as an attempt to transmute the Marxian concept of class, as founded in the relations of production, into an essentially *political* differentiation between those 'who rule' and those who 'are ruled'— a transmutation which was, indeed, in part made possible by Marx's failure to specify in a systematic fashion the modes whereby the economic hegemony of the capitalist class becomes 'translated' into the political domination of the *ruling* class. For if it is simply the case that economic control directly yields political power, the way is open for the assertion that, in socialism, as in capitalism (indeed as in any other conceivable type of complex society), whoever controls the means of production thereby achieves political domination as a ruling class. The movement of history from capitalism to socialism then becomes conceived of as a mere succession of 'ruling classes' ('elites'), as in classical 'elite theory', or more specifically as the emergence of the sort of 'managerial' or 'technocratic' ruling class described in Burnham's writings, and more recently in some of the variants of the theory of the 'technocratic society'.[3]

The points at issue between the Marxian standpoint and 'elite theory' have become further complicated in recent years by the use of concepts drawn from the latter, such as that of 'power elite', as if they were synonymous with that of 'ruling class'. Before examining in some detail the nature of the ties between economic and political power, as this relates to Marx's theory of class, it will be useful to clarify the usage of the terms 'ruling class', 'elite', 'power elite', 'governing class', etc., which involves, in part, looking more closely than in the preceding chapter at the structuration of the upper class.

In the analysis which follows, I shall be interested primarily in developing a set of formulations which illuminate significant conceptual distinctions, rather than adhering to conventional terminological usage—if it can be said, in any case, that there is any conventional practice in a field in which there has been so much confusion.[4] I shall suggest that, given the distinctions set out below, there can exist a 'governing class' without it necessarily being a 'ruling class'; that there can exist a 'power elite' without there necessarily being either a 'ruling' or a 'governing class'; that there can be what I shall call a system of 'leadership groups' which constitutes neither a 'ruling class', 'governing class', nor 'power elite'; and that *all* of these social formations are, in principle, compatible with the existence of a society which is 'capitalist' in its organisation. To begin with, a few elementary remarks are necessary about the notion of 'elite'. As it is sometimes employed, 'elite' may refer to those who 'lead' in any given category of activity: to actors and sportsmen as well as to political or economic 'leaders'. There is evidently a difference, however, between the first and the second, in that the former 'lead' in terms of some sort of scale of 'fame' or 'achievement', whereas the second usage may be taken to refer to persons who are at the head of a specific social organisation which has an internal authority structure (the state, an economic enterprise, etc.). I shall use the term 'elite group' in this latter sense, to designate those individuals who occupy positions of formal authority at the head of a social organisation or institution; and 'elite' very generally, to refer either to an elite group or cluster of elite groups.

In these terms, it can be said that a major aspect of the structuration of the upper class concerns, first, the process of mobility into or recruitment to, elite positions and, second, the degree of social 'solidarity' within and between elite groups. Mediate structuration thus concerns how 'closed' the process of recruitment to elite positions is, in favour of those drawn from propertied backgrounds. Proximate structuration depends primarily upon the frequency and nature of the social contacts between the members of elite groups. These may take various forms, including the formation of marriage connections or the existence of other kin ties, the prevalence of personal ties of acquaintance or friendship, etc. If the extent of social 'integration' of elite groups is high, there is also likely to be a high degree of moral solidarity characterising the elite as a whole and, probably, a low incidence of either latent or manifest conflicts between them. There has never been any elite, however solidary, which has been free of conflicts and struggles; but the degree and intensity of overt conflict has varied widely, and thus it is reasonable to speak broadly of differentials in the solidarity of elite groups.

Combining these two aspects of structuration, we can establish a typology of elite formations.

| | | Recruitment | |
		Open	Closed
Integration	High	solidary elite	uniform elite
	Low	abstract elite	established elite

A 'uniform' elite is one which shares the attributes of having a restricted pattern of recruitment and of forming a relatively tightly

knit unity. It hardly needs emphasising that the classifications involved are not of an all-or-nothing character. The point has been
made that even among traditional aristocracies there was never a
completely 'closed' pattern of recruitment, something which has
only been approached by the Indian caste system—all elites open
their ranks, in some degree, to individuals from the lower orders,
and may enhance their stability thereby. A relatively closed type
of recruitment, however, is likely to supply the sort of coherent
socialisation process producing a high level of solidarity between
(and within) elite groups. But it is quite feasible to envisage the
existence of instances which approximate more closely to the case
of an 'established' elite, where there is a relatively closed pattern of
recruitment, but only a low level of integration between elite groups.
A 'solidary' elite, as defined in the classification, might also appear
to involve an unlikely combination of elements, since it might seem
difficult to attain a high degree of integration among elite groups
whose members are drawn from diverse class backgrounds. But,
while this type of social formation is probably rare in capitalist
societies, at least some of the state socialist countries fit quite
neatly into this category: the Communist Party is the main channel
of access to elite positions, and while it provides an avenue of
mobility for individuals drawn in substantial proportions from
quite lowly backgrounds, at the same time it ensures a high degree
of solidarity among elite groups.[5] An 'abstract' elite, involving
both relatively open recruitment and a low level of elite solidarity,
whatever its empirical reality, approximates closely to the picture
of certain contemporary capitalist societies as these are portrayed
in the writings of the theorists of so-called 'pluralist democracy'.

The distinguishing of different types of elite formation does not,
in itself, enable us to conceptualise the phenomenon of power.
As in the case of class structuration itself, we may distinguish two
forms of the mediation of power relationships in society. The first
I shall call the *institutional* mediation of power; the other, the
mediation of power in terms of *control*. By the institutional
mediation of power, I mean the general form of state and economy
within which elite groups are recruited and structured. This concerns,
among other things, the role of property in the overall organisation
of economic life, the nature of the legal framework defining economic and political rights and obligations, and the institutional
structure of the state itself. The mediation of control refers to the
actual (effective) power of policy-formation and decision-making
held by the members of particular elite groups: how far, for example,
economic leaders are able to influence decisions taken by politicians,

etc. To express it another way, we can say that power has two aspects: a 'collective' aspect, in the sense that the 'parameters' of any concrete set of power relationships are contingent upon the overall system of organisation of a society; and a 'distributive' aspect, in the sense that certain groups are able to exert their will at the expense of others.[6] The mediation of control is thus expressed in terms of 'effective' power, manifest in terms of the capacity either to take or to influence the taking of decisions which affect the interests of two or more parties differentially.

We may conceptually separate two variable factors in analysing effective power (that is to say, power as differentiated from 'formal authority') in relation to types of elite formation. The first concerns how far such power is 'consolidated' in the hands of elite groups; the second refers to the 'issue-strength' of the power wielded by those in elite positions. While the former designates limitations upon effective power, deriving from constraints imposed from 'below', the latter concerns how far that power is limited *because it can only be exercised in relation to a range of restricted issues.* Thus it is often held to be characteristic of modern capitalist societies that there are quite narrowly defined limitations upon the issues over which elite groups are able to exercise control.[7] By combining these two aspects of effective power as exercised by elite groups, we can establish a classification of forms of power-structure. Like the previous typology, this sets out an abstract combination of possibilities; it goes almost without saying that this is no more than an elementary categorisation of a very complex set of phenomena, and the labels applied here in no way exhaust the variety of characteristics which are frequently subsumed under these terms.

| | Issue-strength | |
	Broad	Restricted
Consolidated power	autocratic	oligarchic
Diffused power	hegemonic	democratic

According to these definitions, the consolidation of effective power is greatest where it is not restricted to clearly defined limits in terms of its 'lateral range' (broad 'issue-strength'), and where it is concentrated in the hands of the elite, or an elite group. Power-holding is 'oligarchic' rather than 'autocratic' where the degree of centralisation of power in the hands of elite groups is high, but where the issue-strength of that power is limited. In the case of 'hegemonic' control, those in elite positions wield power which, while it is not clearly defined in scope and limited to a restricted range of issues, is 'shallow'. A 'democratic' order, in these terms, is one in which the effective power of elite groups is limited in both respects.

Finally, bringing together both classifications formulated above, we can set up an overall typology of elite formations and power within the class structure. This makes possible a clarification of the four concepts already mentioned—'ruling class', 'governing class', 'power elite' and 'leadership groups'. It must be emphasised that these partially cross-cut some of the existing usages in the literature on class and elite theory. The Paretian term 'governing class' is here not, as in Pareto's own writing, a replacement for the Marxian 'ruling class'; in this scheme, a governing class is 'one step down', both in terms of elite formation and power-holding, from a 'ruling class'.

	Elite formation	Power-holding
Ruling class	uniform/established elite	autocratic/oligarchic
Governing class	uniform/established elite	hegemonic/democratic
Power elite	solidary elite	autocratic/oligarchic
Leadership groups	abstract elite	hegemonic/democratic

In this scheme, the 'strongest' case of a ruling class is defined as that where a uniform elite wields 'autocratic' power; the weakest is where an established elite holds 'oligarchic' power. Where a relatively closed recruitment pattern is linked with the prevalence of defined restrictions upon the effective power of elite groups, a governing class exists, but not a ruling class. A governing class borders upon being a ruling class where a uniform elite possesses 'hegemonic' power; and comes closest to being a system of leadership groups where an established elite holds 'democratic' power.

Where a governing class involves a combination of an established elite and 'hegemonic' power, it stands close to being a power elite. A power elite is distinguished from a ruling class in terms of pattern of recruitment, as is a governing class from a system of leadership groups. The latter exists where elite groups only hold limited power, and where, in addition, elite recruitment is relatively open in character.

In terms of the mediation of control, this classification leaves undefined the relative primacy of the power of any one elite group over others. This can be conceptually expressed as referring to the nature of the *hierarchy* which exists among elite groups. A hierarchy exists among elite groups in so far as one such group holds power of broader issue-strength than others, and is thereby able to exert a degree of control over decisions taken by those within them. Thus it may be that the economic elite, or certain sectors of the economic elite, are able to significantly condition political decisions through the use of 'influence', 'inducement', or the 'direct' control of political positions—i.e., through the fact that members of the economic elite are also incumbents of political positions. We may refer to all of these modes of obtaining, or striving for, control as the *media of interchange* between elite groups. It is precisely one of the major tasks of the analysis of elite formations to examine the media of interchange which operate between elite groups in any given society in order to determine what kinds of elite hierarchy exist.

It is obvious enough that the forms of elite hierarchy which obtain in a society are not independent of the institutional mediation of power; but it is mistaken to assume, as probably the majority of writers have done, that the two are analytically inseparable. In other words, the basic alignments of economy and polity which make for the existence of classes are compatible with various possible relationships between elites and power—something not adequately allowed for either in the Marxian or the Weberian theory of the capitalist state. The Marxian conception, whether in its simpler or more subtle version,[8] treats the state essentially as an 'expression' of the class relationships generated in the market. Political power 'disappears' when the capitalist state is transcended, because that state either represents or directly coordinates the system of class domination. In general, Marx's treatment of the state is very much steeped in that tradition of nineteenth-century social thought, found equally in political economy and in Saint-Simonianism, which regards the state as subordinate to society, and which consequently tends to consider the former as capable

of being 'reduced' to its conditions of dependence upon the latter—
in Marx's case, to class relationships. This is why there is in Marx
no recognition of the possible existence of the state as an independent
force: he comes close to such a recognition only in arguing that, in
the phenomenon of 'Bonapartism', where there is a 'balance' of
classes, the state becomes temporarily detached from subservience
to the interests of any one class. In contrast, much of Weber's sociology is concerned with the role of the state as an agency acting
upon society. It is not a gross oversimplification to say that, whereas
Marx viewed the state in terms of his presuppositions about the
economic infrastructure of society, Weber tended to view that infrastructure in terms of a paradigm derived from his analysis of the
rise of the state. For Weber the 'class principle' is subordinate to
the 'bureaucratic principle'. Examination of the differences at issue
between the Marxian and Weberian standpoint here is critically
important to the assessment of the factors underlying any juxtaposition of 'class' and 'classlessness'.

Weber does not reject the notion of a 'classless society': while
in his lifetime he resisted the advent of socialism (at least, in its
Marxist form) in Germany, he envisaged it as a concrete, if not a
desirable, possibility. What he specifically repudiated was the
Marxian conception that the elimination of the capitalist class
system could bring about any reduction in 'the domination of man
by man'; rather, it would in fact lead to the further extension of
such domination, manifest not in terms of the constraining or
coercive mechanisms of the market, but in terms of the expansion of
the bureaucratic mastery of the state over the lives of individuals.
The weaknesses in the respective views established by Marx and
Weber on class structure in relation to the state are complementary.
In the Marxian conception, political 'power' exists only in so far
as it 'translates' the coercive asymmetry of class relationships;
in Weber's discussion, on the other hand, any (rationalised) form
of authority system involving the coordination of the activities of
men within the political and economic order necessarily furthers
the subordination of the mass to the dictates of a few. In retrospect,
it seems quite evident that just as Marx drew too heavily upon the
'class principle', Weber overstated the significance of the 'bureaucratic principle', for two reasons. One is simply the prominence which
the question of the 'legacy of Bismarck'—the hegemony of the
Prussian bureaucracy as a result of the dearth of strong political
leadership in Germany—played as a source of stimulus to his
sociological writings. The other reason relates to the importance
of the opposition between (irrational) charisma and rationalisation

in his works. Bureaucracy stands as the application of rationality to the sphere of human activity, and therefore represents one pole of an antithesis which pervades the whole of Weber's sociology.

Without attempting to analyse all of the difficulties raised by Weber's various discussions of bureaucracy, we may identify two problems which are latent in his divergence from Marx over the nature of the modern state. (1) Under what conditions does the state come to be separate from, and thereby not 'responsible to', society? (2) Under what conditions does the state come to express an asymmetry of class interests? In Marx's analysis, these two questions are assumed to be the same; the state is a separate and an 'independent power' only because and in so far as it represents the interests of one class against others. For him, the answer to the first question is given by the answer to the second. For Weber, on the other hand, the answer to the second is only a particular case of that which is given to the first.

In speaking of the 'separate' or 'independent' character of the state in capitalism, and in contrasting this situation with that anticipated in the transcendence of the state under socialism, Marx neither wished to assert that its 'separateness' merely resides in its institutional differentiation from the other structures in society, nor to hold that its supersession signifies its 'destruction' as such a differentiated institution. Hence the sort of naïve criticism commonly offered against the Marxian view—that, in any modern industrial order, whether capitalist or socialist, the range of activities undertaken by the state necessarily grows rather than diminishes, and consequently that it is quite impossible to suppose that the state can be 'eradicated'[9]—is not immediately relevant. The state is 'separate' from society precisely in so far as it is not 'responsible to' it. The question of the transcendence of the state therefore hinges upon the overcoming of the modes whereby the state is made to serve sectional interests rather than those of the collectivity as a whole. The 'bureaucratic problem', for Marx, is one of these modes of the subservience of the state to sectional interests—which means class interests. However limited Marx's analysis of bureaucracy might be in some respects, it is by no means as completely sterile as is generally assumed when it is compared to Weber's formulation at this point; it is Weber's view, that ties the 'separateness' of the state to its character as a bureaucratic system, which appears the more ingenuous and oversimplified. For Marx's standpoint contains various concrete indications as to the contingent character of the 'bureaucratic principle', and therefore also as to the manner of its transcendence with the 'abolition' of the state in socialism.

It can be taken as axiomatic that the institutional form of capitalism (for both Marx and Weber) is manifest as a 'pure type' to the degree that the role of the state is limited to the regulation of contractual obligations. The capitalist state (as both Marx and Weber emphasise) thus necessarily presupposes a dichotomy between the economic order, left open to the play of market forces, and the political order—a dichotomy between 'economic' and 'political man'. The error made by Marx and Weber, from opposed perspectives, is to assume too little flexibility in the range of possible connections between the 'capitalist state', defined in these terms, and the mediation of control. The question of the 'separate' character of the state can neither be adequately understood in terms of the bureaucratic autonomy of officialdom, nor in terms of a series of clearly defined necessities which flow from the free play of market relationships.

2. THE NATURE OF CLASS EXPLOITATION

A class society, in Marx's writings, is not simply a society in which there happen to be classes, but one in which class relationships provide the key to the explication of the social structure in general. Marx's dichotomous model supplies the necessary foundation for the theory of class society; ownership as opposed to non-ownership of the means of production is the fundamental axis along which 'infrastructure' is related to 'superstructure'. But using the Marxian concept of class, in working out the notions of 'class society' and 'classlessness', is not enough: for this leads to the specious conclusion suggested by Dahrendorf's 'trick of definition' that the transcendence of class society is given simply by the formal abolition of private property. The concepts of 'class society' and 'classlessness' thus turn out to be considerably more complicated than they appear at first sight.

Marx's theory of class society obviously depends in large part upon the manner in which he seeks to tie the dichotomous model to a conception of 'exploitation'. Class society is necessarily exploitative in character because the existence of class structure is predicated upon the appropriation of the surplus product of the mass of the population by an unproductive minority. It is important to recognise that, for Marx, however, the class character of capitalism is, in several senses, more clearly defined than in the case of feudalism, in which there still exists a body of free peasantry who are in a certain sense 'outside' the class structure; even the bonded workers retain a large measure of control over their means of production, and economic and political domination are fused within a localised and personalised system of production. In capitalism, the 'class principle' appears as the very kernel of the social structure in general, and it is precisely in virtue of this that, by a process of dialectical transformation, it becomes possible to anticipate the emergence of a classless order. This is so because, in Marx's tendential analysis of the 'movement' of the capitalist mode of production, the dichotomous model of class increasingly loses its character as an abstract type, and merges with the projected reality of capitalist development.

The abandonment of the Marxian dichotomous model necessarily means discarding the differentiation between productive and unproductive labour, and the associated theory of surplus value as the basis by which to compare the exploitative character of class society with a classless order. Marx's own struggles with the concept of productive labour give ample evidence of the problems created by the notion. Thus he criticises Adam Smith for regarding as productive labour only that which creates material goods, and argues in *Theories of Surplus Value* that: 'Included among these productive workers, of course, are all those who contribute in one way or another to the production of the commodity, from the actual operative to the manager or engineer [as distinct from the capitalist].'[10] But Marx himself was not at all consistent in this usage, and subsequent interpreters can hardly be indicted too harshly if they have failed to remark that Marx's conception is distinct from that of his predecessor. Moreover, even if 'productive labour' is interpreted broadly, it seems clear that it must exclude those engaged in distribution, as well as the administrative officialdom of the state.[11]

The inadequacies inherent in the distinction between productive and unproductive labour can to some degree be met by expanding the meaning of 'production' to include not only the activity of those directly or indirectly engaged in the creation of material commodities, but also the various forms of 'intellectual production' involved in service or administrative occupations. Indeed, Marx frequently uses the adjective 'productive' to apply to such a very broad range of activities (speaking, for example, of the criminal 'producing' crime). But this merely glosses over the specific application of the productive/unproductive labour distinction to the theory of exploitation, and compromises the theory of surplus value. The central importance of the latter to the Marxian conception of class is not typically brought out in the controversies to which the concept has given rise since Böhm-Bawerk's critical assessment of Marx's economics at the turn of the century. The rejection of the theory of surplus value by orthodox economists has been based upon its apparent inability to predict prices. But what this rests upon is an explicit or implicit repudiation of the Marxian emphasis upon production as the source of value; value is interpreted in terms of 'marginal utility' in the sphere of consumption. Such an emphasis is not unconnected, of course, with the prevalence of 'distributive socialism' in most of the Western countries: that is, socialism which is predicated mainly upon the attempt to reduce disparities in income. From Marx's standpoint, however, the prediction of prices is very much a secondary consideration, if it is of any significance at all. The import of the theory of surplus value, as the 'secret' of capitalism, is that it demonstrates that the exploitative character of the capitalist order, like that of the class systems which have preceded it, is founded in the sphere of production. The conception of surplus value thus has to be judged not only, nor even primarily, in terms of how far it is able to provide satisfactory answers to the sorts of questions which occupy the focus of attention of modern orthodox economics, but rather in terms of its relevance as a theory of exploitation in class society.[12]

The most helpful way to approach the problem of class exploitation is by tracing the derivation of the theory of surplus value from the conception of alienation established earlier in Marx's writings. It is frequently held that the notion of alienation, as developed by Marx in the *Economic and Philosophical Manuscripts*, hinges upon a philosophical contrast between 'man in nature' (unalienated) and 'man in society' (alienated)—a perspective which he is later presumed to have broken away from in working out a view based upon the empirical analysis of historical development. The question of the place of the concept of alienation in Marx's work, and the closely related scholarly debate over the degree of continuity between Marx's 'early' and 'mature' writings, raise issues which cannot even be touched upon here.[13] But it can be pointed out that the duality suggested above is not in fact true to the main theme of Marx's discussion of alienation in the Paris *Manuscripts*. The analysis given therein is already an historical one. Human faculties, Marx emphasises, are quite different from the static, 'given' appetites of the animal, because they are created through the development of man's culture over time; even the biological exigencies of eating, drinking, etc., become transformed as a result of association in society. Alienation thus has to be understood, not as a secularised version of the 'fall from grace', but as referring to the separation of man from his own (socially generated) faculties and capacities. This makes sense only if it is seen against the backdrop of the overall development of human society from its primitive forms to the emergence of capitalism. While the evolution of society, up to and including capitalism, progressively expands man's productive powers, and therefore the range of his capacities for satisfaction and fulfilment, it does so only under conditions of labour which prevent or inhibit the use of those capacities. This tension between the creative and stultifying aspects of life in society is maximised in the capitalist mode of production, which greatly enlarges productive wealth, but at the same time prevents its utilisation in the service of human needs.

Already in his early writings Marx advanced the view that private property, as generated by the division of labour, is the 'material form' in which alienation is expressed. The development of Marx's thought, from *The German Ideology* onwards, may be seen as an attempt to follow through—by means of concrete analysis rather than philosophical anthropology—the implications of this proposition. The concept of alienation, as used by Marx in the *Manuscripts*, is of an all-embracing character; in the later writings, it becomes differentiated into more specific and precisely defined terms. The theory of surplus value is crucial in this respect, providing as it does the key link between the fate of the wage-labourer and the 'inner' character of capitalism as a system of class exploitation. As a critique of political economy, *Capital* is built upon the supposition that the analyses of the orthodox economists conceal from view that the fact that 'labour is bought and sold at its true value' does not mean that the exchange between capital and wage-labour is not an exploitative one. This is a critique of political economy *in its own terms*; and in this sense capitalism is based upon an exploitative class system in so far as the worker loses part of his product as surplus value. But *Capital* is also a critique of political economy in a much broader sense—one which can only be adequately understood in the context of the earlier writings on alienation. Considered as part of an (unfinished) larger undertaking,[14] the analysis of class relationships contained within the work is the focal aspect of a more generalised separation of 'man the producer' from the 'products' of his activity.

It is this separation, I shall argue, which may be treated as the basis of a theory of the exploitative component of class structures—in a way which departs from the specific economic theorems embodied in Marx's notion of surplus value, and which instead makes use of the Weberian notion of 'life-chances'. I shall define 'exploitation' as *any socially conditioned form of asymmetrical production of life-chances*. 'Life-chances' here may be taken to mean the chances an individual has of sharing in the socially created economic or cultural 'goods' which typically exist in any given society. Now in these terms it is clear that every society, with the possible exception of the most primitive band societies, embodies exploitative relationships. Although the reduction of forms of exploitation may be an objective towards which men may realistically strive, there is no possibility, in this conception, of their final transcendence. In this sense, the view I am suggesting here is distinct from the Marxian treatment of alienation. But it has in common with it the premise that exploitation implies a separation between the social *creation* of human faculties on the one hand, and the social *denial* of 'access' to those faculties on the other. In using the term 'goods' above, I do not mean to propose that 'exploitation' can be equated merely with inequalities in the distribution of material rewards as is inferred in 'distributive socialism'. The point is a more fundamental one of asymmetry in the distribution of the (socially created) faculties for the *use* of available rewards: and, indeed, whether they are seen to be rewards at all. It is evident enough that life-chances are shaped in a basic way by the availability of material rewards (i.e., wealth, income, 'goods' in the conventional sense); but it is not sufficient to be content with this, since the use to which those rewards may be put depends upon other aspects of 'cultural production', interpreted in a broad sense, whereby tastes and abilities are moulded.[15]

While, according to the conception suggested here, every developed form of society embodies relationships of exploitation, it follows that class exploitation represents only one mode of organisation of such relationships. In class structures, the system of exploitation operates through differentials in market capacity. In so far as this is manifest in terms of variations in the level of material reward, there is little problem in pinning down the exploitative character of class relationships. But these variations also tend to be interrelated with other, less directly 'economic' modes of exploitation. Two factors may be mentioned as of particular importance here. The first is that of education. It may be taken for granted that, in a modern society, the educational system is a primary source of the capacities and inclinations of the mass of the population. Differential access to the educational system, or the domination of certain key areas or levels of education by a particular class, is thus a central (and typical) mode of class exploitation. The second is that of the work environment—in other words, the tie which exists between differential market capacity and the nature of the work task in the division of labour. The work situation is of dual significance here: not only may certain kinds of labour be dull and routine, and hence 'dehumanising' in the Marxian sense,[16] but habitual exposure to such conditions of work may itself have the effect of stultifying pre-existing or latent capacities of the worker, as these might be exercised in other areas of his life's activity.

3. THE CONCEPT OF CLASS SOCIETY

Whether or not a society is a 'class society' is neither a simple matter, nor an all-or-nothing phenomenon, but depends upon a complex of factors. It should be clear that, in the scheme of concepts which I have developed in this and the preceding chapters, a society 'without classes' is not necessarily a 'classless' society. Such *is* the case, on the other hand, in Marx's theory of class, as follows from the conception of surplus production: each type of society which succeeds the original 'tribal' form (Ancient society, feudalism and capitalism) is a class society. Tribal society is classless, because there is no surplus product generated which could serve as the basis of a system of class domination.[17] But from the point of view which I have attempted to establish, feudalism is not a class society: it should rather be called a 'pre-class' society, as are other forms of traditional order which have not been brought within the scope of capitalist markets. 'Primitive communism' should also be treated as falling into this category. By contrast, a 'classless society', as I shall use the term, presupposes an advanced economy. In saying this, I do not want to assert that the existence of classlessness therefore presupposes a movement of the order:

$$\text{pre-class} \rightarrow \text{class} \rightarrow \text{classless society.}$$

Rather, a classless society, while sharing certain of the essential characteristics which separate a class order from a pre-class society, is not itself one in which class relationships are pre-eminent in the social structure as a whole.

In using the phrase 'pre-eminent in the social structure as a whole', I wish to maintain the Marxian emphasis upon the *explanatory salience* of class as central to the notion of class society. A class society is not one in which there simply exist classes, but one in which class relationships are of primary significance to the explanatory interpretation of large areas of social conduct. Thus while there were various forms of nascent class relationship in post-feudal society, this only became a class society with the hegemony of the capitalist market. Similarly it still might be possible to identify the existence of class relationships within a society which merits application of the term 'classless'. In both of these cases it will make perfect sense to analyse sectors of the social structure using class concepts; but it will not be possible, by doing so, to illuminate more than certain limited aspects of the social organisation as a whole.[18] It follows from this, however, that there are no absolute dividing lines, in given empirical cases, between 'pre-class' and 'class' society, on the one hand, or between 'class' society and 'classlessness' on the other.

The characteristics which distinguish pre-class from class society can be determined by generalisation of those already touched upon previously with reference to the decline of European feudalism (pp. 82–4). In pre-class society, the allocation of occupational tasks is governed primarily by traditionally established customs or norms, on a basis of 'ascription' rather than 'achievement' or 'performance'. The economy is primarily localised in character, i.e. production is mainly geared to the needs of the local community. The existence of mercantile capital, or of hand-craft production on a small scale, does not generally effect any fundamental alteration in this situation. Because of the essentially local nature of pre-class society, most relationships of domination, and of exploitation, are personalised, and are patterned primarily through kinship affiliations. This means that the spheres of 'economic' and 'political' power, in the modern sense, tend to be inseparable—a proposition which applies even where there is a developed form of state, which is inevitably patrimonial.

The emergence of classes in pre-class society is brought about by the appearance of those factors which Macpherson has spoken of as creating a 'simple market society'—which, however, should be understood as a transitory form, that is not yet a class society.[19] A 'simple market society' is one where customary ascription of tasks has at least in substantial part ceded place to a division of labour in which occupational position is open to the 'free' play of the inclinations or choices of individuals. Such a society has—again in substantial degree—superseded the constraints of localised production/consumption relationships, through the expansion of what Marx calls 'simple commodity production'. In 'simple market society', however, the individual producer retains a measure of direct control over his means of production. The formation of class society is predicated above all upon the dissolution of this control: upon the spread of a competitive market in labour which embraces the mass of the economically active population. In this sense, class society is tied to the emergence of what Marx quite correctly diagnosed as the essential basis of the modern capitalist order. As stated here, this only represents an abstract connection: many factors may play a part, of course, in actually effecting the transition to a fully developed class society.

At this point it is necessary to fill in more concretely the concept of class society. It is clear that the existence of class society depends upon a definite form of the institutional mediation of power: that is to say, it presupposes a 'separation' between economy and polity such that there is at least a substantial scope for the play of market mechanisms independent of active political control. The degree of explanatory salience of class relationships is contingent in a fundamental sense upon how far this is the case; but the one cannot be directly inferred from the other. In other words, within the *general category* of 'class society', there may be considerable variation in the specific modes in which class analysis is relevant to the explication of other aspects of the social structure. Apart from the character taken by the overall connections between economy and polity, we may distinguish four (interrelated, and therefore only analytically independent) sets of factors which determine this: (1) The nature and types of class structuration. (2) The nature and types of class consciousness (or class awareness) which correspond to the forms of structuration. (3) The forms assumed by overt class conflict— how far, for example, this is 'institutionalised' as collective bargaining in industry, or as routinised competition between organised class parties in politics. (4) The typical character of class exploitation.

I stress these points in order to underline the fact that the identification of any given society as a 'class society' does not thereby— as has very often been assumed, particularly by Marxist authors— relieve the analyst of the responsibility of examining in a concrete fashion the nature of the class relationships which pertain within it. This having been said, these four (variable) characteristics may be recognised as the principal distinguishing features of class society. Class structuration, of course, represents the mode by which disparities in market capacity become 'social realities', and therefore condition or influence the social conduct of the individual. But the existence of class structuration always presupposes at least class awareness, if not class consciousness, and hence implies the existence of differential class 'cultures' within a society. As has been indicated previously, the 'visible' aspects of class structuration may play a more significant role than is ordinarily recognised by writers on class theory in the genesis or maintenance of differentials in class awareness and class consciousness—and certainly it is these aspects of class society which are often fastened upon by literary observers or commentators.[20] But of predominant importance in sociological terms are the types of overt conflict which are linked to oppositions of interest entailed by differing forms of market capacity. It may be accepted that, both in the sense of chronic division of interest, and in the sense of the persistent occurrence of manifest struggles, class conflict is endemic in class society. The elimination of class conflict, latent or manifest, can only be achieved by a major process of reorganisation of society: to this degree we must recognise, with Marx, that a classless society is necessarily distinctively different in *type* from a class society. This does not mean to say, however, that the transcendence of class society in any way implies the transcendence of conflict, or even its reduction; it only signifies that such conflict is no longer meaningfully to be described as 'class conflict', and arises from different sources. The same remarks apply to exploitation, the fourth factor. In class society, the class structure is the primary axis around which the exploitative apportionment of socially created 'goods' takes place. Hence, while rejecting the Marxian theory of surplus value, we may agree that class exploitation is inseparable from, and ineradicable within, class society. But the creation of a classless society does not bring about the end of 'the exploitation of man by man', although again the sources, and to some extent the nature of exploitation, will be different.

4. THE NOTION OF CLASSLESSNESS

The theory of the classless society has taken various guises in the history of nineteenth-century social thought. Marx is not by any means the only author to have conceived of the possibility, nor is his version of a classless order the only one which has been envisaged as a feasible future form of social organisation by those living through the period of the 'great transformation'. The Marxian conception, as I have pointed out, was itself quite strongly influenced by Saint-Simon's interpretation of the projected 'one-class' society. This latter conception is undoubtedly the one which, apart from that developed by Marx, has been most frequently advanced by later writers—turning up most recently in the shape of Ossowski's 'non-egalitarian classlessness'. The notion of the 'one-class 'society amounts to something like a reverse perspective to the one which I have suggested here. Whereas, from the point of view which I have developed, feudalism is a pre-class society, and is succeeded (in Europe) by class society, in the Saint-Simonian version (although not in that suggested by Ossowski) feudalism is the very epitome of class society, and is succeeded, prospectively, by a classless society.

It should be evident, therefore, that the conception of classlessness I shall set out in this section owes little or nothing to any variant of the Saint-Simonian standpoint. While a situation of 'non-egalitarian classlessness', even if it were more than, as Ossowksi suggests, a prevalent form of modern ideological imagery, might have effects upon the degree of class structuration in a society, it is not in itself a sufficient condition of classlessness.

The difficulties with Marx's conception of classless society lie not so much in the basic attributes which characterise it, in so far as these are clearly stated at all, but in the features which are assumed to be necessarily tied to them. It is only certain assumptions built into the Marxian standpoint which make plausible the view that the transformation of the capitalist class structure, and the creation of a classless society, will provide a basis for the wholesale reorganisation of the division of labour (and, thus, the transcendence of alienation). The problems derive from Marx's tendency, already discussed above, to conflate various separable factors under the general concept of the 'division of labour'. The result, within the context of the theory of class, is that elements which are in fact contingent aspects of class structuration in capitalism are treated as necessarily tied to the class system (in Marx's sense). The most important of these are what I have previously referred to as 'paratechnical relations'. The weakest point in Marx's interpretation of the contrast between class society and classlessness concerns the proposition that the transcendence of class society either necessarily leads to, or even provides a basis for, radical change in those aspects of the division of labour which are involved in the sphere of paratechnical relations. This latter sphere is of fundamental importance in the structuration of class relationships in capitalist society; but it does *not* follow from this that the abolition of classes will entail any significant alteration in paratechnical relations. The flaws in the Marxian conception at this point stem in large part from a misleading assimilation of 'capitalism' and 'industrialism'— a matter which is discussed at greater length in the next chapter.

In terms of the concepts which I have introduced earlier, it follows that the basic condition for the formation of a classless society is the establishment of a form of the state which transcends the division between the 'economic' and the 'political' characteristic of class society. This definitely involves the abolition of private property in the means of production; but the crucial element underlying this is the replacement of the 'invisible hand' of market mechanisms by the directive control of production and distribution. The institutional mediation of power essential to the existence of

class society, in which the state functions as the guarantor of contractual relationships, is replaced by one in which the state assumes
overall directive control of industrial enterprise. To say this, to
repeat, is not to hold that a classless society can only emerge out
of a fully developed class society—in Marx's terms, that socialism
is predicated upon the dialectical transcendence of mature capitalism.
On the contrary, it will be one of my major arguments in the latter
part of this book that the only forms of society in the modern
world which approach a situation of classlessness are those which
have never been fully developed class societies.

The further characteristics of a classless order can be derived
by implication from the four components designated as the major
attributes of class society. The first is a lack of class structuration.
This is clearly relative rather than absolute, at least as it applies
to any actual society. A classless society shares with a class society
its character as a supra-local,system, with all the economic and social
complexities which this entails; and there is no foreseeable possibility of completely eliminating the operation of market mechanisms.
In any empirical case which approximates to the type of a classless
society there is bound to be a certain development of class structuration. But this will not be either as pervasive or as clearly formed as
is the case in class societies. A further point needs emphasising
here. Several of the sources of class structuration in class societies
may be present in classless systems (for example, as mentioned above,
a comparable set of paratechnical relations). These may play a part
in creating similarities in structure, within certain institutional
sectors of society; but their impact, alternatively, may be quite
different because they do not operate within a framework of *class*
structuration. The case of the influence of paratechnical relations
can actually serve as an illustration of both of these possibilities.
Thus it may be claimed, as I shall in fact claim in the concluding
part of this book, that there are definite parallels in aspects of the
social structures of contemporary class societies, on the one hand,
and classless societies, on the other, which are to be traced to the
fact that they share something of a common system of paratechnical
relations. But this is not a 'necessary' parallel, as is asserted by the
proponents of the idea of the inherent 'logic' of modern industry;
it is heavily conditioned by the circumstances that, in both forms
of society, there is an overwhelming commitment to similar goals
of maximal economic growth and productivity. Moreover, I shall
argue that the connection between class structure and paratechnical
relations which pertains within the class societies entails that little
can be done, given the overall framework of this type of society,

to change the existing system. In the classless societies, by contrast, the potentiality for change is there, whether or not it comes to be actualised.

Similarly, in classless society we would expect to find only a low level of class consciousness, and especially of conflict consciousness. This is not all the same as the absence of 'sectional group consciousness' in other forms, nor is there any reason why this should not, in given circumstances, be expressed as a recognition of divisions of interest between specific categories of individuals or collectivities. There is no type of society, including even the most simple, which is free from clashes of interest or overt conflicts; in classless society, there are necessarily chronic sources of interest opposition, which are bound to lead frequently to manifest struggles. It should hardly be necessary to add that this applies to any conceivable future kind of classless society, as much as to those now extant. Because of the fragmentary and inconclusive nature of Marx's comments on the 'higher stage' of communism—that is to say, the genuinely classless society projected as the successor to the 'transitional stage' in the passage from capitalism to socialism— it is not clear whether or not, in some sense, he anticipated the disappearance of endemic conflict in the fully realised classless society. Certainly some subsequent Marxists have drawn this conclusion, and in some interpretations of the notion of alienation, as the 'estrangement of man from man', if the 'higher stage' of communist society is to bring about the supersession of alienation it is perhaps plausible to argue that this involves the disappearance of social conflict. At any rate, if something of this sort ever was Marx's view, it is completely distinct from that which I have advanced.

Since I have already commented in similar vein upon the nature of exploitation, it is unnecessary to stress at length that these observations apply here. As in the case of conflict, to hold that the transcendence of class society does not bring about the end of exploitation is not to deny the existence of major and highly significant differences in this respect between class and classless society. But these differences have to be examined concretely; and I wish to deny that classless society is *of necessity* less exploitative in character than class society. The rationale for this proposition is, I think, evident in the line of theoretical analysis which is set out in the remainder of this book; and it is closely bound up with problems of the interpretation of capitalist development, which I have so far set aside, but which must now be tackled.

8

THE PROBLEM OF CAPITALIST DEVELOPMENT

1. 'CAPITALISM' AND 'INDUSTRIAL SOCIETY'

The term 'capitalism', almost as much as 'class', has been used in various overlapping senses by sociologists and historians.[1] But it is relevant at this point only to consider certain matters raised by a comparison of the ways in which the concept of capitalism is used by Marx and Weber respectively. Marx, as I have stressed before, employs the term in a specific sense—to refer essentially to a system of production in which labour-power is a commodity exchanged on the market against capital. Weber's conception of capitalism is more complicated, since he uses the notion in two ways: in a very general sense (e.g., 'adventurers' capitalism'), such that capitalist enterprise can be identified at various periods and locales in the past, and in a sense closer to that of Marx ('modern capitalism'), whereby capitalism is peculiar to the post-feudal Western world. But while Weber recognises, as I have described previously, that the creation of a free market in labour, whereby propertyless workers must sell their labour to employers in return for their means of livelihood, is a necessary and basic component of modern capitalism, this does not—as it does for Marx—express its fundamental nature. It is one element allowing for the achievement of a high degree of rational calculability in economic enterprise. This converges with the fact that, according to Weber, the process of 'expropriation' of workers from their means of production is not confined to the sphere of industry but, in terms of separation from the 'means of administration', takes place in all the major institutions of capitalist society. The central trait of modern capitalism is to be found in its character as a system of rationally calculated, routinised production—exemplified in the formally rational principles of organisation in the capitalist enterprise. Most of the significant theoretical contrasts between the interpretations of the general trend of development of the advanced societies, offered by Marx and Weber respectively, flow from this difference.

Neither Marx nor Weber gave a great deal of attention to drawing a clearly formulated distinction between 'capitalism' and 'industrialism'. Weber's stress upon the significance of rational calculability to modern economic enterprise naturally emphasises the closeness of the connections between the development of capitalism on the one hand and the spread of mechanisation, and factory production, on the other. Of the latter two factors, the first represents the rationalisation of technique, the second the rationalisation of human *labour* in relation to the machine. These developments, Weber makes clear, are promoted primarily by the expansionist dynamic intrinsic to modern capitalism. In this particular respect, his view is not essentially different from that of Marx, who argued that the growth of capitalism from the eighteenth century onwards provided the pressure which eventuated in the transmutation of 'manufacture' into 'machinofacture'. Both Marx and Weber, moreover, saw an intricate and necessary connection between machine and factory. As Weber put it: 'The real distinguishing characteristic of the modern factory is in general . . . the concentration of ownership of workplace, means of work, source of power and raw material in one and the same hand, that of the entrepreneur.'[2] The basic difference between the two thinkers is that, whereas for Weber the rationalisation of technique expressed in the machine epitomises the intrinsic character of modern capitalism both as an economic and social structure, for Marx this rationalisation of technique is, in a highly important sense, secondary and subordinate to the core attribute of capitalism as a class system.

Each of these views of the ties between capitalism and industrialism, I wish to hold, is inadequate; neither satisfactorily makes the conceptual distinctions which are called for—each assumes what in fact needs to be demonstrated by concrete analysis. The Weberian conception is deficient because it depends upon a specious link which is drawn between the rationality of technique and the rationalisation of organised conduct (bureaucracy), without allowing sufficiently for the possibility that *both* these aspects of rationalisation are, at least to some degree, contingent upon variations in class structure (that is to say, class society as contrasted with classlessness). The flaw in Marx's standpoint is similar, except that the direction of emphasis is reversed. For Marx, the process of industrialisation is treated as secondary to, and derivative of, 'capitalism' in his sense: it is, as it were, merely the 'logical outcome' of the impulsions which the class character of the capitalist mode of production embodies.[3] Hence, as I have indicated earlier, the influence of technique, and the structure of paratechnical relations, are treated as necessarily dependent upon, and subordinate to, the class system.

The concept of 'industrial society', at least as it has often been used from Saint-Simon onwards, bears certain affinities with the way in which Weber applies his notion of (modern) 'capitalism'.[4] There have been, of course, numerous theoretical approaches in sociology which have employed the idea of 'industrial society' since Saint-Simon, and the views of its nature which these have advanced are quite diverse. But they all share the supposition that what distinguishes the contemporary societies from traditional forms is a complex of economic and social relationships which are ultimately shaped by modern industrial technique. Thus, like Weber's interpretation of capitalism in terms of rational calculability, but in a blunter fashion, the concept of 'industrial society' cuts across the interpretation of the advanced societies in class terms— and, again, tends to lead to a standpoint which takes for granted theorems which actually demand empirical verification.

We need, therefore, to formulate a clear conceptual differentiation between 'capitalism', 'industrialism' (and 'industrialisation'), and 'industrial society'—although I shall not in fact make use of the latter term in this book, for reasons given below. While there have been numerous debates about the conception of the 'Industrial Revolution', there is probably substantial agreement about the core components of industrialism. Industrialism involves, first of all, the transformation of human labour via the application of inanimate sources of energy to productive activity. But while this may be taken as an adequate representation of its most essential feature, other factors appear as conjoined to this, the most important of which is the physical proximity of workers, together with machinery, in a clearly circumscribed workplace: i.e., the factory.[5] I shall therefore define industrialism as *the transfer of inanimate energy sources to production through the agency of factory organisation.* Industrialisation is then the process, or set of processes, whereby industrialism comes to play a major part in the economic life of any given society. In these terms, the notion of 'industrial society' may be applied to designate a social order in which industrialism has come to predominate in the production of marketable goods within the economy. As it is most frequently employed, however, the concept assumes very much more than this. Since I believe

certain of these further assumptions need to be criticised, I shall,
to avoid confusion, use instead the term 'advanced society', in spite
of its possibly dubious connotations of evolutionism, to refer
to any social order, class or classless, which has moved beyond
'simple market society'.

I have previously made it clear that, according to the scheme of
concepts which I have elaborated, there is an intimate connection
between 'capitalism' and class society. But, for reasons already
alluded to, the Marxian conceptualisation of the former will not
do. Not only, in resting upon the general notion of 'mode of production', does it fail to separate capitalism from industrialism
satisfactorily, but—as a related matter—it is very directly bound
up with the Marxian concept of class, and if the latter must be
relinquished, the derivative specification of 'capitalism' must at
least be regarded in a somewhat new perspective. However, in using
the term 'capitalism', it is neither necessary nor desirable to abandon
all of the tenets of Marx's standpoint. The essential traits of capitalism, as I shall subsequently apply the notion, are the following.
Capitalism exists where: (1) Production is primarily oriented to the
realisation, or search for the realisation, of profit accruing to privately
owned capital. (2) This process is organised in terms of a market
upon which commodities, including labour itself, are bought and
sold according to standards of monetary exchange. In substance,
this definition maintains the principal characteristics of the Marxian
notion; save that capitalism here is not a 'mode of production'
(if the phrase were to be salvaged, one might say that 'capitalism'
plus 'industrialism' equals a definite mode of production).[6] *'Capitalist
society'* may be said to exist when, as some Marxists have put it,
capitalism becomes 'hegemonic': that is to say, when the major part
of the economic system of a society is ordered according to the
two sets of principles indicated above. While the existence of capitalist society presupposes a high level of industrialisation, the reverse
does not hold. Strictly speaking, therefore, there is a very significant
distinction between 'capitalism' and 'capitalist society' because,
since the latter involves industrialism, it is of comparatively recent
creation, while the former is not. If for much of the remainder
of this book I use the terms more or less interchangeably, it is for
the sake of terminological variety, not because I have forgotten
the profound difference between them.

The definition of capitalism given above naturally does not
imply that for any actual economy to be called capitalist it must
manifest anything like 'perfect competition'; or that a competitive
market must be found in every sector of production; or that the

state may not directly run large segments of the economy. Moreover, this definition does not prejudice the existence of oligopoly, or even of monopoly, in the capitalist economy. Even in the most 'organised' of the capitalist economies, the private appropriation of profit, through the investment of capital, remains the ultimate regulator of productive activity. Situations of oligopoly or monopoly, involving in some sense the direct 'administration' of prices by producers, may entail a 'reallocation' of revenue on capital from the more to the less competitive industries, but do not directly cut through the conditions of capitalist production.

2. CAPITALISM IN NINETEENTH-CENTURY EUROPE

Many of those who, from the vantage-point of the twentieth century, have criticised Marx's supposed 'predictions' concerning the future of capitalism have done so in a somewhat curious manner. Dahrendorf's discussion of the emergence of 'post-capitalist' society is a case in point. The argument appears to run as follows. In analysing the social and economic structure of nineteenth-century capitalism, Marx was broadly correct in his diagnosis of the main dynamics of capitalist society in general, and in his interpretation of classes and class conflict in particular. But the nineteenth century is not the twentieth century: since Marx's time we have witnessed the occurrence of profound socio-economic changes which have now rendered his views redundant. It is hardly adequate, however, to argue that Marx was in large part right about what was the case in the nineteenth-century context, but that, as applied to the modern world, his views are mistaken (or irrelevant). Unless we believe that whatever determines the course of social development is purely contingent, it follows that Marx must have been, in substantial degree, wrong in the beginning about certain of the essential dynamic characteristics which he attributed to the European societies from whose history he drew most of his observations.

Although a detailed examination of these matters would demand far more space than is available here, it is possible to identify two primary failures in Marx's analysis of nineteenth-century capitalism. The first concerns the mode in which he attempted to relate his 'abstract model' of capitalist development to the actual societies of his day; the second turns upon certain previously discussed flaws in his theory of class. Now although he (but more particularly Engels) devoted some attention to the United States, most of Marx's discussions of the past, and the prospective future, of capitalism are informed by materials taken from three European

countries: Germany, France, and Britain. The philosophical traditions of these three countries, in the stated order, represent the
primary intellectual sources out of which Marx fashioned historical
materialism: classical German philosophy, French socialist thought,
and British political economy. But, in terms of the more concrete
observations which he drew upon in formulating his model of
capitalist development, the British case was of dominant importance.
Capital relies almost exclusively upon documentation relating to
Britain and—after 1850 at least—it was primarily from within the
context of a theory of development derived from British society that
Marx sought to interpret the course of events in the two other countries.

The famous assertion, made in the Preface to the first German
edition of *Capital*, with reference to the German reader who might
reject the relevance of British development to his own country—
De te fabula narratur!: it is of you that the story is told—succinctly
expresses Marx's standpoint. Britain exemplifies the developing
ascendancy of capitalist society in its 'most typical form'.[7] This is
true, it must be emphasised, not merely of the historical observations upon the enclosure movement, etc., but of much of the supportive basis of the economic *theory* worked out in *Capital*. This
is not to propose that Marx was in any sense unaware of the patent
differences in social and economic structure between Britain and
the other two countries; on the contrary, as I have said before, he
always maintained a most direct interest in the contemporary development of his fatherland, and three long historical essays bear
ample witness to the depth of his intellectual involvement in events
in France. But, following up the *dénouements* of 1848, for the bulk
of his intellectual career he adopted the view that the revolutionary
transcendence of capitalist society must, both in terms of theoretical
understanding and practical accomplishment, be predicated upon
the *maturity* of the capitalist mode of production.

The inherent problems in this view, which was shared by many
writers contemporary with Marx, have only become fully apparent
in the light of subsequent experience, both of the later development
of the three European societies and of the modern formation of
societies outside of Europe. The point is, that rather than being
the 'type case' of either capitalist or industrial evolution, Britain is
the exception; or, more accurately, it represents only one among
various identifiable patterns of development in the emergence of
the advanced societies.[8] In Britain—no doubt as the overall result
of a complicated (and still highly controversial) set of specific
historical antecedents—the way was paved in the nineteenth century

for the mutual accommodation of capitalism and industrialism within a general framework of a bourgeois democratic order. Consequently the process of industrialisation took place in an 'undirected' fashion, through the agency of a multiplicity of entrepreneurial activities in a relatively stabilised 'bourgeois society'. France in the nineteenth century, and arguably ever since, was dominated by the legacy of the 1789 revolution. While Marx was perfectly cognisant of this, and indeed regarded the French polity as in certain ways the exemplification of the bourgeois state, he failed adequately to analyse the continuing differences in *infrastructure*[9], as well as 'superstructure', which separated French from British society. French history, throughout the nineteenth century, was conditioned by persisting cleavages between what Marx referred to as 'retrograde' elements—large land-owners, the peasantry, the Church and army, on the one hand, and the large-scale industrial and commercial interests upon the other. The process of industrialisation was not only more attenuated and retarded than was the case in Britain, but it took place within the framework of a society which, far from epitomising the most 'modern' bourgeois order, did not become a fully 'bourgeois society' until the period of triumphant republicanism preceding the turn of the century.

In Germany, of course, the position was different again. It could be said that the very starting-point of Marx's intellectual career is to be traced to a concern, in the early 1840s, with Germany's 'backwardness', in relation (politically) to France, and (in terms of economic development) to Britain. For over half the nineteenth century, Germany remained a loosely organised aggregate of principalities, rather than a nation-state in the modern sense, and its level of economic advancement was low. Marx anticipated that a metamorphosis in this situation could only come about through the generation of socio-economic forces which would be so tumultuous as to very rapidly outstrip the capabilities of control of a momentarily ascendant bourgeoisie in favour of the creation, in short order, of a socialist society. He lived to see the unification of Germany, and the initial period of German industrial expansion. But it is hardly possible to encompass these, or the pattern of development of Germany after his death, within the general framework of his ideas. The political unification of Germany was accomplished, not under the sway of those 'progressive' German states where industry and commerce, or liberal political ideas, were most strongly developed, but under the domination of 'semi-feudal' Prussia. The German nation-state was forged, as Weber emphasised, and made one of the focal points of his thought, through the exercise of military power. The process of industrialisation, compressed within a relatively short period of time, was in substantial degree directed by a state in which traditional, land-owning groupings maintained a strong mastery.

These developments in France and Germany cannot be properly understood if the British experience is treated as the prototype—and especially if this is generalised into a generic, polar contrast between 'feudalism' and 'capitalism'. Marx, as I have stressed previously, departed from the theorists of 'industrial society' in envisaging a threefold progression of feudalism–capitalism–socialism rather than opposition between 'traditional' and 'modern' society. But this latter, twofold, opposition is there in Marx's writings, in the shape of the generalised antithesis between 'feudalism' and 'capitalism' that constitutes the major historical division which he himself observed to have occurred. Nothing is more intrinsic to nineteenth-century thought than this antithesis, versions of which inform the works of virtually all the major social thinkers of the period. There can be no objection to such concepts separating, in some sense, the two sides of the 'great transformation', the 'traditional' and the 'modern', if these are treated as no more than general types,. whose usefulness must be examined in relation to a diversity of cases. But, in fact, both Marx and most of the other thinkers of the time tended to rely heavily upon one empirical case in working out their typologies—and then to proceed (and this applies less to Marx than to certain of the others) to commit the fallacy of 'misplaced concreteness' by treating them as if they could be applied *in toto* to the explanation of specific historical instances.[10]

Perhaps the most important element in Marx's contrast of 'feudalism' and 'capitalism' which blinkered his interpretation of nineteenth-century Europe is that of agrarian or land-owning elite groups. Looking above all to the case of Britain, Marx saw these as either, in the form of· the post-feudal aristocracy, irresistibly swept aside by the advent of capitalism, or, in the form of *rentiers*, making up one sector of the capitalist ruling class. Even in Britain, however, the land-owning aristocratic elite retained a strong economic, and especially political, position longer than Marx foresaw. But in ·Germany, in the shape of the *Junkers*, they continued to play a decisive role until well into the twentieth century: and the examination of how this came to be is essential to the understanding of the social and political development of the country. Germany after the turn of the century would certainly warrant the appellation 'capitalist society'; but its social and economic structure, and its history since the late nineteenth century, in important respects show a closer parallel with Japan than of any other European country. The other side of the coin to this is Marx's relative neglect of the 'retrograde class'—the peasantry. Even prior to the twentieth-century socialist revolutions, the peasantry have played a major role in shaping the form taken by the advanced societies—and, again, the early 'disappearance' of both the bonded and independent peasantry in Britain has proved to be more the exception than the rule.[11]

In a more general sense, specifically *political* factors have played a far more significant part in the latter-day development of the advanced societies than Marx allowed for.[12] The lasting pre-eminence of 'traditional' elements in the capitalist societies at the turn of the twentieth century is closely tied in to the rise of national-ism. It has often been pointed out, correctly, that Marx gave little or no prominence to the possible role of nationalism in influencing the course of modern history. But this is only one among various aspects of the matter. It is not necessary to adopt the extreme view which reduces class conflict to a manifestation of a struggle to acquire political 'citizenship', in order to see that there is a sub-stantial amount of validity in the proposition that the attempt to secure full political incorporation for the working class (and its success) is of basic importance in the development of the capitalist societies. In one sense, Marx was obviously right to regard nationalism and socialism as competing and mutually exclusive principles; but in an *explanatory* sense, in tracing the development of these as the dominating mass movements of the late nineteenth century, it is evident enough that the two both intertwine and, in some degree, feed upon similar sources.

Any account of the development of Britain, France, and Germany in the early years of this century must proffer an interpretation of the fact that, while a strong workers' movement flourished in each of these societies, in the movement in the latter two countries there was a strong component of revolutionary class consciousness, while in the first there was not. Exactly the contrary would be expected if the injunction *De te fabula narratur!* is applied. The dis-crepancy can be understood, however, if it is placed against the background sketched in above. The counterpart to the revolutionary workers' movement, in France, and Germany, was an aggressively nationalistic conservatism. The creation of an established liberal bourgeois order was a protracted process, threatened on two fronts. In Britain (as, in a different context, in the United States) the interpenetration of nascent industrialism with a very specific social structure allowed for a relatively stable accommodation between the various classes; neither revolutionary socialism, nor militant conservatism, became the forces which they were in the other two European countries.

But these phenomena can only be partially interpreted in these terms: at this point it is useful to move on to the second type of factor compromising Marx's treatment of nineteenth-century capitalism. It is a very familiar theme in critiques of Marx that his writings contain a number of key 'predictions' concerning the projected course of capitalist development—predictions which failed to materialise. Now there can be no doubt that, at least for much of his career, Marx expected the demise of capitalist society to occur in the then very near future—even if his expectations as to the character of the likely precipitating situation changed according to the concrete course of events in the European countries. But it is equally clear that most of what have been taken as 'predictions' about the future of capitalism are in fact regarded by Marx as tendential properties of capitalist development, the actualisation of which is influenced by contingent events. To analyse the validity of these hypothesised characteristics of capitalism, it is not enough to indicate divergencies in the actual development of the capitalist societies since Marx's day: an assessment must also be made of the *theoretical* significance of these divergencies to those properties which Marx regarded as immanent in capitalism as a 'mode of production'. Of the tendential characteristics of capitalism identified by Marx, three are of particular importance: (1) the thesis that the evolving maturity of the capitalist economy gives rise to an expanding relative disparity between the economic returns falling to wage-labour and those taken by capital; (2) the theory that capitalism is subject to endemic crises of overproduction, which characteristically become more cataclysmic over time; and (3) the conception that capitalism 'undercuts its own premises' since its continuing operation consolidates processes of the concentration and centralisation of capitals (thereby tending towards—although Marx himself did not use the term—'monopoly capitalism').

Since the latter part of the nineteenth century, the real income of the bulk of that vast segment of the occupational structure which Marx would categorise as 'wage-labour' has increased substantially in all of the capitalist societies. This fact, of tremendous importance if the 'emiseration thesis' is regarded as a specific 'prediction' concerning the future of capitalism, loses some of its significance, at least in relation to the Marxian standpoint, if it is recognised that, according to Marx's economic theory, what is crucial is the chronic incapacity of wage-labour to augment its relative share of the burgeoning productive wealth of capitalism. But that this growing prosperity is inconsistent with that theory is hardly open to doubt. For the main proposition underlying Marx's view is that, because of exigencies generic to the capitalist economic system, the income accruing to wage-labour cannot in the long term rise far above subsistence level. But such a rise has occurred, and it is not to be explained away either in terms of the minor escape-clause which Marx allows, that what is 'subsistence' may be influenced by variable cultural definitions, nor in terms of latter-day Marxist theories of imperialism.[13] As has often been pointed out by economists, it is possible, however, to salvage certain of the relevant tenets of Marx's economic theory, at the expense of sacrificing the conclusion which he wished to draw from it, and thereby to reconcile the former with the fact of the rise in the real income of the wage-labourer. It is a major theme of the Marxian economic theory of capitalism (again, not to be regarded as a concrete 'prediction') that there is a tendency for the rate of profit on capital to decline. Given, therefore, that the rate of surplus value remains constant, it follows that rising productivity of labour must bring about an augmentation in real wages.[14]

Whatever may be the validity of this theoretical interpretation, the facts of the matter today seem fairly clear. Although it was incorrect to suppose that the intrinsic character of the capitalist economy generates an expanding divergence between the returns taken by wage-labour and capital, it was not as far from the truth as many of Marx's critics have held. In spite of the various forms of taxation schemes, aimed at the redistribution of wealth and income, which have been introduced in all the capitalist societies, there have for the most part been only marginal changes in the relative differentials which existed in the latter part of the nineteenth century. What appears to be generic to capitalism is a *stable* disparity between the economic returns accruing to the major classes—within this we can include not only the differentiation between the propertied and the non-propertied, but also that between middle and working class in terms of paid income.[15] Certainly the real income of both of the latter classes has increased very considerably over the past hundred years; but rather than significantly affecting the relative differentials, this process has simply moved virtually everyone upwards in like degree. Particularly important is the apparent fixity in the distribution of property: in spite of the claims which have been made for the advent of a 'peoples' capitalism', distinguished by a widening spread of property ownership, it has become clear in recent years—even in the United States, where this contention has most frequently been advanced—that the reality is rather the marked resilience of the pre-existing concentration of property ownership in the hands of a small minority of the population (although the degree of concentration in this respect has never been as high in the United States as that typically observed in the European countries). If the capitalist societies have changed at their 'upper levels' since the nineteenth century, the case has to be made primarily in terms of declining salience of property ownership for economic control, as a result of the growth of joint-stock companies, rather than in terms of the changing distribution of property as such.

So much has been written about the Marxian theory of capitalist crises that there is no need to do more than recapitulate certain of the major themes here. For many years, it was not an uncommon expectation of Marxists that capitalism would meet its demise in one final, catastrophic crisis—and, up to 1930, this was not an implausible suggestion. In Marx's own writings, however, no such event is specifically foreseen, and indeed the factors actually bringing about crises remain somewhat obscure. Marx did not write anything approaching a comprehensive account of the nature of crises, and probably held that they represent the final outcome of a series of interconnected factors, which cannot be reduced to any simple formula. But the underlying conditions which he diagnosed as producing the general tendency of the capitalist economy to be subject to recurrent crises are clear enough and, broadly speaking, they may be accepted as correct (if, in the light of modern economic analysis, oversimplified). Capitalism differs from pre-class society in virtue of the fact that it breaks the immediate tie between production and consumption which predominates in the latter type of social order, where production is geared to local, known needs. In the capitalist system, via the development of money economy, exchange transactions become governed by the impersonal forces of the market. There is thus an inherent 'anarchy' in capitalism, because there is no definite agency whereby production is adjusted to consumption. The pursuit of profit on capital is the principal mode whereby some measure of equilibrium between production and consumption is maintained; a crisis occurs essentially where a sufficient level of yield on investment is not achieved, and where a significant volume of 'overproduction' occurs, creating a vicious circle of diminution of consumer power through the laying-off of labour, and a further decline in the rate of profit. The occurrence of these processes, Marx pointed out, eventually re-creates equilibrium conditions, but at a lower productive capacity, whence a new upswing in production may then take place.[16]

Marx himself analysed the source of one set of elements which, by only a relatively slight extension of his argument, can serve in part to counter the 'anarchy' of capitalist production: that is, the third series of tendential properties of capitalism mentioned above—the tendency towards concentration and centralisation. In so far as something akin to a monopoly situation exists in any sector of production, economic organisations are potentially able to regulate prices, and therefore profits, in a direct fashion and, if only by the exclusion of alternative products, to regulate the needs of consumers; and the centralisation of the market, as manifest in the domination of a limited number of financial or credit agencies, can introduce an important degree of regulation of market operations. What Marx failed to perceive, undoubtedly in large part because of the inadequacies in his general analysis of the state, was that the developing maturity of capitalism might generate a different form of partial 'undercutting of its own premises' by stimulating an expansion of state intervention in economic life. The brilliance of Keynes' economic writings has tended to lead to a neglect of the fact that the 'Keynesian revolution' was as much an expression of changes which were already proceeding within the capitalist societies as a novel set of measures for reorganising the capitalist economy. Historically, as I have pointed out, the state has in certain capitalist countries played an important role in fostering economic development, and thus from the beginning has been deeply involved in economic life. But it is arguable that, just as the appearance of dislocations or crises stimulates concentration and centralisation, so it also acts to promote state intervention in the workings of the economy. For the operation of 'unfettered' capitalism, first of all, tends to create definite 'weaknesses' in certain sectors of the economy: and these are frequently the sectors into which the state moves. Moreover the very occurrence, and widening scale, of crises makes evident the generic instability of capitalism if no direct control is maintained by the state over certain of the key aspects of economic organisation. To be sure, this is not an exigency created within the mechanics of capitalist production itself; that is to say, it implies a significant degree of conscious recognition on the part of governmental agencies of what has to be done to rectify, or alleviate, the 'pathology' of the system. But this is not, after all, qualitatively different from what occurs in the processes of economic reorganisation, in the shape of concentration and centralisation, in the context of the 'recovery' from crises. State intervention of the Keynesian type does not, of course, eliminate the tendency to crises; but it does mean that this tendency can be converted to one of relatively minor fluctuations of boom and recession.

In the light of subsequent developments even Marx's most stringent critics cannot deny that he was correct in identifying concentration and centralisation as fundamental tendencies of the maturity of capitalist production. What can and must be questioned are the inferences he drew from this in relation to the anticipated transcendence of capitalism by socialism. Marx saw in these processes the incipient socialisation of the market, to be complemented by the rise of a revolutionary working-class movement, which would take over a system that had already progressed a considerable way towards generating the elements of a socialist economy. But if these two sets of changes are not inherently connected—for reasons more fully documented in subsequent chapters—then the resultant picture is very different. What Marx caustically referred to as 'a whole system of swindling and cheating by means of corporation promotion, stock issuance, and stock speculation' becomes, not a transitory phase intervening between 'classical capitalism' and socialism, but the characteristic form of the developed capitalist economy.

3. CAPITALISM AND THE ORIGINS OF STATE SOCIALISM

I have earlier distinguished two types of situation linked (in Marx's writings) with the revolutionary transcendence of capitalism which, although they are necessarily closely tied in his own thinking, may be analytically separated. One of these looks to the emergence of a revolutionary working class within the most developed capitalist societies, the other to the disruptive effects of contact between a 'backward' order and an 'advanced' one, as a result of the rapid socio-economic changes which may be brought into play by such contact. Both, however, presuppose the existence of a highly developed 'capitalist mode of production' (in Marx's sense), since that latter situation only leads to a socialist revolution if it serves to precipitate a process of revolutionary change in the advanced societies themselves. With the advantage of hindsight, we can now see that neither of the 'two Marxian views of revolution' is satisfactory. Each presumes a close connection between revolutionary consciousness and activity on the one hand, and the maturity of capitalist development on the other. The truth of the matter is that the sort

of revolutionary process which has taken place is not only substantially different from what he envisaged but, as a widespread
phenomenon, is associated with the *early stages* of capitalist-in-
dustrial development rather than the later stages. This is not the
place to essay the outlines of a general theory of revolutionary
change, if such a theory is conceivably possible at all. Three observations, however, are relevant here: (1) The (manual) working
class is most likely to achieve a high degree of revolutionary class
consciousness in the initial phase of the industrialisation process.
(2) The nature or form of this class consciousness, however, depends
in a very significant sense upon broad aspects of the socio-economic
framework within which industrialisation occurs. (3) In the kinds
of 'successful' revolutionary change which have occurred since
the turn of the century, the peasantry has typically played an important, and even crucial, role—not as a 'retrograde class', but as a
positive source of impetus to revolutionary activity.

The factors which tend to stimulate a revolutionary class consciousness on the part of the working class in the initial stages of industrialisation are—in the abstract—not difficult to specify. The
development of industrial production involves the emergence of
contradictions which are normally far more pronounced than those
involved in the commercialisation which is typical of the formation
of 'simple market society' within a pre-class order. The paratechnical
relations characteristic of industrial production are not only dramatically different from those of either peasant agrarianism or handcraft
'manufacture', but the transference from the latter to the former,
in the phase of 'take-off' into industrialism, normally occurs with
considerable rapidity. Moreover, this transference involves a wholesale uprooting of labour from the close-knit rural community to
the more disaggregated urban environment. The scholarly debate
over whether, in purely material terms, the standard of living
(in Britain) prior to the Industrial Revolution was marginally
higher or lower than afterwards does not affect the fact that the
changes involved create the potential for a profound *experience* of
deprivation—and for a recognition of possible 'alternative orders'.
Given the nature of the contrast between the paratechnical relations
of agrarian and those characteristic of industrial production, the
attraction of the newly formed working class to socialist ideas is
readily understandable. The labour force, drawn from a productive
system in which the worker maintains a definite degree of control
over his means of production, moves or is thrust into a situation
where he—together with a mass of others, with whom he is in
visible contact—is subject to the 'given' discipline of the factory

and machine.[17] But the specific nature of this class consciousness, how far it remains inchoate or becomes canalised within a workers' movement, and the role of the workers' movement itself, are all in substantial degree dependent upon the overall character of the society in question—upon the two sets of factors indicated previously: the character of the pre-industrial structure, and the 'trajectory' of the industrialisation process.

The forms of revolutionary change which have led to the establishment of state socialism are diverse, and I shall not make any attempt to analyse them here. Undoubtedly these cannot be understood solely in terms of socio-economic presuppositions; political factors have played an extremely significant part—and particularly the impact of war.[18] But there are obvious and striking differences between the character of the societies where state socialist systems have come into being and those which have remained capitalist. In the first place, capitalist society is primarily a creation of the nineteenth century (and earlier); state socialism a product of the twentieth. Most of the contemporary capitalist societies experienced industrial 'take-off' in the nineteenth century, even if very late on in that century. State socialism, on the other hand, is a much more recent arrival: the phrase 'socialism in one country', as applied to the USSR, had a quite literal meaning until less than thirty years ago, and even the October Revolution is only a little over half a century old. With some partial exceptions (the German Democratic Republic and Czechoslovakia), state socialism has come into being in societies which had reached only a fairly rudimentary level of economic development, and where the peasantry constituted the mass of the population. A class-conscious working class may, in Russia, have played a leading role in the sequence of revolutionary change, but only against this backdrop. The character of the advanced state socialist societies varies as much as that of the capitalist ones, and one must avoid overtly simple categorisations of them as much as of the latter. But the conclusion is inescapable that state socialism has served essentially as an alternative framework for the channelling of the industrialisation process to that, or more accurately, those, characteristic of nineteenth-century capitalism— a framework which is particularly apposite in the modern age, given the existence of highly advanced technology, together with the availability of guidelines from the prior experience of the capitalist societies themselves.[19] Later in the book, in referring fairly extensively to Poland and Yugoslavia for illustrative material in order to examine the character of state socialist society, I shall be stretching the phrase 'advanced society' beyond its legitimate frame of reference. But I think that it is necessary to look at these countries in order to document adequately the ideas I wish to propose. I shall, however, concentrate my attention primarily upon the industrialised sectors of these societies, and shall not deal in any detail with their agricultural populations—a dubious, but in this case, I believe, a defensible procedure.

The term 'state socialism' may be used to apply to a broad spectrum of societies which have experienced a socialist revolution, regardless of their level of industrial development. 'State socialism', as I employ the notion here, refers *to any economic order in which the means of production is formally socialised in the hands of the state.* This implies that the state assumes directive control of economic life, and that consequently the ultimate criteria regulating production are determined by political decisions. Such a situation does not preclude, of course, the continued existence of private property in the means of production in certain sectors, nor does it entail (if this were conceivable at all) the abandonment of 'market mechanisms' altogether. I shall later be dealing in some detail with the nature of state socialist society, but at this juncture the discussion must move to a consideration of the significance of the changes which have taken place in the class structure of capitalist society since the turn of the century.

9

THE INSTITUTIONAL MEDIATION OF POWER

AND THE MEDIATION OF CONTROL

1. IS IT STILL CAPITALIST SOCIETY?

Amongst the proliferation of writings on the subject, we may distinguish two primary themes concerning supposed changes in the institutional mediation of power in the capitalist societies since the nineteenth century—each is closely associated with the notion that capitalism has altered so fundamentally over the past seventy years, that we now live in a 'post-capitalist' society. One theme, pointing to the growth of 'citizenship rights', asserts that the application of such rights to virtually the whole of the adult population has transformed the nature of the capitalist state. The other looks more to the economic sphere, holding that the increasing domination of industry by a limited number of very large corporations has radically modified the basic alignments of economy and polity characteristic of 'capitalist society' as such. The latter viewpoint is closely connected to the notion of the 'managerial revolution', if the latter term is understood to include less sweeping interpretations of the 'disappearance of the capitalist' than those of Burnham himself. I shall argue in this chapter, however, that the problem of the 'rise of the propertyless manager' is primarily one to be dealt with as a question of the mediation of control, rather than of the institutional mediation of power.

T. H. Marshall has distinguished three aspects of the growth of citizenship: the civil, political, and socio-economic. The first comprises the 'rights necessary for individual freedom' (freedom of speech, etc.) and equality before the law; the second, rights of political organisation and the franchise; the third, rights of economic welfare and social security. Marshall admits that the early emergence of citizenship rights, particularly those in the first category, formed part of the very creation of capitalist society, helping thereby to consolidate the class structure of capitalism. In the twentieth century, however, this relationship has been reversed, and 'citizenship and the capitalist class system have been at war'.[1] The argument has considerable force, and certainly there is an intrinsic difference between the character of the rights embodied in 'civil' citizenship, and those of the latter two types. By and large the growth of civil rights—as Marx stressed—is a necessary part of the transcendence of pre-class society by capitalism. Formal equality before the law, and freedom of contract, are universal principles which actually sanction the class asymmetry of the capitalist market. The struggle to achieve the universal extension of the other types of citizenship rights typically came considerably later in time, and the effects of their successful implementation appear to have been quite different. As has already been pointed out, the rise of workers' movements, in certain measure, has to be understood in terms of endeavour to secure full incorporation within the capitalist state. The successful achievement of the universal franchise (which, however, occurred at quite widely disparate times in different societies)[2] was in turn a condition of the emergence of social democratic parties and the growth of welfare rights for the mass of the population.

But these facts can be admitted without accepting that the development of citizenship rights has effectively altered the basic nature of the institutional mediation of power in capitalist society. Indeed, I shall argue that in certain important respects, both the second and third types of citizenship right, as well as the first, have served to stabilise class differentials in capitalist society rather than to act counter to them. After all, as has often been pointed out, Bismarck effectively initiated the modern welfare state in order to diminish opposition amongst the working class, and more specifically to counter the revolutionary appeal of the Social Democratic party. The argument can be generalised via the very reasoning of the advocates of the citizenship thesis: namely, that the granting of the twin prerogatives of what Bendix has called the 'plebiscitarian idea' (according to which 'all adult individuals must have equal rights under a national government') and the 'functional idea' (whereby 'the differential affiliation of individuals with others is taken as given and some form of group representation is accepted'),[3] blunted the opposition of the working class to the general conditions of capitalist production. If there is any truth in the idea (advocated strongly by Dahrendorf and others) that the formation of working-class political parties on the one hand, and the establishment of trade unions and recognised modes of collective bargaining on the other, leads to the 'defusing' of class conflict (a thesis which, however, as we shall see, must in a sense be turned upon its head), then this may be seen as consolidating the basic institutional form of the capitalist state—the 'separation' of the spheres of the political and the economic—rather than transcending it by 'post-capitalism'. Moreover, arguments can be raised to suggest that the practical effects of the implementation of citizenship rights of the third sort—welfare and social security provisions—are rather different from what is normally assumed. First, it might be pointed out that the net outcome of the extension of welfare provisions serves the interests of the dominant class by helping to maximise worker efficiency. Second, as various authors have recently claimed, the furnishing of welfare services may not, as it would appear to do, constitute a major cost for those outside the working class. That is to say, costs are met primarily through a 'life-cycle redistribution' process, borne largely by members of the working class itself.[4] While, therefore, it can be acknowledged that the growth of citizenship rights has no doubt brought about significant changes in the capitalist societies since the nineteenth century, it seems reasonable to conclude that these changes represent more of a 'completion' or consolidation of capitalist development rather than an undermining of it.

A more convincing advocacy of the 'post-capitalist' view can be made with reference to the changing character of the economic sphere as such—that is to say, to the significance of the processes of concentration and centralisation. Three sets of problems may be distinguished here, at least in so far as the interpretation of these processes bears upon the institutional mediation of power in capitalist society: the problem of competition and monopoly; the determination of the consequences of the diffusion of property ownership in joint-stock companies; and the evaluation of more recent market 'planning' on the part of the state.

With the partial (and debatable) exception of Japan, where the erstwhile *zaibatsu* domination of the economy was to some degree broken after the war, it is impossible to deny that the general trend of development of industry in the capitalist societies has been towards a very strong concentration of industrial capital.[5] This can easily be demonstrated using various kinds of indices, such as the proportion of workers in the non-agricultural labour force employed in various sizes of enterprise. Thus in Germany, in 1905,

20·3 per cent of the labour force were in firms of over two hundred employees; by 1961, the proportion had risen to 45·1 per cent. In France, in 1906, the percentage of the labour force in enterprises having more than five hundred employees was 11·7; the corresponding percentage in 1958 was 29·8. Figures for the United States show that, in 1909, 15·3 per cent of all employees worked in firms of over a thousand people, while by 1955 this proportion had grown to 33·6 per cent.[6] At the top of this pyramid of industrial concentration, a small number of very large firms, the celebrated 'megacorporations', possess enormous capital assets, and account for a steadily increasing proportion of the productive capacity of major sectors of the economy. Because of the sheer size of its 'megacorporations', as much as because of any special position which the American economy holds in respect of relative degrees of concentration,[7] the United States has most frequently been regarded as the 'type-case' here. In *The Modern Corporation and Private Property*, Berle and Means attempted to chart the growth of the very large companies in the United States and to establish a projection of potential future trends. As they showed, the assets of the two hundred largest corporations had increased annually by 5·4 per cent from 1909 to 1928, but the assets of all firms, taken *in toto*, had grown by only 3·6 per cent per annum. If this pattern of differential growth were maintained, they showed, the two hundred largest firms would by 1970 control all economic activity.[8] While the trend of development has not actually gone to this extreme, it has certainly progressed some considerable way. Thus, by 1962, the five largest American corporations held over 12 per cent of all manufacturing assets: the five hundred largest companies possessed nearly 70 per cent of these assets.

It would be absurd to deny that the growth in concentration has produced quite basic changes in the organisation of the capitalist economies. But to speak, as many Marxists have done, of the arrival of 'monopoly capitalism' is too simple. In the first place, it should be pointed out that there are definite variabilities between the capitalist societies, even the most technologically advanced, in terms of the level of concentration of industrial capital; and, however far the process may have progressed, there is no society which even approximates to Berle and Means' prognosis, and which does not still possess a very large infrastructure of smaller enterprises. Second, there *is* a difference between 'monopoly' and 'oligopoly'— and the latter is the characteristic situation in those sectors of the capitalist economies dominated by the very large companies. 'Monopoly', at least as it has traditionally been conceived within

Marxism, for example by Hilferding, is represented as the transcendence of capitalist competition: the socialisation of the market within the confines of capitalism, heralding the appearance of socialised production. But, in fact, even in monopoly, competition persists; in oligopoly this may often be very severe, since it takes place primarily between two or a small number of competitors who 'face each other' directly. Such competition may take various forms: a struggle to undercut costs in order to maximise profitability *vis-à-vis* the competitor(s), often closely connected with bids to outdo the °others in technological innovation—what Baran and Sweezy call the 'dynamics of market sharing'; competition over what has been termed the 'reputational effect'—the endeavour to build, in the minds of consumers, a particular image of the company as a 'quality' producer; competition between oligopolistic and non-oligopolistic sectors; and 'derived competition', whereby the influence of oligopoly within certain sectors of the economy, by heightening the level of profit within those sectors, intensifies competition in other sectors which operate at reduced rates of profit.

However, none of these modes of competition centres upon prices in the classical manner, and there can be little reason to dispute the proposition that, in conditions of oligopoly, Galbraith's 'revised sequence' prevails. The megacorporation is a 'price maker' rather than a 'price taker', and through advertising and promotion seeks to directly condition the needs of consumers. Moreover, there are two senses in which oligopoly tends increasingly to dominate in modern capitalism, over and above the industrial sectors where some form of price management or 'price leadership' is maintained. First, oligopoly is normally most highly developed in manufacturing, which has a strategic position within the economy since those in the primary industries must usually sell their products to it, and those in the tertiary industries, retailing and commerce, are dependent upon it for their source of goods. Secondly, and in part connected with this first point, the competitive sectors are often satellites of ologopolistic industries: they are either almost wholly dependent for their sales upon the latter, or they buy from them almost exclusively. Thus, in the United States, the highly competitive motor-car parts industry necessarily has to sell most of its output to the four large car firms, and is obliged to follow the lead of these firms in pricing its products.[9]

The implications of these phenomena for the 'managerial revolution', ever since the publication of Berle and Means' book, have remained contentious. In so far as these bear upon the institutional mediation of power, however, rather than the problem of the mediation of control, we may distinguish two major sets of issues here: the question of whether the 'behaviour' of the firm has changed in any essential manner with the rise of the very large corporation, and the more general matter of how far the 'managerial corporation' is still in any sense bound to the interests of property. According to a prominent version of the modern theory of the firm, the very large company contrasts in quite a basic fashion with the traditional 'entrepreneurial' enterprise in virtue of the fact that, while the latter seeks to 'maximise' its profits, the former merely 'satisfices'.[10] According to this view, the megacorporation, or the managerial group which directs it, is concerned only to maintain 'satisfactory' profits; the primary goals become those of fostering the stability and growth of the enterprise, and preserving or expanding its market strength. While the conclusions which have been drawn from this have been various, the more radical versions of the thesis have argued that, at least incipiently, satisficing marks a major departure from the premises of the capitalist market.

In any such radical form, the argument does not stand up to close scrutiny. For one thing, it is not clear what either of the terms involved actually designate, and the view appears to rest in substantial degree upon a misleading comparison between an abstract model (entrepreneurial profit maximisation under conditions of complete market knowledge and optimal rationality) and the postulated 'behaviour' of actual enterprises in the modern economy. If 'maximisation' is interpreted in this way, and anything less is satisficing, then it is evident that satisficing has always been the order of the day, in firms of all sizes. Although the results of a shift from 'profits' to 'growth' may have substantial consequences for neo-classical economic theory, it is misleading to suppose that it signals a major transformation in the character of capitalist enterprise. This conclusion helps to resolve the question of the general role of the large corporation in relation to private property. However widely diffused and fragmented share ownership may be, the megacorporation is necessarily tied to the existence of private property. The most general sense in which this is true is that, whatever its size and its capacity to 'make' prices, the firm remains ultimately bound by the exigency of 'profitability' in relation to securing for shareholders an adequate level of return upon investment. But there is also a more specific consideration, which at least expresses a concrete possibility, that there may be a reverse causal association to that which has normally been presumed to operate in 'managerial' companies—that, if dividends are low in such companies, it is not because they have become detached from the interests of private property, but because firms of this character tend to dominate in those industries in which low dividends and high ploughback have been qualities which particularly promote survival or market success.[11] In sum, while there can be no doubt that the 'managerial revolution' is a major phenomenon within contemporary capitalism, *its significance is primarily relevant to the mediation of control*—a problem to which I shall give attention later in this chapter. At this point, however, it is necessary to consider recent changes which serve to promote the centralisation of the capitalist market through the action of the state.

The typical feature of Keynesianism in the 1930s was the concern to secure something approaching full employment at a given level of productive capacity. While this has been fundamental in blunting the operation of the tendency to periodic crisis, as Schonfield has pointed out, it is rather distinct from the marked trend towards 'planning' which has accelerated since the last war. The characteristic of what he calls the 'new capitalism' is that: 'a variety of independent forces have combined to increase the available powers of control over the economic system and at the same time to keep the volume of demand constantly at a very high level'.[12] That is to say, long-range national planning has replaced the mere technical interventionism of the earlier period. Some indication that this is to some degree distinct from the development of state intervention in economic life of the Keynesian type is given by the fact that the two countries which adapted most easily to Keynes' prescriptions, Britain and the United States, have been among the most laggardly in furthering schemes of state planning. The leading nations in this respect, on the whole, have been those which historically have a strongly developed state apparatus and officialdom. France and Japan are examples, and offer both striking parallels as well as interesting contrasts.[13] The formal authority of the state over economic enterprise is lower in Japan than in the majority of other capitalist societies. In actuality, the strong and complex interconnections of state and industry in Japanese society make possible a high, if somewhat fluctuating, degree of government influence upon business activity through sectoral planning. But there is less nationalised industry than in most European countries. While the state has substantial interests in the operation of communications and transport (without having a full monopoly over the latter) and, more importantly, in banking and finance, it lost many of its former powers as a result of the occupation.[14] The very situation of defeat, however, made both possible and necessary a post-war reconstruction plan of a comprehensive sort, leading on directly to a series of macroeconomic schemes.

Among the European states which have instituted long-range development planning, there are considerable differences in the formal position of the relevant agencies. Two types can be distinguished: one where the planning apparatus is separated from the administrative machinery of government, as in the initial stages in Britain; the other where the body responsible for planning is located within the main core of the institutions of public administration. The latter is the case in France, and undoubtedly reflects the continuity in the *dirigiste* tradition in that country. In a general way it could be said that those societies which fall into the first type have come to recognise the need for trend planning via the short-term management of employment and deflationary policy, while those of the second type have moved in the opposite direction, attempting to assimilate short-term economic management within pre-existing long-term planning schemes. In France, as in Japan, the exigencies imposed by reconstruction following the war provided the stimulus to modern planning. The Monnet schemes, set into being immediately after the war, were oriented mainly towards achieving a rapid revival of certain basic sectors of industry; but from there planning moved to a broader macroeconomic level. Whatever its starting-point, there is virtually no European capitalist society which has not today evolved some sort of commitment to long-range economic planning on the part of the state. In the United States, comparable developments have taken longer to appear.[15] While there is some history of attempts at price and wage management in the early 1960s, it is only very recently that there has been a defined movement towards macroeconomic planning—a phenomenon which in part is to be explained in terms of the greater independence of the American economy in relation to foreign trade as compared to the European countries.

Whether capitalist planning is successful or not in securing high and progressive rates of economic growth and in containing inflation, it is undoubtedly the case that the advent of macro-economic planning is a development of major importance in modern capitalism.[16] But it cannot be interpreted in isolation from the two other sets of phenomena discussed above. The growth of the big corporations, with their orientation towards the 'revised sequence', and their international character, both stimulates and demands new policies on the part of the capitalist state. The economic goals of capitalist planning are generally in accord with the interests of big business, particularly as regards forward investment planning, and often in the overall macroeconomic allocation of resources. On the other hand, the emergence of planning creates a whole series of potential new conflicts between state and industry on the one hand, and within the class structure more generally. There is a close link here with the role of social democracy. Social democratic parties have, at least in many countries, played an important part in initiating, furthering, or supporting planning—for obvious enough reasons. Not only do schemes of macroeconomic growth need the support of the trade unions in particular, and the acquiescence of the working class as a whole, but the ideology of social democracy is particularly conducive to the promotion of centralised economic regulation. Taken together, the conjunction of the rise of social democracy, the megacorporations and oligopoly, and state planning, constitutes a linked series of changes which, while they cannot be accurately represented as 'post-capitalism', are of a significant nature. In referring generically to the capitalism of the post-war period, therefore, I shall make use of the somewhat graceless terms 'neo-capitalism' and 'neo-capitalist society'.

2. THE UPPER CLASS IN CAPITALIST SOCIETY

In examining the character of the upper class in the capitalist societies, we need to look both at the general parameters of class structuration and at the more particular aspects of structuration which I have indicated earlier—specifically, the relationship between the upper class and elite formations. There has been a defined tendency in the literature upon general problems of class theory to assume too high a level of 'closure' in the structuration of the upper class in capitalist societies, particularly in relation to the historical development of these societies. This view readily leads to the conclusion (as stated, for example, by Dahrendorf) that, since the nineteenth century, there has occurred a radical process of the 'decomposition' of the unitary character of the upper class. But, as Poulantzas has rightly emphasised,[17] this 'monolithic' class has never existed. Whether or not it was shared by Marx himself, the tendency to speak in this way no doubt has its origins in the propensity of Marxist authors, most notably Lukács and his followers, to regard classes as 'acting subjects' executing various defined 'historical tasks'. In this way, the 'bourgeoisie' or 'proletariat' appear as homogeneous entities, almost on a par with individual actors. This sort of view has to be abandoned, or its distance from the reality of the historical development of the capitalist societies has to be clearly recognised, if we are to offer an assessment of the validity of the thesis of class decomposition.

The first point which has to be made is one already mentioned in the previous chapter: namely, that any analysis of the development of modern capitalism from the latter part of the nineteenth century up to the present time must recognise the protracted significance of 'traditional', land-owning groups within the class structure. The reaction of such groupings, first to commercialism, and subsequently to industrialism, is the key factor which has influenced the form taken by the structuration of the upper class in the different societies —except in the United States, which did not come to capitalism through the dissolution of feudalism. Japan and Germany again provide one polar type here, since in both cases the transition from a *ständische Gesellschaft* to an industrial society was achieved under direction 'from the top'.

The formation of the upper class in Japan, of course, has to be understood in terms of the long period, stretching from roughly 1600 up to 1867, of domination of the Tokugawa family, which brought the Japanese feudal system to the peak of its development. While the end of the Tokugawa period also signalled the conclusion of Japanese feudalism, the new nation-state was decisively influenced by its residue. The core of the Japanese upper class in the post-Tokugawa era was drawn from the old warrior grouping, not from the merchant class which had reached some considerable economic prominence in the latter stages of feudalism. The history of Japan up to the Second World War is one of the penetration of the upper class by the industrial entrepreneurs, who, remained, however, heavily subordinate to the established ethos. Most of those controlling the great *zaibatsu* combines were drawn from outside the feudal families.[18] The situation in Germany at the mid-point of the nineteenth century was obviously more complicated, both politically, in virtue of the dispersion of the various principalities, and economically, by reason of the contrast between the predominance of small peasant holdings to the west of the Elbe, and the existence of the *Rittergüter*, the large estates, in the east. The fact that Germany became politically unified under the dominance of Prussia made for the ascendancy of the *Junker* element in the upper class until well into the twentieth century—an ascendancy stabilised, as in Japan, by an aristocratic monopoly of the officer corps and the state bureaucracy. As in Japan again, but in a much more ambivalent manner, the social ascent of 'commoner' industrialists into the upper class was very substantially governed by their acceptance of, and orientation towards, the ethos of the land-owning aristocracy. As Landes has expressed it, they 'sublimated their ambitions and assuaged their frustrations in the drive to national unity and aggrandisement'.[19] In both Japan and Germany it would be true to say that the upper class to some degree, as Max Weber remarked of the *Junkers*, 'dug its own grave': that is to say, the predominance of aristocratic elements was eventually inevitably weakened by the successful transition to industrialism. But in neither case did this effectively dissolve their pre-eminence as the basis of the structuration of the upper class. This was in the end only brought about in conjunction with the effects of political change and war.

If these two societies are the primary examples of a process of development which was, in a quite definite sense, directly counter to any sort of trend towards the 'bourgeoisification' of the upper class, the role of landed aristocracy in the structuration of the upper class in the other European societies has also been very considerable. This was perhaps least true of France, which, at least in a formal sense, eradicated its aristocracy in the 1789 revolution. For most of the nineteenth century, land-owners and *rentiers* were the main backbone of the French upper class, scorning business and commerce: if their ethos was bourgeois rather than aristocratic, their ideal was one of *bourgeois vivant noblement*. As in other respects it is probably Britain which is more the polar case as compared to Japan and Germany. The most striking characteristic of the British upper class in the latter half of the nineteenth century is the mutual penetration of aristocracy and those in commerce and industry— for which the way had been paved by a long process of development going back to the seventeenth century. Certainly the dominant ethos remained a 'gentlemanly' one, facilitated by the entitlement of industrialists, or at least of their offspring; but the very creation of the notion of the 'gentleman' was in substantial degree a product of the nineteenth century, and the rise of the public schools was the milieu for effecting this peculiar fusion of the old and the new. In this manner there came about that 'blend of a crude plutocratic reality with the sentimental aroma of an aristocratic legend' which R. H. Tawney described as the feature of the British upper class. Of the world's leading industrial powers, only Britain has a distinguishable aristocracy which, even if stripped of most of its political influence (although by no means completely so), and suitably replenished by a steady influx from below, has maintained a position within the upper class.

The case with the United States is really quite different. Not only the absence of a feudal past, but also the sheer size of the country, its character as an 'immigrant society', and the dynamic nature of its westward expansion in the nineteenth century, all combined to limit the structuration of a clearly defined upper class, except in the southern states. A national upper class only emerged towards the end of the nineteenth century, and even today remains primarily centred upon the eastern seaboard. It has been argued by some writers that the relatively cohesive development of the British upper class around the 'gentlemanly ethic' has, ever since, prevented the creation of values attributing any sort of distinctive esteem to business;[20] what has happened in the United States has been something almost the reverse of this—that is to say, the emergence of what Baltzell terms a 'business aristocracy'. In the United States, as opposed to the European societies, success in business, whether it be in industry, finance or commerce, has commanded the core position in the formation of the upper class. This is not to say that the *nouveau riche* is directly acceptable within the 'business aristocracy': but the dominance of the 'old rich' is founded upon a *long-standing* pre-eminence in business rather than upon any sort of ethos which either condemns or cross-cuts it.

These differences in the general character and degree of upper-class structuration in the capitalist societies undoubtedly still persist today, but in an attenuated and changed form, and the analysis of these changes in detail goes far beyond what can be attempted here. In any fully industrialised society, the role of landed property, even as supportive of a general ethos infusing class structuration, necessarily declines sharply. It does not follow from this, however, that the structure of the upper class in the different societies, any more than the overall form of those societies as a whole, inevitably 'converges', although certain common patterns of change can easily be discerned. In order to analyse the most significant of these, however, it is useful to pass to a direct discussion of what I have previously referred to as the mediation of control.

3. THE MEDIATION OF CONTROL AND THE 'MANAGERIAL REVOLUTION'

A scrutiny of writings on the thesis of the 'managerial revolution', such as those of Dahrendorf, shows that the elements supposedly involved may be helpfully ranged in terms of three aspects of elite formation distinguished in Chapter 7: elite recruitment, 'solidarity', and effective power. First, the emergence of propertyless managers as a segment of the economic elite has been held to be associated with changing rates and channels of social mobility. Thus Dahrendorf writes:

[For managers] . . . there are two typical patterns of recruitment, and both of them differ radically from those of capitalists and heirs. One of these patterns is the bureaucratic career. . . . More recently, a different pattern has gained increasing importance. Today, a majority of management officials in industrial enterprises have acquired their positions on the strength of some specialised education, and of university degrees . . . there can be little doubt that both of these patterns of recruitment—but in particular the latter—distinguish managerial groups significantly from those of old-style owner-managers as well as new-style mere owners.

This tends to produce, according to Dahrendorf, a more open system of intergenerational mobility: as education becomes more important as an avenue of recruitment into managerial occupations, the chances for those from working- or middle-class backgrounds of moving into those occupations improve.

Secondly, the rise of the managers is held to introduce an important source of disaggregation, and potentially of conflict, within the economic elite as a whole. Again Dahrendorf expresses the idea: 'the crucial effect of the separation of ownership and control in industry [is] . . . that it produces two sets of roles the incumbents of which increasingly move apart in their outlook on and attitudes toward society in general and toward the enterprise in particular.'[21] Much has been made, particularly by American writers, of the presumed connotations of this situation. A divergence in ideals and values, it is believed, tends to reinforce differences in styles of life and social contacts: the 'organisation man' is alien to the entrepreneurial capitalist. This in turn supports a certain conflict of interest, not infrequently leading to open struggles—based chiefly upon the fact that the managerial executive is supposed to be concerned less with the pursuit of high returns on capital than with enhancing the productivity and security of the corporation.

Finally, as the core of the thesis, effective power within the large joint-stock companies is believed to devolve into the hands of the managers, the sanctions held by the 'owners' of the enterprise becoming purely nominal. As a result of the growth of oligopoly, this process is often regarded as associated with an increase in the *consolidation* of effective power in the hands of the managers. Those who control, the megacorporations, where the ratio of managerial dominance is most complete, are thereby able to control or influence broad segments of industry and the market. But quite disparate conclusions have been drawn by different authors as regards the results of managerial control in industry for the *issue-strength* of the power wielded by the economic elite. As stated in its extreme form by Burnham, the theory of the managerial revolution entails the conclusion that the economic elite is dominant in the hierarchy of elites: that political decisions are directly or indirectly controlled by the economic elite. But something of a contrary inference has been drawn by the less radical proponents of the theory: namely, that while the managers may hold consolidated power in the economic sphere itself, their capacity to influence the actions of political leaders has in fact become more limited, rather than more extensive, in part because the political elite now increasingly broadens its control over economic affairs.

The view that the advent of the managerial revolution has brought about, or is linked to, an increase in social mobility into positions of economic leadership can be seen as part of a broader conception of the 'democratisation' of access to elite positions in general. The view is difficult to evaluate satisfactorily on an empirical level, because of the lack of materials allowing us to determine typical rates of mobility, either intra- or intergenerational, for anything but quite recent periods. The influence of education upon social mobility into elite positions is undeniable, especially within neo-capitalism, which is typically characterised by a massive expansion of higher education. But it is important to point out that education is a determinant of the differentiation, as well as the homogenisation, of mobility chances. Perhaps the most striking case of this is the creation of the English public schools in the nineteenth century, which served to facilitate a narrow monopoly of access to elite positions, rather than acting to spread the distribution of mobility chances. There certainly are reasons for doubting that there has occurred, in the majority of capitalist countries, a very pronounced expansion of mobility chances for movement into elite positions as a result of the relatively recent growth in higher education. Although detailed comparison is impossible, studies of the social origins of executive managers show that everywhere a majority, and usually a quite substantial majority, of business leaders, whether propertied or propertyless, derive from a narrow background of economic privilege. The same is undoubtedly true of political leaders, and of the higher civil service.[22]

Two general conclusions seem in order from surveying the literature on social mobility: (1) There are significant differences in the degree of 'openness' of mobility into elite positions both between different elite groups within the same society and comparing similar elite groups in different societies. Thus, in Britain, in spite of a quite massive dominance of elite positions by those from a background of socio-economic privilege, there is a significant difference in the degree of upper-class monopoly of elites in such institutions as the Church and army as compared to the economic elite. This seems to be reversed, by contrast, in the United States, where access to elite positions in the army, for example, is much more open than in either the political or economic sectors.[23] Comparing recruitment to higher managerial positions in British and Japanese industry, it would appear that the former is more open than the latter, but the contrary seems to apply in recruitment to the higher civil service in the two societies. Many such contrasts can be found, and there is no indication that they are becoming less pronounced.[24] (2) Those changes which have occurred over the past seventy years, in creating more open patterns of recruitment to elite positions, have almost certainly acted to favour the chances of the middle class—and may even have actually produced a *diminution* in the relative chances of working-class individuals in penetrating to elite positions. All systematic studies of social mobility agree that 'long-range' mobility, intra- or intergenerationally, is very rare in the advanced societies. But again there appear to be significant divergences between different societies in this respect: thus intergenerational mobility from working class to elite positions is considerably higher in the United States and Japan than in the majority of the European societies.[25] While there have been, since the turn of the century, certain unmistakable changes in patterns of social mobility at the lower levels of the class structure in the capitalist societies, so far as mobility into elite positions is concerned the changes which have occurred have in the main been confined to a limited erasure of the margins between the middle and the upper class. There seems to be nothing which excepts the case of economic elites from this general judgement.

But this does not necessarily discredit the idea that, within the economic elite, there has developed a major source of schism centring upon a progressing separation between owners and managers. As in the case of mobility studies, there are difficulties in specifying how far there is a distinguishable trend in the direction presumed, because the relevant historical materials are sparse. But if such a trend were under way, it ought to be observable with particular clarity in neo-capitalism, which has greatly accelerated the development of the megacorporations. Even here, the available descriptive material is rather inadequate as a basis for reaching a substantiated view upon a matter about which such impressive claims have been made.[26] But what data there is does not support the view which Dahrendorf expresses. That there occur conflicts between shareholders and managers cannot be denied; but these do not appear to be any more common than those between shareholding blocs and, if anything, they are probably less so. Rather than indicating that managers and owners 'increasingly move apart in their outlook on and attitudes towards society in general and toward the enterprise in particular', what evidence there is suggests something quite different: that an overall homogeneity of value and belief, and a high degree of social solidarity, as manifest in interpersonal contacts, friendship and marriage ties, is more noticeable than any marked cleavages. In this respect, the opinion expressed by Meynaud in relation to French industry seems to hold good, with relatively minor variations, for other societies also: 'the factors uniting family-style owners and professional managers are much stronger than the elements tending to divide them . . .'[27] To accept this is not to adopt the sort of view set out in Mills' *The Power Elite*, which greatly exaggerates the degree of harmony within the 'higher circles' of American society in general, and within the economic elite in particular. Struggles and clashes between different factions are the rule rather than the exception in the higher echelons of the economic order; nothing is more out of accord with reality than to present a 'conspiracy' picture of an unbroken cooperative consensus (as critics of Western society, like Mills, have tended to do of the capitalist societies, and critics of the state socialist societies have for their part tended to do of the role of the Communist Party in those societies). Moreover, in terms of level of solidarity between elite groups, rather than within the economic elite itself, there can be little doubt that in the United States there is a considerably greater degree of fragmentation, if not necessarily of overt conflict, between elite sectors than in most other societies, and it is not accidental that that country has been the main source of 'pluralist' theories. Judged in relation to the typology of elite formations which I suggested earlier, the United States approximates more closely than any European society, or than Japan, to the case of an 'abstract elite', but is probably more accurately classified as possessing an 'established elite'. Britain, on the other hand, probably ranks at the other pole, still maintaining a 'uniform elite', with most other capitalist societies distributed somewhere between.

The problem of the effects of the rise of the managerial element upon corporate power has been so extensively discussed in recent years—a discussion which has yet again proceeded, necessarily, largely by inference from inadequate and unreliable empirical documentation of the key issues involved—that there is no need to do more here than to isolate some putative conclusions from the debate. First, as many writers have pointed out, even within the most developed neo-capitalist societies, familial enterprises are very far from having disappeared altogether, not excluding companies which rank among the largest in a given economy. Secondly, as Marxist critics have consistently stressed since the first appearance of *The Modern Corporation and Private Property*, even in very large joint-stock companies, where share-ownership is widely dispersed, control of a minority bloc of shares can, and frequently does, yield effective power over the fortunes of the company.[28] By the use of techniques such as the 'pyramiding' of firms, moreover, such control may be ramified considerably beyond the immediate company concerned. Thirdly, the term 'control', in the context of the phrase, 'separation of ownership and control', is ambiguous. If 'control' is taken to mean the execution of the day-to-day administration of the corporation, then it is irrefutably the case that the separation of ownership and control is an accomplished fact in the great majority of the very large companies in all the capitalist societies. If, however, the term is interpreted as 'effective power', the above statement becomes considerably more problematic, since what matters in this case is the capacity and readiness of shareholders to intervene directly in the running of the corporation if they consider it to be necessary in the furtherance of their interests. Fourthly, a not inconsiderable proportion of 'propertyless' managers turn out to be propertied after all, even if the percentage of stock they hold in their own companies is not generally very large (according to Florence's calculations in Britain, the average proportion of ordinary shares owned by directors of very large companies is about 1·5 per cent).

But these four points are all qualifications or riders to the general conclusion, now accepted very broadly by writers of quite differing theoretical persuasion, that the extension of managerial control, in the sense of the effective power of managers to determine the policies which govern the fate of the large-scale corporation, is a characteristic phenomenon in all neo-capitalist economies. In the megacorporations, share-ownership functions as, in Baran and Sweezy's phrase, 'a ticket of admission to the inside', where effective corporate power is held. While there may be some dispute about the precise degree of extension of managerial control, the major problems which are raised concern its consequences for the structure of power within the enterprise, and more especially for the relationship between economic and political elites in neo-capitalist society. As regards the former, there can be no doubt whatsoever that the growth of the megacorporations produces a 'consolidation', in the sense in which I have previously defined that term, of economic power, concentrated in the hands of the managerial grouping— that is to say, in terms of both the degree of directive control within the corporation and in terms of the economic power generated by oligopolistic influence over market conditions. Contrary to Galbraith's theory, there is no reason to suppose that the extension of managerial control is associated with a diffusion of economic power within a new 'technostructure'. According to Galbraith, because of the indispensability of technical and scientific information to the modern corporation, those who possess the specialised mastery of such information increasingly assume power in the organisation: 'It is not the managers who decide. Effective power of decision is lodged deeply in the technical, planning and other specialised staff.'[29] But this confuses indispensability and power, an error which Max Weber pointed out long ago: if being indispensable necessarily confers power, then in a slave economy the slaves would be dominant.

The consolidation of economic power does *not* imply that, in the hierarchy of elite groups, the emergence of neo-capitalism leads to the pre-eminence of the economic over the political elite. Undoubtedly, with the advent of capitalist planning, the media of interchange between elite groups become more unequivocal and immediate. As in so many matters connected with the study of elites, we lack the time series data which could form the basis of a more precise analysis; but it seems plausible to assume that the general trend in the capitalist societies, since the turn of the century, has been towards reducing what I have called the 'direct control' of elite positions, at least as regards the relation between economic and political elites. However, this has been counterbalanced, particularly in neo-capitalism, by the growth of formalised mechanisms for the mutual exertion of influence: that is to say, by the development of statutory and consultative committees linking industry and political policy-making. In the main, these constitute an effort on the part of the polity to expand its control over industry, an endeavour which has met with some measure of success in all the capitalist societies, even in the United States, where the resistance of the economic elite has probably been strongest. The attempt to establish and sustain such institutional sources of elite interchange inevitably produces new frictions and clashes between economic and political leaders, and creates mobile interest coalitions seeking to influence political decisions; but, in general, the main characteristic of the mediation of control in neo-capitalist society is the increasing ascendancy of political control over decision-making in the economic sphere.

Within the polity itself, two major phenomena can be easily discerned as characteristic of neo-capitalism, both the result of the declining salience of elective assemblies: the growing power of the civil service on the one side, and the cabinet, or certain cabinet circles,[30] on the other. These tendencies affect all parties in power, whether or not, as in France, they normally depend upon shifting coalitions or, as in Britain, two parties are massively predominant; but they are particularly fateful for social democratic parties. Much has been written, since Michels, of the tendency of social democratic parties to become 'deradicalised', especially once they have come to attain office. While one important element in this is clearly the need of a party which accepts the existing institutional mediation of power to accommodate itself to the constraints which this necessarily imposes, it is also strongly affected by the decreasing relevance of constituent assemblies. From one aspect, the power of the civil service, which always tends, for reasons specified very plainly by Weber, to resist any substantially innovative attempts to modify the existing socio-economic order, normally acts as a forceful source of pressure towards moderation. Equally important, however, although for different reasons, is the dominant role of the cabinet within the elective assembly. The process of the *embourgeoisement* of social democratic politicians, pointed to by Michels, is typically concentrated particularly strongly among the higher echelons of the leadership.[31] Contrary to his interpretation, however, that social democratic politicians of middle- or upper-class backgrounds are more likely than those of working-class origin to retain a radical outlook, the opposite appears to be the case;[32] and, given that this is so, it follows that effective power in social democratic governments is lodged with those least likely to wish to implement the more radical aspects of the socialist programmes to which the party may be nominally committed.

The categorisations of elite formation and power-holding which I suggested in Chapter 7 are obviously schematic, and are offered primarily as a mode of isolating some of the elements which have normally been confused, or have remained latent, in the confrontation between Marxism and elite theory—and as a means of providing for the fact that there have been, and are, major variations between the capitalist societies in the nature of the connections between the upper class and the mediation of control in the political and economic spheres. This is now readily admitted even by Marxist authors. Thus Miliband writes that:

advanced capitalism has in the twentieth century provided the context for Nazi rule in Germany and for Stanley Baldwin in Britain, for Franklin Roosevelt in the United States and for the particular brand of authoritarianism which prevailed in Japan in the 1930s. Capitalism, experience has shown again and again, can produce, or if this is too question-begging a phrase can accommodate itself to, many different types of political regime, including ferociously authoritarian ones.[33]

On the whole, however, Marxist writers have not been able to successfully analyse these differences within the sorts of theoretical framework which they have adopted: hence the use of such phraseology as Miliband's, that capitalism can 'accommodate itself' to differing forms of 'political regime'. 'Capitalism' is not, and has never been, the sort of monolithic order implied in this quotation; even if defined in purely economic terms, there have been major and continuing differences in the 'infrastructure' of the capitalist societies (a matter discussed further below), and the political systems of these societies, even prior to the advent of neo-capitalism in modern times, have played a basic role in conditioning these differences. The typology of power-holding which I developed earlier can logically be applied to any elite group: but if it be granted that it has particular reference to the political sphere, German and Japanese fascism, two of the cases mentioned by Miliband, approximate closely to the 'autocratic' type. The emergence of fairly comparable 'autocratic' governments in these two societies, however, cannot be understood if these are treated, so to speak, as mere appendages which somehow happen to become in a few instances tacked on to capitalism—any more than they can be explained, as they used to be in older Marxist interpretations, as constituting the 'highest point', or natural end-result, of capitalist development.

In terms of the neo-capitalist societies today, the generalisation could be ventured that political elites for the most part are distributed between the 'oligarchic' and 'hegemonic' categories, with a definite tendency to move in the direction of the latter. The United States probably approaches closest to the 'democratic' pole; and if the picture painted by some of the pluralist political theorists definitely exaggerates both the degree of openness of elite recruitment and elite fragmentation in that society, it is still plausible to regard the mediation of control in the contemporary United States as approximating to that of a system of 'leadership groups'. In most of the other neo-capitalist societies it still makes sense to speak of the continuing existence of a 'ruling' or 'governing class', as I have defined those terms. The terminology is not particularly important; what is significant are the variations in the mediation of control between the capitalist societies, which have to be examined in the following chapters in relation to variations at other levels of the class structure.

In spite of the evidence demonstrating the continuing concentration of property ownership in the capitalist societies, and in spite of the now abundant research which shows the importance of this in the reproduction of life-chances from generation to generation, many writers have asserted that there no longer exists a distinguishable 'upper class'. One reason for this may be traced to the tendency —which is fairly strong in Marxism also, because of its insistence that both feudalism and capitalism are class societies—to draw an implicit comparison between the upper class in contemporary society and status groups (especially the feudal aristocracy) which have existed at previous periods in history. There are strong reasons which tend to impel the latter, often quite deliberately, to accentuate their differentiation from the rest of society. In any form of society where political and economic domination is legitimated in terms of some principle of aristocracy, or 'natural right', it is in the interests of the dominant grouping to ensure recognition of its claims to power by *enhancing* its own social visibility. The case with the upper class in capitalist society is quite different. Veblen's famous account of 'conspicuous consumption', the effete self-display of a pseudo-aristocracy, is the exception rather than the rule; in modern societies, in contrast to previous types of social order, there is a strong pressure upon members of the upper class to deny the operation of the 'class principle', and thereby to deny their own distinctiveness as a separate and isolable class. The 'invisibility' of the upper class in capitalist society is not, however, to be understood as a product of conscious artifice, as the 'visibility' of the aristocracy in prior times to some extent can be understood; rather it is the natural expression of whatever degree of monopoly the upper class maintains over access to elite positions in a form of society in which ideals of political and economic 'equality of opportunity' prevail.

THE GROWTH OF THE NEW MIDDLE CLASS

There is a now famous short passage in the 'fourth volume' of *Capital, Theories of Surplus Value*, in which Marx criticises Ricardo for having neglected 'the constantly growing number of the middle classes, those who stand between the workman on the one hand and the capitalist and landlord on the other'. These middle classes, Marx declares, 'are a burden weighing heavily on the working base and increase the social security and power of the upper ten thousand'.[1] The statement is an enigmatic one, in spite of some recent attempts to make it appear otherwise,[2] because it does not accord with the main weight of Marx's theoretical thinking, either on class in general, or the 'middle class' in particular. It must be attributed to the remarkable prescience of a man whose insights not infrequently broke the bounds of the theoretical formulations whereby he sought to discipline them. That it describes a fundamental aspect of modern social reality is unquestionable; and the same is true of the more characteristic Marxian conception that the tendency of capitalist development is to diminish the proportional significance in the class structure of those whom he normally designated as the 'petty bourgeoisie'. I shall henceforth refer to this grouping, however, as the 'old middle class', using the term 'middle class' without qualification to refer to propertyless non-manual, or 'white-collar', workers.

The decline of the old middle class, while a definite and identifiable phenomenon in the capitalist societies since the nineteenth century, has not proceeded in quite the radical fashion which Marx probably, and later Marxists certainly, expected. Not only are there, even today, important differences between the contemporary societies in terms of the relative size of the old middle class, but its decay has taken the form of a slowly declining curve, rather than a progressive approach to zero. Bernstein and Lederer, two of the first self-proclaimed Marxists to attempt systematically to confront the problems posed for orthodox Marxist theory by the burgeoning of the white-collar sector, were almost as perturbed by the stubborn persistence of the old middle class as by the growth of the new. But, however important the old middle class may remain in certain countries, there can be no doubt that the phenomenon of over-whelming consequence since the turn of the century is the massive relative enlargement of the white-collar sector.[3]

In spite of general agreement upon the decline of the old middle class, statistical comparisons between different countries are ex-tremely difficult to make. Modern economists have not been greatly interested in very small enterprises, and the relevant statistical materials are extremely patchy and incomplete. The figures do, however, suggest a general pattern which applies, although with quite wide discrepancies, to most of the capitalist societies: a pattern of a steady relative diminution of small businesses (including within this category small farms, manufacturing and retailing enter-prises) from the closing decades of the nineteenth century up to the early years of the 1930s; whence the decline continues, but at a considerably reduced gradient. Compared to larger enterprises, however, small businesses typically manifest a very high rate of turnover.[4]

There are also problems in making comparisons between different societies in the overall growth of white-collar labour, but the general trends are so striking that these can be overlooked for present purposes. The relative advance of the white-collar sector has proceeded furthest in the United States, which has recently been hailed as the first 'middle-class society'.[5] Whether or not this is so, in the sense of manual workers being outnumbered by white-collar workers, depends upon the criteria used to make the relevant dis-criminations between occupational categories. Thus one recent estimate (1969) places them at parity, each composing 48 per cent of the total labour force; if, however, only the male labour force is considered, manual workers outnumber non-manual employees by 54 to 41 per cent. Certainly, in terms of the proportion of white-collar workers in the labour force as a whole, few other capitalist countries come near to matching the United States. Figures for Britain for the year 1959 show 29 per cent of the total labour force as non-manual workers, a rise of only 1 per cent over 1951, and 7 per cent more than 1921. In Japan, in 1963, white-collar workers numbered 27 per cent of the non-agricultural labour force, an advance from 24·5 per cent in 1944.[6] It has been commonly assumed that the differences between the United States and countries like Britain and Japan are simply a matter of 'lag', indicative of the lower level of technical development of these countries—and that therefore in this case it is the United States which shows to the other societies 'the image of their own future'. But there are some indications that this may be a mistaken, or at least an oversimplified, conclusion. For there seems to have occurred a levelling off of the relative growth of the white-collar sector in the United States over the past decade; and a similar phenomenon seems also to have occurred in other societies, but at the considerably lower ratios of non-manual workers which characterise these societies as compared to the United States. An illustrative case is that of Britain, quoted above; another is that of France, where the ratio has barely changed over the last dozen years.[7]

But, of course, it is misleading in itself to treat 'white-collar labour' as an undifferentiated category, and the overall expansion of the white-collar sector in the capitalist societies conceals differential rates of growth in various occupational sub-categories. Whereas the relatively early enlargement of the white-collar sector mainly concerned the growth of clerical and sales occupations, in neo-capitalism those occupations usually grouped by census statisticians as 'professional and technical' labour show the highest recent rates of development—although these nowhere comprise any more than a fairly small minority of white-collar workers as a whole.

1. THE CONDITIONS OF MIDDLE-CLASS STRUCTURATION

The differentiation between the market capacities conferred by educational and technical qualifications, as compared to manual skills or pure labour-power, in the capitalist societies has everywhere taken the form not only of quite clear-cut divergences in income, but also in other modes of economic reward. In terms of income alone, while there have been certain important internal changes within the general category of white-collar labour as a whole, there has been an overall stability in the differential between the mean incomes of non-manual versus manual workers—that is to say, if real income distributions at the turn of the century are compared to those of today, since there have been substantial fluctuations in interim periods. Thus, in both Britain and the United States, the differential between non-manual and manual workers was reduced during World War I, and again in the subsequent war, and has since re-established itself.

The significant changes which have occurred, now well-docu-
mented, concern, first, a relative diminution of the income of
clerical workers within the white-collar sector, and, secondly, the
development of some degree of 'overlap' at the margins between non-
manual and manual labour.[8] But out of these changes in the gross
income statistics an enormous mythology has been built, in much
of the technical literature on class as well as in the lay press. The
apparent merging in the economic returns accruing to manual as
compared to non-manual labour looks very different if the facts of
the matter are inspected more closely. In the first place, the traditional superiority of the white-collar worker in terms of job security
has by no means disappeared: in general terms, non-manual workers
continue to enjoy a greater measure of security, even if, for reasons
which I shall discuss in subsequent chapters, there is some cause
to suppose that certain categories of manual workers will increasingly
enjoy more favourable contractual conditions in the future. Secondly,
typical patterns of overall career earnings are quite different in the
two categories. It is not only the oft-quoted fact of the range of
promotion opportunities which are potentially open to white-collar
workers, but are largely denied to manual workers, which is at
issue here. Even leaving this aside, the latter characteristically
experience a 'declining curve' of earnings which the former, often
having guaranteed annual increments, usually do not encounter.
Thus Fogarty shows that, in Britain, unskilled manual workers
reach peak income at an average of 30, and thence drop some
15–20 per cent to retirement age; skilled workers tend to reach their
peak earnings some ten years later, and subsequently drop about
10–15 per cent.[9] In addition, the length of the working week of
manual workers is longer than that of non-manual employees:
in 1966, in Britain, the former averaged 44 hours a week, as compared to 38 hours for white-collar workers.[10] Thirdly, a considerably
larger proportion of those in non-manual occupations are in receipt
of fringe benefits of various kinds, such as pension and sick-pay
schemes: in most countries these workers also gain disproportionately from tax remissions as a result of participation in such
schemes.[11]

While there are variations in these phenomena between different
societies, particularly if we consider the case of Japan, these do not
alter the overall picture. If we consider the totality of economic
returns available to manual and non-manual workers, the idea that
any kind of overall 'merging' of the two groupings is taking place
may be unequivocally rejected. The overlap is confined to segments
of skilled manual occupations on the one hand, and of clerical

and sales occupations on the other. But the major characteristic of these latter occupations is that they are everywhere increasingly monopolised by women—a fact of great importance in considering the nature of the boundary between the working and middle classes (cf. below, p. 194). Thus in Britain, which appears typical in this respect, the proportion of women in white-collar occupations rose from 30 to 45 per cent between 1911 and 1961; but they are almost wholly clustered in clerical and sales occupations—those which Lockwood has referred to, perhaps somewhat archaically now, as 'white-bloused' occupations. In fact, it has recently been claimed, *à propos* of clerical labour, that 'In the future, the few men remaining in clerical jobs will be "juniors" working their way up and the routine male clerk, as a career grade, will become extinct.'[12]

In enquiring into the factors linking these differences in market capacity to class structuration, we are fortunate to possess a number of fairly detailed cross-national studies of social mobility which, whatever the methodological difficulties involved, allow us to reach some quite definite conclusions as regards the mediate structuration of the class relationships differentiating middle and working classes. In the capitalist societies, since the end of the nineteenth century, there has typically been a substantial amount of upward intergenerational mobility across the non-manual/manual line; but this is primarily to be explained in terms of the relative expansion of the white-collar sector. The thesis originally promoted by Lipset and Bendix, however—that rates of intergenerational mobility from manual to non-manual labour tend to be basically similar in the advanced societies—is evidently oversimplified, if not entirely misguided. Thus, as S. M. Miller showed, there are significant differences, even if the state socialist societies are excluded, between countries in terms of the *patterning* of mobility chances. Some societies have low rates of upward and downward intergenerational mobility across the non-manual/manual line; some show considerably higher rates of both upward and downward mobility, while others have yet different combinations of these rates. One of the significant findings of social mobility investigations is that virtually all movement, whether upward or downward, inter- or intragenerational, across the non-manual/manual division, is 'short-range': that is to say, takes place in such a way as to minimise achieved differences in market capacity.[13] Thus there is some sense in speaking, as Parkin does, of the operation of a sort of 'buffer zone' between the two class groupings: most mobility takes place in and out of this zone, which acts to cushion any tendency towards the collapse of mobility differentials separating the two. Those social mobility investigations which include time-series cohort studies indicate that there has not been much change in rates of mobility between manual and non-manual labour over the period since World War I.

Taken overall, the findings of these studies show quite conclusively the importance of mediate structuration as a major source of a class differentiation between non-manual and manual labour in the capitalist societies. But this can only be analytically separated from the various bases of proximate structuration, which in fact help to explain the origins of observed variations in mobility chances. Primary among these is the division of labour characteristic of the productive enterprise, and the paratechnical relations associated with it; and this is obviously linked to, but again has to be analytically distinguished from, the system of authority relationships which pertain within the enterprise.

It is perfectly clear that, since the first origins of the modern large-scale factory, there has come into being a generic disparity between white- and blue-collar labour—suggested by those very terms themselves, as well as by the terminology of 'non-manual' and 'manual' work—in terms of task attributes in the division of labour. As Lockwood has stressed, the clerical worker, with a relatively weak market capacity, has typically shared conditions of labour which have far more in common with higher-level managerial workers than with the workers on the shop-floor. Clerical employees work in the 'office', which is normally materially separated from the shop-floor and often is elevated above it, such that the office workers may physically 'look down upon' the workers. Whereas the nature of manual work-tasks frequently involves strenuous and exhausting labour in conditions which soil the hands and clothing, the clerk normally works in a relatively clean environment, at a task which simply involves the manipulation of symbolic materials. Even clerical workers, quite apart from higher-level management, may have little or no direct contact with the manual workers, since the foreman normally is the principal channel of communication between office and factory-floor. In Lockwood's words: 'The converse of the working cooperation of clerks and management is the social isolation of the office worker from the manual worker. The completeness of the separation of these two groups of workers is perhaps the most outstanding feature of industrial organisation.'[14] Obviously the degree to which this is so varies, both in relation to size of enterprise and to the particular industrial sector involved; but the general principle holds good, and also applies to the case of Japanese industry, where the organisation of the enterprise is in some other respects quite different to that typical of Western societies; although in Japan the separation of white-collar from manual labour in the enterprise has been historically reinforced by the status discrimination between *shokuin and koin*.

In his analysis, however, Lockwood assimilates these aspects of the paratechnical relations of modern factory organisation with the authority relationships of the enterprise. But while these factors may be closely associated within the characteristic form of productive organisation in the capitalist societies, and even in the advanced societies in general, it is important to draw a general distinction between them. For, at the cost of some degree of oversimplification, it can be said that, while any substantial modification of a system of paratechnical relations necessarily involves alteration in pre-existing techniques of production, change in the authority system does not inevitably entail modification in technique—a fact which becomes of major importance in assessing certain possibilities of 'industrial democracy' in both capitalist and state socialist societies. The authority structure of the enterprise should be regarded, neither as an inseparable part of the paratechnical relations of modern industrial production, nor, in Dahrendorf's view, as constituting a 'class system' *sui generis*, but as one factor promoting the structuration of class relationships. From this latter aspect, we may accept Lockwood's designation of authority as a significant element contributing to a general class differentiation between white- and blue-collar labour. In all the capitalist societies, the authority structure of the industrial enterprise is basically hierarchical within management; but manual workers confront management as a grouping subject to directive commands, without themselves being part of a command hierarchy. As Lockwood indicates, even clerical workers participate in such a hierarchy, and correspondingly tend to be regarded by the workers, and to regard themselves, as 'belonging to management': clerks, in Croner's term, participate in the delegation of authority, while even those blue-collar workers with the most favourable market capacity, skilled manual workers, do not.[15]

There has been much debate recently over how far what I have called class structuration is in some sense 'primarily' influenced by relationships established within the enterprise, or alternatively how far it is conditioned first and foremost by factors extrinsic to the productive organisation itself. Even the protagonists in the debate, however, have to admit that there is no question of any simple determinism involved, one way or the other, and for my purposes here it is sufficient to stress that there are necessarily definite *inter*connections between intrinsic and extrinsic factors, which in a more detailed discussion could fairly easily be spelled out more precisely. The most important of these factors in promoting a general differentiation between white- and blue-collar workers are the distributive groupings formed by neighbourhood 'clustering', and certain types of status group formation. The tendency to neighbourhood clustering undoubtedly varies substantially, both in relation to differences in size and density of urban areas, and to differences in the overall social and political structures of the capitalist societies. Thus the existence of a large underclass, as in the United States, partially cuts across any very clear contrast between 'middle-class neighbourhoods' and 'working-class neighbourhoods', although it by no means obviates it altogether. Moreover, neighbourhood class segregation can be counteracted, in so far as national or local bodies intervene in the 'free market in housing' by neighbourhood planning. But the strength of the tendency towards neighbourhood separation is undeniable, especially in the 'old-established' capitalist societies like Britain, and is supported by the fact that greater job security characteristic of white-collar labour generally makes for a wider availability of house loans and mortgages.[16]

Obviously neighbourhood class segregation is never complete, and there are differences between neighbourhoods within the major class categories: as represented, for example, by the existence of so-called rough and respectable working-class neighbourhoods, in which there is an evident recognition (at least on the part of the 'respectable') of a definite status discrimination between types of housing area. But this complicates rather than undermines the predominant line of demarcation, concentrated most strongly upon the white/blue-collar division. Neighbourhood differentiation undoubtedly has an important effect upon the 'visibility' of class relationships, the general significance of which has been alluded to earlier. When people are asked to draw 'phenomenal maps' of city neighbourhoods, these show large blank areas which represent the neighbourhoods of which they have little knowledge—and among which there is normally a pronounced skewing in class terms.

Differences in neighbourhood organisation are directly bound up with the exploitative connotations of class relationships, apart from those pertaining to the economic sphere itself—particularly in so far as these differences influence the distribution of educational chances. The mechanisms which govern the process whereby 'vicious circles' of underprivilege are set up in this respect are by now well understood. Working-class families are larger in average size than those of the middle class, and the amount of direct parental contact is lower—a phenomenon which, in so far as it influences the verbal facility of children, may have lasting effects upon intellectual abilities. Parental attitudes to education among the working class, moreover, often tend to be unfavourable. As regards the schools, poor equipment and poor facilities in the underprivileged areas are associated with badly qualified teaching staff and an educational environment in which problems of control assume precedence over intellectual development as such.

A number of fairly recent, and well-known, studies in the European countries have demonstrated that class awareness, rather than class consciousness, is the typical cognitive perspective of the middle class.[17] The 'image of society', as Willener calls it, of the white-collar worker involves a hierarchical perception of occupational levels distinguished by differences of income and status—an evident generalisation from the hierarchical system of authority in which the non-manual worker is located. Movement up or down this hierarchy is perceived to be decided by the initiative and energy shown by any particular individual. Consistent with this 'individualism' is a general willingness to accept 'deferred gratification' as a necessary investment to secure anticipated future rewards. Such an 'image of society' does not inevitably preclude the possibility of subjective class identification, but it very definitely inhibits the formation of certain levels of 'class consciousness', as I have defined this term previously. Conflict and struggle play a part in this imagery, but primarily in terms of the striving of the individual to secure a social position which accords with his talents and zeal, not as any sort of class confrontation.

The connections which can be presumed to exist between such class awareness and the sources of proximate structuration of the middle class indicated above, are easy to see. But it is equally easy to generalise too readily from the European experience, in two respects: in treating what is again essentially an abstract, or 'ideal-typical', presentation of the class awareness of the white-collar worker as if it applied *en bloc* to the middle class in the different European countries; and in failing to look closely enough at non-European societies where these patterns are less clear-cut. The first point is important with regard to evaluating recent interpretations of changes which some observers believe are occurring at the lower levels of the white-collar sector, and which are in a certain sense 'proletarianising' clerical labour. As in the debate over separation of ownership and control, there is a manifest danger that the extant reality will be contrasted to what is in fact an ideal-typical conception of the past, thus making it appear that much more striking transformations have occurred than have actually taken place. The parochialism of simply taking European examples is readily demonstrated by considering the case of Japan, where the 'individualism' of the white-collar worker in the West is tempered with a strong dose of 'collectivism' in outlook. The Japanese *sararyman* in a large company, while normally having to achieve entrance to the company through intensely competitive examinations, tends to accept an 'image of society' which emphasises the significance of group loyalty rather than individualistic achievement.[18]

2. SOURCES OF DIFFERENTIATION WITHIN THE MIDDLE CLASS

We may distinguish two major sources of differentiation within the middle class as a whole: that having its origin in differences in market capacity, and that deriving from variations in the division of labour. The most significant type of difference in market capacity is undoubtedly between the capacity to offer marketable technical knowledge, recognised and specialised symbolic skills, and the offering of general symbolic competence. The marketability of specialised symbolic skills has normally been protected or enhanced by the systematic enforcement of controlled 'closure' of occupational entry, a particular characteristic of professional occupations. The growth of professional occupations has been particularly marked in neo-capitalist society. In the United States, for example, the proportion of professional workers in the male labour force almost trebled between 1950 and 1970, and a similar trend can be observed in other societies, even if the total proportion of professionals in the labour force does not approach that of the United States (about 15 per cent). While the professions obviously share certain elements in common with other occupational associations, notably the trade unions, which attempt to impose control over the distribution of market capacities, in other respects they are quite distinct from these. The professional association functions not only as a medium of occupational control, but seeks also to establish ethical prerogatives governing general 'standards of conduct'.[19]

Although there certainly are controversial problems of sociological analysis posed by the existence of the professions, professionalisation does not offer major difficulties for class theory. The same cannot be said, however, of other sources of differentiation within the middle class, which have caused many authors to doubt the applicability of any such generic term as the 'middle class' altogether. The term appears to have a definite usefulness in relation to white-collar workers within organisations, where these workers are part of a definite 'office', and consequently of a bureaucratic hierarchy of authority. But what of workers whose tasks are not primarily 'manual', but who are not so clearly involved in any such clearly identifiable hierarchy, and who, while they may often be connected with the professions, are not of them? As C. Wright Mills puts it: 'The old professions of medicine and law are still at the top of the professional world, but now all around them are men and women of new skills. There are a dozen kinds of social engineers and mechanical technicians, a multitude of Girl Fridays, laboratory assistants, registered and unregistered nurses, draftsmen, statisticians, social workers. In the salesrooms, which sometimes seem to coincide with the new society as a whole, are the stationary salesgirls in the department store, the mobile salesmen of insurance, the absentee salesmen—the ad-men helping others sell from a distance.'[20] What, if anything, do such a bewildering variety of occupations share in common with each other, let alone with the white-collar office worker? Adopting Renner's concept, and modifying it for his own purposes, Dahrendorf has argued that the common element is to be found in the fact that white-collar workers constitute a 'service class' which 'provides a bridge between rulers and ruled'.[21] But this is hardly convincing. What it seems to represent is an attempt to find some place for a concept of a 'middle class' within Dahrendorf's more general endeavour to link class theory to a dichotomous authority scheme, and hence shares the flaws inherent in that general conception. But more especially, it fails to deal adequately with the problem of the heterogeneity of 'services' offered by those in the diversity of occupations mentioned by Mills: it is not particularly enlightening to learn that what a draftsman shares with a social worker is that each is part of a 'bridge between rulers and ruled'.

The primary defect in the conception of the 'service class', in this latter connection, is that *it does not distinguish adequately between class and the division of labour*; or, expressed another way, it does not distinguish between two aspects of the division of labour— differentiation of occupations in respect of divergences in market capacity on the one hand, and in respect of divergences in para-technical relations on the other. The second, as I have stressed, should be regarded as one major component of class structuration on the basis of market capacity: if it can be a source of the homogenisation of class relationships, so can it also be a source of *differentiation* in class structuration, even where similar market capacities are involved. The same is true of authority systems, which Dahren-dorf seeks to make the essential axis of class structure itself. Thus a draftsman and a social worker may have a broadly similar market capacity, in relation to the economic returns which their skills may earn them when offered for sale on the market, but their position in the division of labour, in the sense in which I have used the term, may be quite different; and both may differ from the clerical worker in the large organisation in respect of not belonging so clearly to a specific 'level' in a hierarchy of authority.

3. WHITE-COLLAR UNIONISATION

If the relative expansion of the white-collar sector has been a fundamental stumbling-block to Marxist theory, this is in large part because of the fact that non-manual workers have been 'falsely class conscious'. This phrase can refer to at least two sets of dis-tinguishable phenomena: the general predominance of 'class awareness' amongst white-collar workers; and the apparent greater reluctance of white-collar workers to associate in occupational unions as compared to manual workers (together with a reluctance, when they do form unions, to affiliate themselves too closely with those of blue-collar workers).

Rates of white-collar unionism actually differ quite considerably cross-nationally, as does the degree of separation of white-collar from manual unions. It does appear to be almost universally the case that the level of unionisation of white-collar workers, in any given country, is lower than that among blue-collar workers: Japan, however, is one society which may be regarded as a probable exception to this. According to one estimate, of the 9·3 million workers who were union members in Japan in 1963, at least 35 per cent were in white-collar occupations—a higher proportion than that represented by the white-collar sector in the labour force as a whole. Japan also differs from the Western countries in other aspects of unionisation. In general, among the latter countries, it seems to be the case that white-collar unions have taken the lead from manual unions in respect of levels of unionisation. Those countries where blue-collar labour is highly organised, such as Sweden, also tend to have relatively high rates of white-collar unionisation; other societies, such as Britain, show lower levels of both white- and blue-collar unionisation. Even where there has been a fair degree of 'mixed' union membership, that is to say, with non-manual and manual workers belonging to the same unions, it has normally been the blue-collar membership which has played the most active dominating role. But in the Japanese labour movement these roles have been reversed, with the white-collar elements playing a more stable part, while union membership has taken its strongest hold in those sectors of the economy in which the white-collar sector has expanded most rapidly since the war. In contrast to the Western societies, union 'mixing' is the rule rather than the exception in Japan, something which is undoubtedly closely bound up with the fact that it is the enterprise, rather than the occupation, which is usually most prominent in the consciousness of both white-collar and blue-collar workers.[22] As a mass phenomenon, white-collar unionisation in Japan dates primarily from the period after the war, with the membership concentrated in 'enterprise-wide' unions; although about 20 per cent of the total union membership is in solely white-collar unions, these are for the most part in sectors where only non-manual workers are employed. Within the enterprise unions, half the union leadership is drawn from white-collar groupings, and there have been only a small number of instances where white-collar workers have broken away from these unions to form their own associations.[23] While there are tensions within contemporary union organisation in Japan, tensions which spring in substantial degree from divisions between manual and non-manual factions, there is no indication of any pronounced tendency towards the development of a major separatist white-collar union movement.

France is one of the few Western countries in which there is something of a history of a close integration of non-manual and manual workers within the labour movement. It is perhaps significant that, as Crozier has pointed out, the French term *employés*, while normally applied to non-manual workers, can be used to refer to all workers within an enterprise; there is no generic term corresponding to *Angestellte*, or to 'white-collar worker' (or the less commonly used 'black-coated worker'). The early sales and clerical unions, the *Chambre syndicale fédérale des employés*, founded in the latter part of the nineteenth century, were radical in orientation, and the *Chambre* took part in the founding of the central union organisation (CGT) in 1895.[24] In subsequent periods, white-collar unions have played a part in several periods of open industrial conflict, such as the general strikes of 1919 and 1936.[25] Since the war, white-collar unions, like the manual unions, have been divided along ideological lines, according to whether they affiliate themselves to the Communist, Socialist or Christian organisations, with the latter two being most important. In most of the other capitalist societies, however, there is a quite marked degree of separation, and often of antagonism, between white- and blue-collar unions, even where they are nominally attached to the same federations. Britain is a case in point. The white-collar unions in Britain, on the whole, have looked to the manual unions as their model and, with the exception of the National Association of Local Government Officers (until 1964), have generally sought affiliation with the TUC. But they have also for the most part carefully maintained their separate identity, and have remained conscious of the task of protecting their specific interests.

Why are rates of unionisation, in terms of union membership, generally lower amongst white-collar as compared to manual workers? As regards those groupings of white-collar workers who enjoy relatively privileged forms of market capacity, there would seem to be no particular difficulty in providing an answer to this question, since their economic interests, their place in the hierarchy of the enterprise, and their class awareness, all clearly act to distance them from involvement with unionisation or with collective action. But strongly developed, and occasionally militant unions, as opposed to professional associations, are not completely unknown among those with privileged market capacity (for example, airline pilots), even if they are relatively rare. An analysis of the factors influencing the level of unionisation in those occupations whose market capacities are closest to those of manual workers (of whom clerical workers may be regarded as the most instructive case) should also shed light upon these other instances.

It is now well established that, in recent years, a series of changes have affected the economic position of the clerical grouping, as compared with the higher levels of the working class. The most important of these changes are: a relative decline in the income and other economic advantages of clerical workers *vis-à-vis* the more affluent groupings in manual work; and a transformation of the nature of the tasks, and therefore of the paratechnical relations, formerly characteristic of clerical work in the division of labour. It is clear that various long-term factors have weakened the economic differentials between clerical workers and the more 'affluent' sections of the working class. The arrival of near-universal literacy has diminished the market capacity of general symbolic competence; the very expansion of the white-collar sector itself has reduced the 'scarcity factor' involved in access to routine non-manual occupations. It is not only in terms of income, however, that clerical employees have seen their economic circumstances lessened as compared with blue-collar workers: in most countries, the other forms of economic differential which in the past tended to

separate manual and non-manual labour have to some extent
diminished. The very appropriateness of the designation 'clerical'
becomes questionable in the light of the introduction of mechanical
means of carrying out tasks previously involving the 'pen pushing'
of the clerk. The influence of each of these sets of phenomena upon
pre-existing class relationships has frequently been exaggerated,
not only in terms of their statistical significance, but also because of
the effects of the 'feminisation' of clerical labour. But it is impossible
to decry either the reality of these changes, or their connection to
rising rates of unionism, and they provide a clear indication of
some of the conditions governing the unionisation of white-collar
labour in general—conditions which may be treated in terms of
the variable factors of class structuration.

It is evident, in the first place, that there is little or no tendency
to unionisation where superior market capacity is associated with
the possibility of promotion chances up an administrative hierarchy,
and is further supported by a form of class awareness stressing 'individualism', cognitively and evaluatively. Chances of career mobility
are undoubtedly particularly important here. Historically, one
of the characteristics separating the clerk from the manual worker
has been the fact that the former has nominally, and to some degree
actually, enjoyed promotion possibilities which were not open to
the latter. In so far as the position of clerical workers is subject to a
career 'block', such that opportunities of career mobility are only
open to those with specialised academic qualifications, there is
likely to be a strong stimulus to unionisation and to collective
action. The existence of career 'blocks' (so-called balkanisation),
undoubtedly is the major factor influencing unionisation among
those of superior market capacity. Occupations such as school
teaching, where high rates of unionisation are common, even
though the level of income and economic advantages are quite
considerable, are characteristically those in which, once the given
occupational position is reached, the chances of further career
mobility are limited. Thus, in Britain, for instance, school teachers
reach a ceiling income at a relatively early age: and the possibilities
of promotion to a headmastership are, statistically speaking, very
slim indeed.[26]

In all of the capitalist societies there are wide disparities between
different industries in rates of unionisation of white-collar labour,
which are clearly influenced by divergences in the characteristic
form of paratechnical relations. White-collar workers are less often
concentrated in large, homogeneous productive establishments
than manual workers—certainly one factor tending to promote a

high level of unionisation. Administrative centralisation, however, particularly if it is associated with a developed technical rationalisation of working conditions, tends to stimulate white-collar unionisation: thus the civil service normally shows very high rates of union membership in the lower grades. In France, for example, 40 per cent of civil servants are union members, compared to an average of only something like 15 per cent in the private sector; in Japan, the figure is fully 90 per cent. The mechanisation of certain clerical tasks has been widely interpreted as a process of the 'proletarianisation' of the lower levels of white-collar labour, and hence as the principal factor underlying rising union membership; but in fact comparative studies of variations in white-collar unionisation indicate that the centralisation and rationalisation of administration is more important in promoting a high rate of unionisation.[27] The reasons for the relatively low level of unionisation of white-collar workers are obviously not completely distinct from the factors influencing the relationships between non-manual and manual unions. Apart from the case of Japan, it seems to be very generally true, as mentioned previously, that direct contact with blue-collar unions has often provided an impetus to white-collar unionisation: thus with the exception of the civil service, union membership tends to be higher among clerical workers in industries where they are in immediate contact with strongly unionised manual workers, such as mining, engineering or transportation.

4. PROLETARIANS OR NOT? THE THEORY OF THE 'NEW WORKING CLASS'

I have already stressed that it is mistaken, or at the very least misleading, to speak of a class as an 'actor', especially in the way in which, for example, such writers as Lukács and Touraine are prone to do. A class is not even a 'group'; the concept, as I have defined it, refers to a cluster of forms of structuration based upon commonly shared levels of market capacity. This applies with particular force to the position of the middle class within the contemporary capitalist societies, since middle-class individuals normally lack a clear conception of class identity and, even when unionised, characteristically do not embrace any form of conflict consciousness.

Since the turn of the century, when the rate of relative increase in the white-collar sector first became apparent, the idea has been advanced—particularly, of course, by Marxist authors—that this 'new middle class' will become split into two: because it is not really

a class at all, since its position, and the outlook and attitudes of
its members, cannot be interpreted in terms of property relations.
Hence, so the argument runs, the majority of white-collar workers
will become 'proletarianised', as befits their condition of propertylessness, while a small minority will move into the dominant class.
Today, some seventy years later, the facts continue to belie such
expectations. In the contemporary societies, there are two connected
sets of processes which are commonly pointed to in order to support
modern variants of the notion expressed by the cumbersome term
'proletarianisation'. One is the post-war growth in the white-collar
unions, and the other is the influence of mechanisation. As I have
already indicated, each of these expresses significant changes occurring at certain levels in the class structure. But these changes do not
involve any major process of interpenetration of middle and working
classes. As regards the white-collar unions, the evidence indicates
that the process of their growth, which in any case in most instances
is not an increase in 'union density', but an increase which simply
keeps pace with the expansion of the non-manual sector as such,[28]
does not in and of itself carry any particular consequences for the
labour movement as a whole. In other words, this growth tends to
be accommodated within the existing pattern, whatever this may
be in a particular society. Where there are marked divergences and
conflicts between manual and non-manual unions, these persist,
or may even become accentuated; where there is a higher degree of
mutual penetration, the rise in white-collar unionism does not significantly alter such a situation.

The impact of mechanisation is perhaps more difficult to assess.
Certainly it is a phenomenon which dates back a long way, although recent years have seen the introduction of new forms of
computerised techniques into office work. While many discussions
of the conditions of white-collar labour ignore the distinction,
there is just as much need to differentiate 'mechanisation' from
'automation' in the office as in the factory—although in neither case
does the latter form of technology, relating only to a minor segment
of the labour force, have the significance which some (including
Marx, and more recently Marcuse) have wished to claim for it. It
is misleading to suppose, as Marxist authors commonly do, that the
effect of the mechanisation of office work, the beginnings of which
can be traced to the last two decades of the nineteenth century,
has been progressively to eliminate the differences between office
and shop-floor. Mechanisation, as involved in factory labour,
tends to define the total character of the labour task, often reducing
the role of the worker to 'machine-minding'. But this has generally

not been the case with mechanisation in the office, where type-writers, adding machines, dictating machines, etc., appear as ad-juncts to clerical labour, rather than as transforming it altogether. Women, who compose a category within the labour force which is systematically discriminated against in terms of level of income and career opportunities, largely monopolise those occupations which are wholly routinised (e.g., typist, stenographer). For other clerical workers, the judgement offered by a recent researcher aptly summarises the position: 'what these machines really replaced was a great deal of laborious manual effort in checking data and routine arithmetical calculations . . . some understanding of the business continued to be the desirable qualification of the clerical worker, whether his work was done by manual or mechanical means.'[29]

The recent trend towards automating office tasks, by the use of computers in white-collar occupations, does tend to effect a more total reorganisation of office work. But research upon the influence of the adoption of computerised methods upon para-technical relations indicates that, far from serving to promote the 'proletarianisation' of clerical employees, these normally have the consequence of producing a diminished demand for routine workers, increasing the need for more highly-educated and qualified personnel. Thus a study by the US Bureau of Labor Statistics, of twenty offices which introduced large-scale computers, showed that about two-thirds of the office employees stayed at the same job level as prior to computerisation, a third were upgraded to higher-level positions, while no more than 1 per cent were down-graded to more routine jobs. Comparable figures appear in most other studies. As regards those directly involved in the running of office computers—computer operators, programmers, etc.—research indicates that the level of educational qualifications, and the period of training involved, are substantially greater than is demanded of other employees in non-supervisory positions.[30]

We continue to hear the judgement delivered by orthodox Marxist authors that, as it has recently been expressed, 'salaried workers . . . find themselves carefully *separated* from the rest of the proletariat by the artifice of the bourgeoisie, not by scientific analysis [*sic*]. The fact that they wear a white shirt and are paid at the end of the month is hardly sufficient to place in question their *objective* mem-bership of the working class, even if their *subjective* consciousness remains confused.'[31] It is surely time to abandon such naïvetés; and they have indeed been abandoned by some of the more original Marxist writers, and others influenced by them, who have sought to replace the traditional idea of 'proletarianisation' with a conception of a 'new working class', led by technically qualified workers whose conditions of labour would seem at first sight to separate them quite decisively from the bulk of manual workers.

There are in fact several theories of the 'new working class'. Others will be referred to in the following chapter. In this section I shall consider only that conception of the 'new working class' which is linked to the idea that sections of what used to be called the 'new middle class', together with certain groupings of manual workers, are moving towards forming what Garaudy, following Gramsci, refers to as an 'historic bloc', which has a revolutionary potential in neo-capitalism. Unlike the other theories of the 'new working class', this has been mainly worked out by Marxist writers, particularly in France, and received a major stimulus from the events of May 1968 in that country. In contrast to the more traditional Marxist approach, this theory does not attempt to explain away the conduct and values of white-collar workers as 'false class consciousness', or to neglect the general significance of the expansion of the non-manual sector in the capitalist societies, but rather looks for a novel basis for incorporating segments of white-collar labour within the 'working class', defined in a particular way. This is found in the crucial importance of scientific and technical ideas to neo-capitalism: the production and dissemination of scientific knowledge becomes the primary 'force of production' in neo-capitalist society. Engineers, scientists, technicians of all sorts, thus occupy a pivotal place in the socio-economic order. But rather than affiliating themselves with other groupings in the 'middle class', these workers constitute a new vanguard of the working class—not because they are 'proletarianised' in the conventional sense of the term, as regards income and economic rewards; but because they experience, in acute form, a 'contradiction' between their need for autonomous control over their work task (the production of knowledge) and the bureaucratic exigencies of the organisation to which they are subject. As Touraine expresses the notion:

We are not thinking here of the new 'proletarians', of white-collar workers who must carry out tasks as repetitive, monotonous and constraining as those of workers on the assembly-line, but rather of relatively high-grade categories: technical workers, designers, higher level white-collar employees, technical assistants, who do not take part in the bureaucratic game, but who are more directly exposed to its consequences than workers of the traditional type . . .[32]

The necessarily autonomous process of the creation of ('universally valid') technical knowledge clashes with the subordination of such knowledge to the economic aims of the productive enterprise.[33]

Whatever its deficiencies, the theory appears to fit the contemporary trend in the white-collar sector within the capitalist societies, which in some degree has been towards the specific growth of technically specialised occupations. However, it is open to a number of objections. In the first place, one of the premises upon which it rests, the supposition that, in neo-capitalism, knowledge has supplanted technology as the principal productive force, is highly questionable—a matter explored more fully below (pp. 261–2). Even if this were acceptable in the form in which it is put forward, there would be some reason to doubt the overall claims which have been made for the theory, because it tends to exaggerate considerably the degree to which 'scientific and technical' workers have penetrated even those industries making use of highly advanced technique.[34] More important, however, the sense in which the 'new working class' is a 'class' is ill-defined and ambiguous. Sometimes the term is used, in ways akin to Garaudy's notion of the new 'historical bloc', to refer to an integration of the bulk of the (manual) working class with the 'knowledge producers'; sometimes to designate a merging of the latter with those segments of the working class who, because their tasks are becoming automated, become 'controllers' of machinery rather than 'operatives' subject to the dictates of the machine; and sometimes to describe only the new technically qualified experts themselves. But in none of these cases is it clear what the rationale is for calling the grouping in question a 'class'—and, like most previous approaches in class theory, it tends to conflate the two aspects of the division of labour which I have distinguished: scientific knowledge as a basis of market capacity, and as a basis of position in a system of paratechnical relations.

Finally, it should be pointed out that the theory is at variance with reality, if it is to be advanced as a generic interpretation of the rise of a new proto-revolutionary force in neo-capitalist society. In the United States, which boasts the largest proportion of workers who should comprise the 'new working class', there is no sign of the revolutionary potentialities anticipated by the progenitors of the theory. It is not accidental, in point of fact, that the doctrine of the 'new working class' should have been primarily developed by French authors: for, in a certain sense, it could be held that the 'historic bloc' has been seen in action in the happenings of May 1968. But the reasons for this might lie less in the factors specified in the theory, and generalised to neo-capitalism as a whole, than to other characteristics of the structure of French society which, given the long-standing affiliation of white- and blue-collar workers in the union movement, might explain the incidence of both working-class and middle-class radicalism in that country. As I shall try to show in the following chapter, this is indeed the case.

THE WORKING CLASS IN CAPITALIST SOCIETY

I have already indicated that there is reason to treat with some reserve the conventional assumption that all the capitalist societies will, in the near future, tread the path already followed by the United States, by experiencing a growth of the white-collar sector of such magnitude as to equal or surpass the proportion of manual workers in the labour force. But however this may be, it is important to resist the tendency, now quite strong in the non-Marxist literature on classes, to speak as if a 'middle-class society' were an accomplished fact in the capitalist countries. If we understand by this phrase the statistical predominance of white-collar as compared to blue-collar labour, then this is patently false. Virtually all of the capitalist societies are 'working-class societies', with a large majority of the non-agricultural labour force in manual occupations. It is worth emphasising that manufacturing remains in many ways the key sector in the economy, and has a high proportion of manual workers everywhere. Moreover, in opposition to what is often assumed to be the case, the relative decline in manual labour is not in most countries the result of any sort of significant diminution in the size of the manufacturing sector. Thus in Britain, in 1881, 50 per cent of the economically active population was in manufacturing; in 1951 the figure was 49 per cent, with only minor fluctuations in between.[1] In statistical terms, the growth in service occupations is accounted for by the dwindling proportion of workers in agriculture. But it is also important not to neglect altogether the continuing significance of agrarian occupations within at least a considerable number of the capitalist societies. Although in countries such as Britain or the United States the agrarian sector is small, and is in any case highly mechanised, the same is not true of, for example, France or Italy. As in other respects, it will not do simply to discuss these differences as symptomatic of 'backward' economic development without considering their effects upon other (firmly established) aspects of the social structure of the societies in question.

1. THE STRUCTURATION OF THE WORKING CLASS

Factors influencing the mediate structuration of the working class have been dealt with in the preceding chapter. It will suffice to emphasise here that the division between non-manual and manual labour in terms of inter- and intragenerational mobility, continues to be, through the operation of the 'buffer zone', a primary source of class structuration in neo-capitalism. Obviously, however, this does not operate in an undifferentiated fashion; it is very generally the case, for example, that chances of intergenerational mobility out of the working class are heavily concentrated within the skilled manual category.

In the past development of the working class, in the Western societies at least, the influence of neighbourhood and regional segregation has been fundamental to class structuration and to class consciousness. Such segregation has taken various forms. Thus, in all the advanced societies, there are regional variations in the distribution of workers in manual labour, particularly in manufacture. In England, for instance, a line drawn through the centre of the country marks something of a class division, with a strong localisation of the working class in the Midlands and North, and an over-representation of the middle and upper classes in the South, especially in London and the South-East. But there have also been, historically, important divisions between communities. It is with some truth that the archetypical 'proletarian worker',[2] a member of a clearly distinct 'working-class culture', and strongly class conscious, has been associated with industries, such as coal-mining, which have grouped workers together in isolated villages or towns. Also important, of course, are the distinctive types of paratechnical relations which tend to characterise manual labour in such communities, often involving strong attachment to small work groups in a fairly homogeneous 'technical environment'. How far communities of 'proletarian workers' have ever constituted more than a relatively small proportion of non-agricultural manual workers as a whole is open to question; they are probably most characteristic of those societies (particularly Britain itself) which entered the Industrial Revolution early, when the industrialisation process was mainly 'undirected' in character. Although by no means unknown there, the development of this form of class segregation has been rather rare in the United States, especially outside the Eastern seaboard—and for a similar cluster of reasons as those which explain the relatively weakly developed upper class in that society.

It is mistaken to suppose that the formation of large urban areas, because of their presumed high level of anonymity and spatial mobility, necessarily tends to dilute the clarity of working-class structuration. To begin with, this sort of view, in so far as it involves an implicit or explicit contrast with the 'proletarian worker' type of class segregation, exaggerates the historical significance of the latter: the creation of the working class, such as it exists in the capitalist societies, has in substantial degree involved a direct mass migration from rural areas to urban areas. In spite of the importance of 'ecological fluctuations', producing cyclical movements of the rise and decay of urban neighbourhoods, it is possible, in most European cities, to point to areas which have been 'stably working class' for generations. The patterns identified by Wirth as characteristic of a monolithic 'urban way of life' are in fact primarily—although, again, less so in the United States—attributes of the middle class in the cities. Nonetheless, the types of environment in which the initial structuration of the working class takes place, during the course of the industrialisation process, obviously do condition the nature of the 'working-class cultures' which emerge. Duveau's classic work, *La vie ouvrière en France*, for example, identifies four types of working-class milieu in nineteenth-century France: (1) The large city, such as Paris or Lyon, in which the working-class areas, although distinctive and clearly defined, participate to some extent in the wider cosmopolitan life of the city. 'In Lyon, as in Paris, the feeling of solidarity which is created by the city dominates that created by the shop or the factory.' (2) The medium-size urban centre, such as Orléans, in which industry is scattered in location, and product diversified. The worker here resembles Lockwood's hypothetical 'deferential traditional' type, where there may be awareness of class identity, but where the environment does not provide the conditions necessary to effect the maieutic function of heightened class consciousness. Here 'the city orchestrates merely a simple air; we do not any longer hear the sophisticated counterpoint of Paris or Lyon'. (3) The 'company town', like Le Creusot, which is the isolated, homogeneous environment of the 'proletarian worker', where 'the town, without any personality of its own, effaces itself before the factory'. (4) The small, still predominantly rural community, with the worker engaged in handcraft production for the market, or in seasonal factory labour—the latter situation frequently creating a high level of socialist radicalism.[3]

Before moving on to a more detailed discussion of the influence of paratechnical relations upon working-class structuration, and more particularly upon class consciousness, it is worthwhile at this juncture to consider the relationship between the early formation of the working class and the conception of the 'institutionalisation of class conflict', as advanced by Dahrendorf and others. The theory of the institutionalisation of class conflict looks to the numerous, and often violent, episodes of nineteenth-century labour history[4] as the starting-point of its argument. Dahrendorf's advocacy of this theory runs as follows. Marx anticipated, he points out, a cumulative growth of working-class protest with the development of capitalism as the isolated, sporadic uprisings of the sort witnessed in Britain in the early part of the nineteenth century became generalised into a nation-wide class confrontation. But this is not what has happened. The violence of class conflict has declined, and has been replaced by formalised modes of arbitration; if strikes are frequent, they usually take place without violent clashes between the opposing groups. Conflict of interest has been recognised and formalised, and thereby held in check. Most important of all, this has made possible the fragmentation of class conflict into 'industrial conflict' and 'political conflict'. 'Industrial conflict', Dahrendorf writes, 'has been severed from the antagonisms that divide political society; it has been carried on in relative isolation'. Something of a natural counterpart to this idea is Lipset's analysis of the 'democratic class struggle' in capitalist society: the possibility of an overall class confrontation, polarising society, is controlled by the formalisation of opposing interests in the regulated competition of 'class parties' in politics.

Dahrendorf's thesis has been strongly criticised for assuming too strict a disconnection between industry and politics, and certainly some of his statements on the matter are over-drawn: for example, the proposition that, in 'post-capitalist' society, 'membership in an industrial class leaves open to which political class an individual belongs, since independent determinants and mechanisms of allocation are effective in the associations of industry and political society'.[5] I do not wish to question, however, the underlying validity of the assertion that in the contemporary capitalist societies there is a basic isolation of industrial and political conflict, but rather the inferences which Dahrendorf draws from this fact. While Marx *was* mistaken in expecting the cumulative development of overt class conflict with the growing maturation of capitalist society, he was mistaken for reasons other than those implied in the theory of the institutionalisation of class conflict proposed by Dahrendorf.

The latter author's view is explicitly based upon the notion that, whereas in nineteenth-century capitalism, economic and political conflicts were 'superimposed', in 'post-capitalism' they have become separated. Class conflict, in the Marxian sense, is prevented, or rather its effects are blunted, by the dissociation of the two—and this is one of the major social changes providing for the supersession of 'capitalism' as such. The view which I want to suggest here is, in at least an important sense, the contrary of this. It is that the institutional separation of (the *manifestations* of) class conflict in the industrial and political spheres, far from marking the transcendence of capitalism, *is the normal mode of the structuration of class conflict in capitalist society*. The political aspects of worker protest in the nineteenth century, as Bendix has suggested, represent conflicts produced above all by the *lack of incorporation* of the working class within the institutional framework of capitalist society. They are, to use Smelser's term, 'hostile outbursts' whose origins are to be explained in terms of factors (deriving from the 'superimposition' of *contradiction* and class *conflict*) specifically characteristic of the early phases of capitalist industrialisation. The separation of industrial and political conflict, once the incorporation of the working class has proceeded a considerable way, is merely symptomatic of the generic character of capitalist society as predicated upon a fundamental separation of economy and polity. Although influenced by specific forms of working-class structuration, 'conflict consciousness' is in a certain sense inherent in the outlook of the worker in capitalist society; 'revolutionary consciousness' is not.

2. THE ORIGINS OF CONFLICT CONSCIOUSNESS

There have been, and continue to be, various controversies over the connections between differing forms of paratechnical relations and the class consciousness of the working class. It is not my intention to comment upon these, save to emphasise that we cannot expect to find a wholly clear-cut and invariant connection between the two, as some students of the matter seem to have assumed; the influence of any given set of paratechnical relations is necessarily conditional upon other factors which affect class structuration and class consciousness. There is, however, quite evidently a basic difference between the connotation of 'paratechnical relations', as this phrase is applied to the bulk of the working class in capitalist society, and its implications with regard to the work situation of the main core of the middle class: for the labour of the former is very often mechanised, and subordinated to the exigencies of the machine, in a way in which that of the latter is not—hence, of course, the proliferation of studies attempting to examine the influence of technique upon the behaviour and cognitive attitude of the worker.

In fact, in this regard Marx's analysis of the sources of class consciousness among the working class can be accepted—except that this analysis identifies sources of 'conflict' rather than 'revolutionary' consciousness. At least two of the aspects of para-technical relations which Marx specified as heightening class consciousness have been shown, in a variety of twentieth-century researches, to *tend* to have such an influence: namely the congregation of workers in large plants, and their subjection to routinised forms of productive activity. There are difficulties, however, in evaluating the literature on these issues, not only because it is theoretically weak, but in addition because there are wide differences in the meaning attributed to the term 'class consciousness'. Thus most research dealing with 'plant size' has dwelt upon enunciating relationships between size of enterprise and political attitudes, the latter usually as manifest in voting behaviour. Lipset, for example, quotes studies in Germany and the United States which indicate that 'the larger the industrial plant . . . the more leftist the workers', with the connection apparently being a direct and progressive one; the same kind of relationship has been observed in Britain. But in France, it appears that the relationship is curvilinear, rising at each end of the scale, in both small- and large-scale plants. In Japan, there seems to be no significant connection at all between plant size and what the authors of one survey describe as 'awareness of class in the Marxian sense'.[6] Each of the latter cases represents specific instances of broader divergencies in class structuration and consciousness discussed further below.

An enormous amount of research, particularly since the war, has been devoted to the possible influences of differences in types of productive technique upon worker attitudes. There have been numerous classifications of variations in technique offered in the literature. Thus Blauner, in his study of American workers, sets out a fourfold typology: 'craft' industry, of which printing is an example, where there is a low level of mechanisation,[7] and skilled labour predominates; 'machine-tending' industries, with a higher degree of mechanisation, where the worker merely 'minds' the machine; industries involving 'assembly-line' technique, with a very advanced level of job fragmentation, and highly routinised and specific tasks; and 'continuous process' industries, such as the chemicals industry, involving automatically controlled production flows, in which the labour task concerns only the monitoring and maintenance of the machinery.[8] As Dahrendorf and many others have pointed out, Marx was wrong in supposing that the trend of capitalist development was towards the elimination of the skilled worker—although the character of skilled labour has altered, with the 'traditional craft worker', working alone or in a very small productive establishment, being increasingly displaced by skilled labour attached to larger enterprises. Undoubtedly the persistence of skilled labour is an important source of differentiation within the working class as a whole. The market capacity of the skilled worker is typically superior to that of workers at lower skill levels, a factor widely influencing union formation and stimulating inter-union conflict, and (because, for example, of the greater job security of the skilled worker, making for an easier availability of house mortgages, and allowing for a pattern of 'deferred gratification') tending to support divergences in distributive groupings within the working class. These differences in class structuration are in turn connected with fairly generally observed differences in class consciousness: even within large plants, for instance, skilled workers are normally less conflict conscious than other workers. This indicates two sorts of reservation which have to be made in evaluating the influence of technique, such as classified in Blauner's scheme: first, the assessment of effects of differences in industrial technique over the behaviour and outlook of workers is likely to be rather complex, since these never act 'alone'; and, secondly, while the majority of industrial organisations can be classified in a general way according to type of technique, not all the tasks in the division of labour within the organisation will be of the same skill level.[9]

Most of the researchers who have investigated the relationship between technology and worker attitudes, like Blauner himself, have been primarily concerned with the effect of highly mechanised and rationalised technique upon 'job satisfaction', rather than with class consciousness as such.[10] Virtually all of the studies of car assembly-line workers, the most familiar grouping in this research, conclude that, as a consequence of the determined work pace, the extreme repetitiveness and isolated character of the work task, such workers display a high level of 'alienation' from their labour—the word 'alienation' being used, of course, in a way which taps only the surface of the original Marxian connotations of the term. It is often suggested, however, that the prevalence of this type of technique in production is associated with a marked degree of conflict consciousness, as a result of the standardisation of skills and wage returns which it creates. But the gap between 'alienation', as conceived of in these researches, and some defined form of conflict consciousness, is a large one; moreover, some recent studies have failed to discover any direct relationship between types of technique and stated 'job satisfaction'.[11] One flaw in many investigations of the subject, particularly characteristic of the relatively early research, is a failure to separate out adequately the influence of authority relationships. In industrial settings such as that of the assembly-line, the worker tends to be rigidly controlled in his labour, apparently 'by the machine'. But the mode of operation of any type of productive technique always involves some sort of human directive, such as the assumed need to maximise productivity, which is not set by the worker himself. The few observations which have been made in circumstances where it is possible to dissociate, to some extent, paratechnical relations from the character of the authority system indicate the partially independent significance of the latter.

In Marx's analysis, the influences of large-scale industry and mechanisation combine to foster the growth of trade union associations, and these really constitute the main focus for the sharpening and accentuation of class consciousness. Marx did not offer any kind of systematic examination of the sources of unionisation amongst the working class, but it can be argued that there are two potential sources of such unionisation in capitalist society: (1) Unions may represent attempts to offset, as far as possible, the imbalance in market power in the bargaining procedure between worker and employer; (2) Unions may represent attempts to offset, as far as possible, the subordinate control position of the worker in the enterprise in relation to the performance of his task in the division of labour. In so far as conflicts between workers and employers are oriented to the first sort of objective, they concern a struggle over *the modification of market capacity to secure scarce economic rewards*. In so far as such conflicts are oriented to the second type of issue, they concern a struggle over *the mediation of control within the enterprise*. I shall refer to the first of these as an orientation towards 'economism', and the second as an orientation towards 'control'. Struggles over control are 'political' struggles—using this term in a very broad sense—since they necessarily involve attempts on the part of working-class associations to acquire an influence over, or in the most radical context to gain full control over, the 'government' of industry. If the Marxian idea that trade union conflicts tend directly to engender political conflicts (in the more specific sense of the term) has not accorded with the general reality in the capitalist societies, we must ask what mechanisms

typically act *to confine the bulk of industrial conflict to economism.*
For, given the growth of formalised techniques of collective bargaining in industry—i.e., given the recognition of the economic
and political spheres as separate areas of bargaining encounters
in which the working class play an acknowledged role—we still have
to ask what factors explain how this partial 'encapsulation' of conflict is maintained. To put it another way, any sort of major extension of industrial conflict into the area of control poses a threat
to the institutional separation of economic and political conflict
which is a fundamental basis of the capitalist state—because it
serves to bring into the open the connections between political
power in the polity as such, and the broader 'political' subordination
of the working class within the economic order.

It is worth emphasising that union-management clashes involving
economism are in principle reconcilable in a way in which those
over control are not. For while at any given point in time there
is only a fixed amount in the income 'cake' to be divided between
wages and profits, over an extended period the size of the 'cake'
can be increased, and hence wage increases can be exchanged against
productivity agreements, etc. In the long-term, such a process can
only operate—without tending to shift into clashes over control—
if there is a continuous rise in real incomes; but this is exactly what
has been achieved by the capitalist economies in the twentieth
century. This sort of solution is not open in relation to control. It
must be recognised, however, that, in all industrial settings—even
on the assembly-line—workers hold a certain measure of control,
usually informally organised, over their working environment and
labour task. In so far as union action is oriented towards making
their informal control recognised and explicit, it is unlikely to
compromise management interests, and may indeed conform to
them by clarifying the realities of the situation. Action to maintain
'defensive control' is largely distinct from that oriented to issues of
control which involve the possibility of altering existing hierarchies
of authority within the enterprise. We may thus agree with Mann
that 'What we call the *institutionalisation of industrial conflict* is
nothing more nor less than the narrowing down of conflict to
aggressive economism and defensive control'.[12] A high degree of
'aggressive economism' would be expected to characterise unionisation in those industrial sectors in which there is a marked level of
conflict consciousness, with union development both reflecting
and furthering such consciousness; and, in a general way, this is
found to be the case. Thus Kerr and Siegel's well-known study
indicates that 'proletarian worker' communities consistently have

the highest strike rates, as measured by man-hours lost; but strike propensity is also quite high in those industries which combine large-scale plants with a developed level of mechanisation. Strike rates are low, by contrast, in those industries where there is a high average skill factor, where the division of labour in the enterprise is diversified, and where there are many small firms physically dispersed in a larger urban community.[13]

3. UNIONISATION AND ECONOMISM

According to the viewpoint which I have advanced in this chapter, and more broadly in this book, there is no difficulty in dealing with the evident differences between the American labour movement and that characteristic of the Western European societies. The evolution of the labour movement in the United States has posed, of course, something of an intractable problem for orthodox Marxist theory, and more generally for any approach which accepts the view that the maturity of capitalism—apparently developed in its 'purest' form in that society—would lead to an intensification of revolutionary class consciousness.[14] The standpoint which I am suggesting would imply two overall generalisations: (1) That the labour movement tends to be 'socialist' in orientation where it is formed in a society in which there are fairly important 'post-feudal' elements, and will be closely integrated with a political movement to the degree that the active incorporation of the working class within the 'citizenship state' is resisted.[15] (2) That the labour movement tends to be 'revolutionary-socialist' in orientation where each of these conditions apply, but where the 'post-feudal' elements offer a source of marked resistance to emergent capitalist industrialism. The significance of the term 'resistance' in this proposition will have to be clarified below; and the use of the term 'socialist' manifestly begs many questions. In the first category mentioned above, however, I wish to include societies such as Britain, where the labour movement has been linked to forms of socialist ideology which are primarily reformist in nature, having no clearly formulated ideals of the revolutionary destruction of capitalism. In the second category, the most prominent cases are those of France (which I shall concentrate my discussion upon) and Italy, where the labour movement has maintained a strong level of commitment to such ideals— which in practice means mainly a commitment to Marxism itself as a guiding ideology.

The gulf between Perlman's theory of the labour movement and the type of view established by Marx some sixty or so years

earlier expresses, in a way, the differences between the character
of the blue-collar unionisation in the United States and the European
countries. Rather than linking unionisation to awareness of commonly held positions *vis-à-vis* the means of production, and thus
to class structure (in the Marxian sense), Perlman explains the emergence of the American labour movement in terms of an economistic
attempt on the part of workers to improve their market capacity
by seeking to introduce controls upon the supply of labour—a
process initially begun by the craft unions.[16] Certainly it is the case
that the labour movement in the United States has been almost
completely a matter of trade union development, disconnected from
socialist political objectives or cooperative experiments; there has
not really been a 'narrowing-down' of industrial conflict to economism, because this has been the predominant characteristic of the
labour movement from the nineteenth century onwards.

Rather than offering any extensive analysis of the divergences
between the American labour movement and those of the European
countries, I shall concentrate in this section upon the second question
mentioned above: the problem of the origins of a persisting 'social-
ist-revolutionary' posture in the labour organisations which represent working-class interests. For while the labour movement in
the United States does not share the affiliation with socialist political
parties which characterises the European societies, it has more in
common with some of them, such as Britain, than it does with those
in which the labour movement has been strongly permeated by
revolutionary ideas, such as France and Italy. But it is also worthwhile to compare European patterns as a whole to the development
of the Japanese labour movement.

Perhaps the most striking characteristic of the French labour
movement is the persistence of revolutionary ideology through
long periods of social and economic change—both in the society
itself, and in the organisation of the unions more specifically.
While, for example, the pace of economic development at the turn
of the century was slow, as compared with Britain or Germany,
later periods of relatively sharply rising prosperity have not significantly diminished its prevalence; and while the old anarcho-
syndicalist influences have evaporated, they have been replaced by
communism, dominant in the CGT. That the 'official ideology' of
the CGT is not divorced from the attitudes of a substantial proportion of workers is readily indicated by recent investigations
which demonstrate continued existence of revolutionary consciousness among the working class. Thus Hamilton's research
shows that, in the author's words, 'There is a very high level of

sensed injustice among CGT members and an extremely high level of revolutionary sentiment'.[17] But among workers belonging to other unions, even those which are quite strongly, and actively, anti-communist, a sizable minority are found to voice similar attitudes. Moreover, workers who are not members of any union also show, in Hamilton's study, a high development of revolutionary consciousness, even in plants which are completely non-unionised. These findings contrast markedly with those of studies of workers in most other European countries and in the United States. Thus when the 'team-game' analogy is applied, and workers are asked whether or not they and their employers are 'on the same side', a majority of British workers, in various differing types of industrial settings, agree that they are, whereas comparable groupings of French workers hold that they are on opposing sides.[18]

That there is a substantial 'feed-in' from communist-led unionism to worker attitudes is evident from the responses of French workers to probings about the nature of the society which they anticipate or hope will succeed capitalism. For the most part, these tend to iden- tify the objectives of revolutionary socialism with the establishment of a workers' state modelled on the USSR, thus reflecting the strongly pro-Soviet character of the CGT and PCF. But the important fact is that the consciousness of a revolutionary 'alternative society' is closely linked to perception of work deprivation—a phenomenon which provides the beginnings of the explanation of the relative lack of a trend towards economism in French trade unionism, as compared to other European societies in which the labour move- ment has apparently become 'deradicalised' since the turn of the century. This brings us back to the surveys of 'job satisfaction' referred to in the preceding section of this chapter, and, more par- ticularly, to the connection between job satisfaction and unionism. Studies of this phenomenon in Britain and the United States indicate that there is a direct correlation between union participation and stated degree of job satisfaction: those workers, within similar industrial settings, who are active union members are more 'satis- fied' than those who are passive members or who are not unionised. This finding, apparently contrary to Marx's view, but not to Lenin's notion of 'trade union consciousness', is reversed among workers affiliated to the CGT in France, where those active in the union express the highest levels of manifest job dissatisfaction. These workers, as compared to those in reformist unions in France, also see the firms they work in as having little potential to supply them with increased economic rewards, even in enterprises which are in fact prosperous.[19] Thus it may be suggested that there is an important *reciprocal* influence of radical labour leadership and the persistence of revolutionary consciousness among the working class. The tendency towards economism which has characterised the labour movement in most of the European countries is not to be explained only in terms of the *embourgeoisement* of a 'labour aristocracy', or in terms of the tendency of labour leaders to renegue upon the revolutionary ideals of the mass for motives of personal aggrandisement.[20] The point, rather, is that there is a contingent tie between an orientation to control and an orientation to the amelioration of market capacity, a tie supplied by the *manifest political content* of early worker protest movements. In so far as, in virtue of the political incorporation of the working class within a developed system of 'citizenship rights', the capitalist state successfully consummates the institutional separation of economy and polity, the political aspects of conflict become 'hived off', and this tie broken.

One factor influencing this process is clearly likely to be how far the political orientation of the labour movement is initially strongly revolutionary in character. But in the case of France we must seek to explain what creates and *perpetuates* the tie between a revolutionary orientation towards control, and the radicalism of the labour leaders, in that country. The preceding analysis does indicate, however, the *mechanisms* which, from the side of the experience of the working class itself, serve to stabilise the institutional organisation of the capitalist state in the majority of European societies and in the United States. It can be suggested that the primacy of an orientation towards economism is maintained, not because the majority of workers are 'satisfied' with their work, or because, as Dubin has suggested, in modern social conditions work becomes less important as a (potential) source of fulfilment, but because workers are prepared to trade off 'alienating' work experiences for economic rewards. That is to say, from the point of view of experience of, and attitudes towards, work—at least, of workers involved in those industrial settings which tend to be associated with a high level of 'alienation' from the work task or a high level of conflict consciousness—the 'integration' of the working class is based less upon a normative adoption of the ideals and beliefs generally approved of by the middle and upper classes than upon a 'pragmatic' acceptance of the existing industrial order.[21] The importance of this is evident. It does not imply that the absence of what is defined as favourable 'returns' will, of itself, provide the situation for a wholesale revival of revolutionary consciousness in those countries where this is at present largely absent—the theoretical analysis of class consciousness which I have elaborated would indicate this is not the case. But it does carry the implication that the maintenance of the levels of 'integration' which have characterised the last decades, as indexed, for instance, by strike rates, depends very substantially upon the capacity of the capitalist societies to maintain the rising levels of real income which they have achieved in the past, *without introducing measures which will serve to reorient the labour movement back towards problems of control.* But it is arguable (see Chapter 16) that the emergence of neo-capitalism will act to push the course of events in precisely that direction.

This still leaves unresolved, however, the determination of the factors which account for the differences which separate France from most other European countries.* Two interpretations of these differences can be found in the existing literature. One is that set out by recent theorists of 'industrial society', associated particularly with the 'end of ideology' view, and may be called the theory of delayed development; the other, proposed by some latter-day Marxist writers, is a theory of *uneven* development. While these bear certain similarities, they are not the same. The former holds that, where revolutionary tendencies continue to exist among the working class, this is because the society in question, for whatever reason, is not yet 'fully industrialised'—that is to say, like France (and Italy), still maintains a sizable agricultural sector. Since, the argument runs, the working class tends to be revolutionary only in the early stages of capitalist–industrial development, the continuing existence of revolutionary ideals in contemporary societies can be no more than a temporary anomaly, a residue of the past which is soon to be swept away. But although this view may have a superficial plausibility, particularly in relation to Italy, it is not very illuminating. France can hardly be called 'backward' today, using any conventional index of economic development; moreover, the differences in infrastructure which today distinguish France from, say, Britain are ones which are very long-standing; and, finally, the theory can offer no explanation of why there should have been, *historically*, differences in the nature and degree of revolutionary sentiment among the French and British working classes. The conception of 'uneven development' is more sophisticated, and more in line with the reali-

---

* It should perhaps be emphasised that neither in this chapter, nor in other parts of the book, do I discuss the question of the occurrence of revolution as such, in France or anywhere else. This is a matter, of course, which depends not only upon those forces which might constitute (or perceive themselves to constitute) a threat to the existing order, but upon the alignment of groups within that order, and the reactions of the authorities to any concrete attempt to overthrow it. The role of the French Communist Party in the events of May 1968 is illustrative of the point.

ties of the past history of French society. According to this view, which has been generalised by Althusser on to a highly abstract level, the impetus to revolutionary change in a society is generated by a 'merging of contradictions'. In France, the contradictions already inherent in capitalist society converge with others, such as the co-existence of a fairly mature industrial sector with a relatively primitively organised, large agricultural sector.

There is no doubt that there is a considerable element of validity in the theory of uneven development, and in order to pursue this further we must return to what I have earlier held to be the primary determinant of revolutionary class consciousness: not class conflict as such, but class conflict which takes place in the context of 'contradiction' as I have defined it. According to this interpretation, the creation of revolutionary consciousness is likely to be maximised at the point of transition from small-scale, rural labour to factory production: that is to say, in the initial stages of industrialisation. But, first, this does not always happen and, second, in most cases the revolutionary context of working-class consciousness eventually fades. Thus any simply stated theory of revolutionary consciousness, treating this as the inevitable outcome of the migration of rural workers into industrial labour, is clearly insufficient. What determines whether or not 'migratory' workers develop a revolutionary class consciousness? We can of necessity distinguish two relevant possible sets of influences: the character of the pre-industrial setting from which the worker originates, and the nature of the industrial environment to which he moves. Where these 'mesh' closely, there is likely to be no tendency to revolutionary consciousness, or indeed even to conflict consciousness. Thus, as Weber pointed out in his study of agrarian workers in nineteenth-century Germany, some (although a minority of) migrants from the land were able to make a quite easy adjustment to their work environment, since they moved from a setting characterised by patriarchal employer–worker relations to ones in which the same sort of organisation prevailed, within small-scale manufacturing establishments. But where, as Duveau's work shows, rural conditions of labour are associated with a high level of diffuse resentment, this tends to become transformed into revolutionary sentiments if the worker moves to an industrial setting. This, in fact, seems to have been an important source of radicalism in France in the late nineteenth century—a source of adherence, as would be expected, to anarcho-syndicalism as much as to revolutionary socialism. Such was particularly the case with seasonal workers, peasants for half the year and factory labourers for the other half. Of the seasonal worker, Duveau remarks: 'in the same way as he appears in two distinct material settings, his sentiments show two different sides. Sometimes he seems pious and reserved, holding all the social hierarchies in great respect, while at other times he voices radical opinions and declares himself to be a supporter of the "red" republic.'[22] The sort of clash experienced by the seasonal worker on a cyclical basis—maximised when he is involved in the large-scale, mechanised factory—is that which, when it becomes a more permanent migration, tends to lead to a resolution of this 'schizophrenic' attitude in favour of radicalism.

Hamilton's research indicates that rural radicalism continues to be an important influence in contemporary France, and we may accept the conclusion drawn by him and others that it is a phenomenon of basic significance, not only to the early origins of French revolutionary class consciousness, but in its persistence into modern times. This still has to be connected, however, with the broader socio-political development of French society in the nineteenth and twentieth centuries, in order to explain the growth and persistence of revolutionary socialism. The thesis which might be suggested here is a not unfamiliar, but profoundly important one: that socialist ideas are originally born, not out of the growth and maturity of capitalism itself, but out of the clash between capitalism and (post) feudalism. Where this clash assumes a revolutionary character, which may be because of the political intransigence of the aristocracy as such or because of purely economic barriers to capitalist development, socialism will also tend to be revolutionary. Revolutionary socialism (and anarchism), having in part its roots in rural radicalism, will be a more or less chronic characteristic of a society, like France, which manifests 'uneven' development, since such a society has a long history of an unresolved confrontation of 'progressive' capitalism and 'retroactive' semi-feudal agrarianism within a single overall national structure. As has been stressed previously, the 1789 revolution in this sense created more deep-lying social cleavages than it eradicated: while helping to strengthen an urban upper class, it left traditional centres of rural, localised power—a split in some ways epitomised, of course, by the contrast between Paris and the provinces. I have argued before that the decline in revolutionary sentiment among the working class, in other countries, can be interpreted in terms of the effects of its 'political incorporation' upon concern with an orientation towards control in industry. These effects will not occur, however, when the political recognition of the working class within the state is not accompanied by its essential counterpart, the recognition of the legitimate bargaining power of organised labour within the industrial sphere itself. Such tends to be the case in a society split between a progressive and 'revolutionary' polity and a chronically 'resistant' infrastructure, or where employers tend to resist unionisation in favour of a 'semi-feudal' patriarchalism.[23] I should, however, stress at this juncture that I do not wish to revert here to the sort of standpoint which holds that these phenomena are merely residual—simply the result of a lag in capitalism development which will soon be overcome. Rather, I will argue, as a general principle, which applies to the emergence of capitalist-industrialism in any given country, that the mode of rupture with post-feudal society creates an institutional complex, within which a series of profound economic changes are accommodated, *that then becomes a persisting system, highly resistant to major modification.* In other words, the characteristic forms of the state, of political parties and the labour movement, once established, constitute an institutional order, basic elements of which become, as it were, 'frozen' during the process of the transition to capitalist society (as I have defined this latter term).

The view which I have proposed concerning the orientation towards control and the political involvements of labour movements can be examined further in relation to Japanese unionism, although there is no space here to discuss the case of the Japanese labour movement in any detail. The most striking difference between Western and Japanese unions is the relative lack of concern of the latter with anything other than the position of the worker in the immediate enterprise of which he is a member. Enterprise unionism is neither formed out of the 'job consciousness' of the American craft unions, nor out of the alienative conflict consciousness characteristic of many European industrial settings, but upon a facsimile of *buraku* solidarity. As in Germany, but in an even more specific fashion, the supervision of the industrialisation process by an authoritarian, paternalistic state made possible a transfer from agrarian to industrial labour which avoided some of the clashes in modes of experience and conduct that occurred in other societies, a pattern which is continued in the post-war development of enterprise unionism.[24]

In such circumstances the possibilities of pursuing economism are distinctly limited; and on the other hand, any direct linkage between an orientation towards problems of control and broad political objectives is largely forestalled. It would follow, therefore, that there is likely to be a fundamental tension in the Japanese labour movement in so far as it exists on a national level. For it is neither possible to opt to move towards social democracy by stabilising labour

demands around economistic objectives, nor to sustain a revolutionary orientation relating to struggles for control. In fact, even a cursory
glance at the history of the labour movement in Japan shows that
it has been subject to what has been called a 'pendulum-like swing'
from 'realism to utopianism', or from a radical to a moderate
stance.[25] Of course, this is a long-term phenomenon, which pre-
dates the rise of modern enterprise unionism, and has continued
to depend upon other factors besides the latter: but, in the post-war
era, the exacerbation of the 'pendulum-like' character of the labour
movement can to a considerable degree be understood in these
terms.

4. THE 'NEW WORKING CLASS'—AGAIN

Just as the ideas associated with the (putative) development of a
'new working class', as diagnosed by authors such as Touraine and
Mallet, in many ways reflect the character of French society, so
other theories which employ the same phrase express aspects of
variant types of social and economic structure. Two such theories
have received some currency. (1) An approach, identified with S. M.
Miller and other American authors, locates the 'new working class'
not at the upper, but at the lower levels of manual labour. The 'new
working class' here is a case of what I have called generically an
'underclass'; in this instance, the 'ethnic poor' at the bottom of
the American class structure. This conception of the 'new working
class', however, shares more than what might initially appear to
be a mere terminological resemblance to other theories. While it is
connected with poverty rather than, as in the second sort of view
mentioned below, with affluence, it shares with the latter the notion
that recent changes at the margins of the working class are of
major importance in influencing the attitudes and conduct of the
majority of members of that class as a whole. Moreover the new
focus upon the underclass in the United States is part of a conscious
reaction against the assumption that the affluence of the American
worker, in conjunction with other factors, has eliminated the usefulness of the term 'class' altogether in that society.

(2) The notion of the importance of 'affluence' in dissolving the
older forms of class structuration has received particular attention
in the works of authors writing in, or about, both the United States
and Britain. While this notion has taken various guises, at its most
simple it involves the assertion, or the assumption, that rising real
levels of income, particularly marked at the upper levels of the working class, have transformed the traditional class structures. This
view is evidently quite distinct from that of the French writers,

and it is misleading to bracket them together as theories of '*em-bourgeoisement*' (*Verbürgerlichung*), as has occasionally been done. The term is in any case not an especially appropriate one, for in the proposition, 'workers are becoming middle class', 'middle class' refers not to Marx's property-owning bourgeoisie, but to propertyless white-collar employees. As applied in Britain, the view which links ongoing changes in class structure with rising affluence was initially offered in a specific political context. The electoral defeats of the Labour party in the 1950s seemed to many observers to both signify, and result from, a transformation of the affluent sections of the working class. If the belief that the high-income manual worker has become an 'Orpington man' seems rather whimsical today, it was certainly advanced not long ago as a profoundly significant indicator of the erosion of the existing class structure.[26]

(3) There is yet another conception of a 'new working class' which, although not so clearly distinctive as those already referred to, and in part overlapping with them, is worthy of mention. This view proposes that something of a separation has taken place between the position of the worker as producer and his position as consumer. Similar ideas in this respect can be traced in the writings of authors of such otherwise widely divergent persuasions as Dubin, Schelsky and Gorz. In Gorz's phrase, 'Capitalism civilises consumption and leisure to avoid having to civilise social relationships, productive and work relationships.'[27] This standpoint is of course in a sense quite opposed to that of those, such as Dubin, who do not see, as Gorz does, the attractions and pleasures obtained outside of work as 'false' or 'manipulative'. The common thread is to be found, however, in the thesis that the changing position of the working class in neo-capitalist society can be understood in terms of the dissolution of pre-existing divisions between distributive groupings, through making a variety of 'mass' consumer goods and leisure-time opportunities available to virtually every member of the population.

Like the discussion of the significance of the 'affluent worker' in Britain, the debate over the American version of the 'new working class' has been to a considerable degree stimulated by political considerations. The presence of a large underclass has been regarded as having a deep influence upon the political views and conduct of the white working class. It is hardly possible to resist the conclusion that the existence of a quite highly structurated underclass is a fundamentally important phenomenon now conditioning the American experience. Miller's 'new working class' is comprised of blacks plus Puerto Ricans and Mexicans, working in low-wage, non-unionised service industries, and having very high rates of chronic unemployment; the predominantly white 'old working class' is mainly in semi-skilled and skilled occupations, more highly unionised, and employed in the high-income manufacturing and construction industries. The underclass is thus, as compared to the white workers, mainly composed of relatively recent migrants to the urban-industrial areas.[28]

Although it is evident that the emergence of a massive urban-based underclass is, in a variety of ways, a specifically American phenomenon, similar developments, less pronounced in nature, can be witnessed in other of the advanced societies—as a result, for example, of the migration of West Indians and Asians into Britain, and of Algerians into France. There is no indication that these groupings, at least in the near future, are likely to achieve any significant level of entry into the higher reaches of the occupational structure, and there is plenty of evidence to indicate that the same sort of modes of proximate structuration as have acted in the United States—operating especially through quite clearly defined area segregation—have already progressed a long way as regards the coloured minorities in Britain and France. It is of some consequence, therefore, to consider briefly the possible role of this 'new working class' in the United States in terms of the occurrence of somewhat parallel happenings in these European societies.

Two rather inconsistent views have recently been advanced in some quarters concerning the role of the underclass in the social and political structure of the United States: that it is a possible force for revolutionary change, serving as a potential focus for the generation of a surge in class consciousness which will at last activate the white working class; and that it is a factor making for a prevalence of conservative attitudes amongst the white workers. The first view has a certain amount to commend it, both in theory and in fact. As migrant workers, emanating from rural labour, and moving into routinised occupations, it is possible to suppose that the members of the new urban underclass might manifest some sort of revolutionary class consciousness. Moreover, this might appear to receive some measure of support in Leggett's study of Detroit, in which migrant black workers show a high level of what the author labels 'militant egalitarianism' and 'militant radicalism'.[29] But the arguments which suggest that the revolutionary potentiality of the underclass is likely to be severely limited are easy to document. In terms of its size within the overall population of the United States, it can be stated categorically that no broadly based revolutionary labour movement can be sustained by the underclass alone, and if there is anything at all in the second view mentioned above, it follows that there is no foreseeable likelihood that the attitudes of the underclass can act as a catalyst to the white working class. Furthermore, if ethnic divisions may act to promote class structuration they may also act to cut across it: and the underclass is itself fragmented into three major ethnic groupings. Finally, there is little to suggest that the class consciousness of black workers is permeated by revolutionary ideology, in the sense in which I have previously defined this; Leggett's 'radical egalitarianism' and 'militant radicalism' seem to represent nothing more than an extreme version of the egalitarian individualism common among all class levels in the United States.

But we may undoubtedly expect chronic 'hostile outbursts' on the part of members of the underclass in so far as they are denied access to the exercise of 'citizenship rights', on a par with white workers, in the economic and political spheres. It seems fairly clear that the active political incorporation of the mass of the (urban-based) underclass, long retarded among Southern agrarian workers, is now rapidly proceeding. Within industry itself, however, there still remain major barriers to the equalisation of the inequalities in market capacity which differentiate the underclass from the white working class. Certainly one factor in this is the barriers put up by, or indirectly deriving from, the actions of some of the unions, and it is evidently important to ask just how far these actions are guided by general attitudes which might support the political conservatism frequently attributed to white workers. Much of the writing about the matter has been a result of ill-informed speculation rather than concrete investigation, and it is only rather recently that material has become available as a basis for a more well-founded evaluation. Such evidence does not seem to support the conventional view that prejudiced attitudes are concentrated among the white working class, nor the notion that this is the main source of right-wing political attitudes. Thus a survey of the 1964 Presidential election showed that no more than 20 per cent of white manual workers, outside of the South, supported Goldwater, a much lower proportion than among (white) non-manual workers; in the 1968 election, support for Wallace among the non-Southern white working class was no higher than amongst the middle class.[30]

What this evidence does not show is whether the prejudiced attitudes which plainly do exist within the white working class, even if they are no more widespread than within the middle class, are clustered amongst those workers who are, or who believe themselves to be, in the most direct competition with black workers for jobs. If, as might be hypothesised, this is the case, the social implications of these attitudes might be much larger than their statistical distribution suggests. That is to say, the lower-paid white workers, through the resistance they offer to the penetration of black workers to more highly remunerated jobs than their own, or even to securing economic parity, might be held to contribute to the existence of a 'buffer zone' intervening between the mass of the underclass and the bulk of the white working class.

Most of the discussions of the underclass, however, have neglected what may be the most basic phenomena serving to differentiate it from the 'mainstream' working class—phenomena located in the economic infrastructure of neo-capitalism, and which, whatever differences might be found between attitudes towards ethnic minorities on the part of the working classes in different countries, might depend upon characteristics broadly shared by all the capitalist societies. These characteristics can be understood in the context of the emergence of what some economists have called the 'dual labour market'. This is something which, although it could be said to have existed for a long while in Japan, may plausibly be regarded as a rapidly developing feature of Western economies. It can be understood in terms of a distinction between 'primary' and 'secondary' markets.[31] A primary market is one in which available occupations manifest the characteristics traditionally associated with white-collar jobs: a high and stable or progressive level of economic returns, security of employment, and some chance of career mobility. A secondary market is one in which these conditions are absent: where there is a low rate of economic return, poor job security, and low chances of career advancement. In the past, the differentiation between these has tended to follow skill lines within the working class, in the European societies and the United States: skilled workers have enjoyed the advantages of a primary market in labour. Where, however, considerable segments of the working class are affected by an increasing tendency to negotiate long-term contracts collectively, the distinction between primary and secondary markets begins to cut across skill divisions. *The same discontinuity, however, persists.* In other words, the worker possessing the market capacity allowing him only to enter secondary employment is unlikely ever to be able to acquire a job in the primary market. It may be suggested that there are two main sources of disqualification from primary employment which tend to operate even if formal market capacities are otherwise equal. One is a sexual disqualification, resulting in part from social prejudice, but also from the interruptions in labour availability (as a consequence of marriage and child-birth) which still strongly influence the conditions of female labour. The other is an ethnic disqualification, causing the underclass to be heavily over-represented in secondary employment.

The factors which act to raise the level of primary employment in the manual sector can be discerned without much difficulty, and they seem likely to be closely connected with planning for increased productivity characteristic of neo-capitalism, both in macroeconomic terms and on the level of the individual corporation. The planning of production necessarily involves making long-term calculations about the supply of labour, and tends to lead to a stress upon committing workers to loyalty to the enterprise. Since this inevitably raises labour costs, employers may be expected to attempt to isolate secondary occupations in such a way as to complement their long-term labour investment with a pool of highly 'disposable' labour, in which a marked degree of labour turnover may be tolerated or even encouraged. The underclass becomes a main repository of this supply of labour, for two reasons: since the results of the 'vicious circle of underprivilege' affect this grouping more than any other, its members in any case possess only low levels of education or marketable skills; and the splitting-off of secondary occupations is likely to be more acceptable to the working class as a whole if these occupations are in large part the lot of those considered to be ethnically inferior. In many contemporary European societies the lack of an indigenous ethnic minority leads to a 'transient underclass' (which turns out to be not so transient after all) being imported from the outside.[32]

If these changes affect substantial proportions of the working class in the neo-capitalist societies, they are certainly at least as significant in modifying the pre-existing class structure as those which have been hypothesised as deriving from 'affluence', or from alterations in consumption patterns. As Goldthorpe and Lockwood have effectively pointed out, the thesis that the emergence of an affluent sector of manual workers has the result of producing a basic transformation in attitudes and conduct can be questioned on many counts. In the first place, it identifies 'affluence' with 'income', which is only one of the sources of economic reward that have in the past served to separate the market capacity of manual from white-collar workers. It is precisely to such sorts of modifications in the market capacity of these manual workers which we have to look if we expect to find any tendency towards the dissolution of pre-existing class relationships. Important as these changes may in fact be, they still only affect a minority of workers; and where they do occur they leave intact other principal sources of class structuration tending to separate the working class from the middle class. Although, in their investigation of 'affluent workers' in Luton, Goldthorpe and Lockwood identify certain differences in class consciousness between these workers and the (hypothetical) 'traditional worker', there is little apparent diminution in unionisation or in Labour voting.[33] Finally, it should be emphasised that, even if we merely consider income alone, and neglect other considerations, the changes in income differentials which have occurred concern only the margins of the classes; and, to a considerable degree, these can be more adequately interpreted as part of an overall decline in the position of lower white-collar workers rather than as an upgrading of blue-collar workers into the middle class.

The remaining version of the theory of the 'new working class' can be criticised for somewhat similar reasons: that is to say, that it neglects the central focus of class relationships as founded in production. The relevance of this observation applies differently to the various writers involved. For those influenced by Marxism, the effects of the incorporation of the working class within the 'mass consumption' economy act to conceal or to submerge the effects of class relationships, but do not eliminate them altogether. The members of the working class may not be aware of their interests as a sectional grouping in capitalist society, and hence, as in Marcuse's rendition of this view, are no longer a revolutionary threat to the existing order. This is not, however, because of the transcendence of their alienative position in the sphere of production, but because of the fabrication of 'false' consumption needs which mask the deprivations inherent in the class structure. Nevertheless, this standpoint shares the assumption, also set out by non-Marxist authors, that the *salience* of class relationships in influencing conduct and beliefs is radically diminished by the assimilation of the working class into global patterns of consumption common to all members of society.

There are considerable theoretical objections which have to be made to this conception if the ideas I have formulated in this and previous chapters be accepted. But even regardless of these, its empirical basis is highly questionable. It is obviously true that, since they participate in the general rise in real income characteristic of capitalist economies, the members of the working class receive a share of the consumer goods created by modern industrial production. But it cannot be directly inferred from this, any more than it can be from rising affluence itself, that the established differences between distributive groupings disappear. The evidence indicates the contrary; moreover, if the old communities of 'proletarian workers' are in decline, this is not because of any uniformity of patterns of consumption *per se*, but is the result of the waning economic importance of the industries with which these have been associated, and the consequent outflux of younger workers to the larger towns and cities. The influence of the mass media, and the diffusion of 'mass culture' generally, is usually pointed to as a primary source of the supposed 'homogenisation' of patterns of consumption, and of needs and tastes. But research on the 'two-step flow of communication' shows that formally identical content, as disseminated in the mass media, may be interpreted and responded to in quite different ways. Far from being eradicated by the uniform content of the media, existing forms of differentiation in social structure may be actively reinforced by it, as a consequence of such selectivity of perception and response.

I shall not attempt, at this point, to summarise any conclusions of a general nature which can be drawn from the matters that I have considered in the three foregoing chapters. For the theoretical issues raised here are not limited to the capitalist order, but concern the advanced societies as a whole; so I shall now turn to an examination of state socialism, reverting to a more abstract plane of analysis in the final chapters.

1 2

STATE SOCIALISM AND CLASS STRUCTURATION

1. VARIATIONS IN INFRASTRUCTURE AND DEVELOPMENT

If it is misleading to generalise about 'capitalist society' solely by reference to a single country, such as Britain in the nineteenth century, or the United States in the twentieth, it is equally deceptive to generalise about 'state socialism'—as is so often done—solely in relation to the Soviet Union. Not only are there certain essential differences between the development of the Soviet Union and that of the other state socialist societies, but these societies differ considerably among themselves. As in the case of the capitalist countries, these differences may be understood in terms of differing 'paths' of development, arising out of variations in the combination of 'traditional' and 'modern' elements. Much of the early history of Soviet Russia was conditioned by the fact of its isolation in a world of hostile capitalist powers. The struggles leading to the emergence of the Stalinist ideology of 'socialism in one country', of course, express the problems faced by successful revolutionaries who found themselves to be, not the vanguard of a process of socialist revolutionary transformation sweeping through the industrialised world, but the rulers of a largely peasant society. The emergence of state socialism in the other countries of Eastern Europe came about, as in Russia, in the context of the disintegrative effects of world war; but the presence of Soviet military power and economic support was this time itself a major factor making possible the successful assumption of power by the indigenous Communist Parties.

Whereas Russia in 1917 was, according to any indices of degree

of industrialisation or sophistication of productive technique, at a
quite low level of economic development, Czechoslovakia was
relatively highly industrialised at the time at which it experienced
its transition to state socialism—and it is still today (together
with the German Democratic Republic) far ahead, in this respect, of
the rest of the East European societies. In 1948, when overall state
planning was initiated, Czechoslovakia had reached an economic
position comparable to the advanced societies of Western Europe.
Most studies which have attempted to draw comparisons between
rates of economic development and productivity increase in the
capitalist and state socialist countries have, as in other respects,
looked to the USSR as the point of reference; but in many ways
Czechoslovakia provides a more useful basis for contrast.[1]

It is important to recognise, moreover, that the phrase 'state
planning' can cover a number of variable phenomena. In all cases,
the term connotes a massive socialisation of industry and trade
under the directive control of the state apparatus. But the extent
and nature of this control varies. The degree to which private ownership of small-scale enterprises or of landed property is allowed to
persist differs between the state socialist societies. In Poland, for
example, privately owned land, in the hands of independent peasantry, heavily predominates over that which is state-run: only
about 14 per cent of cultivated land is either in the hands of the
state or administered by collectives.[2] No East European society has
been as ruthless in enforcing the collectivisation of the peasantry
as was the case in the Soviet Union during the Stalinist period. In
both Poland and Yugoslavia, policies originally designed to implement a process of mass collectivisation were abandoned in the face of
resistance from the peasantry; although in other societies, such as in
Czechoslovakia and Hungary, the policy of forming agrarian collectives has forged further ahead despite such opposition.

In several of the Eastern European countries there was a fairly
strongly marked history of state involvement in economic life. This
is true of Poland and Czechoslovakia, for instance, which in other
respects differed greatly in socio-economic structure. Pre-war Poland,
which, like Germany in the latter part of the nineteenth century,
lacked a developed and self-confident grouping of industrial entrepreneurs, showed a strong leaning towards *étatisme*, with a considerable level of state ownership of major industrial sectors of the
economy. In Czechoslovakia, a pronounced degree of pre-existing
vertical and horizontal concentration in industry aided the consolidation of state intervention in the economy under the Czech
protectorate.[3] Notwithstanding the influence of the doctrine of the

'unique road to socialism', manifest in the universal importation of Soviet methods of macroeconomic planning and industrial organisa- tion, modes of state direction of industrial production varied considerably. Thus comparing the two most industrialised countries in the initial phases of the socialisation of the economy, whereas in Czechoslovakia by 1949 only just over 3 per cent of the labour force remained in the private sector, in East Germany the *sowjetische Aktiengesellschaften*, the nationalised and cooperative enterprises, together involved only something over two-thirds of the labour force, leaving nearly a third still employed in the private sector. In general terms, however, the socialisation of manufacturing industry and commerce proceeded much more rapidly in Eastern Europe after the war than in the comparable phase in the early development of the Soviet Union. [4]

Pre-existing infrastructural differences, not all equally suited to the enforced impress of modes of economic direction derived from the Soviet experience, together with the generic problems created by tightly coordinated central planning, combined to bring about the modifications in economic policy introduced in most state socialist countries in the late 1950s and again, in rather different form, in the 1960s. While these were to some degree influenced by changes in the Soviet Union itself, they followed varying lines in the different societies. The modes of economic planning which were worked out in the first phase of development of the Soviet Union were specifically related to the need to effect a gigantic mobilisation of resources to promote a rapid process of industrialisation, within an unusual social and political context—one which did not apply directly to the 'underdeveloped' economies of post-war Eastern Europe, such as that of Poland, let alone those of countries like Czechoslovakia. The economic reforms of the late 1950s in the state socialist societies are ordinarily interpreted as involving a relaxation of centralised direction of the economy in favour of a reintroduction of certain market influences. But it is worthwhile distinguishing two partly independent aspects of this relaxation, since it can be argued that the mode in which these are combined has important socio-political implications for the mediation of control in different economies. One aspect is the *decentralisation of authoritative decision-making* in the formulation of planning policies; the other relates to *the determination of prices*, and the degree to which this is allowed to be influenced by consumer preferences. The first concerns, most importantly, how far the formation of planning becomes decentralised in the hands of productive enterprises, or associations of such enterprises—in contrast to the situation in the earlier system, in which economic units were treated merely as instrumental to the realisation of national plans. In so far as such decentralisation does take place, it has significant potential implications for the overall position of the Communist Party within the state. Decentralisation 'at the top' may or may not be complemented by decentralisation 'from the bottom up', working through the toleration or encouragement of the evaluation of the performance of enterprises in terms of profits rather than gross output. There are important possible sources of tension between these.

With certain specific exceptions—the most notable being the stagnation in Czechoslovakia in 1962–4—the state socialist societies have continued to maintain fairly high rates of economic growth, even if these have now tailed off from the earlier phase.[5] In terms of the fostering or extension of the industrialisation process there have been, in most of these societies, major changes in the overall composition of the labour force. One is, of course, a steady decline in the proportion of the economically active population working in agricultural occupations. This still remains high, however, compared with the capitalist societies. Yugoslavia, for example, with some 57 per cent of the labour force in agrarian labour, predominantly at a relatively primitive level of technique, resembles Greece more closely in this respect than it does the advanced societies of Western Europe. Even Czechoslovakia (1961) has some 28 per cent of its labour force working in the agricultural sector. But within the non-agricultural labour force there has occurred the phenomenon familiar in the capitalist societies: the relative expansion of white-collar labour and, particularly, the increase in the proportion of 'professional and technical' workers. The latter grouping compose nearly 6 per cent of the labour force in Yugoslavia, for example, only 2 or 3 per cent below that observed for Britain.

2. DIFFERENTIALS IN MARKET CAPACITY

The paucity of references by Marx to the sorts of social and economic organisation which might characterise the projected order to be built following the dissolution of capitalism has presented a major difficulty for Marxist interpreters of state socialism. It is clear from Marx's writings that there is to be a 'transitional phase', constituting what has come to be called, in orthodox Soviet Marxist thinking, 'socialism', as distinguished from the 'communism' which represents the anticipated 'higher stage' of classless society. But even Marx's comments on the 'transitional phase', mainly to be found in his critical notes upon the Gotha programme of the

German Social Democratic party, and not intended for publication, are brief and generalised in character. The doctrine of 'non-antagonistic classes', as developed by Stalin, represents an attempt to fill in an evident, but poorly elaborated, feature of Marx's ideas about the transitional stage of 'socialism': that, while classes continue to exist after the demise of capitalism, their nature is distinctively different than under the prior system.

In fact, it is not at all apparent that the conception of 'non-antagonistic classes', as originally applied in the Soviet Union, bears much relation to the future situation as conceived by Marx. For even if Marx held that a country such as Russia could provide the stimulus to a process of revolutionary change, he still expected that process to become centred upon the more mature capitalist societies: and the main theoretical basis of the transition to a classless order rests upon the notion of the dialectical *Aufhebung* of the proletariat as the remaining 'one class' in society, following the disappearance of the bourgeoisie. But this situation manifestly does not apply in a society only on the threshold of capitalist development, and the 'non-antagonistic classes' referred to in Stalin's scheme are, of course, the (collectivised) peasantry and the working class.

In Stalinist theory, since the abolition of private property in the means of production eliminates class conflict, there must necessarily be harmony between the classes in post-revolutionary socialist society: the 'exploitation of man by man' is eliminated, and peasantry and working class work 'in harness' (together with the 'stratum' of intelligentsia) toward the furtherance of interests shared by everyone. Recent writers, especially in state socialist countries other than the Soviet Union, have been more realistic, admitting that there may be divisions of interest between the residual classes in the 'transitional stage'. In this phase of development, there are bound to be short-term conflicts of interest in terms of the allocation of scarce resources.[6] All such views, however—inevitably enough—are tied to the Marxian notion of class as deriving from the existence of private property in the means of production. The theory which I have elaborated earlier suggests a different approach. There are two sets of connected problems to be analysed in relation to the existence of classes in state socialist society: how far the conditions promoting class structuration are present, and, in so far as these do exist, whether they are of declining significance or, alternatively, are generic to the society. These problems cannot merely be resolved in terms of any simple comparison of the role of private property in capitalism and its absence in state socialism, although this is indisputably a major source of contrast between the two types of society. Furthermore the rhetoric of the 'transitional stage' cannot be accepted as it stands, since, as I have already argued, the state socialist societies do not represent the transcendence of capitalism, but an alternative mode of development to it. According to the approach which I have elaborated, the class character of capitalist society derives in a fundamental sense from the overall institutional mediation of power given in the separation of the spheres of the 'political' and the 'economic'. Contrasting this with the institutional form of state and economy characteristic of state socialism poses general theoretical issues which I shall confront directly in the following chapter. For the time being, therefore, I shall consider the factors affecting the level of class structuration in the state socialist societies, leaving the broader implications of this for later discussion.

In the market conditions which prevail in capitalist economies, persisting economic differentials have characterised both the division between manual and non-manual labour, and that between industrial and agricultural labour. As Parkin has indicated, in analysing to what extent the state socialist societies diverge from this pattern, it is helpful to distinguish between the immediate post-revolutionary period, which—except in the Soviet Union—may be said to correspond generally to the phase prior to the first wave of economic reforms, and the subsequent period in which certain of the government policies characteristic of the time of 'socialist reconstruction' were liberalised or abandoned.[7] But these are controversial matters, and I do not think we can be as confident in reasoning from the available income statistics as Parkin seems to be. After all, the interpretation of comparable statistics concerning the capitalist countries poses many difficulties, although the information we have at our disposal in this regard is mostly more detailed and comprehensive than that bearing upon the state socialist societies. Moreover, some of the older data is probably intrinsically unreliable, a matter of some significance if one is attempting to infer trends. If, therefore, I broadly follow Parkin's analysis in the next few paragraphs, it is with somewhat greater reservations than he apparently has about the conclusions to be drawn from it.

In most of the Eastern European countries and in the Soviet Union, the post-revolutionary phase was marked by more or less successful attempts at the forceful eradication of key groupings in the pre-existing class structure, including not only the large industrial and financial capitalists, but also, in variable degrees, the 'old middle class' of small property-owners and peasant land-owners. For ideological reasons, and also to secure or maintain the active support of the mass of the industrial working class and the peasantry in the face of the hostile reaction of the dispossessed classes, the post-revolutionary governments introduced a series of sweeping egalitarian measures. In the Soviet Union, in the years prior to 1931, the revolutionary state initiated major policies aimed at improving the economic position of the industrial working class in relation to other propertyless groupings in society. Although the income of the collectivised peasantry is difficult to estimate for comparative purposes, there seems no reason to doubt that in the early post-revolutionary phase, as is still the case today, the economic rewards available to the working class were considerably higher than those of the workers on collective farms. But differentials in income and other forms of economic return between those categorised as *fizicheskii* ('physical', or manual, workers) and *umstvennyi* ('intellectual', or non-manual, workers) were markedly reduced in the period after the revolution;[8] as were those between skilled and unskilled workers.

In 1931, Stalin launched a reversal of policy, against economic egalitarianism, under the stimulus of the problems of productivity and massive turnover of labour witnessed under the first Five Year Plan. As a consequence, income differentials began to expand again in the Soviet Union, along a pattern broadly comparable to that characteristic of the capitalist societies. In recent years, however, this trend has again been reversed as a result of deliberate political policy: minimum wages have been raised, tax reforms favouring the lower income groupings introduced, and the overall differential between manual and non-manual labour has again been narrowed.[9] Whereas in 1940 the incomes of skilled manual workers were slightly below those of the lower-level white-collar workers, today the wages of the former are very substantially higher—and, since the proportion of women in the labour force is both larger and more evenly distributed throughout the occupational system than in the capitalist societies, this cannot to any great degree be explained away in terms of a concentration of female workers in the lower non-manual occupations.[10] The pattern in the other state socialist societies appears to have been broadly similar, although the variations between the general distribution of economic differentials in different periods seems to have been less pronounced than has been the case in the Soviet Union. The immediate post-revolutionary phase was succeeded by one in which differentials in economic returns became stretched; this process appears recently to have been reversed by political intervention which has restructured the shape of the labour market. In most of the contemporary state socialist societies, it now appears to be the case that the economic rewards, not merely of skilled workers, but, expressed in terms of median earnings, of manual workers *as a whole*, are higher than those of clerical and lower-level administrative employees.[11]

It seems legitimate to conclude from these considerations that the forms of differentiation in market capacity which operate in the capitalist societies are considerably modified as a result of the institutional mediation of power which prevails in state socialism. Of course, the factors which affect market capacity in capitalist economies by no means disappear altogether: the possession of manual skills remains a major source of differentiation in market capacity within the ranks of manual labour in general, and the possession of *specialised* symbolic skills yields superior market capacities to those associated with manual skills. Nevertheless, we may be fairly confident that the separation in market capacity which has historically characterised the capitalist societies is less conspicuous in state socialism. There are two aspects to this: one is the higher relative income of manual workers, measured in terms of wages alone; the other is that lower white-collar workers do not enjoy the same pronounced advantages in terms of other forms of economic return—job security, fringe benefits, etc.—which have traditionally distinguished manual and non-manual labour in the capitalist countries.

3. LEVELS OF CLASS STRUCTURATION

There is a dearth of materials upon intergenerational mobility which would make possible anything approaching a precise statistical comparison of variations in levels of mediate structuration among the state socialist societies. However, tentative contrasts can be drawn on the basis of the information which does exist, and these can also serve to formulate certain conclusions about how far typical patterns of mobility in state socialist society differ from those characteristic of capitalism. Patterns of mobility obviously differ between the state socialist societies which are highly industrialised, such as Czechoslovakia, and those which have large peasant sectors, such as contemporary Poland, or the USSR prior to the last war. In the latter two countries, a considerable proportion of both manual and non-manual workers come from agrarian backgrounds: the rate of movement into non-manual labour, however, seems to have been higher in the Soviet Union than in Poland. Research indicates that, in Poland itself, rates of mobility from

agrarian backgrounds into non-manual occupations in the post-
war period (1956–68) are markedly higher than before the war.[12]
But this is almost certainly to be traced to the expansion in level
of industrialisation, and the resultant changes in the occupational
structure: the same study shows that in the later period rates of
intergenerational movement from manual to non-manual occupations in industry are not very different from those pertaining prior
to the war. Moreover, rates of downward mobility from non-
manual to manual labour are low, indicating relatively little 'interchange' mobility. Poland ranks towards the extreme in this respect,
however; and certainly rates of downward mobility appear to be
markedly higher than this in Czechoslovakia.[13]

In terms of gross rates of mobility between manual and non-
manual occupations, it might seem that there are few significant
differences between the generality of capitalist and state socialist
societies. But such a conclusion would be a superficial one. Mobility
from manual to non-manual labour in the Eastern European societies and the Soviet Union typically differs from that in the capitalist
societies in that 'long-range' mobility is more common—that is to
say, mobility which 'jumps' the clerical and lower white-collar
occupations. This clearly relates to the different alignment of
market capacities which characterises the state socialist societies.
It indicates that the lower non-manual occupations do not form
the sort of 'buffer zone' which they do in the capitalist order, and
undoubtedly serves in part to cut across the tendency of mediate
class structuration to be concentrated upon a division between
blue-collar and white-collar labour. But again there seems to be an
important time factor involved, linked to the contrast between the
post-revolutionary phase and the later period. In the phase succeeding the assumption of power by the Communist Party, two sets
of phenomena facilitated 'long-range' mobility. One was the *déclassement* of large numbers of men who occupied higher administrative
positions, as a result of the revolution itself. The other was the
promotion of policies calculated to favour the chances of educational
achievement for the sons of manual workers and peasants, through
the use of educational quotas. These were distinctly successful in
breaking through the domination of higher education by individuals
from white-collar origins. In latter years, however, there are clear
indications that this process is being reversed; the quotas have
mostly been abandoned, and there is an increasing imbalance in
recruitment to higher education, militating against the chances of
those from manual or peasant backgrounds. It has been assumed
by many that this will lead to a system of 'educational inheritance'

directly comparable to that observed in the capitalist societies. But how far such will be the case still remains to be seen.

Patterns of intragenerational mobility might also initially seem to be indistinguishable from those which pertain in most capitalist societies. The availability of channels of mobility from the shop floor into a managerial 'career hierarchy' is not apparently any greater in state socialism than it is in capitalism. But this again would be a misleading conclusion, if it is simply offered as a straightforward comparison, for the 'career content' of both the upper levels of blue-collar labour and the lower levels of white-collar labour differs from that characteristic of the capitalist societies. In most of the state socialist societies, there exist considerable chances of career mobility from the unskilled to the skilled categories. These possibilities seem most highly developed in Yugoslavia where, according to Milić, well over 80 per cent of skilled manual workers had received their training after entering employment;[14] but in other state socialist countries the availability of mobility chances within the ranks of manual employment is generally considerably above that offered by similar vocational schemes in the majority of the capitalist societies in which, with the exception of Japan, high rates of labour turnover have discouraged firms from investing in on-job training. The position is something like the reverse in the case of white-collar occupations. The relatively high rates of intergenerational mobility into higher managerial positions in the state socialist societies are closely linked to the importance which is placed upon the possession of specialised educational qualifications. While these are undeniably of major significance in this respect in the capitalist societies also, it is still true in the latter that entry to lower white-collar occupations provides some prospect of career mobility into the higher echelons of the management hierarchy. If there is an ongoing 'convergence' here of patterns of mediate structuration between the capitalist and the state socialist societies, it is perhaps one in which the former are moving towards the latter more than vice versa. For it may be the case that it is not only increasingly difficult for the worker who starts his career in routine office work to achieve promotion, but that, in the differentiation between primary and secondary employment, firms will tend more and more to invest in training a 'stable' body of workers loyal to the enterprise. Whatever 'convergence' has occurred, however, has hardly eliminated what we may accept as constituting a basic dissimilarity between the capitalist and state socialist societies—one which is further emphasised by the relative absence in the latter of certain aspects of proximate structuration which promote a generalised division between the working and

middle classes in capitalism. The main characteristics of the variations in paratechnical relations which tend to separate manual and
non-manual employees within the enterprise are closely intertwined
with the technical organisation of modern industry, and exist
in all of the advanced societies. 'Office' work is physically separated
from the conditions of labour on the 'shop floor'; the nature of
the tasks involved in the manipulation of symbols, whatever the in-
roads which might have been made by the mechanisation of clerical
tasks, necessarily tends to cut off the work experience of the white-
collar employee from that of the vast majority of manual workers.
Other elements in the physical segregation of white- and blue-collar
workers frequently found in capitalist society, such as the use of
separate works entrances, canteens, etc., are normally absent in
state socialist factory organisation. But two additional influences
are important, or potentially important, in dissolving the 'cumulative
effect' of the differences in paratechnical relations of the sort
characteristic of the capitalist societies. One is the existence of status
distinctions which are general to the Eastern European countries
and the Soviet Union, and which tend to follow the established
pattern of variation in economic rewards: skilled manual workers
typically are accorded a more elevated status than lower-level
white-collar employees, who do not share the same sort of status
affiliation to managerial and professional workers usually found
in the capitalist countries. Particularly significant, however, and
worth discussing in some detail, is the influence of forms of authority
relationship in industry.

4. MANAGEMENT AND AUTHORITY IN THE ENTERPRISE

I have pointed out, in previous chapters, that it is a mistake to
assimilate paratechnical relations and patterns of authority in
industry, as many authors tend to do. However, it is not surprising
if these are frequently portrayed as a single aspect of the structure
of the enterprise, since this is how they tend to appear within the
organisation of industrial life in the capitalist societies. I have
suggested that this is a necessary characteristic of the institutional
mediation of power in these societies, in which the economy is
'non-politicised'. In state socialism, these conditions do not pertain,
and it should follow that the nature and dynamics of industrial
authority are correspondingly distinct. I wish to argue that this is
indeed the case, and that apparent similarities in the character of
systems of management in the two types of society actually conceal
significant differences. These differences are of basic importance,

I shall propose, in diagnosing major sources of tension in state socialist society. While discussion of this matter must be deferred to the next chapter, it will be useful at this point to sketch in a background to problems taken up there.

In several of the Eastern European societies, the transition to the new order was accompanied by the appearance of 'works councils' which claimed directive control in industry; but these were transitory, and were followed by a general patterning of industrial organisation on orthodox Stalinist lines. As in the Soviet Union, the need to ensure 'labour discipline', especially in those countries, such as Poland, where the objective of the government was to promote a rapid expansion of the industrial sector, became paramount over the 'social experimentation' of the revolutionary period. The principle of 'one-man management' reintroduced a system of industrial authority in which manual workers were effectively as subject to authoritative commands from 'above' as their counterparts in the capitalist societies. Before 1948, in Poland, Hungary and Bulgaria, with a fairly large private sector still in existence, the unions played a leading role both in seeking to complete the socialisation of the economy and in controlling managerial decision-making. After this date, however, with the introduction of Soviet-type policies, the unions increasingly became little more than agencies helping to ensure the subordination of the work-force to the sovereign authority of management. Yugoslavia, in fact, adopted the 'one-man management' principle as early as 1946. But after the break with the Soviet Union, and the movement towards a system of economic decentralisation after about 1954, workers' councils began to acquire an expanding degree of real influence in plant management. Whatever the validity of the assertions that the workers' councils are effectively controlled by Communist Party members, the result is undoubtedly to break away from the conjunction of manual labour and 'exclusion from authority' within the enterprise which, in capitalism, has been one of the major factors in proximate class structuration. The workers' councils assume responsibility for the hiring of all grades of management personnel, and also are involved in the formulation of production norms and wage rates.[15]

While the Yugoslavian system of councils was fostered by the central government, those in Poland, and, at a later date, in Czechoslovakia, which I wish to use for comparative purposes, were initially formed almost solely on the basis of spontaneous movements at the level of the enterprise, and were only subsequently given the formal approval of the Communist Party.[16] Thus in Poland in

1956, in a number of scattered industrial plants, such as the car factory at Zeran, meetings of manual and non-manual workers collectively drew up proposals for the introduction of 'workers' autonomy' in factory management.[17] Two sorts of result emerged. In the so-called 'experimental enterprises', the participation of workers was to be encouraged via the setting of target plans and sharing in realised profits. But more general, as in the case of the Zeran factory, was the trend towards the revitalisation of the work-ers' councils which had made a brief appearance in the phase of reconstruction just after the war. The impetus behind the renewal of the workers' councils was to counter the role of the unions as 'the second government', and as such was closely linked to diffuse political objectives of the reform of the Party and state organisation. In late 1956, after Gomulka had come to power, decrees formally recognising the existence of the workers' councils were passed at about the same time as those designed to promote economic de-centralisation by enlarging the autonomy of the individual enterprise. Neither the enlargement of workers' control nor the decentralisa-tion at the level of the enterprise proceeded anything like as far as in Yugoslavia, and there was only a short time during which the councils had much effective influence over managerial decisions. In Czechoslovakia, attempts at the creation of schemes of workers' self-management, which had a vigorous early history prior to the forcible disbandment of workers' councils in 1949, occurred spor-adically in 1966–7. In 1968, the rapid spread of such schemes forced the problem of workers' control into the forefront of public attention. The Communist Party 'Action Programme' of April in that year explicitly acknowledged that: 'There is a need for democratic bodies in the enterprises with well-defined powers in relation to management. The directors and top executives should be responsible to these bodies for overall performance and would be appointed by them.'[18] It has been estimated that, by early 1969, workers' councils repre-senting not far off a million workers had been established. The Polish workers' councils have received much less attention in the literature than the Yugoslavian experience, or than the brief episode in Czechoslovakia. I shall argue in the next chapter, however, that the Polish case is equally instructive in illuminating generic aspects of the position of workers in state socialist society.

5. THE GROWTH OF THE INTELLIGENTSIA

With the exception of Czechoslovakia, and to some extent the GDR and Soviet Russia, the state socialist societies have undergone a process of accelerated industrial development at a much later time in history than the capitalist societies—even including relative 'newcomers' such as Japan. Hence the rapid creation of 'technical cadres', able to supervise the introduction of advanced industrial technique into previously 'underdeveloped' societies, has been a major aim of the state socialist governments; the formation of a 'technically trained popular elite' was all the more pressing in Eastern Europe since several of these countries had been heavily drained of the relevant categories of personnel as a result of the war. It was partly in response to this need that schemes for the on-job training of skilled workers were established. But these were accompanied by a rapid expansion of technical and university education—supplemented by the practice of sending students to complete their technical education in the Soviet Union.

The term 'intelligentsia' has been employed in varying ways. But the most useful mode of applying the term, within the context of the state socialist societies, is to refer very broadly to all those individuals who have received some form of specialised higher or technical education which has allowed them to secure access to professional or managerial occupations. According to orthodox Soviet Marxism, the position of the intelligentsia in state socialist society is held to differ quite decisively from that of comparable workers in the capitalist order. In the latter, the place of the intelligentsia in the class structure is affected by mutually opposed influences: as propertyless employees, the intelligentsia, in common with lower white-collar workers and manual labourers, is separated from the property-owning ruling class; but in so far as the members of this grouping play a major role in the very coordination and direction of that rule, and affiliate themselves with the ruling class rather than the proletariat, they may be regarded as an adjunct of that class. The 'new intelligentsia' is distinctively different, both because its previous role as hand-maiden to the bourgeoisie is necessarily dissolved with the abolition of private property, and because it receives a large infusion of individuals drawn from a background of manual labour.

There can be little dispute as to the facts of the 'proletarian origins' of a considerable proportion of the intelligentsia in the state socialist societies. Comparison of the social origins of students in higher education between state socialist and capitalist societies provides some striking contrasts, especially if the situation in the former is compared to that pertaining in the Western European countries. In Zagorski's study of Poland, for instance, it is shown (1969–70) that well over half of those in higher education are from manual or peasant backgrounds; a rather higher ratio than this is reported in an earlier Hungarian study; and investigation in the Soviet Union showed that about 50 per cent of students in higher education were from manual or peasant origins.[19] Similar results appear if the class background of members of the intelligentsia is examined directly. Milić's survey in Yugoslavia (1960) indicates that, of those in managerial positions, over 60 per cent were from manual or peasant origins; while the proportion from similar backgrounds in professional occupations is lower than this, it still reaches nearly 50 per cent.[20] Such findings, of course, stand in quite sharp contrast to comparable mobility studies in the capitalist societies—although, because we have little information on downward mobility, no precise assessments can be made here.

However, certain qualifications have to to be made in interpreting the significance of this contrast. In the first place, the level of 'proletarianisation' of the intelligentsia is less marked if distinctions are made within the general rubric of 'higher education'. This appears quite clearly, for example, in the research in the Soviet Union mentioned above. The figure indicating that about half of those in higher education derive from 'proletarian' origins becomes rather less impressive when it is shown that students from such a background are disproportionately clustered in the technical and vocational institutions rather than those of university level. Secondly, notwithstanding the relatively high proportion of members of the intelligentsia who are drawn from manual and peasant backgrounds, it still normally remains the case that a man from a white-collar background stands a considerably higher chance of entry to the ranks of the intelligentsia than one from humbler origins.[21] Finally, and potentially at least, most important of all, it appears to be very generally true that the ratio of 'proletarianisation' is declining. There are obvious reasons why such a trend might be expected to occur. The sort of circumstances which originally fostered the mobility of large numbers of individuals from the lower levels of the class structure were to some degree historically specific, involving as they did the existence of many posts whose former incumbents had for one reason or another been removed from the scene, and the hothouse creation, bolstered by a still fresh ideological vigour, of a 'new intelligentsia'.

CLASS AND PARTY IN STATE SOCIALIST SOCIETY

1. THE CONCEPTION OF THE 'NEW CLASS'

It is not a novel conjecture that the advent of a type of society founded upon the socialisation of the means of production would generate a new ruling class, a class perhaps even more firmly established in its position than those which have preceded it in history. Such a view was expressed at the turn of the century, by Machajski and others, many years before any society of this kind actually came into being. In more recent times, however, the theory of the 'new class' has come to be associated particularly with the analysis of the contemporary state socialist societies set out by Milovan Djilas. In the words of the latter, 'the Communist states have seen, in the final analysis, the origin of a new form of ownership or of a new ruling and exploiting class . . . the Communist revolution, conducted in the name of doing away with classes, has resulted in the most complete authority of any single new class'.

The view is derived in part from a standpoint resting upon the sort of distinction made by Dahrendorf between the 'narrow' and 'broad' senses of property. The transition to state socialism has abolished legal titles to private property in the means of production, but control of property still remains in the hands of a minority grouping. This new class is composed of those 'who have special privileges and economic preference because of the administrative monopoly they hold', and its position derives from the dominant role played by the Communist Party in political and economic life. It is a 'bureaucratic class', created out of the monopoly of power exercised by the Party, but increasingly undermines the role of the Party itself: 'The once live, compact Party, full of initiative, is disappearing to become transformed into the traditional oligarchy of the new class, irresistibly drawing into its ranks those who aspire to join the new class and repressing those who have any ideals.'[1] The 'new class' is in an important sense a 'political class', because its ownership privileges stem directly from the fusion of the spheres of the political and the economic characteristic of state socialist— as opposed to capitalist—society. In capitalism, Djilas points out, politicians may use their government posts in order to secure personal financial rewards; but in state socialism, access to political positions yields control of the means of the distribution of economic advantages as a whole. Both the tremendous power wielded by the new class, and the economic rewards which its members appropriate to themselves, are contingent upon this fact.

As several recent authors have stressed,[2] there is some factual basis for Djilas' view. Although much of the Communist Party leadership in the pre-revolutionary period in the state socialist societies was drawn from the ranks of professionals and intellectuals, the mass of the Party membership was composed mainly of manual workers and non-independent peasantry. But in subsequent years the proportion of such workers in the Party has everywhere declined: and this decline far outstrips that which might be predicted on a purely statistical basis as a result of the sheer growth of the relative size of the white-collar sector in general. Moreover, the members of the intelligentsia tend more and more to dominate the upper echelons of the Party leadership, and are disproportionately represented among Party activists. The character of the alteration in general Party membership can be documented by fairly recent studies carried out in several of the state socialist societies. Thus in the Soviet Union, in 1959, industrial manual workers made up some 48 per cent of the membership of the CPSU, and collective farm peasantry a further 31 per cent; non-manual workers comprised only 20 per cent of the total. By 1968, however, the proportion of manual worker members had declined to 39 per cent, and that of collective farm peasantry to 16 per cent, while the ratio of white-collar workers had more than doubled, rising to over 45 per cent of the total membership. The intelligentsia are particularly prominent within the last category; examined in terms of occupational categories, data shows that there is a direct relationship between occupational level and Party membership—a large majority of those at the higher levels are Party members, but rates of membership tail off sharply towards the lower levels. Similar trends have been shown in surveys in Poland, Czechoslovakia and Yugoslavia. In Poland, for instance, a study in 1961 showed that those having experienced higher education were three times as likely as others to be PUWP members, and were ten times as likely to be prominent among Party activists. More recent figures on the social background of Communist Party members in the state socialist countries show that what are referred to as 'civil servants and intelligentsia' comprise at the lowest (in Rumania) 23 per cent of total Party membership, and at the highest (in Yugoslavia) not far off 70 per cent.[3]

But various objections can be levelled against Djilas' ideas. In the first place, if there is a 'new class' which has become the ruling class in the state socialist societies, its composition would seem to be different to that indicated by Djilas. According to his interpretation, the core of the 'new class' is made up of those who occupy political-bureaucratic positions in the Party apparatus—that is to say, of full-time Party officials. But if there is any important area of incipient class structuration in state socialism, it concerns the division between the intelligentsia and other groupings in the population. In this sense it would not be apt to say, as Djilas does, that the Party itself tends to decline in importance as the 'new class' becomes a 'bureaucratic class'; rather the reverse is the case: the basis of the formation of the 'new class' would appear to be the penetration and domination of the Party by those with higher education, who increasingly oust the older 'Party men'. Moreover, as many critics have observed, there is a fundamental difference between control over collective property, such as is held by Party officials in state socialist society, and the rights of disposal enjoyed by the owner of private property in the capitalist societies. The former does not allow, as the second does, the direct transmission of economic advantages across the generations. If there is a high degree of closure in the mediate structuration of the 'new class', it must operate via the 'inheritance' of educational advantages.

Djilas himself holds that the pattern of recruitment to the 'new class' is quite different to that of the upper class in capitalist society: 'The social origin of the new class lies in the proletariat just as the aristocracy arose in a peasant society, and the bourgeoisie in a commercial and artisan's society . . . it cannot ever lose its connection with the proletariat.'[4] Although, as I have pointed out previously, it seems to be the case that the level of 'proletarianisation' of higher white-collar workers is declining, this still constitutes one of the most significant contrasts with the situation in the capitalist societies. There is some basis for supposing that this decline is unlikely to reach proportions which would create a level of mediate structuration comparable to that characteristic of the upper class in most capitalist societies. In the latter, a relatively high level of structuration is maintained in substantial degree by the advantages conferred by the ownership of private wealth—this either facilitates the 'direct entry' of sons of upper-class fathers into the higher-order occupations (most obvious in the type-case of where a son is made a director in his father's business) or helps to gain access to the educational advantages which can lead to a similar end-result (most clearly the case where there is a developed system of private schools and universities). In the state socialist societies, these phenomena are largely absent. What is likely to become of increasing importance is the operation of the 'vicious circle' of economic and educational underprivilege which affects the lower levels of the class structure in the capitalist societies. But, given the relative lack of class structuration on the basis of a division between manual and non-manual labour, this will probably assume a different form in state socialism. Individuals from skilled manual backgrounds are likely to do well in terms of intergenerational mobility into the intelligentsia; those most handicapped will be of peasant or semi- and unskilled manual origins. It follows, therefore, that we may expect to find, on a long-term basis, higher rates of fairly 'long-range' mobility in state socialist society. This is not really compatible, as Djilas seems to hold, with a high level of class structuration in the upper echelons of the society. Given the other respects in which his view may be questioned, it is reasonable to conclude that the thesis of the 'new class' is over-stated. While there are undeniably conditions promoting incipient class structuration at the upper levels of the state socialist societies, these are counteracted by the factors which set off the latter from the capitalist order.

2. ELITE FORMATIONS AND THE MEDIATION OF CONTROL

What holds for positions in the intelligentsia in general holds for elite positions in particular. That is to say, it is quite clear that the state socialist societies manifest a much more 'open' system of elite mobility than that which characterises the capitalist societies as a whole. Thus the ten members of the Soviet Presidium in 1957, who were at the same time Central Committee Secretaries, all originated from peasant or manual backgrounds. Of the members of the Central Committee elected in 1961, over 85 per cent came from such backgrounds. Information about the origins of those in elite positions in other spheres in the Soviet Union is difficult to come by; however, it appears to be the case that, while access to these positions is typically much more 'open' than in most of the capitalist societies, they are less dominated by those from peasant or blue-collar backgrounds than are posts in the political elite. This seems to be particularly true of the economic elite: among Soviet military leaders, the proportion deriving from 'proletarian' backgrounds is only slightly below that characterising the political leadership.[5] One of the few comprehensive studies of the backgrounds of elite groupings in a state socialist society is to be found in a recent investigation of so-called opinion-makers in Yugoslavia. The investigation included 'opinion-makers' in various spheres in Yugoslavian society: political and economic leaders as well as those prominent in scientific, artistic and literary fields. The results showed a generally similar pattern to that characteristic of the Soviet Union, save that a rather higher proportion of members of the economic elite was drawn from peasant or manual backgrounds than in the case of the political elite (71 per cent as compared to 68 per cent). In the other groupings, by contrast, a majority of individuals came from non-manual backgrounds.[6]

As in other aspects of state socialist society, it is possible that these characteristics are relatively transitory, deriving mainly from the short-term changes introduced by the turnover in elite personnel with the assumption of power by the Communist Party. The apparent increasing 'takeover' of the Party by those in non-manual occupations, it might be presumed, will eventuate in the replacement of the 'first generation' by a new generation of individuals from white-collar backgrounds. But although it seems probable that the relatively open character of elite mobility will to some degree decline in the future, there is reason to believe that access to positions in the political elite will remain less restricted in character than is typically the case in the capitalist societies. While those in non-manual occupations, and more specifically the intelligentsia, may come to dominate Communist Party *membership* as a whole, the situation with the higher administrative posts within the Party itself is somewhat distinct from this. As Brzezinski and Huntington point out with regard to the Soviet Union, there is probably some considerable amount of 'selection out' by the sons of the white-collar intelligentsia in recruitment to an *apparatchik* career. The career process required to reach an elevated political position demands the sort of personal and ideological commitment which is likely to be less developed among those from higher-level backgrounds; the ideological orientation of the existing Party leadership, together with the patterns which have been established to date, are likely to continue to make a full-time Party career an attractive and a realistic proposition for ambitious individuals from peasant or manual backgrounds.[7]

In terms of the classification of elite formations which I developed earlier, elite groupings in the state socialist societies approximate to the type which I have characterised as a 'solidary elite'. Whatever changes may occur in the future, elites in state socialism have, up to the present, been recruited, for the most part, from individuals drawn from a broad spectrum of social backgrounds; but they have also been closely unified by the general influence of Soviet Marxist ideology. Each of these aspects of elite formation is to be traced largely to the role of the Communist Party, which is dominant in the hierarchy of elites in all of the state socialist societies. There can be little dispute that the effective power wielded by the Party elite considerably outstrips that held by the political leadership in any of the capitalist societies—a proposition which applies both to the 'issue-strength' and the degree of 'consolidation' of that power. In relation to the scheme which I have outlined in Chapter 7, it is evident that the system of domination characteristic of the state socialist societies tends towards the 'power elite' type. It is often emphasised that the power of the Communist Party in the state socialist societies rests upon a tight grip of the means of the production and dissemination of ideas. This is correct enough. But it must also be stressed that the role of the Party in the mediation of control depends upon its central place within a system of closely knit elite integration: that is to say, its monopoly, through the holding of posts in various arms of the administrative apparatus, of the key positions in various institutional spheres.

Partly in the light of the economic reforms introduced fairly recently in most of the state socialist societies, it has been suggested by some writers that this position of monopoly will increasingly come under pressure. According to this view, the intelligentsia—or, more accurately, the scientific and technical intelligentsia—are coming to form the leading source of opposition to the Party apparatus, and will eventually displace the *apparatchiki* as they have existed hitherto.[8] Those with specialised education will not share the same ideological outlook as the Party bureaucrats; and they will undermine the power of the latter because, in any highly industrialised society, those with technical expertise gain more and more power. This theory obviously has close links to general theories of 'technocracy', criticised more fully below: as such, it can be attacked upon very broad grounds, as I shall indicate subsequently (pp. 255–64). As regards the state socialist countries, the view has normally been advanced mainly with reference to the Soviet Union, and in that society there appear to be certain facts which support it. Thus there has been a discernible tendency recently for Soviet government officials to be drawn from technically trained personnel. The Soviet political leaders who have followed Khrushchev —Brezhnev, Podgorny and Kosygin—all graduated from technical institutes.[9] But it may be doubted that this constitutes evidence of the rise of a new technocratic elite within the government apparatus. The theory—as Parry expresses it—of 'the new class divided' presupposes that the technocrats are a distinctive grouping within the elite, separable from the old-style Party functionaries. However, it does not really seem to be the case that the 'technocrats' constitute such a grouping, in terms either of education or outlook. On the contrary, the entry of those with a technical education into higher positions, at least within the political sphere, has been largely controlled by the Party apparatus itself. The use of Party schools as a filter for qualification to leading positions serves to underline the split between elite recruitment to the political and other elites mentioned previously. Those who become the higher Party officials, even if they have received a specialised technical education, tend to undergo a transformation in outlook and attitudes in the course of pursuing a successful bureaucratic career.

Thus, while it may be argued that there is an important emergent source of schism among elites in the state socialist societies, this is not to be understood as simply involving a confrontation of Party officials versus 'technocrats', or as necessarily foreshadowing the demise of the old-style *apparatchik*—a sort of 'end of ideology' thesis in miniature. If there is a generic source of opposition and conflict within elites, it is one which to some degree cross-cuts the influence of technical education as such, and which centres upon a division between the higher political administration, which seeks to maintain a strongly centralised control over economic life, and the pressure towards the decentralisation of decision-making in the economic sphere.[10]

3. SOURCES OF TENSION IN STATE SOCIALIST SOCIETY

State socialism is founded upon the attempt to impose political directives upon economic activity—political directives which, in all of the Eastern European societies, were originally modelled in a very direct way upon the pre-existing mode of economic organisation prevailing in the Soviet Union. This has in the past, *in a certain sense* at least, made the state socialist societies more homogeneous among themselves than is the case among the capitalist societies. That is to say, the overall similarity in the structure of the Communist Party, in its mode of domination of the polity and economy, and the economic policies followed in the initial period after the war, served to produce an apparent homogeneity in socio-economic structure between the various societies. Thus Seton-Watson wrote in 1955: 'I am convinced that in all the sovietised countries the trend of government is identical, and that the differences are being rapidly removed. It is similarly.between the regimes, and the close imitation by all of the past history of the Soviet Union, which needs to be stressed.'[11] It is the very imposition of a 'monolithic' type of politico-economic system upon differing societies which has created one of the major sources of internal strain within them. Seton-Watson's statement could not be made with the same force today but, with the partial exception of Yugoslavia, the state socialist societies continue to manifest a strong general similarity in 'superstructure'.

It is particularly in the more industrialised Eastern European countries that this is in itself one of the primary sources of tension. But we may also distinguish two other variable factors (or sets of factors) which influence the internal social structure of the state socialist societies, directly related to the two aspects of 'decentralisation' mentioned in the previous chapter. One is the nature of the control exerted by the polity over the direction of economic life; the other is the mediation of control at the lower levels of the economic enterprise. While there are elements involved in each of these which affect all of the state socialist societies, their operation is conditioned in substantial degree by the *variation in the 'rapport' between the imposed superstructure, deriving from the first post-revolutionary phase, and the existing infrastructure*. Most of the discussions which have examined the changes which are presumptively occurring in state socialism have looked to the Soviet Union for their source of data. But, if the Soviet Union provided the (consciously followed) 'type case' of the early development of state socialist society, it is arguable that the situation is now quite different. For there are several fairly evident ways in which the East European societies differ from the Soviet Union, as well as among themselves. In the Soviet Union, the Communist Party came into power as a result of a process of internal revolutionary change; with the exception of Yugoslavia—which, significantly, deviated from the 'imposed pattern' at an early stage—the 'socialist revolutions' occurring in the other countries were either facilitated or directly brought about by the use of Soviet military power. Thus there is not only an incipient nationalism which threatens any attempt to foster 'one socialism' in the Eastern European countries, but it is very generally true that the legitimacy of the governmental apparatus is less strongly founded than in the Soviet Union. In at least some of the societies of Eastern Europe moreover (again, most notably in Czechoslovakia), there was a more developed and a more firmly entrenched white-collar middle class than existed in Russia before 1917. Such a grouping offers a potential source of counter-revolution, and may resist the fragmentation into 'lower white-collar personnel' on the one side and 'intelligentsia' on the other, which tends to be the result of the maturation of the state socialist societies. Finally, the process of the 'socialisation of the means of production' has, for the most part, proceeded less far in the Eastern European societies than in the Soviet Union, especially in agriculture, and this may also make for the persistence of interests divergent from those of the centralised government.

It has become a conventional assertion today that both the Soviet Union and the Eastern European societies are undergoing a major process of transition, which is producing, or will produce, quite profound changes in their social organisation.[12] The most common view is that which holds that the system of political power character-istic of state socialism, involving the 'monolithic' domination of the Communist Party, must cede place to a more 'pluralistic' order. This is not necessarily based upon a conception of the 'con-vergence' of industrial societies, although frequently it is. The under-lying theme of this sort of view is easily stated: that, while the auto-cratic role played by the Communist Party may be important, and even necessary, during the rapid transformation of an agrarian into an industrialised society, once this goal has been achieved the running of a complex, modern economy demands a diversification of centres of control. This type of standpoint is often closely linked to the idea that the 'technocrats', disposed towards pragmatic social and economic engineering rather than towards the ideological con-siderations which guide Party officials, are emerging as the new elite.[13]

In spite of the widespread acceptance which it has achieved, the thesis is not a convincing one. Each of the premises upon which it rests is questionable: that the continued domination of the Commun-ist Party in political and economic life is 'functionally incompatible' with the organisation of an advanced society or economy; and that, given the existence of such an 'incompatibility', state socialism will necessarily move in the direction of pluralism (or experience revolutionary outbreaks which will forcibly transform society 'from below'). The first premise can be countered by the assertion of its—equally plausible—opposite: that the complex character of an advanced society demands a *centralisation* of directive agencies, in order to coordinate and integrate the complicated workings of the modern social and economic order. In fact, such an opposition of views oversimplifies the matter at issue and, as I shall argue below, there are certain respects in which these apparently contrary notions each has an element of validity. But even if the first premise were acceptable, which as it stands it is not, the second would not follow in the sort of crude manner in which it is normally advocated. In most of these accounts, the idea of 'functional incompatibility' remains unexamined. When the concept is scrutinised more closely, as it is applied in this particular context, it turns out to concern one or more of the following propositions: that the existing *apparat* lacks the individuals who possess the specialised knowledge necessary to administer a modern economy (i.e., the 'technocracy' thesis again); that economic life cannot be (efficiently) directed by a basically *political* organisation, but must be controlled by managers rather than politicians, however technically competent the latter may be; that the broad ideological conceptions of Marxism and of the intro- duction of a classless order actually or nominally adhered to by state socialist governments have no place in a modern industrial economy; that the dominant position of the Communist Party derives from the transient, relatively fluid social conditions which prevailed when the Party first came to power, and that its influence must therefore decline with the 'routinisation' which occurs in the post-revolution- ary society; and finally, as a general underlying assumption, that the existence of one or several of these circumstances necessarily leads to the occurrence of changes in the pre-existing system.

The latter proposition may be accepted, with the rider that in no case is the response to 'functional incompatibility' an automatic one, as is often implied. A mode of social and economic organisation which breeds definite tensions does not on that account necessarily undergo change, and even if such change does take place, the direc- tion which it follows is not inevitably towards 'adaptation', in any simple sense: if some of the propositions stated above are accurate, the response of the Party organisations, or the state socialist govern- ments more generally, might be to retrench the position of the Party more strongly than is the case at present, and it is not at all obvious that such a path of action is foredoomed to ultimate failure.[14] It is naïve to assume, for example, that if it is true that a highly centralised economy creates productive 'inefficiency' in certain major areas of economic activity, this leads directly to pressure for some sort of fundamental modification of economic life. Such pressure must involve the active and effective opposition of par- ticular groupings to the current state of affairs, and this in turn depends upon the 'visibility' of the phenomena in question; it can be said that one of the major flaws in much of the literature debating contemporary trends in the development of the state socialist

societies is that it involves not merely a questionable 'social functionalism', but a completely illegitimate 'economic functionalism'.

Of the propositions distinguished above, the second and the fourth
are the most plausible. The first one, the modified version of the
technocratic thesis, stands up to close examination no better than
other aspects of this type of viewpoint. It is debatable how far those
responsible for taking the most general decisions affecting political
and economic life need to possess specialised technical competence,
as opposed to being able to seek the advice and utilise the expertise
of those who do have this competence. Indeed, such a situation
is practically unavoidable, since the range of decisions which must
be taken is very wide, and no individual or small group of individuals could master the enormous body of potentially relevant
specialised knowledge—even within a modern large-scale corporation, let alone within the economy or polity as a whole. While there
is likely to be a trend towards the rise of technically 'informed'
men within Party elites—such as already referred to in the Soviet
Union—this is altogether different from the 'rule of experts' predicted by many commentators, and need not bring in its train any
basic alteration in the dominant position of the Party, for reasons
which have previously been mentioned.[15] The third proposition,
asserting the 'functional incompatibility' of the Marxian theory of
classlessness with an advanced industrial order, is equally suspect.
Marxism in the state socialist societies is no longer simply an intellectual theory of society, but an ideological canopy which legitimates
the leading role of the Communist Party; as an ideology, its degree
of persuasiveness cannot be directly reduced to the level of 'scientific'
validity which might be claimed for it by the Western observer.
Whether or not a classless order, such as anticipated by Marx,
comes into being in the state socialist countries carries no definite
consequences for the future of orthodox Soviet Marxism as an under-
pinning political ideology; after all, Christianity survived for many
hundreds of years in societies having very pronounced inequalities
of wealth, notwithstanding its strong emphasis against avarice
and pride in possessions (although perhaps not too much should
be made of this example!).

The remaining two assertions, concerning the overall relationship
between polity and economy, and the 'time-bound' character of
the domination of the Communist Party, are more important,
and each of these can usefully be connected to the problem of
'centralisation' versus 'devolution' in polity and economy. I have
at several points previously referred to factors involved in the 'routinisation' of the state socialist societies, and undoubtedly there are

processes at work here which are significantly modifying the character of the Party structures in the different countries as they seek to
cope with the issues posed to an elite in power, as compared to the
very different demands which face a subordinate organisation
seeking to attain power. But the processes of change which are
taking place are less likely to diminish the monopoly of the Communist Party over political and economic life as a whole than to open
up new sources of schism within it. This is most typically not a schism
between 'bureaucrats' and 'technocrats', but one between two
types of 'Party men'—namely activist Party *members*, increasingly
drawn, as we have seen, from the intelligentsia, and the Party elite,
who are full-time officials. The implications of this (which does not
exclude the existence, of course, of struggles between factions *within*
the elite deriving from the 'succession problem', etc.) can be further
developed in relation to tensions stemming from the attempt to
subject economic life to the direction of the polity: and in analysing
these we may return to some of the ideas I have sought to elaborate
in the discussion of the capitalist countries.

I have noted earlier that there are two aspects of the 'decentralisation' of economic control resulting from the new economic policies
adopted in most of the state socialist countries from the late 1950s
onwards (or, more accurately, as a potential result of these reforms,
since many of the latter have been more widely discussed than they
have actually been implemented). Each aspect has quite direct
parallels in the capitalist societies, but the nature of the elements
involved is in other respects quite different in the two forms of
advanced society. One concerns the mediation of control at the upper
levels of economic organisation, the other the mediation of control
at the lower levels. In the socialist societies there are connections
between these two levels which are largely absent in capitalism.
In the capitalist countries, the debate over the problem of 'ownership
and control' has been for the most part carried on separately from
that regarding the character and future of the contemporary labour
movement, as if these were two largely distinct sets of issues. To a
substantial degree, this in fact mirrors reality. The mechanisms
facilitating economism tend to 'block off' the labour movement
from an orientation to control. In the state socialist societies,
however, the situation is different. Issues affecting the mediation of
control at both levels of the enterprise tend to be closely connected,
such that the modification of economic organisation at either level
has immediate consequences for the other. Moreover, the separation
of economy and polity, characteristic of capitalist society, limits
the repercussions which any tensions or changes in the economic

structure create in the political system, and vice versa; although such repercussions nearly always make themselves felt, they are very often indirect and diffuse. In capitalism, the existence of private property legitimates the independent operation of the enterprise.[16] This principle is not affected by the fragmentation of share ownership in the joint-stock company, or by any of the other phenomena connected with managerialism. In state socialist society, on the other hand, economic conflict necessarily has directly political implications.

Now the pressure towards according more independence of control at the level of the enterprise, as part of the general movement towards economic decentralisation in the late 1950s, originated in the perception of economists and other intellectuals that the tightly structured command economy, inherited from the early development of the Soviet Union, led to various sorts of economic waste and inefficiency. It was thus largely 'technical' considerations which prompted 'Libermanism' and which fostered its expanding influence. In those societies in which such reforms were introduced, they were mostly sanctioned by the Party leadership in 'technocratic' terms, as economic techniques having little or no intrinsic ideological significance. This is, of course, one of the factors which has prompted so many observers to speak of the rise of a new technocratic grouping challenging the dominance of the Communist Party. But it is actually in the interest of the *apparat* to foster such a legitimation of an extension of the independence of managerial control of economic life, because it is the only one which is really compatible with the present level of 'accountability' to the Party. The main point I wish to argue here, however, is that *there is a fatal antinomy between the two aspects of decentralisation which I have distinguished previously* (devolution of economic control in the hands of managers, and increased responsiveness to price mechanisms), *and that this is to be explained in terms of the lack of 'blocking off' in the mediation of control at the upper and the lower levels of the enterprise.*

The introduction of greater managerial independence, as justified in 'technocratic' terms, and involving an orientation to profits, is everywhere likely to meet strong resistance from the general body of workers in the enterprise. This is so precisely because there is no possibility of an orientation towards economism on the part of manual or lower non-manual workers in the state socialist societies. There is probably only one form of justification of independence of managerial control which is likely to be acceptable to the workers within the organisation: that is, *if this is linked to some form of workers' self-management.* This is why the transient emergence of the Polish workers' councils is particularly interesting, as giving evidence of this tendency, and as forming a basis for comparison with the Yugoslavian experience. (Very recent Polish history offers new sources of material here: thus, for example, the demands of the Szçzecin dockworkers, presented to the government in December 1970, called for the dismissal of the existing trade union leadership, and the creation of autonomous workers' councils.) For, in the majority of state socialist societies, any pressure towards the effective introduction of workers' self-management is likely to be strongly resisted by the central Party bureaucracy, since this offers much more of a potential threat to the existing system than that posed by 'technocratic' elements. In Yugoslavia, the introduction of the workers' councils was directly encouraged by the central government after the break with the Soviet Union, as a means of securing mass support for the new economic and political policies introduced. The result has been the creation of a viable form of 'market socialism'. The Yugoslavian experience demonstrates that 'dual devolution'—a fair degree of managerial independence, together with workers' councils (even if the reality deviates somewhat from the stated ideals)—is not impossible to reconcile with the maintenance of the overall domination of the Communist Party. But it is clear enough that such a system could not now be introduced in the other state socialist countries without a substantial reorganisation of the existing Party structures—a reorganisation which took place at an earlier, and more fluid, phase of development in Yugoslavia. Hence it may be argued that there is something of a paradoxical situation pertaining in the majority of state socialist societies. A 'technocratic' legitimation of decentralisation at the level of enterprise management, which is likely to be most amenable to the continuance of the existing dominance of the Party in political and economic life, will tend to stimulate a resurgence of demands for the extension of workers' management—and thus to produce a 'counter-communism', based upon ideas of localised cooperatives and genuine worker participation in the exercise of authority in industry. This is why it is not the 'technocrats', but the activist Party members, who are likely to be a potent source of opposition to the existing governmental structure of power: this grouping offers a source of leadership which, while committed to communism, may question the fixity of orthodox Marxism. The occurrence of serious confrontations between such dissident groupings and the higher echelons of the Party organisation is probably least likely to take place in the Soviet Union itself. This is not because the same generic strains do not make themselves felt, of course, but because of the

factors already alluded to: in most of the Eastern European societies
the dominance of the *apparat* is less strongly established than in the
Soviet Union. The level of industrialisation prior to the transition
to state socialism is a major element, although not the only one,
affecting this.[17]

4. INDUSTRIALISM AND SOCIAL CHANGE: A SUMMARY

State socialism, as I have emphasised earlier, does not represent
the transcendence of capitalism, but an alternative mode of promoting industrialisation or achieving high rates of economic growth.
But, as such, it is founded upon a quite distinct institutional mediation of power from that characteristic of capitalist society. In capitalism, the separation of economy and polity, whereby major
sectors of economic life are left open to the movement of market
mechanisms, is the condition of the existence of classes. In state
socialist society, on the other hand, the economy has been made
subordinate to the directive control of the political administration,
via the abolition of private property, and this has undoubtedly
created very basic differences as compared to capitalism.

State socialist society lacks a distinctive form of upper class such
as characterises the capitalist order. In this respect, it may be con-
cluded that Djilas' term, the 'new class', is not an appropriate mode
of designating the place of the Party in this type of society, or of
the system of privilege which has become built up around it. The
power exercised by the higher Party officials considerably outstrips
that wielded by political elites in the capitalist societies; and Party
positions may be, as Djilas emphasises, means for the attainment of a
distinctively high level of economic reward. But to admit the factual
validity of these statements is not to demonstrate the emergence of a
class formation comparable to that typical of capitalist society. Nor
can such a case be plausibly made out for the intelligentsia. The
abolition of private property limits the emergence of class structuration 'at the top' in state socialist society primarily because it limits
the degree to which the transmission of advantages can be monopolised across the generations. Similarly, the division between manual
and non-manual labour does not have the same class significance in
state socialist society as in capitalism, either in terms of the sheer
differentiation of economic rewards, or in terms of class structuration.

But this is not in any sense compatible with the 'withering away'
of the state, or with the orthodox view of state socialist governments
that the present position is one which is merely a transitional stage

in the movement towards the eventual elimination of 'the exploitation of man by man' in the higher stage of communist society. On the contrary, the relatively low level of class structuration in the state socialist societies has been bought at a considerable cost to human liberties, and is dependent upon a high degree of centralised political control over economic life. There is a genuine dilemma here, concealed by Marx's assumption of some sort of inevitable linkage between 'classlessness' and the supersession of the state. For the elimination of the 'class principle' depends upon the subjection of market forces to political direction; but this consolidates rather than reduces the power of the state. Some indication of the probable results of the decentralisation of power, allowing more scope for independently formed economic policies at the level of the enterprise, is provided by the 'market socialism' of Yugoslavia, where the introduction of the new economic system seems to have brought about an expansion in differentials in market capacity since the 1950s, and may be fostering a hardening of class structuration.[18]

In any case, it is unlikely that any other Eastern European country will lean so far as Yugoslavia in the direction of 'market socialism'. The most probable course of development of the state socialist societies, in the near future at least, will be one veering from the relaxation of political controls over the economic order back to the reimposition of a tight hierarchy of political command. If this conclusion is correct, it means that the situation in the advanced societies is substantially different from that suggested by either of the versions of the idea of 'convergence' which held sway until a few years ago. The Soviet Marxist view of this, of course, maintains the position that state socialism represents the 'future' of capitalism, a supersession of the capitalist system through which, via a process of revolution or evolution, the capitalist societies themselves must sooner or later pass. The Western version, as stated by authors such as Sorokin, Rostow and Kerr, looks primarily to an updated interpretation of the theory of 'industrial society'.[19] As set out by such authors, the idea has been presented in various forms. Probably the most commonly stated view is that which assumes, explicitly or otherwise, that the state socialist societies will move in a direction such that their overall social and economic organisation will come more and more to resemble that of the capitalist countries (which usually means, effectively, the United States). The rather more sophisticated version recognises a mutual coming-together of the two types of advanced society, as the one reintroduces some degree of market autonomy and the other is forced to adopt centralised planning. Each of these interpretations, however, is essentially based upon a naïve exposition of industrialism as a synthesising force which promotes homogeneity between all societies which undergo it. In this respect, curiously, such authors take a leaf out of Marx's own book, and continue the nineteenth-century view of the state as a mere adjunct to, and as determined by, the nature of economic organisation. The very mode of development of the state socialist societies demonstrates the inadequacy of such a standpoint. Thus in the Soviet Union—as, under a different set of circumstances, in Germany and Japan—political power was used to channel and direct the industrialisation process, and there is little ground for the assertion (borrowed from Saint-Simon) that the advent of an industrial society necessarily brings about a reversal of this relationship. The case of Czechoslovakia is a peculiarly apposite illustration of this point, since in this example an already fairly highly industrialised society has been substantially transformed by the imposition of a new system of political power—although the post-war history of this country at the same time indicates some of the *limits* of the political direction of social and economic life.

14

CLASSES IN CONTEMPORARY SOCIETY

1. CRITIQUE OF TECHNOCRATIC THEORIES

The idea of the (coming) obsolescence of property is one which pervades nineteenth-century social theory. Thus we find this as a leading theme in the works of Saint-Simon; and again in those of Marx, in the vision of the revolutionary transformation of capitalism. Aspects of the Saint-Simonian doctrine later re-emerge in Durkheim's writings: for Durkheim, the influence of property is eliminated by the abolition of inheritance—just as the transmission of the advantages conferred by aristocratic blood-right has been abolished, so will the transmission of the advantages given by the possession of property. In its most up-to-date rendition, however, the conception of the obsolescence of property is expressed in a whole cluster of technocratic theories of society.

We may refer to contemporary technocratic theories generically as theories of 'post-industrial society' (a term apparently coined by Bell, but also used by Touraine), although a variety of other terms have been employed to refer to much the same thing: 'technetronic' society (Brzezinski), 'post-modern society' (Etzioni), 'post-cultural society' (Steiner) and even 'post-civilised' society (Boulding)—among others. Although these differ among one another in several ways, they share certain basic characteristics, and we may discuss the ideas of Bell and Touraine as largely representative of what the majority of such authors have to say.

Like other proponents of the conception of 'post-industrial society', Daniel Bell is acutely conscious that most aspects of the notion can be traced back to the early years of the nineteenth century.[1] This may be construed as indicating that the theory has a reputable ancestry; but it is also something of an embarrassment, for the point of the idea of post-industrial society is to attempt to encompass some of the most 'modern' features of the advanced societies. According to Bell—as the phrase 'post-industrial society' suggests—the contemporary world stands on the verge of a fundamental social and economic reorganisation which is relegating 'industrialism' to past history. Since the United States is the most developed country in terms of technique, it follows that this reorganisation has progressed farthest there. The first characteristic of post-industrial society is that manufacture, or the production of commodities, is no longer the overwhelming concern of the labour force; manufacture is increasingly displaced by service occupations. Bell uses the latter term in a much broader sense than is conventional, however, since he includes within it all forms of white-collar labour: the 'service sector' comprises 'trade, finance, insurance and real estate; personal, professional, business and repair services; and general government'.[2] The distinctive aspect of such occupations is that they require the exercise of symbolic rather than physical capacities, the possession of knowledge rather than of manual labour power. In a certain sense it would be true, Bell goes on to argue, that in post-industrial society possession of knowledge confers power in the way in which ownership of property did in the nineteenth and early twentieth centuries in industrial society. But it is more accurate to say that in post-industrial society a new *form* of knowledge comes more and more into prominence. This is 'theoretical knowledge': knowledge of an abstract and highly codified character, which can be applied to a wide range of diverse circumstances.

The specific importance of theoretical knowledge to post-industrial society resides in the fact that it allows for continual innovation and self-sustaining growth. The development of computerised systems of information-processing and social planning makes the control and direction of technical progress on a previously unparalleled scale both possible and necessary. This is a phenomenon upon which Touraine also lays particular stress. 'Post-industrial society', he asserts, could just as well be labelled the 'programmed society', since perhaps its most essential characteristic is that its course of development is governed by the systematic application of technical knowledge to predetermined social and economic ends.[3] It is for this reason, both Bell and Touraine argue, that the university, which is the main locale in which theoretical knowledge is formulated and evaluated, becomes the key institution in the newly emerging society. If the factory was the epitome of industrial society, as the main source of the production of commodities, the university (not, as Max Weber held, the office), as the source of the production of theoretical knowledge, is the central focus of the post-industrial order. This is not to say, Bell continues, that in post-industrial society the mass of the population will become 'technocrats'. The point is that the technocrats increasingly replace industrialists or business leaders as the grouping responsible for taking the policy decisions which affect the whole of society. That is, the formation of policies concerning industry and the economy devolves into the hands of technical specialists employed by the political authority. Because of the multiplying complexities of modern social and economic organisation, all forms of decision-making take on a technical character.

In Touraine's view, the 'technocrats' become the new dominant class in emergent post-industrial society. Class conflict does not vanish with the disappearance of industrial society (a view apparently different from Bell's), but its sources and its nature become significantly altered. Whereas in industrial society, class struggles centre upon the appropriation of economic returns, in post-industrial society they concern the alienative effects of subordination to technocratic decisions. While the more traditional forms of class conflict, involving the labour movement, persist, and while the ideologies associated with them may continue to some degree to inspire the new antagonisms, the working class is no longer, in Touraine's words, 'a privileged actor' on the modern scene. Economism becomes less and less relevant to the much more all-enveloping alienation from technocratic control which is the principal source of conflict in the post-industrial world. 'The stake in the struggle is no longer merely profit-making, but control of the power to make decisions, to influence, and to manipulate.'[4] This type of conflict is evidently not likely to be confined to capitalist society, since the technocratic imperatives make themselves felt in any society which is sufficiently advanced in terms of technique. Again somewhat in contrast to Bell, Touraine emphasises the importance of conflicts between the technocrats and the old dominant class; in contrast to this latter class, the technocratic grouping are often liberal (or even socialist?) in their political views, as befits a rising class just acceding to power.

Both Bell and Touraine agree that a technocrat is more than just a technician. They therefore separate their views from those of Veblen, who looked to replacing industrialists and financiers, who pursue their own private interest at the expense of that of society in general, with engineers who would rationally pursue technical goals which would benefit all. Technocracy is not just the application of technical methods to the solution of defined problems, but a pervading ethos, a world-view which subsumes aesthetics, religion and customary thought to the rationalistic mode. In Bell's words:

> In its emphasis on the logical, practical, problem-solving, instrumental, orderly, and disciplined approach to objectives, in its reliance on a calculus, on precision and measurement and a concept of a system, it is a world-view [which] . . . draws deeply from the Newtonian world-view, and the eighteenth-century writers who inherited Newton's thought indeed believe, as Hume has Cleanthes say in his *Dialogues Concerning Natural Religion*, that the author of Nature must be something of an engineer, since Nature is a machine; and they believed, further, that within a short time the rational method would make all thought amenable to its laws.[5]

Only in post-industrial society, however, does this ethos become all-inclusive. There are clear echoes here, not only of Weber's interpretation of the spread of rationalisation and bureaucracy in the modern world, but of more recent Frankfurt social philosophy. Marcuse's 'one-dimensional society' is one in which, through the encompassing control of the conduct and attitudes of the mass, the old class conflicts become, if not eliminated, at least planed out by the prosperity generated by modern technique. As Habermas seeks to document at length, the technocratic mode, centred upon technical legitimation of policy-making, is in fact 'ideological'. These authors agree that the nature of class conflict has become basically changed since the nineteenth and early twentieth centuries, and that the working class can no longer be looked to as the carrier of the hopes of a future transformation of society.[6] Although in some respects it is misleading to identify them as exponents of the theory of 'technological society', they tend to argue that the technocratic mode dominates, or is likely to dominate, in both the capitalist and the state socialist societies.[7] For these writers, however, the modern technocratic universe generates the possibility of creating a new type of social order having the characteristics which Marx held would distinguish the socialist order of the future.

Neither Bell nor Touraine take such a stance, although Touraine's position is much closer to this than the view expressed by the American author. But it obviously follows from their ideas that the main type of opposition to technocratic rule will emphasise 'participation' in decision-making, and will frequently assume a *cultural* or, as Roszak and others put it, a 'counter-cultural' form. Given the overall orientation of technocratic theories, this allows an apparently ready-made explanation of student unrest and New Left politics—and can easily lead to a condemnation of these as essentially 'irrational', since they seem to represent a protest against reason itself, or rather against the systematic application of reason in the technocratic ethos.[8] This is not, however, Touraine's view. For him, since the university in post-industrial society is the main 'productive agency' for the creation and dissemination of technical idea-systems, it follows that the antagonisms bred by the new form of society will tend to find their most acute expression there. This is not merely an unreasonable protest against the necessary conditions of modern existence; it is a genuine struggle against the propensity of post-industrial society to regard individuals as nothing more than 'means' to the achievement of technical imperatives.

No one dreams of saying that now the students are the dominated class or even that they alone are the militant avant-garde of the oppressed. But students are more than the spokesmen for unaware or inarticulate groups. They are the representatives of all those who suffer more from social integration and cultural manipulation directed by the economic structures than from economic exploitation and material misery.[9]

Technocratic theories are attractive precisely because they appear to encapsulate some of the most striking and distinctive features of the contemporary world. The burgeoning of technical innovation, the massive scale of modern social and economic planning, the expansion of higher education, on the one hand, and the spread of student protest and the attempted construction of a 'counter-culture' on the other—these are the phenomena which form the starting-point of such theories and whose influence in the advanced societies they seek to explain. And yet the very fact that technocratic theories are not new, that they date back to the early origins of industrialism in nineteenth-century Europe, should warn us to be suspicious of their claim to separate out what is novel in the emergent 'post-industrial' universe from the merely 'industrialised' era of recent past history.[10]

In the first place, any conception of 'post-industrial' society suffers from the same defects as that of 'industrial society'. The picture portrayed by the theory of post-industrial society is that the new form of social order succeeds industrial society in much the same way as the latter supposedly succeeded feudalism. But while the notion of 'industrial society', as I have indicated previously, may be validly applied if it is used in only a limited sense, from Saint-Simon onwards it has normally been used in a fashion which carries the strong implication that the predominance of 'industry' rather than 'agrarianism' in any society means that it can automatically be classified with others as a unitary type. This carries with it two further ramifications: that the course of development of a society is in some sense 'determined' by its general economic organisation, or, in the cruder versions, by its level of technological sophistication; and that consequently the most industrially 'developed' society shows to others the image of their future. The first of these three assumptions dominated most nineteenth-century social thought in the guise of the idea that the transformations which have affected the modern world can be usefully understood in terms of a twofold polarity (*Gemeinschaft/Gesellschaft*, mechanical solidarity/organic solidarity, folk society/secular society, etc.). The second assumption, also prominent, but equally misleading, represents the general perspective according to which the state is a mere epiphenomenon of society.[11] These are both perpetuated in the concept of 'post-industrial society': it compounds the inadequacies of the old dichotomies by simply adding a third type supposedly coming to supersede the second; and it continues the fallacious assumption that the level of industrial or technological development 'in the last instance' (to borrow Engels' phrase) determines other aspects of social and political organisation.[12]

It is because these assumptions are built into the notion of 'post-industrial society' that it is possible for most authors to propose that the trend towards the emergent new society is most highly advanced in the United States. This view is urged strongly by Bell, and stated even more uncompromisingly by Brzezinski, according to whom: 'Contemporary America is the world's social laboratory. . . . It is in the United States that the crucial dilemmas of our age manifest themselves most starkly . . . '[13] No one doubts that the United States is, in terms of technique, the most 'advanced' of the 'advanced societies'. No one would wish to deny that some forms of technique currently being widely employed or pioneered in America will subsequently be introduced into, or appropriated by, other industrialised countries. But this is altogether different from the proposition that the United States, in terms of broad aspects of its social and political structure, represents the prototype of a new type of society emergent in the modern world. As in the instance of the Soviet Union among the state socialist societies, a good case can be made for the view that the United States has been, is, and will continue to be, quite distinct in its socio-political organisation from most of the other capitalist societies. The sheer size of the country; the fact that, until recently, it has been an immigrant society; the possibilities of upward mobility (probably perceived rather than real, recent research indicates) which existed because of the westward expansion of the population to areas rich in material resources; the absence of a feudal past; the presence of a very large underclass—all of these factors tend to separate the development of the United States from Western European capitalist countries and from Japan. Moreover (as again has been the case, in much more rigidly defined fashion, in the relation between the Soviet Union and the Eastern European countries) in so far as the United States does constitute a model for the rest of the advanced societies, this is as much because of its political power and its economic penetration of other countries, as because of the 'internal logic' of its technological development.

These observations can be generalised. Even if we confine our attention to the development of technique, we can conclude that there is a flaw in any perspective which assumes that technological progression (or, alternatively, 'lag') can be adequately understood in the manner suggested or implied by most proponents of technocratic theories. The correct view, I wish to suggest, is what might be called a 'leap-frog' conception of technological progress. The image of the future which the technologically advanced society shows to the less developed society is often one of an *avoidable future*. This may be so because of consciously taken decisions on the part of governmental bodies or other agencies, responding to observed effects of the form of technique in question. But *even strictly within the domain of technocratic imperatives*, the 'leap-frog' effect tends frequently to occur. What happens is that the adoption of a given technological mode serves to concretise and to stabilise an existing socio-technical system within a given society or type of society; advancement beyond this then tends to occur in a society which is more 'retarded', but which, precisely because of this, is able to jump ahead of the other because it can introduce more radical technological innovation. Technologies which at one period are 'advanced' often at a later time become a brake upon further progress; this may take place in either the short or the long term.

In large part, recent technocratic theories are founded upon the idea that there is occurring a radical departure from pre-existing technique in the harnessing of *science* to production: science, or technical knowledge in general, passes from being an adjunct to the productive process to becoming itself the primary productive force. 'Industrialism' is a system for the production of goods; 'post-industrialism' is qualitatively different because the production of knowledge assumes primacy. Again, this is certainly not a novel idea, and it is questionable how far the reality itself is novel. Modern technique may be staggering in its scale, its complexity, and in the feats of conquest of time and space which it makes possible. But there is nothing which is specifically new in the application of 'theoretical knowledge' to productive technique. Indeed, as Weber stressed above all, rationality of technique (rather than 'capitalism' in the Marxian sense) is the primary factor which from the beginning has distinguished industrialism from all preceding forms of social order. If one takes a Marxian standpoint on the evolution of capitalism, one tends to overstress the degree to which industrialism can be characterised as the production of commodities (partly because of already noted difficulties with 'unproductive mental labour'; but Marx was too perceptive a thinker not to remark upon the fact that, in capitalist technology, 'science itself becomes a productive force'. In a more general sense, Marx was probably mistaken to regard tool-using and production as the basic quality of human as opposed to animal life. What more distinctively characterises human culture is that man is what Mumford calls 'a mind-making, self-mastering, and self-designing animal . . .'[14]). It is a myth that industrial man was made by the machine; from its first origins industrialism is the application of calculative rationality to the productive order. In this sense, modern technology is not 'post-industrial' at all, but is the fruition of the principle of accelerating technical growth built into industrialism as such.

However, in a more specific sense, the theory of post-industrial society is stimulated by the general decline in the proportion of the working population in manual labour in the advanced societies—and, particularly, of course, by the fact that, within the overall expansion of white-collar labour, rates of growth of professional and technical occupations have been especially high. This brings us back directly to the question of the role of property in the modern social order. The idea that 'knowledge is power' is an old one, and is subject to various well-known difficulties. The most obvious of these resides in the fact that the equation tells us little about who holds (effective) power in any given situation: it is manifestly not always, or even generally, the case that those with *specialised* knowledge hold power themselves. The 'expert', as Weber pointed out, is undoubtedly a creation of modern times; but from time immemorial monarchs and rulers have relied upon those with specialised skills in order to maintain their rule. The 'functional indispensability' of the expert in the political and economic administration of the contemporary advanced societies no more necessarily gives him power than was the case in the pre-industrial world.

In this respect Wiles' laconic comment upon Bell's thesis: 'new techniques merely give governments more choices', is perfectly apt; this may be expressed alternatively in Sartori's observation that there is a fundamental difference between a situation in which 'the powerful have knowledge' and the sort of circumstance predicted in most technocratic theories, according to which 'the knowledgeable have power'.[15]

This is why we must be equally suspicious of the notion that, in the advanced societies, power is becoming 'diffused downwards' among those with specialised technical expertise, as we must of the idea that the 'technocrats' (however this term is interpreted) constitute a newly emergent dominant class. Galbraith's 'techno-structure' (cf. pp. 172–3, above) suggests the former view. It may be admitted, as the conventional sociology of organisations suggests, that technical specialists in the modern large-scale enterprise tend to possess a definite autonomy over their own particular fields of competence which takes them partially out of the vertical 'line' of authority. But this very fact inhibits the exercise of a significant ratio of effective power on their part, because it limits the generality ('issue-strength') of the decisions which are under their sway. Significant power, within any type of organisation, consists in the capacity to determine or shape *policy*, and this virtually always lies in the hands precisely of 'non-specialists' who head the organisation. Decisions taken in the 'technostructure' facilitate, or limit, the *competence* of the policies forged by the top-level agencies, but they do not normally constitute a major limitation upon their capability to enact those policies.

A stronger case can be made for the view that the technocrats form a nascent ruling class in the advanced societies. This view does not identify the 'technocrats' as technical specialists as such—i.e., those who apply technical expertise in specific areas of knowledge—but as those with a general background of technical education who apply the 'technocratic world-view' in pursuit of general matters of economic or political policy. According to this perspective, technical education tends increasingly to form a *qualification* for access to positions of power. But the evidence of the upper class and elite formations in the advanced societies simply does not support this. The most plausible case for such a view can be made out for the state socialist societies; but, as I have already sought to demonstrate, even there it does not stand up to examination. In the capitalist societies, the educational qualifications associated with recruitment to elite groupings still tend to be very much those associated with a background of material privilege. What influences elite recruitment is not that the aspirant recruit possesses a degree in physics or in engineering, but that the degree is conferred at Oxford or at Harvard; and, whatever the variability which may exist in degree of 'closure' of elite recruitment between different societies, it is everywhere true that ownership of wealth and property continues to play a fundamental part in facilitating access to the sort of educational process which influences entry to elite positions. The existence of a property-owning upper class, even if this is not necessarily a 'ruling class' as I have defined that term, is a basic phenomenon separating the capitalist from the state socialist societies, and no concept, whether it be one of 'industrial society' or of 'post-industrial society', that obliterates this difference (which, of course, reflects the essential underlying contrast in the institutional mediation of power between the two types of advanced society) is acceptable.

To deny the usefulness of the concept of 'post-industrial society' does not mean suggesting that there are not significant changes affecting the character of the advanced societies in the contemporary world. The point is that these changes cannot be satisfactorily interpreted in terms of the suggestion that 'industrialism' is being supplanted by 'post-industrialism'. The facile rhetoric of technocratic theories actually covers a general failure to get to grips with problems which need a precise and concrete analysis; the idea that one all-embracing type of social order, that is, 'industrial society', is being replaced by another such overall system glosses over the need to examine the interconnections and sources of conflict between the sub-groups—and classes—of which societies are composed.

2. TECHNIQUE AND THE MODERN SOCIAL ORDER

Nothing lends itself more easily to sweepingly banal observations than the 'global unity' of modern man. The dramatic development of modes of communication and the dissemination of information, allowing virtually instantaneous contact between places on opposite sides of the world, and the rapidity of air transport, annihilate previous social meanings of time and space. It needs a superabundance of the imagination to believe, however, that these phenomena create a 'single world' in and of themselves; and it is a failure of the imagination not to see that the process of creating a single world is a dialectical one, which both unifies and fragments. The theory of the obsolescence of the nation-state is as old as that of the obsolescence of property (and not infrequently, as in Marx's writings, the two ideas have been connected). Internationalism certainly has a new meaning in the twentieth century. Not only the advances in transport and communications, but the formation of supra-national economic and political networks, and the increasingly international character of the megacorporations, are specifically modern phenomena. But although all of these affect the functioning of the nation-state, they do not signal the end of its existence, and in some ways they act to strengthen its autonomy. The primary unit of sociological analysis, the sociologist's 'society'—in relation to the industrialised world at least—has always been, and must continue to be, the administratively bounded nation-state. But 'society', in this sense, has *never* been the isolated, 'internally developing' system which has normally been implied in social theory. One of the most important weaknesses of sociological conceptions of development, from Marx onwards, has been the persistent tendency to think of development as the 'unfolding' of endogenous influences within a given society (or, more often, 'type' of society). 'External' factors are treated as an 'environment' to which the society has to 'adapt', and therefore as merely conditional in the progression of social change. In part, this view often results from the use of organic analogies—such that social development is assumed to be parallel to the growth pattern of a youthful organism, which 'unfolds' its potentialities in a process of predictable maturation. But such a view also tends to be associated with the notion that it is the techno-logical or general economic level of development of a society that 'in the last resort' determines the processes of change which affect it. In fact, any adequate understanding of the development of the ad-vanced societies presupposes the recognition that factors making for 'endogenous' evolution always combine with influences from 'the outside' in determining the transformations to which a society is subject. We may distinguish, analytically speaking, two sorts of influences here: the transmission of material and ideological 'cul-ture' from one society to another, and the (often coercive) *political* domination or subordination of one society by another or others. The second is often the most important, since it is frequently the channel whereby the first is brought about. But the first has received much more attention than the second, because it fits much more neatly with the assumption that technique, or 'economic organisation', broadly defined, is the ultimate motor of social development.

The pervasiveness of this latter notion in sociology may be seen as reflecting some of the essential characteristics of capitalist society itself—in particular separation of the 'economic' and the 'political', and the very degree of autonomy accorded to the former. Even Marx, the radical critic of capitalism, failed to escape from this perspective. The lesson has not yet been learnt, either by most subsequent Marxists or by the majority of their opponents—including many of the technocratic theorists. But it is a lesson which should hardly need teaching in the modern world. 'Industrial society' may not be the militaristic society which feudalism was; however, while in this respect Saint-Simon may have been correct, he was not right in believing that the advent of industrialism implies the end of coercive political power, bolstered by military force. Were it not for the dominance which the endogenous model of development has held in sociology, it would hardly need emphasising how much politico-military power has shaped the character of the advanced societies. Successive world wars have accelerated the progress of technological development in all the advanced societies, and have provided the vehicle of the contemporary pre-eminence of the United States as the leading industrial power in the world; they have served to accomplish what the transition to industrialism failed to bring about in Germany and Japan—the disintegration of the hegemony of traditional land-owning elites; and they have provided the theatre for the processes of revolutionary change which have created state socialist society, first of all in the Soviet Union, and subsequently in other societies of Eastern Europe.

In analysing the influence of technique, and technological development generally, in the advanced societies of the contemporary world, therefore, we must examine inter-national relationships and conflicts in conjunction with the character of the 'internal' industrial development of particular societies or types of society. These considerations are crucial in contrasting the development of the capitalist and the state socialist societies. Marx, of course, anticipated the revolutionary transformation of capitalism as a ramified process of an international character, creating a supranational socialist commonwealth. The fact that state socialism came into being, not as the supersession of capitalism within the industrially developed societies, but as an alternative mode of social and economic organisation to the capitalist order, has produced an altogether different set of circumstances. The political isolation of the Soviet Union in the early years of its existence, together with the premium which was placed upon industrialisation, gave rise to a society based upon the complete subordination of economic activity to the centralised control of the state. Considered together with the rising prosperity of the capitalist countries, the result—strengthened with the emergence of the Eastern European state socialist societies—has been the creation of an international situation in which economic progress and, more particularly, rates of industrial growth have come to be of pre-eminent importance, and are regarded as indices of the relative 'superiority' of the competing types of social order.

Again this is a reason why theories of 'industrial society' (and 'post-industrial society') have a continuing specious attraction. The primacy which has come to be accorded to securing high rates of economic growth places economic 'efficiency' in the forefront, and thereby stimulates the sorts of parallel industrial development which appear to emanate from an immanent 'inner logic' of industrialism drawing together the capitalist and the state socialist societies. Uncritically applied conceptions of 'industrial society' necessarily tend to imply that the existence of forms of technique shared by most or all of the advanced societies means, *ipso facto*, that they share similar structural and dynamic properties. There are two points to be made here. First, while the prevalence of technological similarities between different societies or types of society entails similarities in systems of paratechnical relations, the significance of these may vary according to the broader socio-political context in which they are embedded. Secondly, even where there are broad parallels in social structure between societies, it does not follow that these are 'necessary', in the sense that they are *called into being* by observed parallel developments in technique.

Each of these comments is germane to a general consideration of the influence of industrial technique in the capitalist as compared to the state socialist societies. Thus the state socialist societies are experiencing the same sort of progressive transfer in the labour force, involving the relative expansion of the non-manual sector, as has occurred in the capitalist countries in consequence of technological development in industry. Moreover, within the general category of non-manual labour, the expansion is fastest, in both types of society, among professional and technical occupations involving some form of higher educational qualification. But the impact of these changes, in certain major respects, is quite different in each form of society. In the capitalist societies, such changes must be interpreted against the backdrop of an historically deep-rooted cleavage in class structuration which has separated the manual and the non-manual worker. Among the state socialist societies, on the other hand, the capacity for political control of economic organisation generated by the institutional mediation of power has brought about a different situation; the 'tail end' of non-manual workers has become detached from enclosure within a 'middle class'. The expansion of higher education in these societies has led to the creation of a fairly distinctive grouping, the intelligentsia, which does not really have a direct counterpart in contemporary capitalist society. This is only in part because the manual/non-manual division does not have the same significance in terms of class structuration: it also results from the absence (or relative absence) of private property in state socialist society. In the capitalist societies, the continuing concentration of property in the hands of small minorities of the population heavily influences career process and elite recruitment, even though it does not 'determine' these in any simple sense.

The problematic role of technique is nowhere better illustrated than by the character of industrial authority in capitalist and state socialist societies. Here, as I have stressed, there are obvious parallels between the two types.[16] Most of the state socialist countries are very far from creating the conditions looked for by Marx as involved in the transcendence of bourgeois political democracy: the elimination of the dualism of political 'participation' in the state and subjection to capitalist-managerial domination in the sphere of economic activity. In the Soviet Union, even under Lenin, but particularly under Stalin, industrial discipline geared to increasing productivity became the keynote, as a necessary element in the achievement of rapid industrialisation. The result was a system of authority relations in industry which, quite deliberately, borrowed from managerial structures evolved in the West, and which differed little from the latter in respect of the imposed character of the demands to which workers were subject. Since a similar system of industrial authority was instituted in the Eastern European societies, it appeared as if the authority relations characteristic of the capitalist industrial order were an intrinsic element in modern industry, regardless of context, save that workers in the state socialist societies lacked the collective power given by the right to strike. But such a view would be deceptive. If the analysis I have set out in previous chapters be accepted, it follows that apparent similarities in authority relations in industry between the two forms of society actually conceal major differences in structure and dynamics. The right, and the propensity, to strike is *not*, as it has so often been regarded by socialist thinkers, a mechanism which (potentially) threatens the integrity of the capitalist order. Rather, it is a focal element in maintaining the orientation to economism which allows for the persistence of the prevailing system of industrial authority, and more generally for the continuing separation of economy and polity which Marx rightly noted as a distinctive feature of capitalist society. In spite of the prevalence of overt manifestations of conflict which necessarily characterise this type of industrial order, it can be argued that it is in fact inherently more stable than that which exists in the state socialist societies, which is subject to the occasional, but much more deep-rooted eruption of worker antagonism involving an orientation to control.

3. THE RELEVANCE OF CLASS ANALYSIS

The irrelevance of class analysis to contemporary capitalist societies has been proclaimed by two quite different schools of thought in modern sociology. Each in a definite sense agrees that class relationships were basic to nineteenth-century capitalism, but considers that today this no longer holds true. One such school of thought is to be found among certain of the technocratic theorists—notably Marcuse and, in a slightly different version, Habermas. According to Marcuse, the transformation of nineteenth-century capitalism into a 'one-dimensional' or 'totalitarian' society has not eliminated classes—the class basis of exploitation identified by Marx has not disappeared—but it has effectively undermined the form of class conflict such as it existed in the nineteenth century, upon which Marx's anticipation of the revolutionary overthrow of capitalism was predicated. In the 'one-dimensional' society, labour unions and labour parties become integrated within the existing order, and do not offer any alternative to it.

The second school of thought—associated particularly with the writings of certain contemporary American sociologists—tends to be of a different political persuasion and to argue a quite different case. According to this view, which in some respects also mirrors the notion of 'post-capitalist' society expressed by Dahrendorf, class analysis is no longer relevant to the modern social order, not because it becomes increasingly 'one-dimensional', but, on the contrary, because it becomes more 'pluralistic' or diversified. Various factors are adduced as promoting such diversification. The idea of the obsolescence of property is once again of some significance here. These writers point to the rise of managerialism as evidence that property no longer confers power in the large corporation; to the extension of the franchise and the growth of modern political parties as indicative of the fact that political power has become detached from the ownership of property; and, above all, to the diminished importance of property as a source of income, and its replacement by occupational position. The latter point is usually linked to the view that 'inheritance' of occupational position cannot occur in the same way as the inheritance of property, and hence that the family is of less and less significance as the locus of the transmission of economic advantages from generation to generation; the family, it is emphasised, is isolated from the world of labour and the life-chances of men in the labour market.[17] This thesis, therefore, asserts that contemporary capitalist society is diversified in two basic senses: in terms of the sources of economic and political power and, more particularly, by the graduated hierarchy of socio-economic differences built into the occupational structure. As Parsons has expressed the latter point: 'There is, of course, an hierarchical dimension to the occupational system . . . but, especially in the upper ranges, it is only one of several dimensions of differentiation. It is particularly important that there is no clear-cut break between an upper and a lower "class"; even the famous line between manual and non-manual work has ceased to be of primary significance.'[18]

The writings of Marcuse have their origin in a disillusionment with 'classical' Marxism. Together with the other Frankfurt social philosophers, Marcuse has relinquished the desperate obtuseness with which orthodox Marxists attempt to hold to the traditional views of the conflict of bourgeoisie and proletariat, and the immanence of revolution. In this stance, the Frankfurt thinkers are certainly justified. The poverty of the main prop used to bolster orthodox Marxist class theory—the idea that the revolutionary potential of the working class has been stifled, and emiseration (temporarily) overcome by the imperialistic involvement of the capitalist societies with the 'third world'—has long been apparent. There has been no shortage of exploitative imperialism, in one guise or another, over the past century, but it is patently mistaken to suppose that the fruits of such exploitation, or the 'translation of the class struggle to the conflict between rich and poor nations', can explain why the course of development of the capitalist societies has not conformed to Marx's anticipation. The overwhelmingly important factor explaining the rise in the real income of workers over the past century is rising productivity, brought about primarily by technological change; and we have to look to other factors, in any case, to explain why the class structure of contemporary capitalism differs from that which is portrayed in the Marxian view. Theories of imperialism, whatever their validity in other respects, have simply served as a rationale for avoiding any direct confrontation with problems posed by the internal processes of change experienced in the capitalist countries since the nineteenth century.

In not being content with such an escape-route, and in recognising the need to comprehend changes which have intervened in capitalist society since the turn of the century, Marcuse's analysis makes a valuable break with the more orthodox forms of Marxism. But it is a break which is both not radical enough and too radical. It is not radical enough in that Marcuse tends to accept the sort of view which holds that Marx was basically correct in his diagnosis of his own time, but has been falsified by events which have occurred since then. Marcuse writes as a Marxist compelled to accept that the working class has not fulfilled, and looks unlikely to fulfil, the revolutionary role in the transformation of capitalism which it gave promise of in the nineteenth century. But he does not accept that this is above all because of the mistaken or misleading aspects of Marx's analysis which were there from the beginning. What German writers describe as *Spätkapitalismus*, meaning among other things that the 'high point' of capitalism has now been passed, is better regarded actually as the maturity of the capitalist order; 'high capitalism', as they describe it, is one phase in the full institutionalisa-tion of the separation of economy and polity which is the hall-mark of capitalist society. The fundamental error, to put it another way, which is taken over from Marx, is *to identify 'bourgeois society' and capitalism.* On the other hand, Marcuse's view is too radical because since an intrinsic link is presupposed between the working class and the revolutionary potential to create an entirely different order from that prevailing in capitalist society, the absence of such a potential is taken to show that class relationships have today lost their significance—or, more accurately, have become submerged within the unified 'one-dimensional' totality.

Such a conclusion is as unacceptable as its opposite, that the de-gree of diversity within modern societies precludes the recognition of 'classes'.[19] The expansion of managerial control in the large corporations undoubtedly represents a significant development within modern capitalism—albeit one which Marx himself pointed to one hundred years ago. It may be doubted, for reasons already mentioned, whether or not the level of effective managerial control in the large firms in the contemporary capitalist economies is as complete as is normally asserted; but that the phenomenon exists on a quite broad scale cannot be disputed. In such circumstances, by definition, the property owner does not wield direct economic power, and in this sense there is a diversification of the sources of power. But, as I have already argued, this is a long way from estab-lishing that it no longer makes sense, or is no longer useful, to speak of the existence of an 'upper class' in capitalist society; and this question should in any case be treated as partially separable from the relationship of such a class to the means of domination, that is to say, whether or not it is a 'ruling class'. In terms of the distribu-tion of power, however, property ownership remains of primary importance within the economic order, in two respects. First, whatever the degree of managerial control in the corporations and the extent of the diffusion of share ownership, it remains true that possession of property very often gives direct access to economic power; second, and most significantly, in spite of the vast extension of the public sector in neo-capitalist society, it is still true that the pursuit of returns from investment of one sort or another is the basic motor of the economic system as a whole. Within the political order, it is evident enough that property rarely 'buys' power as it did in the nineteenth century. But to suppose that the connections between property ownership and political power have been completely broken by the development of the modern franchise and party system simply ignores the strong ties which exist in all the capitalist countries between business and the conservative or liberal parties. In these ways, property remains a fundamental element in the system of power in capitalist society, even when, as in the United States, elites are not clearly integrated within a 'ruling class'.

The argument which refers to the graduated character of the occupational structure rests upon rather different premises from those relating to the distribution of power. There are actually two propositions involved here: that the economic order constitutes a graded hierarchy which shows no clear-cut 'breaks'; and that the chances of an individual achieving a given position on this hierarchy are no longer primarily governed by the position of the family from which he originates. The latter point may be dealt with first. The thesis here is reminiscent of Durkheim's assessment of 'internal' and 'external' inequalities: external inequality is characteristic of the transitional stage in the evolution of the modern type of society, and disappears when the inheritance of wealth or property is abolished; qualities transmitted through the family are then completely detached from the determination of success in the occupational order.[20] But this states a Saint-Simonian ideal which has not in fact come to realisation, and in the light of recent research upon social mobility and educational opportunity we do not have much difficulty in showing why this is so. The basic reason is that the distribution of talents and capacities in a society (that is to say, of 'internal' inequalities') is itself heavily conditioned by variations in family organisation; but in addition, studies of social mobility demonstrate quite unequivocally that the family of origin influences the chances of occupational mobility even where manifest ability is held constant.[21] It is, of course, true that, in contemporary society, the family 'contracts' in terms of the degree to which kinship ties provide a basis for the formation of economic relationships. But this was, after all, one of the principal elements involved in the very beginnings of the development of capitalist society, and was a condition of the transcendence of feudalism; the formally 'open' character of economic opportunities in the capitalist economy has been, and continues to be, divergent from the differential life-chances which it actually creates—*this is precisely the basis for the existence of classes.*

The problem of class 'boundaries' has constantly hampered the theory of class. The difficulties here, as I have suggested previously, stem from two misleading assumptions which have dominated much of the literature on the subject. The first rests upon the implicit or explicit attempt to draw too close a parallel between the social and economic structure of feudalism and that of capitalism, as if the divisions between classes could be as clearly drawn and specific as those between feudal estates. If the point may be repeated, the very creation of 'classes', as opposed to 'estates', presupposes the dissolution of the sorts of criteria which were applied within the feudal order. Marxian theory has actually played a leading part in fostering such a misleading view since, in its most characteristic emphasis, it holds that both feudalism and capitalism are class systems founded upon the same principle of minority ownership of the means of production: it thus appears that the dominant class in capitalism should be as clearly distinct a grouping as the feudal aristocracy. But, in the nature of the case, this cannot be so. This leads to the second matter: the failure to analyse what I have called 'class structuration' as a *variable* phenomenon involved in the interconnections between economy and society. Class divisions cannot be drawn like lines on a map, and the extent to which class structuration occurs depends upon the interaction of various sets of factors. It should be emphasised that this is *not* the same as saying that class is a 'multidimensional' phenomenon which can be analysed as an aggregate of several hierarchical 'dimensions', as is sometimes claimed by certain of those (mis)interpreters of Weber who identify 'class' and 'stratification'. In the history of the capitalist societies, class structuration has been most strongly developed at three levels, separating the upper, middle and working classes. How far this will continue to be the case is a question which has to be taken up in the concluding chapter. But I should emphasise that there is no opposition between the idea that capitalism is intrinsically a class society, as I have set it out in this book, and the notion of 'pluralism'—at least, as the latter term is understood by some authors, such as Kerr, for whom pluralism implies an orientation towards 'a reliance on markets and plans and group bargaining; towards several or even many centres of power rather than more or only one; towards infinitely complex mixtures of rationality and irrationality, morality and immorality, principle and pragmatism; towards many managers and even more who are managed; towards many conflicts over rules and rewards'.[22] The mistake is to link this complexity of phenomena crudely to 'industrialism'.

THE FUTURE OF CLASS SOCIETY

1. RATIONALISATION, CLASSES AND BUREAUCRACY

Most recent technocratic theories, wittingly or unwittingly, borrow a good deal from Max Weber. In some respects it is obviously mistaken to regard Weber as an advocate of the technocratic standpoint, since for Weber it is not the technical specialist or engineer who is the characteristic figure in modern culture, but the administrative expert; moreover he was careful to indicate that the bureaucrat is normally subject to the rule of the 'non-specialist' who has a broader vision than that conveyed by the mastery of administrative or technical skills. But the conception of rationalisation, as Weber employed it,[1] depends upon an interpretation of the fundamental significance of technique in modern social life. There is a clear connection in Weber's thought between technique, as the application of instrumental rationality to the material world, and bureaucratic organisation, as the application of technical reason to social activity. Thus Weber frequently compares bureaucracy to the smooth-running 'machine', in which the rule-governed conduct of the bureaucratic official represents the cog in the machinery. Rationalisation entails more, however, than simply the extension of technical reason —that is to say, the instrumentality of the correlation of the most 'effective' means to defined 'ends'. The process of the expansion of technical rationality is accompanied by two other phenomena: the 'disenchantment' of the world, and the concomitant replacement of religious or mystical norms by abstract 'rational-legal' imperatives. These twin series of changes have a curiously opposed outcome. On the one hand, religion, magic, mysticism, become inevitably squeezed out of the organisation of human conduct in the major institutional spheres of society; on the other hand, the predominant forms of social protest become utopian, futile outbursts against the imperatives of rationalisation, and themselves assume a 'mystical' character.

The polarity between rationalisation and charisma which runs through Weber's writings provides a vindication of this point of view. Charisma, the main element tying together protest movements throughout history, has, in Weber's words, a 'specifically irrational' character. But this means two things, which are not clearly distinguished in Weber's writings. Charisma, in other words, is set off against reason in two senses: it is a departure from routinised or technically applied reason (in the type case, the rationalisation inherent in technique, or, more specifically, in bureaucratic procedure), and it is a departure from rationalisation in the sense of the rational-legal validation of action (that is to say, it substitutes religious or mystical value-imperatives as the basis of the overall legitimation of action). It is the fact that these are not separated which allows Weber to place the most diverse forms of movement and belief within the single category of the 'charismatic' and which, more important in the present context, serves to categorise modern forms of political ideology (including the normative components of Marxism) with religion and mysticism as 'irrational'. As Marcuse has pointed out with some force, the 'domination of man by man' involved in the bureaucratic systematisation of activity thus appears as inseparable from the pursuit of 'rational'—that is to say, non-religious or non-mystical—values. Marcuse's own response to this is to take up the second aspect of the two types of rationalisation, and to counterpose to it the vision of a new social order founded upon a new rationality.

Marcuse's analysis is not convincing, however, precisely because it does not take up the issues posed by rationalisation in the first sense and, in the conception of 'one-dimensional society', basically accepts the Weberian idea of the rationalisation of the modern world inherent in the conception of bureaucracy.[2] The difference is that what Weber believes to be the inexorable fate of modern man, Marcuse holds to be open to change; but the latter author provides little in the way of indicating how the projected revolutionary reorganisation of society can feasibly be brought about, and in lieu of this his ideas appear as utopian—a vision of a new world as out of touch with existing social reality as the religious visions to which Weber himself would have connected it. In order to understand the influence of rationalisation in modern culture, we have to consider each of its aspects mentioned above—and the sorts of counter-response which each tends to generate.

It may be readily accepted that the initial emergence of capitalist-industrialism in eighteenth-century Europe both presupposed and greatly accelerated the transmutation of religious world-views, replacing them by rationalised representations of, and legitimations of, the social universe. Marx expressed this in his customary blistering style, writing·that, '[The bourgeoisie] has drowned the most heavenly ecstasies of religious fervour, of chivalrous enthusiasm, of philistine sentimentalism, in the icy water of egotistical calculation. . . . In one word, for exploitation, veiled by religious and political illusions, it has substituted naked, shameless, direct, brutal exploitation.'[3] Like other nineteenth-century rationalists, Marx dismissed the forms of revivalism and mysticism which appeared sporadically as a hangover from the preceding era, or as irrationally *expressed* protests against the alienation inherent in the capitalist order.[4] But in this respect, Weber was surely right: the growth of a rationalised representation of social and natural reality is dialectically linked with the chronic possibility, certainly not of any sort of full-scale revitalisation of organised religion, but of the upsurge of diverse types of religious revivalism, mysticism, and irrationalism in art, literature and philosophy. Forms of social protest based upon beliefs developed in such contexts necessarily tend to assume a 'total' character; that is to say, they question the dominant ethos in its entirety. Weber was led to the view, which also is found in the writings of many of the technocratic theorists, that such kinds of social protest movement may be classified together with politically oriented movements as (ultimately futile) responses to rationalisation. But while it is true that there are bound to be affinities between the two, and the one is likely to feed upon the other, we must recognise that there is a form of political response to rationalisation which does not attempt to discredit rationality as an overall cultural ethos, and which, indeed, is very profoundly based upon acceptance of this ethos; it is a response which is part of Marxian as well as of other forms of socialism and anarchism. It is founded upon a *rejection* of rationalisation in the first meaning distinguished above: or, expressed more accurately, it depends upon the premise that 'rationalisation', in the sense of the rational transmutation of the modern cultural ethos, provides men with the understanding necessary to control 'rationalisation' in the sense of the dominance of technical rationality in social life.

Weber's portrayal of the 'steel-hard cage' to which the expansion of bureaucratisation condemns modern man—without hope of reprieve—gains much of its plausibility from his assimilation of the two aspects of rationalisation. For it is difficult to resist the idea that the rationalisation of culture is a cumulative process which is unavoidable (although always bound to provoke resistance, and the attempted construction of 'counter-cultures'); and thus it seems as though what Weber called the 'parcelling-out of human life', epitomised by bureaucracy, is equally inevitable. Now, in this view, socialism appears doomed to futility. On the one hand, socialist theory advocates an increasing organisation of social relationships, by placing the direction of economic life under central control; on the other hand, a primary underlying theme of socialist thought is the idea of enabling men to escape from the consequences of the systematic organisation of social life involved in the modern division of labour.[5] The outcome of the implementation of socialist policies would thus undercut some of the very ideals which inspire socialist thinkers specifically, those concerned with extending the freedom and autonomy of the individual from social constraints. This might seem to support Weber's conclusion that revolutionary social-ism is essentially 'utopian', and hence is a secular version of religious ideals which have inspired men to question the existing world at previous points in history. But we may accept that there is a paradoxical element in socialist theory without holding that its aims are unrealisable in the face of the necessary rationalisation of modern social life. What is inexorable in the modern world is the advance of the rationalisation of culture; and the sorts of protest which both reflect and seek to abolish such rationalisation are indeed doomed to failure, short of some kind of catastrophic occurrence which destroys contemporary civilisation altogether. But the same is not true of movements oriented towards the other aspect of rationalisation, for which Weber found the prototype in bureaucratic organisation. The problem is that, if Weber's treatment of bureaucracy in general, and the modern rational state in particular, is unsatisfactory, so are the interpretations of these phenomena in the major branches of socialist theory—includ-ing Marxian theory. The analysis of the modern state is perhaps the crucial issue here, but the questions involved spill over to the other major institutions in society.

What I wish to suggest at this point is that the two aspects of rationalisation which I have distinguished (one could, of course, make more refined analytical discriminations) appear as two inter-woven themes within Marxian socialism. One theme involves a call for the overall extension of the rational understanding and control of social life which, according to Marx, is lacking in capitalism. The capitalist mode of production sweeps away the alienated forms of human consciousness represented by religious belief systems,

but substitutes for these the 'hidden god' of the market. The irrationalities traced by Marx in the functioning of the capitalist economy
express this. Socialism, based upon the rational control of economic
life, provides a mode of completing the process of rationalisation
on the plane of the overall organisation of the social activity of man.
Now I have earlier advocated the view that the origins of socialism
are bound up, not merely with the advent of capitalism itself,
but more specifically with the clash between capitalism and feudalism.
The second theme inherent in socialist thought, I wish to propose,
derives its level of intensity (and level of support) primarily from
the degree to which this clash is pronounced and sharp. This theme,
bearing upon the other aspect of rationalisation, is concerned with
the *liberation* of men from the coercive imposition of the will of other
individuals. Its most characteristic expression is the Saint-Simonian
idea, developed by Marx, of the transcendence of the 'political'
power of the state in the projected socialist society.

The paradox in socialist ideology lies at the heart of the Marxian
theory of the capitalist state. We may dismiss the view, as incompatible with the thought of a man of Marx's intellectual stature,
that Marx held a conception of the 'disappearance' of the state
directly akin to that which appears in some cruder versions of
anarchist philosophy. Marx did not believe in the 'destruction'
of the state, but in its *Aufhebung*, which meant the remerging of
the state with society, and the subordination of the state to society.
How he considered this could be accomplished is indicated in his
discussion of the Paris Commune, as I have said before, since this
was to involve revocable officials, serving for only short terms,
and elected from the mass of the people.[6] From this it is only a
short step to the notion, which was, however, never precisely
outlined by Marx, of 'industrial democracy', operating along similar
lines.[7] But these prescriptions were not elaborated in detail anywhere in Marx's writings, and it seems plausible to infer that they
represent an attempt to construct a concrete and defensible basis
for a more diffuse set of ideas which Marx assimilated, in the first
stages of his intellectual career, from earlier socialist thinkers:
ideas concerned with the eradication of the 'domination of man
by man', as set forth by Saint-Simon and by many other prior and
contemporary socialist writers. Such a credo is frequently expressed
in Marx's earlier writings, as where *The Communist Manifesto*
asserts that 'the free development of each is the condition for the
free development of all'.[8]

The difficulty of reconciling this sort of conception with the consequences which flow from the proposition that the irrationalities of

the capitalist economy must be transcended by the consciously directed organisation of production, are apparent enough not to require discussing at length. But a similar problem exists even in the more complex rendition of the possibility of the transcendence of the state. For in order to assume directive control over the production and distribution of goods in society, in such a way as to correlate production with need, the state must be in some degree set off from and set 'above' society. This has to be so, because the state (or other directive agency) has to be responsible for the implementation and coordination of decisions affecting society as a whole. The inevitable partial separation of the state from society, and its superiority over society, depends both on the necessity of applying specialised 'expertise' in administration and upon the exigency of administrative concentration in decision-making. These aspects appear, in a basic way, as distinct strands in Marx's writings on the theory of capitalist development. One part of the economic theory of capitalism concerns the identification of mechanisms whereby the capitalist market conquers its inherent irrationality—but only by undercutting the very principles upon which, as a system of production, it is founded. That is to say, Marx traces the changes whereby the competitive, 'anarchical' structure of early capitalism gradually cedes place to a system which is poised for transformation to socialism, through the processes of the centralisation and concentration of capitals. The theory of classes, and of the development of the revolutionary potential of the working class with the evolution of capitalist society, providing eventually for the emancipation of man from the constraints of class society, constitutes the other strand. In Marx's writings, of course, the two are conjoined, because the development of capitalism is presumed to relate them in an integral fashion: the changing character of the capitalist economy makes for the concrete possibility of the centralised coordination of production, which is realised by the revolutionary action of the working class.

The actual character of the evolution of the capitalist societies is radically different from this. While the maturity of capitalism involves the sort of outcome generally in accord with Marx's expectations with regard to the first set of processes, it does not do so with regard to the second. The revolutionary potential of the working class depends upon the initial encounter with capitalism, not upon the maturity of the capitalist mode of production. In a sense, however, this has concealed the paradoxical element which Marx's thought shares with other forms of socialist theory, since it has meant that the revolutionary transformation of capitalism has not come to fruition; the nature of the problem is only fully apparent in the state socialist societies.

The ambiguity in Marx's theory of the state, and the frailty of his interpretation of the origins of bureaucratic authority, bear witness to the intellectual consequences of the two divergent planes in Marxian thought. I have already indicated (pp. 51–2) the two elements in Marx's conception of the state: on the one hand, that the existence of the state is contingent upon class domination, from which it follows that the abolition (transcendence) of the state is accomplished above all through the abolition of classes; on the other hand, that the state is the vehicle of the administrative needs of a complex society and economy. The Marxian interpretation of bureaucracy is weak because it links the existence of bureaucratic domination only to the first of these propositions; the Weberian conception of bureaucracy, by contrast, is flawed because, by assimilating the two aspects of rationalisation, it addresses itself almost wholly to the second.

The suggestion that, with the abolition of capitalism, the state will be reabsorbed in society is only defensible in reference to the proposition that the state is an expression of that asymmetry of class interests; moreover we must recognise that the question of the class 'bias' of the state is separable—but by no means completely so—from the question of the factors which determine the level of bureaucratic rationalisation of the state apparatus. In capitalism, as Marx (and Weber) insisted, the character of the state necessarily reflects the distribution of class interests, in two senses: by insulating the sphere of the 'political' from the 'economic', and recognising rights of 'full and equal participation' only in the former; and by sanctioning and protecting the existence of private property as the legitimate principle of economic enterprise. There is genuine validity in the Marxian view that each of these serves to separate state from society, and to promote the emergence of the state as an 'autonomous power'. But these are partly distinct from the bureaucratic separation of state and society. Marxist theory of the transcendence of the state is based upon the premise that, through the abolition of private property in the economic sphere, making possible the merging of the 'political' and the 'economic', specifically 'political' power will necessarily disappear. The disappearance of 'political' power, however, can be interpreted in two senses. In a dialectical sense of the phrase, the sphere of the 'political' can be said to be eradicated when it is no longer clearly separable from that of the 'economic'. In this sense, the state is abolished when the conditions of political democracy characterising the capitalist order are transcended by the socialisation of the means of production. But, in the light of the historical example of the state socialist societies, what this leads to is quite evident: an accentuation of the *bureaucratic* separation of state from society, as Weber predicted. The idea that classlessness and the transcendence of the 'political' are, in this fashion, intrinsically linked, is not pure sophistry; for the institutional mediation of power created by the integration of economy and polity, as I have discussed at length previously, does provide an escape from class society. However, it is obvious that what happens in such circumstances is that the disappearance of the 'political' becomes equated, not with the abolition of the state, but with the domination of the state apparatus over economic life, and thus with the entrenchment of bureaucratic power.

2. CLASSES, CLASS CONFLICT

Since the beginnings, in the late eighteenth century, of the vast series of social transformations epitomised by the two forms of 'revolution' which characterise the modern epoch—'political revolution' and 'industrial revolution'—men have envisaged the arrival of a new age in which major conflicts and cleavages in human society will finally be eliminated. Such a vision appears in the works of Saint-Simon and Comte; in most influential form, in those of Marx; and in the writings of a host of more minor figures in nineteenth-century thought. The disasters of two world wars have helped to make twentieth-century thinkers less sanguine about the future than those of the previous era. But interpretations of the trends of development in the advanced societies continue to raise such possibilities, in much lower key, and in the guise of sociological analysis rather than revolutionary chiliasm. Conceptions of the 'end of ideology', and most versions of technocratic theory, express the view that, in contemporary society, the deep-rooted social conflicts of the past have been left behind in favour of a general 'consensus of ends'. More specifically, of course, it is held that the class struggles which punctuated nineteenth-century European history, and which Marx made the centre-piece of his theoretical scheme and of his practical project for the revolutionary reorganisation of capitalism, have today become dissolved. In this respect, some of those who have attempted to formulate a 'critical theory' of contemporary society, seeking to preserve the vision of a radically new feature for industrial man, have shared the assumptions of the authors who proclaimed the 'end of ideology'. In the face of such a chronic tendency in social thought to foresee the incipient decline, or the disappearance, of the fundamental conflicts which have set men against each other in the past, we must insist upon the ubiquity of conflict in social life. Conflict is the irremediable fact of the human condition, the inescapable source of much that is creative, as well as destructive, in human society. To say this, evidently, is not to say that the nature and sources of present-day conflicts may not have changed significantly from those which moved men in previous times.

The view that class conflict, such as characterised the nineteenth and early twentieth centuries, is no longer an important feature of capitalist society is based upon a commonly accepted set of empirical observations, and upon an interpretative standpoint concerning the evolution of capitalism over the past one hundred and fifty years. Among the empirical observations, four are particularly relevant: (1) violent confrontations between labour and employers, relatively common in the nineteenth century, have declined in favour of routinised forms of strike activity and collective bargaining; (2) the revolutionary posture taken by the labour movement in its early history, in several European countries, has become translated into reformist social democracy; (3) the working class has diminished, and is continuing to diminish, in size relative to the middle class; (4) union membership has not increased over the past two or three decades. Of these four statements, only the final one can be questioned on a strictly factual basis although, as I have previously mentioned, certain reservations might be made concerning the third proposition indicated here. The stabilisation of union membership, a matter with which some authors have made great play,[9] is a phenomenon which seems to be confined to the United States; in the European societies, and in Japan, rates of union membership have tended to rise.

However this may be, what I really wish to take issue with is the theoretical interpretation of such observations. This is a convenient place to offer a summary exposition of one of the primary contentions which I have advanced in this book. I have already pointed out the inconsistency involved in the ideas of those authors who argue as if, while the Marxian interpretation of capitalism was valid enough for the nineteenth century, it has been falsified by subsequent processes of social change. Behind this inconsistency, common enough as it is, there can be found a view of the development of capitalist society over the past century or so which is almost universally shared. This is essentially a conspectus originally worked out, or latent, within classical political economy, and clarified by Marx. The theorems involved can be easily stated. They are: that the essential component of 'capitalism' is the unfettered competition of a multiplicity of producers; that any movement towards a diminution in the number of competitive producers, in respect of capital, or towards the collective organisation of workers, in respect of labour, serves to threaten the hegemony of the capitalist system; and consequently that the decline of capitalism can be charted by the degree to which these latter two sets of processes are seen to take place. To these we may add the notion that the functioning of capitalism, as an economic and as a social order, is inhibited by the intervention of the state in economic life.

If these theorems are accepted, then it follows that the latter half of the nineteenth century already shows capitalism to be in its decline. Violent confrontations between employers and workers then appear as the outcome of capitalism in its 'pure' form, and the so-called institutionalisation of class conflict, by departing from the original premises upon which the capitalist economy is based, seems to represent, as many authors (somewhat contrary to Marx) have supposed, a mechanism of containing the effects of the class conflict inherent in unfettered capitalism. Such an interpretation seems to be supported by the fact of the protracted struggles which labour organisations had to endure in order to achieve recognition of the legitimacy of collective bargaining, and of labour parties to achieve recognition within the fully enfranchised democratic polity. This in turn leads to the idea that the late nineteenth century was generally the period when class struggles were most highly marked; and that, over the past seventy years, the process of development in the majority of the capitalist countries has manifested a progressive decline in the intensity and the social significance of class conflict.

The perspective I have set out is distinctively different from, and in a way almost wholly opposed to, this. What is typically considered to be the peak of capitalist development is more usefully seen as the early phase in the emergence of *capitalist society*. It is important to stress the term at this point, although I have used the terms 'capitalism' and 'capitalist society' almost interchangeably in previous chapters. For the emergence of capitalist society presupposes, not merely a series of economic transformations involving the formation of industrial and financial capital, and production for a market, but in addition profound social and political changes creating a specific form of institutional mediation' of power. There are two primary components involved: one concerns the polity. In political economy, and in Marxian theory, as I have often stressed, the nature of the modern state is treated in highly inadequate fashion—an offshoot of the general assumption of the primacy of economic organisation in influencing capitalist development. The 'abstract model' of capitalist society—capitalist society in its 'purest' form—restricts the operation of the state apparatus to the function of ultimate guarantor of contractual obligations. Such a model is misconceived in relation to the factual development of the capitalist societies, since it only comes close to reality in the case of a few countries, with Britain being the prime example; and is impossible to sustain upon a more general theoretical level.

If the thesis I have described in Chapter 12 is correct, there is an inherent connection between capitalism and liberal democracy which goes beyond that ordinarily assumed. In Marx's thinking, the ethic of 'freedom of opportunity', which comes to prevail in the economic sphere with the transition from post-feudal society, is directly tied in with the emergence of ideologies of political democracy. But, as Marx makes clear in an early critique of Hegel, bourgeois political democracy is a sham because (among other reasons) only a small minority of the population are actually able to participate in the electoral system. The fact that working-class organisations are able to bring pressure to bear to extend the franchise constitutes a weakness in the overall structure of capitalist society, since it makes possible the rise of mass labour parties which, at least in certain countries, can actually accomplish the revolutionary overthrow of the capitalist order by operating within the existing political framework. The view which I have developed in earlier chapters suggests that such an interpretation is mistaken—in part, precisely because it ignores, in a particular way, a fundamentally 'political' aspect of the nineteenth-century labour movement. The working class, or the political organisations which represented it, had to struggle to secure full incorporation within the polity of the modern nation-state; the result of this incorporation, however, has not been to weaken, but to stabilise, or complete, the institutional mediation of power in the capitalist order. *Social democracy, in other words, is the normal form taken by the systematic political inclusion of the working class within capitalist society.* What has to be specifically accounted for is not the 'reformist' tendency of the political arm of the labour movement once it has been accepted within the liberal democratic order—that is, when the separation of the 'political' and the 'economic' has become recognised not merely as a formal principle, but as an institutionalised reality—but those cases (the United States) where the labour movement has not been strongly linked to socialism of any sort, and those cases (France) where a revolutionary orientation has in fact become strongly marked.

I have consistently stressed that the basic structural trait of capi-

talist society is that of an institutional mediation of power involving a separation of the 'political' and the 'economic', such that
the characteristic modes of participation in one sphere are not
determined by those in the other. Another way of expressing this
is by saying, as Macpherson does, that capitalism is a 'system
in which production is carried on without authoritative allocation of
work or rewards, but by contractual relations between free individuals (each possessing some resource be it only his own labour-
power) who calculate their most profitable courses of action and
employ their resources as that calculation dictates'.[10] In such a
system there is always a certain tension between state and economy;
the 'separation' of the two spheres always involves at the same
time a mutual dependence, and changes in one sphere call into
play reciprocal or counter-developments in the other. This is why
it is not contradictory to say that the maintenance of the insulation
of the 'political' and the 'economic' depends upon the existence of
definite interconnections between them. State 'intervention'—the
term is of course itself misleading, but by now conventional—in
economic life is in this sense not only compatible with capitalism;
it is intrinsic to it. The decline of *laissez faire*, and the rise of the
modern welfare state, must be understood in terms of such mechanisms of mutual realignment of polity and economy. The role of the
state in fostering taxation schemes, limiting monopoly, influencing
labour use and labour mobility, and even, in neo-capitalism, of
introducing long-term planning, may significantly alter the conditions under which contractual relationships are established and
maintained; but none of these modes of intervention transgress the
essential character of the organisation of economic activity.[11] The
use of a term such as 'maturity' has its disadvantages, since it
suggests, speaking of the 'maturity' of capitalist society, that the
latter has a natural cycle of growth, maturity and decay, which we
are in a position to predict. Such a view is certainly entailed in the
Marxian standpoint, with its portrayal of the progressive internal
transformation of 'classical' capitalism culminating in socialist
revolution, as well as in other schools of socialist thought. But
capitalism has proved to be a resilient economic system, capable of
undergoing major internal modifications without promoting the
sort of revolutionary cataclysm which Marx anticipated. While
it is obviously true that where the 'high point' of capitalist development is placed depends upon how the concepts of 'capitalism' and
'capitalist society' are defined, in the terms which I have suggested
it is perfectly appropriate to consider this as coinciding with the
most recent generic type: what I have called neo-capitalism.

As regards the phenomenon of the 'institutionalisation of class conflict', the view which I have sought to establish is again distinct from, and in a sense the contrary of, the prevailing orthodoxy, which accepts Marx in order to refute him. The existing idea is a simple one, and may be expressed as follows. There is an inherent tendency towards class conflict in capitalist society which, if left 'unregulated', produces a revolutionary working class which pits itself against the rest of society in violent class warfare. The recognition of divergent class interests, formalised in collective bargaining, serves to control and to provide mechanisms of outlet for such conflict, and thus undermines the revolutionary potential of the working class. The interpretation which I have advocated, however, holds that revolutionary consciousness tends above all to characterise the point of impact of post-feudalism and capitalist-industrialism, and is not endemic to capitalist society itself. The 'institutionalisation of class conflict' is not a process minimising the occurrence or the effects of class conflict, negating its potential revolutionary significance, but is the characteristic form in which class conflict expresses itself in developed capitalist society. Again, it is the presence of revolutionary class consciousness, rather than its absence, which demands special explanation.

3. OLD CLASSES AND NEW CONFLICTS: THE PROBLEM OF NEO-CAPITALISM

As in many areas of class theory, two (at least) rather divergent views have been taken of the consequences of the relative expansion of the white-collar sector, and the closely connected technological changes affecting lower-level non-manual occupations. Many authors have simply assumed that the growth in the white-collar sector which has taken place over the past decades heralds the arrival of a 'middle-class society' in which the continuing enlargement of the middle class increasingly weakens, and eventually eliminates, the forms of class structuration which have previously existed. This represents a sort of latterday restatement of a theory of classlessness, akin to Saint-Simon's idea of the 'one-class' society: society becomes classless in so far as everyone becomes middle class. A second standpoint, mainly advanced by Marxist authors in recent times, looks to the occurrence of a split within the ranks of white-collar workers, dividing those in routinised jobs, who are plunged into the working class, from those in higher-level occupations who tend to affiliate themselves with the upper class.

The objections which can be raised against the former viewpoint are so fundamental that it is hardly necessary to discuss it in detail. In the first place, it is based upon a projection into the future rather than upon a present actuality. Secondly, it is once more predicated largely upon the explicit or covert assumption that the United States can be treated as the exemplar of the prospective development of the other capitalist societies. But, as I have frequently emphasised, there are definite reasons why the level and character of class structuration in the United States has always differed from that characteristic of the majority of capitalist countries. Thirdly, in the United States as elsewhere, a high proportion of lower-level white-collar occupations, including particularly those which have become modified by the introduction of mechanisation, together with many newly created forms of service work, are staffed by women. Given that women still have to await their liberation from the family, it remains the case in the capitalist societies that female workers are largely peripheral to the class system; or, expressed differently, *women are in a sense the 'underclass' of the white-collar sector.* They tend to monopolise occupations which not only have a low economic return, but which are lacking in subsidiary economic benefits, have limited security of tenure, and offer little in the way of chances of promotion.

Finally, and in theoretical terms most important of all, the typical modes of class structuration, and the pervasiveness of class awareness, within the middle class inevitably tend to diminish the specific social (or cultural) influence of the latter in relation to the centrifugal pull of the working class on the one side, and upper class on the other. This means that *the middle class rarely tends to play a direct role in manifest class struggles.* But it is important not to confuse this with the notion that, in relation to class structuration itself, a new process of 'polarisation' is taking place which is effectively swelling the working class through a massive *déclassement* of routinised white-collar labour. The fact that most of the occupations in question have become dominated by women workers probably acts to solidify as much as to dissolve the 'buffer zone' between the working and middle classes, and certainly must lead us to reject any of the more sweeping assertions about the 'proletarianisation' of the lower levels of the white-collar sector. Probably less important than any process of routinisation is the partial closing-off of possibilities of career mobility for men in certain ranges of non-manual occupations. As I have already suggested in an earlier chapter, this is a principal source of rises in white-collar unionisation and militancy. How far white-collar unions become integral to the labour movement, however, and how far their militancy involves any sort of revolutionary consciousness, is dependent upon the same factors which determine the character of the labour movement as a whole in any given society.

In neo-capitalist society, the sort of changes pointed to by most authors, affecting the traditionally established division between manual and non-manual labour,[12] are of less far-reaching significance than two other sets of phenomena which are increasingly likely to influence the nature of class conflict: the emergence of a manual underclass, and the ramifications of long-term state planning. In the United States, the underclass is composed primarily of three ethnic groupings, the largest of which is in no sense a newcomer to the country, whilst the others are relatively recent arrivals (Mexicans and Puerto Ricans). The proportionate size of the underclass in the United States, and the fact that the majority element within it has been part of the society, although not assimilated culturally within it, for a very long period of time, again sets that country apart from other capitalist societies in which it is possible to point to a nascent, but identifiable, underclass. However, even in the United States it is only relatively recently, as a result of the mass migrations to the northern cities, that a mass of black workers has become finally drawn into the industrial labour force.

It may be suggested that the emergence of an underclass in a society has both a radical and a reactionary potential. Since members of the underclass are likely to be drawn from rural labour, and move into an urban-industrial environment, they constitute a possible source of an upsurge of revolutionary consciousness. But this is extremely unlikely to penetrate the working class as a whole—least of all in the United States—and will almost certainly, because of the clash of interests involved, serve to produce an opposing effect. We may question the proposition that the working class, as a result of cultural 'authoritarianism', is the main repository of irrational sentiments of prejudice against ethnic minorities. But it is evident that there is a basic division of interest, which in all probability will become more and more pronounced in the future, between those in the new 'reserve army' of capitalism, in insecure occupations yielding only a low rate of economic return, and those in the more stable, high-yielding manual occupations.

Even in those societies which do not develop a distinctive underclass, there is reason to suppose that similar exigencies will operate, although with less divisive consequences than where ethnic differentiation is involved. These phenomena are directly bound up with the types of economic planning characteristic of neo-capitalism, and may act to produce a schism within the working class which partially cuts across the older forms of division between skill levels. There has always been a strong tendency for skilled employees to enjoy a substantially higher degree of job security than other manual workers. Firms have normally regarded skilled labour as an important form of capital investment, and have been prepared accordingly to offer superior employment conditions to such employees. This has invariably been a major factor influencing the character of craft unions and creating an 'aristocracy of labour'. As a result, however, both of the increasing dominance of the megacorporations in the economy and the emergence of state planning, it is likely that a greater level of job security will become extended to some types of non-skilled workers within the enterprise. State planning in neo-capitalism differs in a very basic manner from the directive control of economic activity characteristic of state socialist society. In neo-capitalist society, indicative planning and prices and incomes policies necessarily have to be based upon securing the support of the economic leadership and of organised labour; the degree of direct control which can be secured by political elites over the latter two groupings is normally quite restricted. Much of the impetus towards the development of capitalist planning stems from the fact that, in certain respects, the state and the megacorporations have parallel interests in promoting stable and progressive economic development and in regulating inflation. But these objectives can be successfully pursued only with the involvement of the labour unions. The 'purchase price' of union support is certainly likely to be mainly—initially at least—an economistic one; that is to say, such support might be proffered only if guarantees are given that the working class will be able to reap its share of the benefits created, by progressive economic growth. It must rapidly become obvious that the surest way to seek to achieve this is by making it possible for workers to participate on a regular basis in the corporation: by negotiating long-term contracts. Such a development is, however, likely to be consistent with the needs of management in the large firm, who will wish to invest in a core labour force which is economically committed to the organisation—hence clarifying the distinction between primary and secondary employment.

The results of such a process may be expected not only to foster the structuration of an underclass separated from the working class as a whole, but also to provide new sources of tension or contradiction within the existing class framework in neo-capitalist society. In earlier chapters, I have suggested that the institutional mediation of power typical of capitalist society, up to the recent past, has been stabilised by the operation of factors acting to restrict union activity to an orientation towards economism (plus 'defensive control'). This has been, of course, a fragile stability which is—depending also upon other characteristics of any given society—potentially liable to be threatened by the resurgence of movements directed towards the reorganisation of industrial control. The balance of economism and conflict consciousness which has characterised the former phase of capitalist development must come under pressure with the economic changes which are implied in neo-capitalism. For it is difficult to suppose that the sorts of linkage between state and economy involved in macroeconomic planning can be formed without stimulating a redirection of the labour movement back towards an orientation to control. There are several reasons for this. One is that union leadership may be reluctant, or directly resistant, to entering into the sort of liaison with economic and political elites which is implied in neo-capitalist planning. This is likely to be especially true with regard to attempts, on the part of the polity, to implement policies designed to regulate monetary circulation and to check inflation. If the interests of the megacorporations and the modern capitalist state are generally convergent, it follows that the endeavour to moderate inflation will tend to be directed mainly towards the regulation of incomes rather than prices—although conflicts over price controls between economic and political elites are bound to occur. Union leadership may regard any type of attempt to regulate incomes with disfavour, but will certainly resist the implementation of policies which seek to restrict rises in incomes without placing comparable limitations upon rises in prices.

We must therefore expect to witness a growth in the level of official strike activity, consequent upon a struggle between the labour unions and the state. But this can normally take place within the confines of existing structures; of potentially greater significance are the possible consequences which may result as regards the relationship between the unions and the mass of workers in those economic sectors or industries particularly affected by neo-capitalist planning. For, in an important sense, the forms of economic bargaining called into play in neo-capitalism are likely to clash with an orientation towards economism. The confinement of class conflict to economism, as I have tried to make clear in the earlier analysis, depends upon the capacity of capitalism to generate a regular increase in money-wages, and a general overall augmentation in real wages (which, because it is less visible, may be more staccato than the former without endangering the existing system), in conjunction with a cluster of attitudes, towards work and towards the wider society, which serve to close off the perception of the possibility or the need to reorganise the character of industrial control. Any pressure for the external regulation of wages, even if having official union sanction, will thus tend to be resisted in and for itself. The negotiation of long-term collective contracts by the unions offers a mode of meeting such resistance: but the result of this is likely to be precisely to stimulate a renewed consciousness of problems of control among the rank-and-file. For the attempt to secure labour agreements implies both that the worker recognises a long-term commitment to the corporation, at the same time as it recognises a commitment to him, and that he comes to acknowledge an extension of collective bargaining into a sphere concerning a much broader aspect of the contractual relation than the monetary one. To the degree in which union leadership seeks to continue to operate within a framework of economism and 'defensive control', it is likely to face an increasing disaffection within its own membership, or have to adopt a stand which to some extent abandons economism in favour of an orientation to control.

In such a situation we may anticipate a revival of interest in schemes of workers' self-management. Thus there may be a parallel element here between neo-capitalism and the state socialist societies—but the social processes involved in each case are clearly in most respects quite different. In neo-capitalist society, there are likely to be a number of basic emergent tensions associated with attempts to implement economic planning, none of which is reproduced in the same form in state socialism. One centres upon the differentiation between primary and secondary employment, which may become particularly significant where there is a distinct underclass. This, as I have said, may conceivably represent a significant source of schism within the lower orders of the class structure, partly cutting across the traditionally established lines of class conflict. Where there are not major tensions at this level, conflict may become transferred to the more familiar division between skilled and non-skilled workers within the working class: craft unions are not likely to welcome unambiguously contractual agreements which to some degree cut across the old differentiations in economic advantages. In so far as oppositions of interests are involved at these levels of the class structure, and open conflicts occur, any tendency towards the ramification of class conflict involving the mass of the working class, and breaking away from the orientation to economism, will be weakened. The possibility, however, of the renewal of class conflicts relating directly to the nature of industrial control, and thus spilling over into the political sphere, is a strong one. But how far such conflicts will take the form of a major revolutionary confrontation of the working class with the existing structure of the capitalist state is not a matter which can be inferred from their generic character. In this sense recent Marxist previsions that the full-scale revolutionary transformation of capitalist society is finally at hand are no more realistic than they have been in past generations. There are instances where such an occurrence is conceivable: but these are those (France, Italy) whose development has, for specific reasons, created a class system which is not representative of that of the majority of the capitalist countries.

4. EXPLOITATION AND CLASSLESSNESS

I have suggested that there are two strands in socialist theory, which give it a paradoxical aspect. These can readily be related to the conditions which originally generated socialism (and sociology) as a coherent body of thought—the tug of war between post-feudalism and emerging industrial capitalism. The vision of an escape from the exploitation of man by man, the prospective entry into a new realm of human liberty, is one which was stimulated by the sloughing-off of the constricting social, economic and moral bounds of the traditional order. In this sense, anarchism and socialism feed from similar sources.[13] Anarchism is socialism freed of its paradox; but it is precisely this which makes the former nothing more than an irresolute *promesse de bonheur*, conjured up in recent times by the brilliantly pathetic slogans of May 1968—*Sous le pavé, la plage!* In the revolutionary schools of socialist thought, there is more than an echo of the religious spirit which in previous ages had awakened the imagination, and had created other-worldly images of a universal human freedom. But socialist theory is far more than a secularised version of the antecedent religious worldview, however much the latter may have contributed to it as a source of ideological inspiration. The advent of 'simple market society', and its imminent transcendence by capitalism, produced a series of genuine social and economic freedoms, when viewed in the perspective of the preceding order, which stimulated both a perception of the potential malleability of human society and the idea that future transformations could complete the emancipation already apparently begun by the emergence of new social forms. In this regard, socialism is aptly viewed as a radicalisation of bourgeois ideology, and has to be seen as part of a reaction to a feudal past.

In its other aspect, socialism comprises a quest to complete the rationalisation of human society by making possible the application of technical rationality to social organisation itself. This in part explains the strong affinity between most branches of socialist thought and the outlook of natural science. No socialist, of course, could accept that form of social theory which elaborated only the positivistic features of Saint-Simon's thought—Comtean philosophy —and which consequently emphasised regulation and control within a new corporate state. But the tendency to identify socialism with scientific rationalism, as itself a legitimating norm of *Praxis*, which is thus absolved of the necessity of any independent moral or normative sanction save its own scientific validity, has inevitably been very strong.

However, the search for the elimination of exploitation comes into blunt opposition to the endeavour to rationalise social organisation through the conscious direction of social and economic life. The dilemmas inherent in this antagonism are not resolved in Marxian theory, nor have they been resolved by the practical development of the advanced societies since the close of the nineteenth century. The contradiction which Marx identified in capitalism is itself contradictory! The present-day confrontation of capitalist and state socialist society has in effect given concrete shape to the issues involved. In capitalist society, the class system continues to constitute the fundamental axis of the social structure, and remains the main channel of relationships of exploitative domination. The state socialist societies, on the other hand, have genuinely succeeded in moving towards a classless order, but only at the cost of creating a system of political domination which has altered the character of social exploitation rather than necessarily diminishing it. The challenge to socialist thought today, or rather to those forms of political philosophy which seek to advance beyond the traditional confines of socialist ideas without abandoning them altogether, is to explore the lin. 's of the opposition between rationalisation in each of its aspects, a. ⁴ then to attempt to build a new reconciliation between them.

POSTSCRIPT (1979)

Although it is only six years since this book first appeared, during that period there have been major changes in the intellectual climate of the social sciences. I wrote the book in the context of the rise to prominence of the 'New Left', and the challenge which it posed both to orthodox Marxism and to the established varieties of 'academic sociology', especially to structural-functionalism. At that time it was necessary to defend the centrality of the concepts of class and class conflict in the analysis of the industrialised societies, against the views of writers associated both with the New Left and with academic sociology. Each group of authors tended to see class division and particularly class struggle as of diminishing significance in the industrially advanced world, but for different reasons (see especially pp. 269–74, above). A commonly shared standpoint among academic sociologists—and one which still has its defenders today—connected the decline of class to the increasing internal diversification of the advanced societies. This view, I tried to show, was closely affiliated to an interpretation of the development of capitalist-industrialism which for a long while had offered a rival analysis to that of Marxism: the 'theory of industrial society'.[1] Many proponents of the New Left, on the other hand, influenced by Marcuse, traced the declining relevance of class analysis to the 'one-dimensional' character of the industrialised societies. These apparently opposed views, one emphasising diversification, the other consolidation, actually shared a good deal in common. Both accepted that the 'institutionalisation of class conflict' radically undermines the role which class divisions used to have, as a focus of economic and political strife, in earlier phases of the development of the industrialised countries.

In dissenting from these views, I did not want merely to revert to an orthodox Marxist standpoint, of the sort proposed by Soviet

Marxism, or by most Western Communist Parties in the late 1960s. It seemed to me that the attacks of the New Left against 'obsolete Communism'[2] contained elements of fundamental sociological and political importance—concerning, above all, problems of 'rationalisation' and bureaucracy as sources of domination in contemporary society, capitalist and state socialist. The most appropriate strategy for studying such problems seemed to be that of attempting a creative appropriation from Max Weber as well as from Marx. The position I developed in the book owes considerably more to Marx than to Weber, but I did not hesitate to submit Marx's works to substantial critical analysis. I wanted, and still want, to be free from several sorts of dogmatism which have traditionally afflicted many orthodox Marxist writings. One is a dogmatism of the text: the presumptions of certain authors that they have a privileged access to the true meanings of Marx's texts, and that these texts are never ambiguous or inconsistent. Another might be called the dogmatism of the quotation: the supposition that, in order to validate a thesis about a particular state of affairs in society, it is enough to conjure up a quotation from Marx which appears consistent with that thesis. A third is scholastic dogmatism: the assumption that all the answers to contemporary questions of social analysis are to be found in Marx's works, if we but look hard enough. These are all related to a fourth type of dogmatism, which might be termed that of dogmatic purification: the dogma that Marxism is unique and self-enclosed, and hence must be protected against contamination from 'bourgeois thought'.[3]

Since its initial appearance this book has been subject to a variety of critical appraisals. The intervening period has also seen the publication of a number of important works that bear directly upon issues that it raised. In this discussion, I shall give particular attention to the following among such issues:

1. The relation between Marx's conception of class and the Weberian analysis of class as 'market situation'.
2. The problem of the 'new middle class' in capitalist society.
3. The relation between capitalist development and bureaucracy.
4. The nature of the capitalist state, and its relation to class conflict.

1. MARX AND WEBER: CLASS SOCIETY AND CLASS STRUCTURATION

In this section I shall concentrate upon certain misunderstandings of my views that have quite often appeared in the critical literature: misunderstandings that certainly derive in some part from faults in

my presentation. One of the most frequent interpretations that has
been made of the book is that, since considerable space is devoted to
discussion of Max Weber, and Weber's ideas are given serious
consideration, its standpoint is a Weberian, or a 'neo-Weberian'
one.[4] But I did not intend to defend a Weberian standpoint as
against a Marxist one, nor did I intend to produce some sort of
synthesis of Marx and Weber in respect of problems of class structure.
In case this is not clear, I should emphasise that I do not think such a
synthesis is either desirable or possible. Of course, the question of the
intellectual connections between the writings of Marx and Weber is
not at all easy to resolve, since there are interpretative problems on
both sides.[5] But there can be no doubt at all that there are very
deep-lying divergencies between both their overall methodological
views and their more substantive writings, and that these are reflected
directly in their respective analyses of capitalism, class and class
conflict.[6]

The significance of Weber's work for class analysis, when juxta-
posed to that of Marx, is that it identifies a number of important
areas which are relatively undeveloped in Marx's writings. These
include aspects of each of the four issues I have distinguished above.
In all of these, as I tried to show in the book, Weber's work raises
questions that must be directly confronted: 'the market' as a mediim
of class formation; the social and political significance of the 'new
middle class' in capitalism; the importance of bureaucracy as a form
of domination; and the character of the state as a focus of political
and military power. But in none of these instances did I adopt
Weberian *solutions*.

A good deal of the criticism that has been levelled against *The
Class Structure of the Advanced Societies (CSAS)* has focused upon
my introduction of the concept of 'market capacity'. Critics have
alleged that, in my analysis, 'the (Weberian) notion of "market capacity" replaces the (Marxist) relation to the means of production';[7]
or again: 'it is apparent that Giddens' principal concern is the
definition and analysis of class at the level of market encounter'.[8]
But neither of these statements accurately describes my concerns;
they really amount almost to gratuitous misreadings of the position
I developed in the book. I placed a great deal of emphasis, in discussing the emergence of the modern class system, not upon markets
as such,[9] but upon the nature of the *capitalist market*. My object in
doing so was to seek to underline the distinctiveness of capitalist
society in contrast to pre-existing types of social formation. Although
I would no longer see the characterisation I offered of 'pre-class
society' as either accurate or adequate, I still hold to the overall

standpoint I established. Capitalism is a 'class society' in a more
fundamental sense than feudalism or other types of society that have
previously existed in history. For only with the advent of capitalism
does an exploitative class relation become part of the very mechanism of the productive process itself—a phenomenon which has
important implications for assessing the scope of Marx's 'historical
materialism' and the base/superstructure problem.[10] In pre-capitalist
societies, the exploitative process involves the appropriation of
surplus production, but the relation of exploitation is not merged—as
it is in capitalism—with the labour task itself. The formation of
capitalism is not merely brought about by the expansion of commodity markets in what, following J. B. Macpherson, I called
'simple market society' (see pp. 133–4 above). The development of
trade and commerce was a significant factor in the dissolution of
localised production/consumption relationships in post-feudal
society, but in 'simple market society' the producer maintained a
considerable amount of control over the labour process. The distinctive feature of capitalism, which constitutes it as a class society,
is the intersection of commodity and labour markets within the
process of production itself. As Marx emphasised so strongly in the
first volume of *Capital*, the development of capitalism thus presupposes the creation of a mass of formally 'free' wage workers;
labour-power becomes a commodity to be bought and sold. Without
wishing to play the game of Marx-quotations, it might nevertheless
be worthwhile repeating the passage from Marx referred to on pp.
84–5 above:

The historical conditions of its existence (i.e., the existence of capitalism)
are by no means given by the mere circulation of money and commodities.
It can spring into being *only when the owner of the means of production and
subsistence meets in the market with the free labourer selling his labour-
power.* And this one historical condition comprises a world's history.
Capital, therefore, announces from its first appearance a new epoch in the
process of social production. [my italics]

Labour-power becomes 'a commodity like any other': at the same
time, it *cannot* be a commodity like any other because it involves the
activities of living beings. Property, as capital, confers a definite
range of rights or capacities upon its owners or possessors, in the
context of capitalist production. But the 'propertyless' are not
merely inert objects to be disposed of at the will of the owners of
capital. The possession of 'mere labour-power' also makes possible
certain capacities of action for its possessors, in relation to capital.
In using the term 'market capacity', I did not intend to follow

Weber's equation of 'class situation' with 'market situation'. I wanted rather to stress the centrality of the *labour contract* to the capitalist system. From the side of the capitalist, the labour contract involves the need to coordinate and control the activities of human beings over whom he has no prerogatives of the kind involved in feudal relations of fealty (nor a direct capability of physical coercion). From the side of the worker, the labour contract provides a basis for resisting the dominance of the employer, through attempting to operate sanctions upon the conditions under which labour-power is hired. The collective withdrawal of labour-power, or its threat, thus comes to constitute a major feature of capital–labour conflicts.

To suppose that, in capitalism, product and labour markets can be severed from the process of production is simply foolish or doctrinaire.[11] Moreover, it is useless to conjure up the ritual incantation that class relations are founded in the 'relations of production', if that phrase is left unexplained. Rather than substituting the concept of 'market capacity' for 'relations of production', I wanted to identify what the main components of the relations of production are within the capitalist economic order: and to show how these are involved in the structuration of class relationships (pp. 107–12, above). The phrase, 'relations of production', is often used to run together three sorts of socio-economic relationships that I thought it important to distinguish. These are those involved in:

1. The division of labour within techniques of production (para-technical relations).
2. The authority relations within the enterprise.
3. The connections between production and consumption, as involved in 'distributive groupings'.

Each of these has to be grasped in the overall context of the capital/ wage-labour relation. Max Weber tended to separate each from the class structure of capitalism, by regarding the first two as elements of a general process of 'rationalisation' of economic life, and relating the third to the sphere of 'status groups'. It is here precisely that Weber's view of 'class situation' as equivalent to 'market situation' is most consequential, as compared to Marx. In contrast to Weber's conception, my account of class structuration seeks to analyse these three sets of elements as integral to capitalism as a class society. I specifically set out to criticise (rather than merely to ignore, as many Marxists have been prone to do) the Weberian standpoint that 'starts from an assumption of the inherent rationality of technique which is viewed as the generator of a global process of rationalisation'.[12]

In discussing class structuration, I attached a good deal of importance to a fourth factor, social mobility. I see no reason to revise this as a theoretical emphasis, although arguments about the relevance of mobility to class formation continue. It is important to see that a certain conception of social mobility, as 'equality of opportunity', has been central to the theory of industrial society.[13] Rejection of the theory of industrial society does not, however, entail repudiating the significance of connections that exist between levels and modes of mobility and class structuration.[14] This has been acknowledged even by Poulantzas, who perhaps comes closest among modern class theorists to taking a view like that of Schumpeter (see p. 107, above). Although Poulantzas in a recent work speaks dismissively of 'the stupidity of the bourgeois problematic of social mobility',[15] he goes on later in the same book to recognise—albeit rather grudgingly—the relevance of both inter- and intra-generational mobility to class formation and class consciousness in capitalist society.[16] Of course, the importance of mobility does not simply depend upon the actual distribution of mobility chances, but also upon the ideological implications of notions of 'equality of opportunity', etc.

Before leaving the question of 'Weberianism' and moving on to more substantial issues, it might be worthwhile re-emphasising certain of the main themes of *CSAS*. The book is sometimes regarded as expressing a similar standpoint to Frank Parkin's *Class Inequality and Political Order*, which first appeared at about the same date. But in fact our views are quite distinct—as regards the characterisation of both capitalism and state socialism, although I shall only refer to the first of these here. Parkin's conception is much closer to an unreconstructed Weberian position than my own. Parkin's overall emphasis, as he makes clear, is upon the distribution of inequalities or 'rewards' associated with class relations. The significance of private property as capital is barely analysed by Parkin at all. Where he does mention property, which is very briefly,[17] it is in terms of the economic rewards that property ownership may confer. His 'dominant class' is not defined in terms of property, but as non-manual workers. My conception—drawn from Marx—of the centrality of the labour contract to the capitalist class system, and thus of the significance of market capacity to class structuration, diverges substantially from Parkin's views. Throughout the book I was concerned to demonstrate the essential importance of private property to the organisation of capitalist society. Although I thought, and still think, it justifiable to defend a three-class model of capitalist society, the whole of my analysis is predicated upon accepting the capital/wage-labour relation as integral to the 'structural principle'[19] dominant in capitalism.

2. THE PROBLEM OF THE 'NEW MIDDLE CLASS'

Questions concerning the 'new middle class' have brooked large in discussions of class analysis ever since the debates over Marxist revisionism in the German Social Democratic Party. In the book I distinguished three main interpretations of the relative expansion of 'white-collar' occupations. One such interpretation, particularly favoured by some American authors, was that the relative increase in white-collar work heralds the arrival of a 'middle-class society'. This kind of view was linked to the idea that established forms of class conflict progressively disappear as the process of *embourgeoisement* becomes more complete. It stood in direct contrast to a second interpretation, the attempt of Mallet and others to appropriate some of those in these intermediate occupations to a potentially revolutionary 'new working class', rather than to a 'new middle class'. The third view was that of orthodox Marxism: that most of those in white-collar occupations are being downgraded rather than upgraded, in a process of proletarianisation, so that neither a new middle class nor a new working class exists at all. I rejected all of these views, although not *in toto*. Both of the first two, it seemed to me, derived in some part from over-generalisation from specific societies, one of the tendencies I was concerned to criticise throughout *CSAS*. The very same occupational categories supposedly involved in the revolutionary vanguard of the 'new working class' in France, where that conception originated, were taken by writers in the United States to be among the most stable and quiescent sectors of the 'middle-class society'. The third view simply seemed to fly in the face of the evidence, which just does not conform to traditional ideas that white-collar workers are (finally!) becoming thrust down into the proletariat.[20]

Marxist authors however have in recent years devoted considerable attention to developing accounts of the distinctive characteristics of a white-collar middle class. Among writings worthy of mention are those by Carchedi, Wright and Poulantzas. Of these the least interesting, marred as it is by a peculiarly unrepentant form of functionalism, is that offered by Carchedi.[21] Carchedi defines capitalist production as involving a reciprocity of functions between capital and wage-labour. To 'perform the function of labour' is to participate in the process of generating surplus value; to 'perform the function of capital' is 'to take part exclusively in the surplus value producing process', which means participating in the 'control and surveillance' of labour.[22] Those who perform the function of labour make up the 'collective worker'. In contemporary capitalism, dominated by large

monopolies, the function of capital is no longer performed by
individuals, but collectively: the counterpart to the collective worker
is thus the 'global capitalist', composed of those who carry out the
'control and surveillance' of workers. The new middle class is then
identified as those who carry out functions of both collective worker
and global capitalist. This refers, Carchedi says, only to the
'economic identification' of the new middle class: such an identification, he argues, has to precede more complicated analyses which
could be arrived at (but which he does not attempt) if 'ideological
and political dimensions' were introduced.

The new middle class, in Carchedi's view, is a specific development
of the emergence of the large corporations. Accepting the managerial-
ist thesis, which he calls the 'ideological description of the emergence
of the global function of capital', Carchedi argues that the new
middle class is a phenomenon of the diffusion of the control of
capital. The function of capital is no longer carried out by 'the
capitalist class', but by the propertyless middle class also. Because
the members of the new middle class do not have 'real ownership' of
the means of production, the global function of capital is not always
dominant over that of the collective worker; the latter may dominate
over the former. Members of the new middle class, in sum, 'are
partly on the side of capital and partly on the side of labour. This
is the contradiction inherent in their position. Moreover, even when
they are on the side of capital, they are both exploiters (or oppressors)
and oppressed. This is an element of further contradiction inherent
in their position'.[23]

Carchedi's views have a certain similarity to those of Wright, as
the latter admits.[24] According to Wright, the new middle class can
be understood as comprising 'contradictory class locations' in
capitalist society. The class relations involved in capitalist production, Wright argues, can be analysed in terms of three basic sets
of elements: control of labour-power, control of the 'physical means
of production', and control of capital allocation. The class division
between capitalist and worker can be seen as involving a unity of
each of these elements. The capitalist controls capital allocation, the
uses to which the means of production are put, and the authority
relations to which labour is subject; the worker is excluded from
each of these forms of control. 'Contradictory class locations', by
contrast, are those which do not cluster at either of these poles, but
involve mixes of the three sets of elements. Thus middle managers in
industry, for example, have little or no say in the allocation of capital
investment, but enjoy a certain degree of control over their means of
production and over the labour-power of others. Top managers are

in contradictory locations 'at the boundary of the bourgeoisie', while foremen and line managers are in contradictory locations 'at the boundary of the proletariat'.[25] Clerical workers and other lower-level white-collar workers, Wright says, occupy contradictory locations between the petty bourgeoisie, or old middle class, and the working class. He hedges his bets on proletarianisation: 'It remains to be shown whether the net effect of these two tendencies— the expansion of white-collar employment and the proletarianisation of white-collar work—has increased or decreased the contradictory locations between the working class and the petty bourgeoisie'.[26]

The writings of Carchedi and Wright are significant in so far as they mark a break with the tendency of Marxist writers to deny that there is anything at all distinctive about the class position of white-collar workers as compared to the mass of the working class— although, as I have said, it should be remembered it was Marxist analysts (mainly 'revisionists') who were among the first to give detailed attention originally to the 'new middle class'.[27] But there are substantial objections that can be brought against the ideas of both Carchedi and Wright. I should wish to reject every sort of functional-ism, whether Marxist or otherwise.[28] Quite apart from this, however, there are serious limitations to the mode of analysis pursued by Carchedi. His approach is an objectivist one, which presumes that classes can be 'identified economically' in separation from class conflict and class consciousness; Carchedi seems to assume that classes can be regarded as economically formed prior to their entry into 'ideological and political' relations.[29] Poulantzas among others has provided a convincing critique of this type of standpoint—as I also tried to do in *CSAS*. More important in the present context, Carchedi's formulation of the functions of the global capitalist and the collective worker appears to elevate the 'control and surveillance of labour'—i.e., authority relations or power—to a central place at the expense of the ownership of capital. Carchedi's equation of the global capitalist with 'a hierarchical and bureaucratic structure'[30] comes oddly close to the views of Dahrendorf and Galbraith. What Carchedi insistently calls 'real ownership', as opposed to legal ownership, is conceptualised in such a way as to conflate property and authority.[31] A whole series of issues, which I conceptualised as involving the relation between 'the institutional mediation of power' and the 'mediation of control' are swept under the carpet of the concept of the 'global capitalist'. Carchedi only discusses Dahrendorf's analysis very cursorily. But, in respect of the character-isation of the new middle class, he differentiates his conception from that of Dahrendorf only in so far as Carchedi holds that members of the new middle class perform both the 'global function of capital' and that of the 'collective worker'; whereas Dahrendorf distinguishes two segments of the new middle class, one affiliated to capital, the other to wage-labour. Carchedi seems to have no qualms in assimilating his 'global capitalist' to Dahrendorf's dominant class, which is defined in terms of 'authoritative control'.[32]

Although he echoes criticisms of my standpoint as 'Weberian',[33] Wright's discussion actually in some ways quite closely resembles my analysis of the major factors involved in class structuration—save that he gives no attention to phenomena outside the workplace as relevant to class formation (i.e., 'distributive groupings'). 'Control of labour power', as Wright uses the phrase, refers to authority relations in the setting of the productive enterprise; control of the 'physical means of production' is not too different from what I called 'paratechnical relations'. However, we may doubt that it is useful to refer to white-collar occupations as involving specifically 'contradictory locations'. The concept of 'contradiction' is used in a very loose way by many writers, and is often treated as merely a synonym for 'conflict' or 'antagonism'. I think it is necessary and important to distinguish conflict and contradiction, although I would no longer follow exactly the same differentiation which I made between the two in *CSAS*.[34] However this may be, the basic nexus of contradiction in capitalism, as Wright would certainly agree, is to be found in the relation between capital and wage-labour. All class relations, as he acknowledges, are contradictory: those involving the new middle class are therefore 'doubly contradictory'.[35] But this is at best misleading. For surely it is the *working class*, rather than the new middle class, which experiences and embodies most acutely the contradictory character of capitalist production. The 'most contradictory' class locations, Wright says, 'are occupied by middle managers and what can loosely be termed "technocrats" '.[36] But Wright does not see these groups as potentially revolutionary, in the manner of the new working class of Mallet. The term 'contradictory', as applied by Wright to the structuration of the new middle class, is a misnomer.

There are at least three further respects in which both Carchedi's and Wright's analyses seem to me deficient as interpretations of the class relations involved in white-collar labour. First, neither author gives sufficient attention to the influence of the labour market upon class structuration. Several aspects of the market capacity of white-collar workers have been important historically in respect of class formation, as I attempted to show in detail: the possession of educational qualifications of various sorts, the level of job security and other benefits, and the chances of promotion up a 'career' hierarchy. There is no doubt that these have been eroded in some degree, especially when those in lower-level white-collar occupations are compared with skilled workers. But there is also no doubt about their continuing significance, and their relevance to class conflict and class consciousness. Second, both authors downplay the importance of manual/non-manual divisions (in contrast to Poulantzas). The separation of manual and non-manual labour has sometimes been regarded as one of the most fundamental concerns of Marxist theory.[37] In the more immediate context of class structuration, it is of consequence both materially and ideologically, as an aspect of the division of labour. 'Relations of production' has to include not merely who controls the 'physical means of production', as Wright puts it, but the influence of the material character of the labour task and the work environment upon social relationships. The significance of manual/non-manual differentiations is not that some workers do not perform 'mental operations' whereas others do, but that 'paper-work' normally implies a different (and usually physically separate) work environment (the 'office') from 'manual labour' (the 'shop-floor'). Third, both writers ignore the participation of women in the white-collar labour force. The declining economic conditions of work of clerical occupations and the 'mechanisation of the office' have everywhere been accompanied by the expansion of what I called in the book a female 'underclass of white-collar labour'. The double discrimination suffered by women—discrimination within a segmented labour market plus subjection to domestic drudgery—still awaits adequate theorisation in terms of class analysis. But the fact that the proletarianisation of lower-level white-collar labour has at the same time involved its feminisation has probably consolidated rather than dissolved pre-existing divisions between the working and new middle classes (see p. 288, above). Whether this is so or not, it is quite illegitimate simply to pass over the connections between class exploitation and sexual exploitation in respect of market capacity.

Poulantzas's discussion of the new middle class or, as he prefers to call it, the 'new petty bourgeoisie', continues the general theoretical emphases he introduced in *Political Power and Social Classes*.[38] Unlike Carchedi, he does not hold that an 'economic identification' of classes can precede an examination of their political and ideological dimensions: classes are formed in a conjunction of economic, political and ideological 'levels' (and always defined in and through class conflict).[39] The main economic criterion Poulantzas applies to distinguish the new petty bourgeoisie from the working class is the differentiation of unproductive from productive labour: the prole-

tariat comprises those involved in productive labour. His primary
'political' criterion is supervisory as compared to non-supervisory
positions. His chief 'ideological' criterion is the division between
non-manual and manual labour. Since he emphasises that classes
cannot be defined in purely economic terms, Poulantzas is prepared to
accept that some types of productive worker are not working class:
political/ideological criteria may place them in the new petty bourgeoisie. Moreover, Poulantzas specifically disputes the sort of
conclusion reached by advocates of the proletarianisation thesis:
white-collar workers are clearly separated from the working class,
Poulantzas says, by virtue of participating in the ideological domination of manual by mental labour.[40] One of the distinctive features of
Poulantzas's analysis, and a reason why he speaks of the 'new petty
bourgeoisie' rather than 'new middle class', is his claim that the new
and old petty bourgeoisie (old middle class) can be categorised as a
single class. This is not because they are the same economically,
according to him, but because they share a common politico-ideologi-
cal position and outlook: here Poulantzas mentions some of the
features I called (pp. 111 and 185–6, above) 'class awareness'.

In *CSAS* I rejected the theory of surplus value and the associated
distinction between productive and unproductive labour in favour
of a broader conception of exploitation. I think today that my
rejection of these notions was too categorical; and although I
should still want to locate the theory of surplus value within a wider
conception of exploitative domination in class society, the definition
of exploitation that I offered (pp. 130–1) was quite inadequate. However, Poulantzas's attempt to use the productive/unproductive
labour distinction as a basic economic criterion for distinguishing
between working class and 'new petty bourgeoisie' is open to major
objections. Poulantzas's version of the concept of productive labour
is a particularly restrictive one. Productive labour, for Poulantzas, is
labour which creates surplus value through the production of
material commodities. If productive labour, thus conceptualised, is
connected to Poulantzas's other criteria, it leads to the curious conclusion that the advanced capitalist societies are more dominated by
the middle class than even the most enthusiastic proponents of the
emergence of a 'middle class society' have believed. Thus according
to Wright's calculations, if Poulantzas's criteria are applied to the
American labour force, the new petty bourgeoisie constitute 70 per
cent of the economically active population, whereas the working
class form only some 20 per cent.[41] Quite apart from this statistical
argument, there are other reasons to doubt that the productive/
unproductive labour distinction is an appropriate basis for differenti-

ating the working and new middle classes.[42]

Poulantzas's claim that the 'old and new petty bourgeoisie' can be treated as belonging to a single 'middle class' is especially unconvincing. There is no doubt that in certain respects, and at certain conjunctures, the members of old and new middle classes do share common interests and forms of class consciousness. But the divisions between them are at least as deep as characteristics they might have in common. The economic circumstances of the old middle class are chronically threatened by the large capital of the megacorporations; whereas the growth of the large corporations is a major element promoting the expansion of remunerative white-collar 'careers'. Small capital is often in opposition to the spread of the activities of the state, which however again tends to contribute to economic changes favouring certain categories of propertyless white-collar workers. Moreover, the 'class awareness' of white-collar workers, often geared towards career mobility within large-scale organisations, may be only marginally related to the independent individualism of the small entrepreneur. Poulantzas's conceptual merging of the old and new middle classes also points to unresolved difficulties in his general theoretical standpoint, in respect of his attempt to avoid 'economism'. In combining 'economic, political and ideological levels', Poulantzas claims to maintain the primacy of the economic domain. But it is hard to see that he does so in respect of the postulated unity of the old and new middle classes: for these have different economic bases, and form a single class for Poulantzas only because of their supposed 'ideological' affinities.

In sum, notwithstanding the interest of some of the formulations of the authors I have mentioned in this section, I do not think their work would lead me to make substantial alterations in the analysis of the new middle class offered in *CSAS*. The sources of class structuration of the new middle class are more heterogeneous than those of either the dominant or working classes; and, as I emphasised (p. 288, above), the new middle class rarely features prominently in manifest class struggles. But in all the advanced capitalist societies, its social and political significance is considerable: that this is so is at least more widely acknowledged today by Marxist authors than was the case some years ago.

3. CAPITALIST DEVELOPMENT AND BUREAUCRACY

One of my main aims in *CSAS* was to explore the relations between property and authority, or between what I would now call generically 'allocation' and 'authorisation', as structured resources constituting forms of domination.[43] The classical Marxian texts lack an adequate theory of bureaucratic domination, and Marxist authors have rarely given sufficient attention to integrating the critical analysis of class domination with the critical analysis of bureaucratic domination.[44] Weber's interpretation of the rise of modern capitalism as intrinsically promoting the spread of bureaucracy, and his linkage of bureaucratisation to a broader 'process of rationalisation' have to be directly confronted here. I did not pretend to offer an exhaustive analysis of Weber's notion of rationalisation,[45] but attempted to distinguish, as separable sources of class structuration, phenomena which Weber bound together along the dimension of rationalisation —bureaucratisation. Weber's analyses draw direct connections between paratechnical relations and the authority system of the productive enterprise; and between the authority system of the enterprise and the capitalist state. The rationality of technique is treated as integrally involved with the rationality of bureaucratic domination in the specification of these connections. Weber quite often compares bureaucracy directly to a machine (cf. pp. 275ff., above): both are the most 'technically-rational' means of harnessing energies to the fulfilment of specific tasks. An individual within a bureaucratic organisation, Weber says, 'is only a single cog in an ever-moving mechanism which prescribes to him an essentially fixed rate of march'.[46]

Two basic questions suggest themselves. How far is the rationality of technique specifically an outcome of capitalist class domination? How valid is Weber's analysis of bureaucratic organisation, as implying the inevitable concentration of power within 'imperatively coordinated associations'? The connecting point between these questions is to be found in the concept of the division of labour.[47] At the time when I wrote *CSAS* only a few general analyses of the division of labour in capitalist production, most notably that by Georges Friedmann,[48] were available. Since then, however, a major contribution dealing with this problem has appeared, Braverman's *Labor and Monopoly Capital*.[49]

Braverman's starting point is the sale of labour-power as a commodity: in selling their labour-power to the capitalist, workers cede control of the labour task. The consolidation and expansion of this control is the first imperative of 'management'.[50] The division of labour plays a crucial part in this process, but not the division of labour in general. Braverman insists upon the importance of distinguishing between the social and technical division of labour. The social division of labour, which involves the separation of tasks devoted to the making of whole products, is found in all societies;

the technical division of labour, involving the detailed fragmentation of the labour task into repetitive operations carried out by different individuals, is specifically characteristic of capitalist production. The progression of the technical division of labour, Braverman argues, is central to management control of the labour process, since it enables knowledge of and command over the labour process to be taken more and more completely out of the hands of the worker. Taylorism, or 'scientific management', is the most developed and comprehensive form which this takes: the operations carried out by the worker are integrated into the technical design of production as a whole. The 'sieving off' of knowledge of and skill in work that is maximised by the application of Taylorism, according to Braverman, has today become intrinsic to the technological development of capitalism. Subsequent changes in management ideology which might seem to have replaced Taylorism, such as the emergence of the 'human relations approach', are in fact only of marginal significance. Taylorism has become the secular organising creed of capitalist production.

Braverman's analysis, as against that of Weber, allows us to show that the rationality of technique in modern industrial enterprise is not neutral in respect of class domination. The importance of this can scarcely be over-emphasised. Industrial technique embodies the capital/wage-labour relation within its very form. Class domination is shown to be the absent centre of the linkage Weber drew between the rationality of technique and the rationality of the most 'technically effective' form of authority: bureaucracy. Although Braverman's use of Marx's differentiation between 'the division of labour in society' and 'the division of labour in the workshop'—the social and technical division of labour—can be questioned,[51] his emphasis upon the integration of the capitalist division of labour and management control is illuminating. Moreover, it offers the possibility of reconnecting the Marxian theme of 'alienated labour' directly with a socio-economic analysis of the nature of capitalist production.

This having been said, there are substantial limitations to, and objections that can be made against, Braverman's approach. I shall confine my discussion here to those which have some bearing upon issues raised by Weber's conception of bureaucracy.

First, although Braverman's discussion radically alters the nature of the connections Weber draws between technique and bureaucratic administration, Braverman has little to say about the 'internal' organisation of managerial authority in capitalistic enterprise.[52] Hence it is not clear what becomes of the knowledge and control of the labour process that is taken from the worker. To say merely that it is appropriated by 'capital' is as vague and unsatisfactory as talking of the 'global function' of capital as being that of the 'control and surveillance' of labour.'

Second, Braverman describes the 'sieving off' of knowledge and skill from the worker as largely a one-way movement. The result, curiously, is an analysis which underestimates the consciousness and capabilities of workers as compared to management and which, notwithstanding its divergence from a Weberian model of progressive 'bureaucratic rationalisation', portrays a process seemingly as irreversible as that envisaged by Weber. In Braverman's work, this consequence derives in some part from his declared attempt to concern himself only with the ' "objective" content of class', and not with the 'subjective will'.[53] But a great deal of his book is actually about the 'subjective will' of *management*, as manifest in Taylorism, etc. It is impossible to sever 'objective' and 'subjective' components of class in the manner in which Braverman tries to do, as if the first can be analysed separately and the second added in later[54]—here there is a definite similarity between the approaches of Braverman and Carchedi. Workers' knowledge of the labour process is not confined to the nature of the work task: the implications of technological change have been grasped by workers as well as management, and actively resisted by them. Historical studies of the American working class indicate not only that Taylorism had considerably less impact than Braverman suggests, in large degree because of worker resistance, but that the expansion of more 'humanistic' conceptions of industrial relations was also in some part an outcome of working class opposition to Taylorism.[55]

This point can be generalised, and focused back upon Weber's interpretation of bureaucracy. Most Marxist authors who have discussed Weber's treatment of bureaucracy have been insufficiently critical of the way in which Weber actually characterises bureaucratic hierarchies. That is to say, they have accepted that bureaucratic systems of administration do have the traits which Weber attributed to them, but treat these as an outcome of the class relations of capitalism. However, it is important to develop a more frontal attack upon Weber's thesis that the advance of bureaucratisation inevitably produces an increasingly rigid hierarchy of power within an organisation.[56] As Crozier has shown, the relations between offices in bureaucratic organisations offer spaces of potential control for subordinates that are not available in smaller, more traditional collectivities.[57] The generalised contrast which Weber tended to draw between the autonomy of action enjoyed by actors in traditional communities and the 'steel-hard' nature of developed bureaucratic systems is not justifiable. In fact it is plausible to argue that the more tightly knit and inflexible the formal relations of authority in an organisation, the more they can be circumvented and manipulated by those in subordinate positions to their own advantage. Successful struggle for the maintenance of elements of control by subordinates is much more prevalent than Weber acknowledged.

The significance of struggle on the level of day to day practices is frequently left untheorised in Marxist analyses, both on the level of bureaucratic hierarchies and that of the shop-floor: Braverman's work is actually rather conventional in this respect. This tendency, especially pronounced among the more orthodox Marxist writers, is undoubtedly related to the 'failure' of workers in advanced capitalist countries to have produced a successful proletarian revolution. Less dramatic forms of worker resistance are thereby ignored or written off as insignificant. In *CSAS* I tried to sustain the claims that the successes of the labour movement have been very considerable, and that they have provided the major impetus transforming the 'liberal state' into the 'liberal-democratic state' (cf. pp. 284-7, above). Worker resistance is however important in regard of two other characteristics of the development of the working-class over the past century: the prominence of what I called 'conflict consciousness', as distinguished from 'revolutionary consciousness'; and the persistence of skill differentiations among manual workers. The prevalence of conflict consciousness is not surprising given the 'defensive' nature of the attempts of workers to maintain or recover aspects of control over circumstances of their labour that are excluded from the labour contract and materially eroded by technological development. Rejection of the routines of oppressive labour may take various forms, including absenteeism, sabotage, etc.[58] It would be quite mistaken to see the variety of day to day worker resistance as secondary and unimportant because it does not promise the imminent demolition of the capitalist mode of production.

I still think it correct to argue, as I did in *CSAS*, that the continuing internal differentiation of the working class is fundamentally important to the social and political development of the capitalist societies since Marx's day.[59] A significant contribution to the analysis of this issue has recently been made by Andrew Friedman.[60] Friedman suggests that in anticipating a progressive homogenisation of labour through the dissolution of skill differentials, Marx did not allow sufficient weight to the power of worker resistance at the level of the firm, and the need of capitalists and managers to build the fact of such power into their managerial strategies. Labour-power insistently refuses to be a commodity like any other. Friedman distinguishes two main types of managerial strategy which may be used to control the labour force. One such strategy he calls 'responsible autonomy'. Here managers allow workers substantial independence of action in the work situation, so as to encourage them to adapt to technological and other economic changes in a manner that conforms to overall management objectives. The other strategy is that of 'direct control', which tries to harness labour-power by close supervision, the maintenance of strict labour discipline, and the minimising of worker responsibility through Taylorist techniques. Braverman, Friedman argues, over-emphasises the second of these strategies, as many Marxist authors have tended to do. This over-emphasis follows from 'a failure to appreciate the importance of worker resistance as a force provoking accommodating changes in the mode of production', a mistake which 'leads to a technological deterministic view of capitalist development'.[61]

Friedman argues that employers tend to divide workers into two categories, and apply differing strategies to them. Some categories of labour are regarded as essential to the long-run profitability of the firm. Others are treated as more peripheral. Central workers enjoy greater job security than peripheral workers, and are allowed 'responsible autonomy' in the work situation; peripheral workers are more prone to be subject to 'direct control' of one form or another. Since peripheral workers are likely to be divided off from central workers along sexual or ethnic lines, Friedman's distinctions help to elucidate the significance of dual or segmented labour markets for class analysis (cf. pp. 219–20, above). But the distinguishing of central from peripheral workers, in conjunction with an emphasis upon struggle 'at the micro-level', also illuminates processes whereby skill differentials are sustained in the face of technological innovation. Central workers are often able to protect their 'skilled' position even when technological change has simplified the nature of the actual labour tasks they perform; or they are able to use their privileged market capacity to appropriate new skills which may be demanded by processes of technological change that destroy old skills. 'Centre-periphery relations', Friedman concludes, 'demonstrate the fundamental inequality among workers which is generated through struggle as part of the *normal* development of capitalist societies'.[62]

4. THE NATURE OF THE CAPITALIST STATE AND ITS RELATION TO CLASS CONFLICT

In *CSAS*, although I made no claim to produce a comprehensive analysis of the modern state, I set out to question a well-established conception of the relation between polity and economy in contemporary capitalism. The view is one which has been particularly closely associated with the writings of the leading figures of the 'Frankfurt School' (Horkheimer, Adorno, Marcuse) but it is by no means confined to those authors. According to this standpoint (see pp. 284ff., above), the high point of capitalist development is to be found in the nineteenth century—epitomised by Victorian Britain. Since the state does not intervene extensively in economic life, economic activity is largely unfettered; in these circumstances, class conflict is manifest and acute. With the further development of capitalism, however, the economy becomes increasingly politicised, and class struggle loses its prime place as a dynamic source of transformative change. Such a conception shares more than a superficial similarity with the theory of industrial society as developed in the 1950s and 1960s. The proponents of the theory of industrial society placed more emphasis upon the 'institutionalisation of class conflict', or upon the acquisition of citizenship rights, than upon state intrusion into economic life; but all shared a picture of a society which, for worse or for better, had successfully eliminated the transformative potential of class conflict. This view seemed to me to be wrong, in whatever version it might be held, for two reasons: it accepts too unquestioningly the 'case' of nineteenth-century Britain as the exemplar of capitalist development; and it is based upon misleading premises of classical political economy. So far as the first of these is concerned, it has become apparent that British history, in several important respects, is more of a 'deviant case' of the development of industrial capitalism than an exemplary one. So far as the second is concerned, the basic mistake is to identify 'capitalism' primarily with competitiveness in labour and commodity markets, as the classical economists did. As the state expands the range of its economic activities, and as the sectors dominated by monopoly or oligopoly grow, so it appears that the mechanisms of capitalist production identified by Marx become superseded. It seemed to me right to claim that capitalist society is predicated upon an institutional separation of the economy and polity, but wrong to equate this separation with the competitiveness of markets.[63] The 'insulation' of economy and polity persists as a fundamental feature of neo-capitalism, although the modes in which such insulation is sustained clearly differ from those characteristic of earlier phases of capitalist development.

In discussing the insulation of economy and polity in capitalist society, I think today that I concentrated too one-sidedly upon its internal form within the nation-state. The insulation of economy and polity operates externally as well as internally, in the relations between nation-states in the context of what Wallerstein has called the 'modern world-economy'.[64] While there are criticisms that can be made against certain of his arguments,[65] Wallerstein's discussion can be usefully drawn upon to complement the analysis I provided. According to Wallerstein, the European world-economy, which has its origins in the late fifteenth century, is quite different from the empires that have preceded it. In such empires, the relations between the metropolitan centre and subordinate regions were predominently political in character; the collection of taxes by the imperial state was the principal basis of economic connections within the imperial domains. The economic, in other words, was fused with the political. But with the development of the capitalist world-economy, the sphere of the political becomes confined to the nation-state, which commands a monopoly of law and the means of violence; while the wider connections between nation-state are primarily economic. 'Capitalism', Wallerstein says, 'as an economic mode is based on the fact that the economic factors operate within an arena larger than that which any political society can totally control'.[66]

One of Max Weber's most important contributions to social analysis was to emphasise the significance of the formation of the state in the development of Western capitalism, where the state is defined in terms of its monopoly of law and the means of violence within specified territorial boundaries. This emphasis stands in contrast to one of the dominant trends in the social thought of the nineteenth century and early twentieth century: the presumption that the exchange relations involved in modern industry are fundamentally pacific (thereby contrasting with the 'militaristic' nature of feudal society).[67] For Weber, the concentration of a repressive apparatus in the hands of the state is closely tied to his general analysis of technical rationality and bureaucratisation, as one institutional form which the centralisation of the 'means of administration' assumes. But just as this analysis can be broken down and connected to the class structure of capitalism on the level of bureaucracy and the division of labour, so it can be also in respect of the state. I have only the space here to set this down in the briefest outline. The emergence of the absolutist state in Europe, through the concentration of power in the hands of the monarchy, was the condition for the internal and external insulation of economy and polity, which in turn was the condition for the formation of the capitalist market. Internally, the consolidation of the state had as its counterpart the creation of civil society as a distinct sphere from that of the polity. Externally, the emergence of the state clearly delimited the scope of the polity in respect of the territorial sovereignty of others. The nature of the capitalist world-economy was established as part of the same process that created the conditions for the initial expansion of capitalistic enterprise internally—prior to the occurrence of 'bourgeois revolutions' as such.

It seems plausible to argue that the concentration of the means of repression in the hands of the state was closely related historically to the evolution of the capitalist labour contract. In the *Ständestaat*, 'law' was still substantially embedded in the traditionally established rights and obligations of the estates, as was the capability of using force to uphold those rights and obligations.[68] The (legitimate and actual) capability to employ means of violence to ensure performance of economic duties was directly involved in the relation between dominant class and subordinate producers. This was also the case in empires, in so far as tax collection was directly bolstered by the threat or use of force. The capitalist labour contract involves only the 'economic' exchange of 'free' labour-power for a wage, and embodies no other rights or obligations: the employer hence is no longer able to discipline a labour force through the *direct* control of violence or its threat. The spread of capitalist markets can thus be seen as both condition and consequence of the 'extension' of control of the means of repression from the social relations involved in the productive process, and their appropriation by the state. Of course between the absolutist state and the modern nation-state there is an extended process of development; but I think the analysis I have just sketched in could provide a basis for relating capitalist development intrinsically to the internal/external insulation of the economic and political, and to the role of political violence in modern history.

In recent years there has been a welcome, and long overdue, recognition by Marxist authors that the capitalist state is not a mere shadowy epiphenomenon of the 'economic base', and a break away from what I called (p. 51, above) the 'instrumental' conception of the state. There are major limitations, however, to discussions of the state by Poulantzas, Mandel and others. However much 'relative autonomy' may be accorded the state, the state is still regarded only 'negatively', in terms of how it sustains (even if only in the long term) the hegemony of capital.[69] The state is treated only from the point of view of its involvement in the reproduction of capitalist social relations. But as against this type of analysis, we can argue that, if the state is not neutral in respect of class domination, neither is it unilaterally involved in the perpetuation of capitalism. The state participates in the primary contradiction of capitalist society, between private appropriation and socialised production.[70] A notable contribution to the analysis of the contradictory nature of the capitalist state has been made by Claus Offe in his various writings.[71] Offe makes a distinction between 'allocative' and 'productive' activities of the state. Allocative activities are those involving resources controlled by the state, and include Keynesian forms of state intervention in the economy. Productive state policies, which are characteristic of the contemporary phase of development of capitalist countries, are directed to intervention in the accumulation process itself. Productive state activities are 'market replacing', and are organised with a view to 'managing' the crisis-tendencies of capitalist production. Both types of state intervention involve the state in contradictions, because in each the state is impelled in the direction of socialising economic activity in the very process of protecting the interests of private capital; but the contradictory character of the state is accentuated in so far as it undertakes productive rather than allocative policies. 'The *existence* of a capitalist state presupposes the systematic *denial* of its nature as a *capitalist state*'.[72]

This view may be regarded as logically equivalent and substantively connected to Marx's analysis of joint-stock companies, as representing 'the abolition of the capitalist mode of production within the capitalist mode of production itself' (see pp. 35–6, above). The joint-stock company expresses in a concrete way the primary contradiction of capitalism, representing an anticipation of a new mode of economic organisation yet being part and parcel of the old one. The same may be said of the productive activities of the state. The 'decommodification' of sectors of economic life through socialisation under the direction of the state is a material anticipation of a new society at the same time as it helps to sustain capitalistic enterprise. 'The state's attempts to maintain and universalise the commodity form require organisations which cease to be subject to the commodity form in their own mode of operation'.[73]

To point to the importance of Offe's work is not to accept it in its entirety, since Offe, in company with Habermas, holds that 'traditional' capital/wage-labour conflicts are considerably less significant in contemporary capitalism than I think is the case. Although they see neo-capitalism as more strife-ridden than the 'older generation' of Frankfurt writers, they nevertheless accept that the labour movement has been successfully 'incorporated' into the polity in the advanced capitalist societies. Curiously, Habermas appears to think modern capitalism more stable than Daniel Bell does.[74]

The question of the 'incorporation' of the working class within capitalist society, of course, is at the heart of debates between

Marxists and non-Marxists about the contemporary evolution of capitalism. Although it has been criticised both from the Right and the Left, I should not be inclined to modify the position I set out in *CSAS* in any basic way. This standpoint involved three main ideas.

(1) The character of labour movements and their relation to the formation of political parties and other organisations is strongly influenced by the specific experience of different societies in 'critical phases' of the early development of capitalist-industrialism. The famous question of 'why there is no socialism in the United States' cannot be discussed separately from that of the long-established radicalism of labour movements in countries such as France and Italy. It still seems to me essential to distinguish between 'conflict consciousness' and 'revolutionary consciousness', and to see that the second is not simply an extension of the first. Class struggles in the United States have certainly been as pronounced and bitter as in any European country, in spite of the relative absence of revolutionary consciousness in the American labour movement. As one American commentator has recently noted, 'Taking tough-as-nails stands on economic battlefields is not the same thing as radical class consciousness. Consequently, it is necessary to probe elsewhere to discover why economic militancy (in the United States) did not broaden out to become widespread political radicalism despite pressures in that direction'.[75]

(2) The attempts of labour movements to secure full political rights for the working class within the framework of liberal capitalism have been very consequential for the evolution of the advanced capitalist societies in the twentieth century. I sought to question two opposed interpretations of this process. On the one hand, Marxist authors have often been dismissive of the achievement of 'citizenship rights' on the part of the working class as of little consequence in altering the character of the capitalist state. On the other hand, writers such as Bendix and Roth have advanced the thesis that the basic divisions which Marx attributed to class conflict are in fact the outcome of the exclusion of the working class from participation in the state; with the attainment of the franchise, the main basis for class conflict disappears. Neither of these standpoints seemed to me to be correct. The view I set out, and which I should still wish to defend today, owes a good deal again to the various writings of Macpherson. This involves seeing the insulation of the 'political' and the 'economic' in advanced capitalism as having been formed in a two-stage process. The consolidation of the capitalist market economy was associated with the replacement of the absolutist state by the 'liberal state', the first phase of 'hegemonic capitalism'. The

liberal state, in Macpherson's words, 'was a system of alternate or multiple parties whereby governments could be held responsible to different sections of the class or classes that held a political voice . . . the job of the liberal state was to maintain and promote the liberal society, which was not essentially a democratic or an equal society'.[76] The 'liberal democratic' state was only achieved through the struggle of the working class to achieve the franchise. There can be no doubt that the emergence of liberal democracy has been a major stabilising influence in modern capitalism. The fact that liberal or social democracy—rather than fascism, as seemed to be the case to many Marxists in the 1930s—is the 'normal political form' of advanced capitalism has extremely important sociological and political implications. The connections between capitalism and liberal democracy are much more profoundly embedded than is suggested by those interpretations which trace the limitations of the attainments of social democratic parties to the defects of their leadership.

(3) The elements of validity in the conception of the 'institutionalisation of class conflict' have to be acknowledged, at the same time as the underlying logic of that conception is rejected. The notion of the 'institutionalisation of class conflict' has been closely linked with the theory of industrial society and has been held in two main versions.[77] In both, class conflict, in the sense of active class struggles, is regarded as characteristic of the early period of the development of industrial capitalism. According to one version, however, the establishment of normatively accepted modes of industrial bargaining is only part of a more general process of institutional differentiation characteristic of an industrial order. In this view, not only does class conflict disappear with the maturity of industrialism, but the concept of class loses its application.[78] The second version is a more cautious one, and is that associated with Lipset, Dahrendorf and others. According to such writers, the 'institutionalisation of class conflict'—which is closely connected by them to the achievement of 'citizenship rights'—undermines the transformative potential of class conflict, without eliminating class struggle altogether. The separation of 'industrial conflict' from 'party conflict' is the condition of the disappearance of such transformative potential. Although I have no sympathy with the first type of viewpoint, I do think there is something of significance in the second. But whereas the authors who have proposed this second verion associate it with the final dissolution of the transformative potential of class conflict—and see the objectives of the labour movement as being exhausted by the achievement of rights of industrial bargaining and the franchise—I see the 'institutionalisation of class conflict' in quite

different terms. The separation of 'industrial conflict' from political participation in the distinct sphere of 'the polity' I consider to be the generic form which the insulation of the economic from the political assumes in developed capitalist industrialism. We have to admit that, in conjunction with the intervention of the state, the institutional isolation of economic bargaining from the mechanisms of political participation has proved to be a stabilising influence in capitalist society. But at the same time it depends upon social conditions which are chronically subject to pressure—even in those societies where the labour movement has been least revolutionary. These conditions turn principally upon the confinement of economic bargaining in the workplace to 'economism', as opposed to an 'orientation towards control'. I might repeat here what I argued in the text (p. 206, above):

any sort of major extension of industrial conflict into the area of control poses a threat to the institutional separation of economic and political conflict which is a fundamental basis of the capitalist state—because it serves to bring into the open the connections between political power in the polity as such, and the broader 'political' subordination of the working class within the economic order.

CONCLUSION: CAPITALISM AND SOCIALISM

If I have thus far not discussed the state socialist societies, this is not because I regard the chapters dealing with them as more satisfactory than those concerning the capitalist countries. Rather, the opposite is the case; the sections dealing with the societies of Eastern Europe now seem to me in need of greater revision than the rest of the volume. I continue to hold to a basic conviction I had when I wrote the book: that it is no longer plausible to write critiques of capitalism that do not at the same time attempt to come to grips with socialism as a current reality, not just as a 'deferred utopia'. I still think it correct to refer to the Eastern European societies as 'state socialist' rather than as 'state capitalist' societies. I would also continue at the same time to maintain the view that, as Mallet has expressed it, 'The "socialism" of the Eastern countries, even in its liberal version, is to socialism what the monsters of the paleolithic era are to present animal species: clumsy, abortive prototypes'.[78] State socialism, to repeat my argument in the book, cannot be regarded as the transcendence of capitalism, but as an alternative social formation promoting industrialisation and economic growth.[79] However, I would no longer today speak of 'the paradox of socialism'. The phrase has too negative a ring to it, and does not conform to the views which I am currently attempting to elaborate in some detail, but which I had not adequately worked out at the time of writing *CSAS*. What I called 'the paradox of socialism' is the same in logical form, although not in substantive content, as the contradictory nature of capitalism: socialism also has its contradictions.

REFERENCES AND NOTES

Wherever full bibliographical details are not given, please refer to Works Cited (pp. 347–54).

Introduction

1. Alvin Gouldner, *The Coming Crisis in Western Sociology* (London 1971); Norman Birnbaum, 'The crisis of Marxist sociology', *Social Research* 2, 1968.

2. For various different statements of this idea, see Ralf Dahrendorf, *Class and Class Conflict in Industrial Society* (Stanford 1959) and 'Out of utopia: toward the reorientation of sociological theory', *Essays in the Theory of Society* (London 1968); John Rex, *Key Problems in Sociological Theory* (London 1961); David Lockwood, 'Some remarks on "The Social System"', *British Journal of Sociology* 7, 1956; 'Social integration and system integration', in G. R. Zollschan and W. Hirsch, *Explorations in Social Change* (London 1964).

3. cf. John Horton, 'The dehumanisation of anomie and alienation', *British Journal of Sociology* 15, 1964, and 'Order and conflict theories of social problems as competing ideologies', *American Journal of Sociology* 71, 1965–6.

4. cf. Robert Friedrichs, *The Sociology of Sociology* (New York 1970).

5. See in particular Dick Atkinson, *Orthodox Consensus and Radical Alternative* (London 1971); but the present success of 'ethnomethodology' is also significant in this regard.

6. See, *inter alia*, Erich Fromm, *Marx's Concept of Man* (New York 1963).

7. I have set out to deal with some of the background to this in a series of recent publications on the history of social thought. See especially: *Capitalism and Modern Social Theory* (Cambridge 1971); *Politics and Sociology in the Thought of Max Weber* (London 1972); Introduction to *Emile Durkheim: Selected Writings* (Cambridge 1972); 'Durkheim's political sociology', *Sociological Review* 19, 1971; 'Four myths in the history of social thought', *Economy and Society* 1, 1972.

8. cf. 'Four myths in the history of social thought', op. cit., *passim*.

9. However, Parsons was clearly very conscious of these matters, and produced various discussions of the German social structure.

10. On the historical origins of the concept of class, see Rudolf Herrnstadt, *Die Entdeckung der Klassen* (Berlin 1965).

11. Page wrote in 1940, 'in the United States, the word "class" is symbolic of stereotyped conceptions, and is apt to convey the impression that the person who speaks of "class" is moving outside the boundaries of American culture, or indicating an allegiance to the "foreign" doctrine of Marxism'; see Charles H. Page, *Class and American Sociology* (New York 1969), p. xi. See also Robert Nisbet, 'The decline and fall of the concept of social class', *Pacific Sociological Review* **2**, 1959, for an *apologia* for the view which relegates the concept of class to the lumber-room of social antiquity. A more recent discussion which is critical of the fact that 'American sociologists have continued to evade and to avoid the class dimension in their analyses . . .' is given in Leonard Reissman and Michael B. Halstead, 'The subject is class', *Sociology and Social Research* **54**, 1970.

Chapter 1. Marx's theory of classes

1. See Georges Gurvitch, 'La sociologie du jeune Marx', *La vocation actuelle de la sociologie* (Paris 1950), for a forceful advocacy of the significance of Saint-Simon's ideas in the evolution of Marx's thought.

2. Saint-Simon, *La physiologie sociale* (Ed. Gurvitch, Paris 1965), p. 141.

3. This is obviously a sweeping statement: exceptional cases readily spring to mind—such as Maurice Halbwachs, *The Psychology of Social Class* (London 1958).

4. Marx and Engels, 'Manifesto of the Communist Party', *Selected Works* (London 1968), p. 35.

5. *Capital*, vol 3 (Moscow 1959), pp. 582ff.

6. I shall use the term 'technique' in preference to 'technology', since the former has a broader sense; but I shall preserve the adjective 'technological', since 'technical' has an established and divergent meaning.

7. cf., for a detailed analysis along these lines, Nicos Poulantzas, *Pouvoir politique et classes sociales de l'état capitaliste* (Paris 1970).

8. See *Capital*, vol. 1 (Moscow 1958), p. 446; 'Manifesto of the Communist Party', *Selected Works*, p. 44; *Capital*, vol. 3, p. 532.

9. Marx and Engels, *The German Ideology* (London 1965), p. 61.

10. ibid., p. 95.

11. Marx and Engels, *Werke*, vol. 3 (Berlin 1962), p. 62 (from *The German Ideology*).

12. ibid., p. 79.

13. 'Preface to the first German edition of *Capital*', *Selected Works*, p. 231.

14. *German Ideology*, p. 95.

15. *Capital*, vol. 3, p. 429.

16. ibid., vol. 1, p. 645.

17. 'Wage Labour and Capital', *Selected Works*, p. 84.

18. 'Modern industry has converted the little workshop of the patriarchal master into the great factory of the industrial capitalist. Masses of labourers, crowded into the factory, are organised like soldiers. . . . The more openly this despotism proclaims gain to be its end and aim, the more petty, the more hateful and the more embittering it is.' 'Manifesto of the Communist Party', *Selected Works*, p. 41.

19. *Capital*, vol. 1, p. 644.

20. 'Manifesto of the Communist Party', pp. 56–7.
21. 'Introduction to *The Civil War in France*', *Selected Works*, p. 252.

Chapter 2. The Weberian critique

1. Theodor Geiger, *Die Klassengesellschaft im Schmeltztiegel* (Cologne 1949); Karl Renner, *Wandlungen der modernen Gesellschaft* (Vienna 1953); Dahrendorf, *Class and Class Conflict in Industrial Society*.
2. For a cogent representation of this view, see W. G. Runciman, 'Class, status and power', in J. A. Jackson, *Social Stratification* (Cambridge 1968).
3. See my *Capitalism and Modern Social Theory*, pp. 185ff. and *passim*.
4. I ignore here the philosophical and methodological questions which are involved in Weber's critique of 'philosophies of history'. See Max Weber, *The Methodology of the Social Sciences* (Glencoe 1949), pp. 68ff.
5. *Economy and Society*, vol. 2 (New York 1968), pp. 926–40, and vol. 1, pp. 302–7.
6. ibid., vol. 2, p. 928.
7. ibid., p. 930.
8. ibid., p. 927.
9. Marx actually makes the same point (*Capital*, vol. 1, pp. 135–6), and mentions that similar struggles between debtors and creditors occurred in the Middle Ages. But he argues that 'the money relation of debtor and creditor that existed at these two periods reflected only the deeper-lying antagonism between the general economic conditions of existence of the classes in question'.
10. Herbert Marcuse, 'Industrialisation and capitalism', in Otto Stammler, *Max Weber and Sociology Today* (Oxford 1971). According to Weber, 'capitalistic accounting presupposes rational technology, that is, one reduced to calculation to the largest possible degree, which implies mechanisation' (*General Economic History*, p. 208).
11. See my *Politics and Sociology in the Thought of Max Weber* (London 1972), pp. 34ff.
12. *Economy and Society*, vol. 1, pp. 110–11.
13. ibid., p. 305.
14. See Wolfgang J. Mommsen, *Max Weber und die deutsche Politik, 1890–1920* (Tübingen 1959), pp. 280–304.
15. *Economy and Society*, vol. 2, pp. 930ff.

Chapter 3. Some later theories

1. The German edition of *Class and Class Conflict* was published in 1957. See also, Dahrendorf, *Marx in Perspektive: die Idee des Gerechten im Denken von Karl Marx* (Hanover 1953, doctoral dissertation).
2. *Class and Class Conflict*, pp. 28ff.
3. ibid., pp. 30–1.
4. ibid., p. 56.
5. See Dahrendorf, *Conflict after class*, Nöel Buxton lecture (Essex 1967).

6. *Class and Class Conflict*, p. 62. Here, as elsewhere in this volume, I adopt the practice of using the adjective 'Marxian' with reference to what I take to be Marx's own ideas and contributions; I shall use the terms 'Marxist' and 'Marxism' to refer generically to the writings of subsequent authors who are self-professed followers of Marx.

7. ibid., p. 165.

8. Dahrendorf recognises, however, that 'The changes that separate capitalist and post-capitalist society are not wholly due to the effects of class conflict, nor have they merely been changes in the patterns of conflict.' (ibid., pp. 245–6).

9. ibid., p. 275.

10. Raymond Aron, *Democracy and Totalitarianism* (London 1968); *18 Lectures on Industrial Society* (London 1968); *Progress and Disillusion* (New York 1968); and especially *La lutte des classes* (Paris 1964).

11. *La lutte des classes*, pp. 22–3; cf. also *18 Lectures on Industrial Society*, pp. 73–6.

12. *La lutte des classes*, pp. 23–4.

13. ibid., pp. 51–2.

14. ibid., p. 95.

15. ibid., p. 78. See also Aron, 'La classe comme représentation et comme volonté', in *Les classes sociales dans le monde d'aujourd'hui, Cahiers internationaux de sociologie* **38**, 1965.

16. ibid., p. 356.

17. Stanislaw Ossowski, *Class Structure in the Social Consciousness* (London 1963).

18. ibid., p. 27.

19. W. L. Warner and P. S. Lunt, *The Social Life of a Modern Community* (New Haven 1941).

20. Ossowski, op. cit., p. 70.

21. ibid., pp. 69ff.

22. ibid., p. 114.

23. ibid., p. 184.

Chapter 4. Marx's critics: a critique

1. T. B. Bottomore, *Classes in Modern Society* (London 1966), p. 21.

2. cf. Lukács' earlier writings, especially *History and Class Consciousness* (London 1971), pp. 1–26.

3. *Class and Class Conflict*, p. 129.

4. *German Ideology*, p. 39.

5. Dahrendorf writes: ' "The history of all societies up to the present is the history of class struggles". This seemingly empirical sentence is in reality but a reformulation of the philosophical postulate that links alienation (and thereby all known history), private property, and the classes' (*Class and Class Conflict*, p. 31).

6. As Dahrendorf himself certainly stresses: 'Although the heuristic purpose and general approach of [Marx's] theory of class can and must be sustained, this is not the case with respect to most other features of this theory' (ibid., p. 126).

7. ibid., p. 168.

8. Lenski has also offered a concept of class which recognises a plurality of classes; and his ideas are open to similar objections. See Gerhard E. Lenski, *Power and Privilege* (New York 1966).

9. Dahrendorf has apparently come more recently to recognise some of the difficulties inherent in the views developed in *Class and Class Conflict in Industrial Society*. In 1967 he remarks: 'the problem of the direction of change (and, probably related to it, the substance of class interests) . . . escapes my attempt to reformulate class theory' (*Conflict After Class*, p. 27).

10. Ossowski, op. cit., pp. 34–7.

11. Ossowski recognises this (e.g., p. 35), but he does not develop the point.

12. ibid., p. 79.

13. The main groups in question here are blacks, 'poor whites', and landowners. See, for example, J. A. Dollard, *Caste and Class in a Southern Town* (New Haven 1937).

14. W. L. Warner, *Social Class in America* (Chicago 1949); Ossowski, op. cit., pp. 47ff.

15. Ossowski, op. cit., p. 176. 'For example, where Soviet ideologists see two non-antagonistic classes and a "stratum" of intelligentsia, an American sociologist or a Russian *emigré* will perceive six or ten classes as the levels of social stratification' (p. 177).

16. *La lutte des classes*, pp. 69–70.

17. cf. Theodor Geiger, *Die soziale Schichtung des deutschen Volkes* (Stuttgart 1932), pp. 2ff.

18. e.g., Lukács. See Georg Lukács, op. cit.

19. Thus Aron refers at one point to 'the fiction that control of the means of production determines the relation of classes. . .' (*Progress and Disillusion*, p. 39).

20. ibid., p. 33.

21. Dahrendorf, however, specifically warns against confusing 'class' and 'stratification'.

22. *Economy and Society*, vol. 2, p. 927.

23. ibid., p. 930. The 'talented author' in question is apparently Lukács.

24. ibid., p. 929. Of course, an historical analysis of this matter is contained in the detailed studies of the 'world religions'.

25. Although Weber adds, cryptically, that this holds 'with some oversimplification' (ibid., p. 937).

26. This does not mean to say, however, that legal criteria become *irrelevant* to status discriminations with the disappearance of estates; on the contrary formally defined 'equality' before the law is a condition of 'conventional' status differences (and also a condition, as I shall emphasise in subsequent chapters, of the existence of *class society* itself).

Chapter 5. The Marxian standpoint reassessed

1. See Marc Bloch, *Feudal Society* (London 1961).

2. C. B. Macpherson, *The Political Theory of Possessive Individualism* (London 1964), p. 51.

3. Walter Ullmann, *The Individual and Society in the Middle Ages* (Baltimore 1966), pp. 40–1.

4. Bloch, op. cit., p. 148.

5. ibid., pp. 353ff. Bloch remarks that 'It was perceived that the dominant characteristic of the town was that it was inhabited by a special type of human being'.

6. Georges Gurvitch, *Le concept de classes sociales de Marx à nos jours* (Paris 1954).

7. See, for instance, Henri Pirenne, 'The stages in the social history of capitalism', *American Historical Review* **19**, 1913–14. According to Pirenne: 'before the thirteenth century we find a period of free capitalistic expansion' (p. 506).

8. *Capital*, vol. 3, p. 914.

9. ibid., vol. 1, p. 170.

10. According to the famous statement of this matter: 'At a certain stage of their development, the material productive forces of society come into conflict with the existing relations of production, or—what is but a legal expression for the same thing—with the property relations within which they have been at work hitherto. From forms of development of the productive forces these relations turn into their fetters. Then begins an epoch of social revolution' ('Preface to *The Critique of Political Economy*', *Selected Works*, p. 182).

11. cf. H. B. Acton, *The Illusion of the Epoch* (London 1962), pp. 162–4.

12. *The Poverty of Philosophy* (London n.d.), p. 92.

13. See, for example, the analysis in 'Wage labour and capital', *Selected Works*.

14. *German Ideology*, p. 32.

15. This has created major interpretative problems for Marxist scholarship. Most of Marx's early followers took a fairly simple view of the matter, assuming a high level of generalisation. More sophisticated accounts (e.g., Lukács') take a much more cautious view.

16. I have elsewhere referred to this as 'technological alienation', distinguishing it from 'market alienation'. See *Capitalism and Modern Social Theory*, pp. 228–9.

17. *German Ideology*, p. 45.

18. *Grundrisse der Kritik der politischen Ökonomie* (Berlin 1953), p. 592.

19. Engels, 'On authority', *Selected Works*, vol. 1 (Moscow 1958), p. 637.

20. 'The civil war in France', *Selected Works* (1968 ed.), p. 294.

21. For a discussion of some relevant problems, see Paul Sweezy *et al.*, *The Transition from Feudalism to Capitalism* (London 1954).

22. 'Manifesto of the Communist Party', *Selected Works*, p. 36.

23. cf. Maurice Godelier, 'Structure and contradiction in *Capital*', in Ralph Miliband and John Saville, *The Socialist Register* (1967).

24. See below, pp. 112–13.

25. I am aware that this statement is something of a controversial one, if one takes the view (which I do not accept) that millenarian beliefs are phantasmic representations of class revolution.

26. George Lichtheim, *Marxism* (London 1964), p. 172.

27. Thus he wrote, speaking of his *Principles of Political Economy*, that if he were to rewrite the chapter on value, 'I should acknowledge that the relative value of commodities was regulated by two causes instead of by one, namely, by the relative quantity of labor necessary to produce the commodities in question, and by the rate of profit for the time that the capital remained dormant, and until the commodities were brought to the market' (*Letters of David Ricardo to John Ramsey McCulloch*, New York 1895, p. 71).

Chapter 6. Rethinking the theory of class (I)

1. Marx's usage is variable on this point: he often speaks of the 'working classes', 'ruling classes', etc.
2. See, for example, David Lockwood, *The Blackcoated Worker* (London 1958), pp. 202–4; Frank Parkin, *Class Inequality and Political Order* (London 1971).
3. See Robert A. Nisbet, 'The decline and fall of social class', op. cit.
4. What I call class structuration, Gurvitch calls negatively 'résistance à la pénétration par la société globale'. Georges Gurvitch, *Le concept de classes sociales de Marx à nos jours* (Paris 1954), p. 116 and *passim*.
5. We may, however, agree with Schumpeter that 'The family, not the physical person, is the true unit of class and class theory' (Joseph Schumpeter, *Imperialism, Social Classes*, Cleveland 1961). This is actually completely consistent with the idea that mobility is fundamental to class formation.
6. See below, pp. 264–9.
7. Lockwood, *The Blackcoated Worker*, op. cit.
8. It might be pointed out that it would easily be possible to break down the notion of status group further: according, for example, to whether the status evaluations in question are made primarily by others outside the group, and rejected by those inside it, etc.
9. This is not, of course, the same as Lukács' 'class-conditioned unconsciousness'; but I believe that Lukács is correct in distinguishing qualitatively different 'levels' of class consciousness. Lukács, op. cit, pp. 52ff.
10. cf. Poulantzas, op. cit. It is misleading, however, to speak of *classes sans conscience*, as Crozier does. See Michel Crozier, 'Classes sans conscience ou préfiguration de la société sans classes', *Archives européenes de sociologie* 1, 1960; also 'L'ambiguité de la conscience de classe chez les employés et les petits fonctionnaires', *Cahiers internationaux de sociologie* 28, 1955.
11. Or, to use another terminology, where there is 'overdetermination' (Louis Althusser, *For Marx*, London 1969, pp. 89–128).
12. Marx's *Lumpenproletariat*, according to this usage, is only an underclass when the individuals in question tend to derive from distinctive ethnic backgrounds. Leggett has referred to the underclass as the 'marginal working class', defining this as 'a sub-community of workers who belong to a subordinate ethnic or racial group which is usually proletarianised and highly segregated' (John C. Leggett, *Class, Race, and Labor*, New York 1968, p. 14).
13. cf. Alain Touraine, *La conscience ouvrière* (Paris 1966), p. 17: 'il existe un grand nombre de combinaisons possibles entre les trois principes dont un assemblage très particulier constitue la conscience de classe: le *principe d'identité* qui est, plus encore que la définition d'un groupe d'appartenance, la définition d'une contribution, d'une fonction sociale et donc le fondement des revendications; le *principe d'opposition*, c'est-à-dire la définition du groupe antagoniste et plus précisément celle des obstacles au contrôle des travailleurs sur leurs œuvres; le *principe de totalité* qui definit le champ social dans lequel se situe la relation definie par les deux principes précédents'.
14. See my *Capitalism and Modern Social Theory*, ch. 14 and *passim*.
15. This may perhaps be regarded as a particular case of Lockwood's distinction of problems of 'social integration' and 'system integration'.
16. cf., however, Engels' observation that 'poverty often dwells in hidden

alleys close to the palaces of the rich; but, in general, a separate territory has
been assigned to it, where removed from the sight of the happier classes, it may
struggle along as it can' (Friedrich Engels, *The Condition of the Working Class
in England in 1844*, London 1968, p. 26).

17. See below, pp. 185–6.

18. V. I. Lenin, *What is to be Done?* (Oxford 1963), p. 63.

Chapter 7. Rethinking the theory of class (II)

1. Poulantzas, op. cit., p. 69.

2. Most subsequent Marxist authors have either been content with the most
generalised assertions about this issue, or have wanted to have their cake and
eat it by insisting that capitalism is dominated by a ruling class who do not
actually 'rule'; cf. again Poulantzas, op. cit., pp. 361ff.

3. See below, pp. 255–9.

4. In this section of this chapter I have drawn upon part of my article 'Elites
in the British class structure', *Sociological Review* 20, 1972.

5. See below, pp. 241–3.

6. cf. Talcott Parsons, 'On the concept of political power', *Proceedings of the
American Philosophical Society* 107, 1963. The error in Parsons' analysis, however, is to take insufficient account of the fact that the 'collective' aspect of
power is asymmetrical in its consequences for the different groupings in society.

7. As in Keller's 'strategic elites'. See Suzanne Keller, *Beyond the Ruling
Class* (New York 1963).

8. See pp. 51–2 above.

9. This is the sort of criticism made by Durkheim (although not specifically
against Marx): see *Professional Ethics and Civic Morals* (London 1957), pp. 51ff.

10. *Theories of Surplus Value*, vol. 1 (London 1964), p. 152.

11. ibid., pp. 389–400.

12. It is clear that a 'paradigm difference' is involved here; the critique of the
theory of surplus value given in orthodox economics involves first and foremost
a shift in orientation, rather than a confrontation with the Marxian view on
its own terms.

13. For one of the most sophisticated of recent discussions, see Ernest Mandel,
The Formation of the Economic Thought of Karl Marx (London 1971).

14. *Capital* forms only one strand of an encyclopaedic project conceived by
Marx in his youth which was to result in 'a number of independent brochures'
complementing the critique of political economy with the 'critique of law,
morals, politics, etc.' (T. B. Bottomore, *Karl Marx, Early Writings*, New York
1964, p. 63).

15. cf. Gorz: 'in a given society at a given level of development the notion o
poverty designates the totality of possibilities (notably cultural, sanitary, medical)
and of wealth which are denied to an individual while at the same time being
held up to him as the norm potentially valid for all' (André Gorz, *Strategy for
Labor*, Boston 1968, p. 22).

16. cf. ibid., pp. 125ff.

17. The 'Asiatic mode of production' is not regarded by Marx as a class
society. It has been argued, nevertheless, that it should be seen as such, even

using strictly Marxian premises. See Karl A. Wittfogel, *Oriental Despotism* (New Haven 1957).

18. This observation is relevant to many contemporary 'underdeveloped' [*sic*] societies. There have been many attempts to force class analysis beyond its useful limits in, for example, studies of the 'new nations' in Africa.

19. Macpherson, *The Political Theory of Possessive Individualism*, pp. 51–3. However, we might question Macpherson's statement that 'For purposes of economic analysis the most essential features are those peculiar to the full market society' (p. 51).

20. Marx's fascination with Balzac's novels undoubtedly derived from the acute and trenchant character of that writer's observations upon the mores of the French bourgeoisie. Marx intended to carry out a study of Balzac as the 'anatomist of bourgeois culture'—although this was one project he never even managed to begin.

Chapter 8. The problem of capitalist development

1. A not inconsiderable number of economic historians, of course, have denied that the concept has any useful historical application at all. cf. R. H. Tawney's Preface to 2nd ed. of *Religion and the Rise of Capitalism* (London 1948), pp. vii–xiii.

2. *General Economic History* (New York 1961), p. 224ff.; also Jean Baechler, 'Essai sur les origines du système capitaliste', *Archives européenes de sociologie* **9**, 1968.

3. cf., for example, the more recent interpretation by Oliver C. Cox *The Foundations of Capitalism* (London 1959), p. 407: 'We may state hypothetically that the conditions of the industrial revolution were inherent in the societal organisation of existing [eighteenth and nineteenth centuries] capitalist communities. It had become one of the inevitable developments of capitalism.'

4. One of Weber's most explicit statements is that elucidating the connection between capital accounting, central to his characterisation of modern capitalism, and machine technology: 'capitalistic accounting presupposes a rational technology, that is, one reduced to calculation to the largest possible degree, which implies mechanisation' (*General Economic History*, p. 208).

5. For more extended discussions of industrialism, see, for example, Bert F. Hoselitz and Wilbert E. Moore, *Industrialisation and Society* (The Hague 1968); William A. Faunce, *Problems of an Industrial Society* (New York 1968); Georges Friedmann, *Industrial Society* (Glencoe 1955); and, on an altogether different plane, Lewis Mumford, *The Myth of the Machine* (London 1967).

6. cf. Adorno, 'die gegenwärtige Gesellschaft durchaus Industriegesellschaft ist nach dem Stand ihrer Produktivkräfte.... Demgegenüber ist die Gesellschaft Kapitalismus in ihren Produktions*verhaltnissen*' (Theodor W. Adorno, *Aufsätze zur Gesellschaftstheorie und Methodologie*, Frankfurt 1970, p. 157).

7. *Capital*, vol. 1, p. 8.

8. For two relevant, and partially overlapping, analyses see Barrington Moore, *The Social Origins of Dictatorship and Democracy* (London 1969); and Alan Touraine, *Sociologie de l'action* (Paris 1965).

9. I use this term without attempting to pin down its meaning very precisely, to refer to the basic patterns of economic organisation (technological level,

form of industrial structure, and modes of exchange of commodities) prevailing in a given society. I have already mentioned some of the difficulties to which the use of this concept gives rise in Marxian theory. I employ it here with qualifications which have been noted previously—in particular with the understanding that the theory of class must analytically separate out those characteristics of infrastructure which I have distinguished as the sources of class structuration.

10. There are, of course, methodological issues of an important sort raised by this statement; but these cannot be analysed here. For an account which questions the use of established dichotomies of the 'traditional' and 'modern', see Reinhard Bendix, 'Tradition and modernity reconsidered', *Embattled Reason, Essays on Social Knowledge* (New York 1970).

11. cf. Barrington Moore, op. cit., pp. 453–83 and *passim*.

12. A strong advocacy of this view is given in Reinhard Bendix, *Nation-Building and Citizenship* (New York 1964).

13. The most sophisticated recent Marxist examination of these problems is Ernest Mandel, *Marxist Economic Theory* (London 1968, 2 vols.).

14. For an exposition of this point of view, see Joan Robinson, *An Essay on Marxian Economics* (London 1966), p. 36.

15. The measurement of the distribution of wealth and income, of course, is a contentious issue and such a broad generalisation obviously has to be put in the perspective of the various controversies which surround this matter. According to Kalecki, however, in Britain the share of wages in the national income was 41 per cent in 1880 and 42 per cent in 1935; another estimate indicates that, in the period 1870–1950, the share of wages never rose above 42 per cent, and on occasion declined to 37 per cent. M. Kalecki, 'The distribution of the national income', *Essays in the Theory of Economic Fluctuations* (London 1939); E. H. Phelps Brown and P. E. Hart, 'The share of wages in national income', *Economic Journal* 62, 1952.

16. As Marx expresses it, crises are 'momentary and forcible solutions of the existing contradictions. They are violent eruptions which for a time restore the disturbed equilibrium' (*Capital*, vol. 3, p. 244).

17. cf. Alain Touraine, *La conscience ouvrière*, op. cit.

18. As Bendix has pointed out, the effects of war have been more effective than industrialisation in destroying traditional forms of social structure in some of the capitalist countries: most notably so in Germany and Japan. Bendix, *Nation-Building and Citizenship*, op. cit., p. 212.

19. In saying this, I do not wish to imply that the experience of the capitalist societies is necessarily unique to the nineteenth century, or to the European context; still less do I want to suggest that the state socialism of Eastern Europe offers the only general pattern of industrial development which can be followed by the 'underdeveloped' societies today.

Chapter 9. The institutional mediation of power and the mediation of control

1. T. H. Marshall, *Class, Citizenship and Social Development* (New York 1964), p. 84; see also 'The welfare state: a sociological interpretation', *Archives européennes de sociologie* 2, 1961.

2. cf. Dahrendorf: 'while in the United States the notion of citizenship had a

practical significance ever since the Declaration of Independence, if not before, its realisation was still in its initial stages in Europe 120 years after the French Revolution'; 'Recent changes in the class structure of the European societies', in R. Graubard, *A New Europe?* (London 1965), p. 295. To accept the validity of this, however, does not entail adoption of Lipset's thesis that the absence of socialism in American politics depends upon 'the fact that egalitarianism and democracy triumphed *before* the workers were a politically relevant force' (Seymour Martin Lipset, *The First New Nation*, London 1964, p. 341).

3. Bendix, *Nation-Building and Citizenship*, op. cit., p. 101.

4. Parkin, *Class Inequality and Political Order*, p. 125.

5. In the post-war 'dissolution programme' in Japan, 325 large firms were supposed to be covered; in fact, only 11 were actually dissolved. Rates of concentration are again climbing: the aggregate capital of the 100 largest corporations in 1964 composed 39 per cent of total corporate capital in 1966, as compared to 32 per cent in 1953 (M. Yoshino, *Japan's Managerial System*, Cambridge, Mass. 1968, p. 124).

6. Quoted in Ernest Mandel, *Marxist Economic Theory*, vol. 2, pp. 395–7.

7. For a comparative account of industrial concentration, see Joe S. Bain, *Industrial Organisation* (New York 1968).

8. Adolph A. Berle and Gardiner C. Means, *The Modern Corporation and Private Property* (Chicago 1932), pp. 40–1.

9. Alfred S. Eichner, 'Business concentration and its significance', in Ivar Berg, *The Business of America* (New York 1968), p. 192.

10. cf. R. Marris, *The Economic Theory of 'Managerial' Capitalism* (London 1964), pp. 266–77.

11. A possibility suggested by P. Sargant Florence, see *Ownership, Control and Success of Large Companies* (London 1961), p. 190.

12. Andrew Schonfield, *Modern Capitalism* (London 1969), p. 64.

13. ibid., pp. 71–87 (Schonfield does not discuss the case of Japan in any detail). The tradition of *étatisme* in France is clearly related to the strong influence which theories of 'technocracy', from Saint-Simon up to the present day, have enjoyed in that country.

14. cf. William W. Lockwood, 'Japan's "new capitalism"', *The State and Economic Enterprise in Japan* (Princeton 1965), pp, 492–511 and *passim*.

15. However, as Speier pointed out in 1937, microeconomic planning has a long history in the United States: Hans Speier, 'Freedom and social planning', *Social Order and the Risks of War* (Cambridge, Mass. 1969).

16. For a Marxist assessment of the implications of planning, see Bill Warren, 'Capitalist planning and the state', *New Left Review* 72, 1972, 16ff; for a substantially different view, see Michael Kidron, *Western Capitalism Since the War* (London 1970). As Warren points out, the stock Marxist opinion that the maintenance of full employment in a capitalist economy depends heavily upon the production of armaments cannot really be reconciled with the fact that the level of arms expenditure has generally been low in Western Europe, as a proportion of the gross national product; and this expenditure has declined without significant economic effects.

17. Poulantzas, op. cit., p. 325. As Poulantzas also emphasises: 'la conception marxiste rigoreuse de la classe dominante n'implique nullement la concentration empirique des diverses fonctions politiques entre les mains des membres d'une classe. . . .' (ibid., p. 361).

18. cf. John M. Maki, *Government and Politics in Japan* (London 1962), pp. 15ff. See also J. C. Abegglen and H. Mannari, 'Leaders of modern Japan:

social origins and mobility', *Economic Development and Cultural Change* **9**, 1960; R. P. Dore, 'Mobility, equality, and individuation in modern Japan', *Aspects of Social Change in Modern Japan* (Princeton 1967).

19. David S. Landes, 'Japan and Europe: contrasts in industrialisation', in Lockwood, op. cit., p. 145. As Landes notes, one major distinction between the Japanese and German upper classes in the late nineteenth century was that, in Japan: 'land ownership never became the symbol of social eminence and prestige, the hallmark of quality, and hence did not have the attraction for new wealth that it had in the West, so that when Japan entered on the path of industrialisation, the successful businessman, whatever his social origin, did not feel it necessary to put the seal on his economic assent by placing a good part or all of his fortune into estates' (p. 170).

20. J. P. Nettl, 'Consensus or elite domination: the case of business', *Political Studies* **13**, 1965.

21. *Class and class conflict*, p. 46. 'Capitalists' in the first quotation are those who found and control their own enterprises; 'heirs' are those who are born to such a position.

22. Out of a vast recent literature, the following works may be indicated as illustrative, J. C. Abegglen and H. Mannari, op. cit.; Akira Kubota, *Higher Civil Servants in Postwar Japan* (Princeton 1969); W. L. Guttsman, *The British Political Elite* (London 1963); R. K. Kelsall, *Higher Civil Servants in Britain* (London 1955); N. Delefortrie-Soubeyroux, *Les dirigeants de l'industrie française* (Paris 1961); G. William Domhoff, *Who Rules America?* (New Jersey 1967); Reinhard Bendix, *Higher Civil Servants in American Society* (Boulder 1949).

23. Morris Janowitz, *The Professional Soldier* (New York 1960), p. 209.

24. All such comparisons, of course, are tenuous in the absence of more adequate materials than exist at the present time. There is an interesting contrast, however, between the role of the universities as avenues of mobility into the higher civil service in Britain and Japan. In Britain, Oxford and Cambridge provide about 48 per cent of recruits to ranks of assistant secretary or above in the civil service, but recruitment seems less open, in terms of socio-economic background, than in Japan, where nearly 80 per cent of the equivalent grades come from Tokyo Imperial University. See Kubota, op. cit., p. 71 and *passim*. On the social background of business leaders in the large corporations in post-war Japan, see Yoshino, op. cit., pp. 85–117.

25. Peter B. Blau and Otis Dudley Duncan, *The American Occupational Structure* (New York 1967), p. 434.

26. Nichols has quite properly remarked: 'we still severely lack studies of the relationship between the manager's personal motivations and beliefs and the interests of shareholders. . . . It follows from the absence of such empirical data . . . that, for the most part, *all* participants in the ownership-control controversy have been forced to rely upon *inferences* drawn from industrial and social structure' (Theo Nichols, *Ownership, Control and Ideology*, London 1969, p. 62).

27. Jean Meynaud, *La technocratie* (Paris 1964), p. 169.

28. Estimates of the typical proportion of shares necessary to achieve this, however, vary widely. Whereas some authors regard anything over 5 per cent bloc ownership as potentially yielding control, others (cf., for example, Sargant Florence, *Ownership, Control and Success of Large Companies*, op. cit.) place the proportion as high as 30 per cent. It is obvious, however, that any such statistical criterion has a largely arbitrary character; the significance of a given percentage of shares will depend upon numerous variable characteristics of particular companies.

29. John Kenneth Galbraith, *The New Industrial State* (London 1967), p. 77.

30. R. H. S. Crossman has recently argued that what Bagehot perceived as the 'efficient secret' of British politics, government by the cabinet behind the façade of parliamentary democracy, has now become supplanted by 'prime ministerial' government. But even if this case could be substantiated for the British polity, it is dubious how far it could be generalised to other cases. But, on the more general point, cf. Luhmann: 'Politische Planung ist daruber hinaus ein Prozess, mit dem die Grenze zwischen den beiden wichtigsten Teilsystemen des politischen Systems, Politik und Verwaltung, uberschritten wird . . .': Niklaus Luhmann, *Politische Planung* (Opladen 1971), p. 81.

31. For documentation on Britain, see Guttsman, op. cit.

32. cf. Parkin, op. cit., pp. 130–6.

33. Ralph Miliband, *The State in Capitalist Society* (London 1969), p. 21.

Chapter 10. The growth of the new middle class

1. *Theories of Surplus Value*, vol. 2 (London 1969), p. 573.

2. cf. Martin Nicolaus, 'Proletariat and middle class in Marx: Hegelian choreography and the capitalist dialectic', *Studies on the Left* 7, 1967. The author's analysis of Marx's problems with the 'middle class' turns upon what I consider to be a mistaken separation between Marx's concern with 'the market' in his early writings and with the theory of surplus value in his later works.

3. The attention given to what Lederer and Marschak called 'Der neue Mittelstand' in Germany in the 1920s and early 1930s obviously relates to the internal problems of Social Democracy and the rise of Nazism. It might be pointed out that the 'official' theory of the right-wing, anti-semitic *Deutschnationale Handlungsgehilfen-Verband* emphasised the significance of the participation of the white-collar worker in the delegation of entrepreneurial authority, and the existence of promotion opportunities, as distinguishing him from the manual worker. For the basic sociological works of the period see Emil Lederer and J. Marschak, 'Der neue Mittelstand', *Grundriss der Sozialökonomik*, vol. 9 (I), 1926; and Lederer, *Die Privatangestellten in der modernen Wirtschaftsentwicklung* (Tübingen 1912).

4. For some cross-national comparisons, see Bert F. Hoselitz, *The Role of Small Industry in the Process of Economic Growth* (The Hague 1968).

5. *Vide* Joseph Bensman and Arthur J. Vidich, *The New American Society* (Chicago 1971), for an exposition of the latest in a long line of putative 'revolutions' stretching from Burnham onwards: the 'revolution of the middle class'.

6. Figures for the USA calculated by Gavin Mackenzie from US census data; the additional 4 per cent and 5 per cent represent farm-workers. Other data are taken from Guy Routh, *Occupation and Pay in Great Britain, 1906–60* (Cambridge 1965); and Solomon B. Levine, 'Unionisation of white-collar employees in Japan', in Adolf Sturmthal, *White-Collar Trade Unions* (Urbana 1966).

7. Michel Crozier, *The World of the Office Worker* (Chicago 1971), pp. 11–12; and 'White-collar unions—the case of France', in Sturmthal, op. cit., pp. 91–2.

8. cf. Routh, op. cit.; Robert K. Burns, 'The comparative economic position of manual and white-collar employees', *The Journal of Business* 27, 1954; US Department of Labor, *Blue-Collar/White-Collar Pay Trends. Monthly Labor Review*, June 1971; and Crozier, *The World of the Office Worker*, pp. 12–15. For

an assessment of how far progressive income tax affects these income profiles, see Parkin, *Class Inequality and Political Order*, pp. 119–21.

9. M. P. Fogarty, 'The white-collar pay structure in Britain', *Economic Journal* **69**, 1959. Hamilton points out that statistics concerning skilled manual workers often include foremen, whose wages are normally markedly higher than those of skilled workers as such; foremen are more appropriately regarded as supervisory, non-manual workers: Richard Hamilton, 'The income difference between skilled and white-collar workers', *British Journal of Sociology* **14**, 1963. As regards the 'declining curve' of income, however, Mackenzie indicates that this probably holds for a certain proportion of clerical workers, as well as manual workers: See Gavin Mackenzie, 'The economic dimensions of embourgeoisement', *British Journal of Sociology* **18**, 1967, p. 32; this article critically examines the preceding work by Hamilton.

10. George Sayers Bain, *The Growth of White-Collar Unionism* (Oxford 1970), p. 59.

11. A survey in Britain in 1961 showed that, whereas 86 per cent of white-collar workers were involved in sick pay schemes, only 33 per cent of manual workers were so covered: HMSO, *Sick Pay Schemes* (London 1964). See also The Industrial Society, *Status and Benefits in Industry* (London 1966); aspects of this work are criticised in Bain, op. cit., p. 64.

12. Enid Mumford and Olive Banks, *The Computer and the Clerk* (London 1967), p. 21.

13. S. M. Miller, 'Comparative social mobility', *Current Sociology* **1**, 1960. Blau and Duncan show that, in the American social structure at least, the first job has a basic influence on achieved mobility: while the gross amount of mobility experienced by those starting their careers in white-collar occupations may be about the same as that of those starting in manual jobs, the former tend to experience much greater *net* mobility, even judged in relation to parental occupation (Peter M. Blau and O. D. Duncan, *The American Occupational Structure*, New York 1967).

14. David Lockwood, *The Blackcoated Worker*, p. 81.

15. Fritz Croner, *Die Angestellten in der modernen Gesellschaft* (Cologne 1962), pp. 34ff.

16. An interesting example of an attempt to reduce class differentiation in housing in Britain is given in Leo Kuper, *Living in Towns* (London 1953). While recognising the existence of class segregation in neighbourhood organisation in Japan, Dore stresses in his study of a Tokyo ward that, as he puts it: ' "Japanese-ness", as opposed to "Western-ness", is still a criterion of some importance for dividing men from their fellows and one which does not necessarily follow economic status lines' (R. P. Dore, *City Life in Japan*, London 1958, pp. 12–13).

17. The leading works are: Alfred Willener, *Images de la société et classes sociales* (Berne 1957); Heinrich Popitz et al., *Das Gesellschaftsbild des Arbeiters* (Tübingen 1957). See also Dahrendorf, *Class and Class Conflict*, pp. 280–9; John Goldthorpe et al., *The Affluent Worker in the Class Structure* (Cambridge 1969), pp. 116–56; Hansjürgen Daheim, 'Die Vorstellungen vom Mittelstand', *Kölner Zeitschrift für Soziologie und Sozialpsychologie* **12**, 1960; Siegfried Braun and Jochen Fuhrmann, *Angestelltenmentalität* (Neuwied 1970). This latter work, however, questions some of the traditional views.

18. cf. Ezra F. Vogel, *Japan's New Middle Class* (Berkeley 1963), pp. 142–62; and Chie Nakane, *Japanese Society* (London 1970), pp. 115ff.

19. Terence J. Johnson, *Professions and Power* (London 1972), pp. 54ff.

20. C. Wright Mills, *White Collar* (New York 1951), p. x.

21. Dahrendorf, 'Recent changes in the class structure of European societies', op. cit., pp. 248–9.

22. According to Taira, 87 per cent of Japanese unions are of the enterprise type, and about 80 per cent of organised labour belongs to them. Koji Taira, *Economic Development and the Labor Market in Japan* (New York 1970), p. 168.

23. Solomon B. Levine, 'Unionisation of white-collar employees in Japan', in Sturmthal, op. cit., p. 238. On the development of enterprise unionism, see also Levine, *Industrial Relations in Postwar Japan* (Urbana 1958).

24. cf. Édouard Dolléans, *Histoire du mouvement ouvrier* (Paris 1953), vol. 2, pp. 13–56.

25. According to Crozier: 'it is from this period (1919–20) that we can date the deep allegiance of the French white-collar world to the workers' cause. To be sure, this unity would remain extremely vague and would accommodate itself to much opposition. Officially, however, it could never again be brought into question. The Catholic unions, which until then remained dubious, had at last shown that at the decisive moment they took sides with the strikers. Even the white-collar employees in banks, those last bastions of bourgeois respectability, had followed . . .' (*The World of the Office Worker*, p. 46).

26. cf. Asher Tropp, *The School Teachers* (London 1957).

27. cf. Lockwood, op. cit., pp. 89ff.

28. For figures on Britain, see Bain, op. cit., pp. 38–9.

29. Jon M. Shepard, *Automation and Alienation* (Cambridge, Mass. 1971), p. 43. cf. also Dorothy Wedderburn, 'Annäherung von Angestellten—und Arbeitertätigkeiten?', and subsequent contributions in Günter Friedrichs, *Computer und Angestellte*, vol. 2 (Frankfurt 1971).

30. US Department of Labor, *Adjustments to the Introduction of Office Automation*, Bulletin no. 1276 (Washington 1960). Other contributions to a now very large literature include Leonard Rico, *The Advance against Paperwork* (Ann Arbor 1967); H. A. Rhee, *Office Automation in Social Perspective* (Oxford 1968); Enid Mumford and Olive Banks, op. cit.; W. H. Scott, *Office Automation* (OECD 1965).

31. Maurice Bouvier-Ajam and Gilbert Mury, *Les classes sociales en France*, vol. 1 (Paris 1963), p. 63.

32. Alain Touraine, *La société post-industrielle* (Paris 1969), pp. 82–3.

33. Serge Mallet, *La nouvelle classe ouvrière* (Paris 1963); Pierre Belleville, *Une nouvelle classe ouvrière* (Paris 1963). See also Mallet, 'La nouvelle classe ouvrière en France', in *Les classes sociales dans le monde d'aujourd'hui*, op. cit.

34. cf. Stanley Aronowitz, 'Does the United States have a new working class?', in George Fischer, *The Revival of American Socialism* (New York 1971), p. 203.

Chapter 11. The working class in capitalist society

1. George Sayers Bain, op. cit., pp. 15ff.

2. David Lockwood, 'Sources of variation in working class images of society', *Sociological Review* **14**, 1966.

3. Georges Duveau, *La vie ouvrière en France sous le Second Empire* (Paris 1946), pp. 226, 227 and 228.

4. For the most fruitful analysis of the British experience, see E. P. Thompson, *The Making of the English Working Class* (London 1963); a critique of this work

is given in R. Currie and R. M. Hartwell, 'The making of the English working class?' *Economic History Review* 18, 1965.

5. Dahrendorf, *Class and Class Conflict*, pp. 277 and 271.

6. Seymour Martin Lipset, *Political Man* (London 1969), p. 237; Eric A. Nordlinger, *The Working Class Tories* (London 1967), pp. 205–9; Richard F. Hamilton, *Affluence and the French Worker in the Fourth Republic* (Princeton 1967),. pp. 205–28; Shin-Ichi Takezawa, 'The blue-collar worker in Japanese industry', in N. F. Dufty, *The Sociology of the Blue-Collar Worker* (Leiden 1969), pp. 190–1; for an overall survey, Geoffrey K. Ingham, 'Plant size: political attitudes and behaviour', *Sociological Review* 17, 1969.

7. There is actually some difficulty in reaching a satisfactory definition of the deceptively simple term 'mechanisation'. One recent attempt is: 'any technological change which increases output per worker (or man-hour), i.e., change which cuts labor requirements per unit of output' (A. J. Jaffe and Joseph Froomkin, *Technology and Jobs*, New York 1968, p. 17).

8. Robert Blauner, *Alienation and Freedom* (Chicago 1964), p. 7.

9. cf. Joan Woodward, *Industrial Organisation: Theory and Practice* (London 1965).

10. See, however, John H. Goldthorpe, 'Attitudes and behaviour of car assembly workers: a deviant case and a theoretical critique', *British Journal of Sociology* 17, 1966.

11. cf., for instance, Arthur N. Turner and Paul R. Lawrence, *Industrial Jobs and the Worker* (Boston 1965). There are obvious difficulties with the notion of job 'satisfaction', since what constitutes 'satisfaction', or its opposite, is clearly subject to relativities of expectation.

12. Michael Mann, *Consciousness and Action Among the Western Working Class* (London 1973), p. 21. The analysis which follows in this chapter owes, at certain points, a considerable debt to this work, and to conversations with Michael Mann.

13. Clark Kerr and Abraham Siegel, 'The interindustry propensity to strike—an international comparison', in Arthur Kornhauser *et al.*, *Industrial Conflict* (New York 1954).

14. cf. Werner Sombart, *Warum gibt es in den Vereinigten Staaten keinen Sozialismus?* (Tübingen 1906), for the classic analysis of the problem. For more recent historical analyses, James Weinstein, *The Decline of Socialism in America, 1912–25* (New York 1967); John H. M. Laslett, *Labor and the Left* (New York 1970).

15. It is important to emphasise the phrase 'active incorporation', because although in some countries a mass franchise was introduced relatively early on it often was little more than a sham. The theorem stated here applies with particular cogency to the early socialist leaders. As Kautsky pointed out, socialism 'was something carried into the class struggle of the proletariat from the outside, namely by middle-class intellectuals'—such individuals were very often most distinctively 'caught' between advancing capitalism and the reaction of 'semi-feudal' land-owning groupings.

16. Selig Perlman, *A Theory of the Labor Movement* (New York 1928). For a more recent attempt at a distinctively comparative analysis, see Everett M. Kassalow, *Trade Unions and Industrial Relations: an International Comparison* (New York 1969).

17. Hamilton, *Affluence and the French Worker in the Fourth Republic*, pp. 229–30. See also Touraine, *La conscience ouvrière*, pp. 150–84 and 277–301.

18. cf., for example, Dorothy Wedderburn and Rosemary Crompton, *Workers'*

Attitudes and Technology (Cambridge 1972), p. 43; and Odile Benoit, 'Statut dans l'entreprise et attitudes syndicales des ouvriers', *Sociologie du travail* 4, 1962. It should be noted, however, that this analogy does not of itself provide an adequate basis for distinguishing conflict and revolutionary consciousness.

19. Hamilton, op. cit., pp. 220–5.

20. cf. J. A. Banks, *Marxist Sociology in Action* (London 1970), pp. 87–138, on union leadership in the mining and iron and steel industries in Britain.

21. For a more detailed analysis, see Michael Mann, 'The social cohesion of liberal democracy', *American Sociological Review* 35, 1970.

22. Duveau, op. cit., p. 229; cf. also Hamilton, op. cit., pp. 258ff.

23. cf. Ehrmann's important study of employers' associations in France. As the author points out, there have been only a few studies of employers' associations, compared to the massive literature on the labour movement, but the former might be of major importance in affecting the character of the latter (Henry W. Ehrmann, *Organised Business in France*, Princeton 1957).

24. cf. Solomon B. Levine, *Industrial Relations in Postwar Japan*, pp. 59ff and *passim*; James C. Abegglen, *The Japanese Factory* (Glencoe 1958), pp. 77–80. For a critique of Abegglen, which he says 'relies almost wholly upon management sources', see Robert E. Cole, *Japanese Blue Collar* (Berkeley 1971). This is an important book, because Cole shows that the 'uniqueness' of the Japanese industrial system should be interpreted, not merely in terms of its traditional 'culture', but in terms also of the characteristic form of the economic infra-structure. There are strong economic pressures, for example, maintaining the *nenko* wage system (the seniority principle). See also Taira, op. cit., for a partly overlapping analysis.

25. Robert A. Scalapino, 'Labour and politics in postwar Japan', in W. W. Lockwood, op. cit., p. 673.

26. See Dahrendorf, *Conflict after Class*, op. cit.

27. André Gorz, 'Work and consumption', in Perry Anderson and Robin Blackburn, *Towards Socialism* (London 1965), p. 349.

28. S. M. Miller, 'The "new" working class', in Arthur B. Shostak and William Gomberg, *Blue-Collar World* (Englewood Cliffs 1965), p. 7.

29. Leggett, op. cit., p. 80 and *passim*.

30. Richard F. Hamilton, 'Liberal intelligentsia and white backlash', *Dissent*, Winter, 1972, pp. 228–9.

31. Peter B. Doeringer and Michael J. Piore, *Internal Labour Markets and Manpower Analysis* (Lexington 1971), pp. 164–83 and *passim*.

32. cf. Stephen Castles and Godula Kosack, *Immigrant Workers and Class Structure in Western Europe* (London 1973). As the authors point out: 'Virtually every advanced capitalist country has a lower stratum, distinguished by race, nationality, or other special characteristics, which carries out the worst jobs and has the least desirable social conditions' (p. 2).

33. Goldthorpe *et al.*, op. cit., vol. 3, pp. 157–9.

Chapter 12. State socialism and class structuration

1. cf. Jan M. Michal, *Central Planning in Czechoslovakia* (Stanford 1960), p. 1.

2. Bogusław Galeski, 'Sociological research on social changes in Poland's rural areas', in J. Szczepánski, *Empirical Sociology in Poland* (Warsaw 1966), p. 80.

3. cf. Alfred Zauberman, *Industrial Progress in Poland, Czechoslovakia, and East Germany* (London 1964), pp. 1–2.

4. Nicholas Spulber, *The Economics of Communist Eastern Europe* (New York 1957), pp. 86–7 and *passim*.

5. cf., for a brief evaluation, Gregory Grossman, 'Economic reforms: a balance sheet', in George R. Feiwel, *New Currents in Soviet-Type Economies* (Scranton 1968).

6. The most sophisticated discussions of these matters, keeping within a fairly orthodox Marxist framework, are by Polish sociologists and political theorists. cf. Szczepański, op. cit. Contrast this with a typical recent Soviet view, repeating the dogma that, following the October Revolution, 'The working class and the peasantry became entirely new classes, previously unknown in history. A new, people's intelligentsia arose and developed. In the Soviet Union the interests of workers and peasants engaged in manual labour and the interests of intellectuals are not antithetical . . .' (A. N. Maslîn and G. V. Osipov, 'Trends towards the combination of intellectual and manual labour', in G. V. Osipov, *Industry and Labour in the USSR*, London 1966, p. 181).

7. Parkin, *Class Inequality and Political Order*, pp. 141ff; and also, 'Class stratification in socialist societies', *British Journal of Sociology* 20, 1969.

8. Maslin and Osipov, op. cit., p. 181 and *passim*. See also L. Kostin, *Wages in the USSR* (Moscow 1960); Mervyn Matthews, *Class and Society in Soviet Russia* (London 1972), pp. 72–107.

9. For relevant analyses, cf. Alex Inkeles, 'Social Stratification and mobility in the Soviet Union', and Robert A. Feldmesser, 'Toward the classless society?', in Reinhard Bendix and Seymour Martin Lipset, *Class, Status, and Power* (London 1967); David Lane, *The End of Inequality?* (London 1971), pp. 31–2 and 54–79. The debate upon income inequality continues in the state socialist countries. Thus a recent Soviet author writes: 'We should not be afraid of the deepening of wage differentials as something which collides with our aims of social development. It is true that in the end wage differentials of working people should be erased. However, there is a danger here in running ahead groundlessly' (J. Volkov, *Literaturnaya Gazieta*, no. 19, Moscow, June 1972).

10. Lane, op. cit., p. 73; cf. Norton T. Dodge, *Women in the Soviet Economy* (Baltimore 1966). In the Soviet Union, the rate of participation of women in the labour force is nearly double that in the United States. About 80 per cent of Soviet women between the ages of 20 and 39 years—the major phase of child-bearing and child-rearing—are employed (compared to about 33 per cent of American women in their late twenties). While women make up a high proportion of those in white-collar occupations, they are not so clustered in the routine jobs as in the Western countries: 53 per cent of those in the professions, including science and engineering, for instance, are women.

11. cf. P. J. D. Wiles and Stefan Markowski, 'Income distribution under communism and capitalism', pts 1 and 2, *Soviet Studies* 22, 1970–1, and Lidia Beskid, 'Real wages in Poland during 1956–1967', *Eastern European Economics* 7, 1969. For general surveys of changes in income distribution in both capitalist and state socialist societies, see Jean Marchal and Bernard Ducross, *The Distribution of National Income* (London 1968).

12. W. Wesolowski, *Struktura i dynamika spoleczeństwa polskiego* (Warsaw 1970). On Czechoslovakia, see Zdenek Strmiska and Blanka Varakova, 'La stratification sociale de la société socialiste', *Revue française de sociologie* 13, 1972 (a discussion of Pavel Machonin *et al.*, *Ceskoslovenska spolecnost-Sociologicka analyza socialni stratifikace*, Bratislava 1969).

13. cf. Daniel Kubat, 'Social mobility in Czechoslovakia', *American Sociological Review* 28, 1963. Kubat claims, however, that overall rates of mobility are declining.

14. Vojin Milić, 'General trends in social mobility in Yugoslavia', *Acta Sociologica* 9, 1965, p. 131; on the Soviet Union, M. Kh. Liberman and V. V. Petrov, 'An analysis of systems of vocational training in industry', in Osipov, op. cit.

15. There is now a large literature on the Yugoslavian workers' councils. See, for instance, ILO, *Workers' Management in Yugoslavia* (Geneva 1962); Adolf Sturmthal, *Workers' Councils* (Cambridge 1964); Paul Blumberg, *Industrial Democracy* (London 1968).

16. cf. Sturmthal, *Workers' Councils*, pp. 119–39; André Babeau, *Les conseils ouvriers en Pologne* (Paris 1960).

17. 'La courte expérience des conseils ouvriers en Pologne', *La documentation française*, no. 2453, 26 August 1958.

18. Quoted in Robert Vitak, 'Workers' control: the Czechoslovakian experience', *The Socialist Register, 1971* (London 1971), pp. 254–5.

19. Russian figures are from a study in Sverdlovsk, quoted by Lane, *The End of Inequality*, pp. 112–13.

20. Milić, op. cit., pp. 125ff.

21. Research by Widerszpil in Poland showed that, of schoolboys from manual worker backgrounds, only 7 per cent aspired to university education; the corresponding percentage for those of non-manual origins was 30 per cent. Quoted in Zygmunt Bauman, 'Economic growth and social structure', in Jerzy J. Wiatr, *Studies in Polish Political System* (Warsaw 1967), p. 23.

Chapter 13. Class and party in state socialist society

1. Milovan Djilas, *The New Class, an Analysis of the Communist System* (New York 1957), pp. 35–6, 39 and 40.

2. See, for example, Parkin, *Class Inequality and Political Order*, pp. 150ff; Lane, *The End of Inequality*, pp. 116ff.

3. Zygmunt Bauman, 'Economic growth, social structure, elite formation', *International Social Science Journal* 2, 1964. A more recent study in Poland shows that the proportion of the PUWP membership represented by the intelligentsia in 1970 was 43 per cent: Adolf Dobieszewski, *Wybrane problemy teorii i praktyki funcjonowania partii* (Warsaw 1971) p. 289; *The Problems of Peace and Socialism*, no. 9, 1970.

4. Djilas, op. cit., p. 41.

5. Zbigniew Brzezinski and Samuel P. Huntington, *Political Power: USA/USSR* (New York 1964), pp. 135–40.

6. *International Study of Opinion Makers*, 1969 (Yugoslavian section), quoted in Lane, op. cit., pp. 116–18.

7. Brzezinski and Huntington, op. cit., pp. 139ff.

8. cf. Albert Parry, *The New Class Divided* (New York 1966); see also Aron, *La lutte des classes*, pp. 331ff.

9. John S. Reshetar, *The Soviet Polity* (New York 1971), pp. 360–1.

10. Thus we must mistrust such blunt statements as 'In socialist society the key antagonisms occurring at the social level are those between the Party and state bureaucracy on the one hand and the intelligentsia on the other' (Frank

Parkin, 'System contradiction and political transformation', *Archives européennes de sociologie* 13, 1972, p. 50).

11. Hugh Seton-Watson, *East European Revolution* (London 1955), p. xvi.

12. cf. Daniel Bell, 'Ten theories in search of reality', *The End of Ideology* (New York 1961); David Lane, *Politics and Society in the USSR* (London 1970), pp. 175–96.

13. For an exposition of divergent ideas about the probable trend of development in the Soviet Union, see Zbigniew Brzezinski, *Dilemmas of Change in Soviet Politics* (New York 1969); for a more wide-ranging discussion, cf. Stephen Fischer-Galati, 'East Central Europe: continuity and change', *Journal of International Affairs* 20, 1966.

14. cf. Robert Bass, 'East European Communist elites: their character and history', ibid., pp. 114–17.

15. cf. Jeremy Azrael, *Managerial Power and Soviet Politics* (Cambridge, Mass. 1966), who argues that the managers conform to the general ideology of the system, and do not constitute a force for radical political change; and George Fischer, *The Soviet System and Modern Society* (New York 1968), who identifies the rise of what he calls the 'dual executive', who is schooled in technical skills and in Party work.

16. cf. on this point Ernst Halperin, 'Beyond Libermanism', in Brzezinski, op. cit., pp. 105–6.

17. Bauman has recently argued, to my mind quite unconvincingly, that the major sources of tension in state socialist society can be understood in terms of an 'early stage of industrialisation' hypothesis (Zygmunt Bauman, 'Social dissent in East European politics', *Archives européennes de sociologie* 12, 1971, p. 41). For other contributions to a debate upon this issue, see the articles by Kolakowski in the same volume and by Lane and Parkin in the subsequent volume of the same journal; Aron offers comments on these in 'Remarques sur un débat', in the latter volume.

18. Parkin, *Social Stratification and the Political Order*, pp. 172–4; cf. also Georg von Wrangel, *Wird der Ostblock kapitalistisch?* (Munich 1966), pp. 219–28.

19. See Pitrim A. Sorokin, *Russia and the United States* (London 1950), and 'Mutual convergence of the United States and the USSR to the mixed sociocultural type', *International Journal of Comparative Sociology* 1, 1960; C. Kerr *et al.*, *Industrialism and Industrial Man* (London 1960). For a general discussion, see Bertram D. Wolfe, 'The convergence theory in historical perspective', *An Ideology in Power* (New York 1969).

Chapter 14. Classes in contemporary society

1. cf. Daniel Bell, 'The measurement of knowledge and technology', in Eleanor Sheldon and Wilbert Moore, *Indicators of Social Change* (New York 1969); 'Technocracy and politics', *Survey* 16, 1971; and 'Labour in the post-industrial society', *Dissent*, Winter, 1972.

2. Bell, 'Technocracy and politics', p. 4.

3. Alain Touraine, *La société post-industrielle*, op. cit.

4. ibid., *The May Movement* (New York 1971).

5. 'Technocracy and politics', p 10.

6. Jürgen Habermas, 'Zwischen Philosophie und Wissenschaft: Marxismus als Kritik', *Theorie und Praxis* (Neuwied 1967).

7. cf. Claus Offe, 'Technik und Eindimensionalität: eine Version der Technokratiethese?', in Jürgen Habermas, *Antworten auf Herbert Marcuse* (Frankfurt 1968).

8. cf., for example, Zbigniew Brzezinski, *Between Two Ages* (New York 1970), pp. 222–36. For Marcuse and Habermas, of course, this is a 'false reason'.

9. Touraine, *The May Movement*, p. 355.

10. Most of the works on technocracy, for rather differing historical reasons, are either French or American. From a very large literature, the following may be mentioned as representative: Georges Gurvitch, *Industrialisation et technocratie* (Paris 1949); Henri Lefebvre, *Positions: contre les technocrates* (Paris 1967); Jean Meynaud, *Technocracy* (London 1968); C. Koch and D. Senghaas, *Texte zur Technokratie–Diskussion* (Frankfurt 1970); Daniel Bell, 'Toward the Year 2000: Work in Progress', *Daedalus*, 1968.

11. cf. Gramsci: 'The success of sociology is related to the decadence of the concept of political science and political art which appeared in the nineteenth century . . .' (Antonio Gramsci, 'Notes on Machiavelli's *Politics*', *The Modern Prince and Other Writings*, London 1957, pp. 181–2). But this judgement also applies to Marxism itself, save for Gramsci and those recently influenced by him.

12. Bell admits that, 'Just as an industrial society has been organised politically and culturally in diverse ways by the USSR, Germany, and Japan, so too the post-industrial society may have diverse political and cultural forms' ('The measurement of science and technology', op. cit., p. 158).

13. Brzezinski, op. cit., p. 196; cf. Lipset: 'instead of European class and political relationships holding up a model of the United States' future, the social organisation of the United States has presented the image of the European future' (Seymour Martin Lipset, 'The changing class structure and contemporary European politics', in Graubard, op. cit., p. 338).

14. Lewis Mumford: op. cit., p. 9.

15. Peter Wiles, 'A comment on Bell', and Giovanni Sartori, 'Technological forecasting and politics', *Survey* 16, 1971, 41 and 66.

16. cf. Reinhard Bendix, *Work and Authority in Industry* (New York 1956).

17. cf. Arthur Stinchcombe, 'Social structure and organisations', in James G. March, *Handbook of Organisations* (Chicago 1965).

18. Talcott Parsons, 'Equality and inequality in modern society, or social stratification revisited', *Sociological Inquiry* 40, 1970, p. 24.

19. Parsons in fact continues to use the term 'class', but redefines the term as virtually equivalent to 'status group' (and uses the term 'status' to mean 'position'). He proposes 'to define *class status*, for the unit of social structure, as position on the hierarchical dimension of the differentiation of the societal system; and to consider *social class* as an aggregate of such units, individual and/or collective, that in their own estimation and those of others in the society occupy positions of approximately equal status in this respect' (ibid., p. 24).

20. Émile Durkheim, *The Division of Labor in Society* (Glencoe 1964), pp. 375–88.

21. cf. the observation made recently by a labour economist that 'decisions made within the family determine who will seek work, for how long, and where. Family members allocate labor and income among themselves by personal criteria, with little reference to private market allocation procedure. The children alone do not decide whether they will work. The wife alone does not choose between a part-time and a full-time job. Or when to quit the labor force. Family

pressures for income and other goods enter into all these decisions' (Stanley Lebergott, 'Labor force and employment trends', in Sheldon and Moore, op. cit., p. 98).

22. Clark Kerr, *Marshall, Marx and Modern Times* (Cambridge 1969), p. 78.

Chapter 15. The future of class society

1. cf. my *Politics and Sociology in the Thought of Max Weber*, pp. 45ff.

2. Marcuse, 'Industrialisation and capitalism in the Thought of Max Weber', in Otto Stammler, *Max Weber and Sociology Today* (Oxford 1971).

3. 'Manifesto of the Communist Party', *Selected Works*, p. 36.

4. Thus the 8th thesis on Feuerbach declares: 'All mysteries which lead theory to mysticism find their rational solution in human practice and in the comprehension of this practice.'

5. cf. Durkheim's analysis in *Socialism* (New York 1962), pp. 55–63 and *passim*.

6. 'The civil war in France', *Selected Works*, pp. 292–4.

7. There are various hints about this scattered through the 3rd vol. of *Capital*.

8. 'Manifesto of the Communist Party', *Selected Works*, p. 53.

9. cf. Bell's discussion of Irving Bernstein, 'Union growth and structural cycles', in Walter Galenson and Seymour Martin Lipset, *Labour and Trade Unionism* (New York 1960), pp. 89–93.

10. C. B. Macpherson, 'Post-liberal democracy?' *Canadian Journal of Economics and Political Science* 30, 1964.

11. cf. Macpherson: 'The state may, as states commonly do, interfere by way of differential taxes and subsidies, control of competition and of monopoly, control of land use and labor use, and all kinds of regulation conferring advantages or disadvantages on some kinds of production or some categories of producers. What the state does thereby is to alter the terms of the equations which each man makes when he is calculating his most profitable course of action. Some of the data for the calculation are changed, but this need not affect the mainspring of the system, which is that men do act as their calculation of net gain dictates. As long as prices still move in response to these calculated decisions, and as long as prices still elicit the production of goods and determine their allocation, we may say that the essential nature of the system has not changed' (Macpherson, 'Post-liberal democracy?', op. cit., p. 494).

12. ibid., p. 495. cf. Hörning's conclusion, surveying different theories of the 'new working class', 'Die Verbürgerlichungs-und Integrationshoffnungen sind unbegründet. Gleichermassen scheint aber auch die Euphorie über eine "Neue Arbeiterklasse" unangebracht' (Karl N. Hörning, *Der 'neue' Arbeiter*, Frankfurt 1971, p. 8).

13. cf. the defence of the *Makhnovchina* in Gabriel and Daniel Cohn-Bendit, *Obsolete Communism, the Left-Wing Alternative* (London 1969), pp. 220–32.

Postscript (1979)

1. cf. my 'Classical social theory and the origins of modern sociology', *American Journal of Sociology* **81**, 1976.

2. Gabriel Cohn-Bendit and Daniel Cohn-Bendit: *Obsolete Communism, the Left-Wing Alternative* (Harmondsworth: Penguin 1969).

3. For two views on this question, see Martin Shaw, *Marxism versus Sociology* (London: Pluto Press 1974); and T. B. Bottomore, *Marxist Sociology* (London: Macmillan 1975).

4. See, for instance, Rosemary Crompton and Jon Gubbay, *Economy and Class Structure* (London: Macmillan 1977), pp. 29–40 and *passim*; David Binns, *Beyond the Sociology of Conflict* (London: Macmillan 1977), pp. 47–54; Richard Ashcraft, 'Class and class conflict in contemporary capitalist societies', *Comparative Politics* **11**, 1979.

5. cf. 'Marx, Weber and the development of capitalism', in my *Studies in Social and Political Theory* (London: Hutchinson 1977).

6. For a brief discussion of these contrasts, see 'Marx and Weber: problems of class structure', in *Studies in Social and Political Theory*, op. cit.

7. Wini Breines and Margaret Cerullo, Review of *The Class Structure of the Advanced Societies, Telos* **28**, 1976, p. 235.

8. Binns, op. cit., p. 48.

9. cf. Karl Polanyi *et al.*, *Trade and Market in the Early Empires* (New York: Free Press 1957).

10. cf. my *Central Problems in Social Theory* (London: Macmillan 1979), ch. 4.

11. See, for instance, Crompton and Gubbay, op. cit.; Goran Therborn: *What Does the Ruling Class Do When it Rules?* (London: New Left Books 1978). pp. 138–43. The crude nature of the opposition which Therborn draws between a caricatured Weberian position and a dogmatically presented quasi-Althusserian interpretation of Marx is characteristic of this sort of standpoint. cf. Laclau's observation that 'The emergence of the free labour market is the decisive factor in the appearance of capitalism,' noted in critique of Althusser's and Balibar's formulation of the notion of mode of production (Ernesto Laclau, *Politics and Ideology in Marxist Theory*, London: New Left Books 1977, p. 75).

12. Terence Johnson, 'The professions in the class struggle', in Richard Scase, *Industrial Society: Class, Cleavage and Control* (London: Allen & Unwin 1977), p. 94. An accurate representation of my position in respect of the rationality of technique and authority is given in Louis Maheu, 'Rapports de classe et problèmes de transformation', in Louis Maheu and Gabriel Gagnon, *Changement social et rapports de classes* (Montreal: Presses de l'Université de Montréal 1978), pp. 21ff.

13. cf. 'Classical social theory and the origins of modern sociology', op. cit.

14. Some writers have, however, questioned the empirical validity of certain of the assertions I made about social mobility. cf. Karl Ulrich Mayer, 'Ungleiche Chancen und Klassenbildung', *Soziale Welt* **4**, 1977; John Goldthorpe and Catriona Llewellyn, 'Class mobility in modern Britain: three theses examined', *Sociology* **11**, 1977.

15. Nicos Poulantzas, *Classes in Contemporary Capitalism* (London: New Left Books 1975), p. 33, and again on p. 284.

16. See, for example, pp. 261ff and 282ff. See also the interesting study by Daniel Bertaux, *Destins personnels et structure de classe* (Paris: Presses Universitaires 1977). Bertaux seeks to replace the term 'social mobility' with that of an 'anthroponomic process' of the 'production, distribution and consumption of human beings' (p. 45).

17. Frank Parkin, *Class Inequality and Political Order* (London: Paladin 1972; first published in 1971).

18. ibid., pp. 23–4. Parkin seems to have altered his views more recently, however. See his article, 'Social stratification', in Tom Bottomore and Robert Nisbet, *A History of Sociological Analysis* (New York: Basic Books 1978), especially pp. 608–16. Since the Postscript was written, Parkin's *The Marxist Theory of Class: A Bourgeois Critique* (London: Tavistock 1979) has appeared. I have discussed this book in 'Classes, capitalism and the state', *Theory and Society* (forthcoming).

19. *Central Problems in Social Theory*, op. cit., pp. 103ff.

20. According to Mallet, one must admit, 'like every man endowed with common sense, the diminishing qualitative and quantitative importance of the traditional proletariat' (Serge Mallet, *Essays on the New Working Class*, St Louis: Telos Press 1975 p. 80). In Sweezy's view, 'the first effects of the introduction of machinery – expansion and homogenisation of the labour force and reduction in the costs of production (value) or labour power – have (in contemporary capitalism) been largely reversed'(Paul M. Sweezy, *Modern Capitalism*, New York: Monthly Review Press 1972, p. 160).

21. Guglielmo Carchedi, *On the Economic Identification of Social Classes* (London: Routledge & Kegan Paul 1977). Carchedi's name for his functionalism is 'dialectical determination'. For an informative critique of Carchedi, see R. W. Connell, 'Complexities of fury leave . . . a critique of the Althusseriah approach to class,' *Theory and Society* **8**, 1979.

22. ibid., p. 4.

23. ibid., p. 118. Carchedi's account is actually very much more complicated than this description of his main themes suggests. As Connell says, Carchedi's book is marked by a veritable 'categorical frenzy'.

24. Eric Olin Wright, *Class, Crisis and the State* (London: New Left Books 1978), p. 62. Wright comments on Carchedi at greater length in his 'Class structure and income inequality' (unpublished Ph.D thesis, University of California, Berkeley 1976).

25. Wright, *Class, Crisis and the State*, op. cit., pp. 77–8.

26. ibid., p. 81.

27. Emil Lederer and J. Marschak, 'Der neue Mittelstand', *Gundriss der Sozialökonomik*, vol. **9** (I), 1926.

28. cf. *Central Problems in Social Theory*, op. cit., pp. 111–15 and 210–22.

29. cf. T. Johnson: 'What is to be known? The structural determination of class,' *Economy and Society* **7**, 1977, who argues that 'Carchedi's levels of abstraction ultimately involve an economic essentialism'.

30. Carchedi, op. cit., p. 6.

31. This point is made in an article by Urry, quoted by Carchedi on pp. 33–6 of the latter's book; Carchedi's reply to the criticism is less than persuasive.

32. Carchedi, op. cit., note 66 to ch. 1, pp. 114–15.

33. Wright, op. cit., p. 90, note 75.

34. See *Central Problems in Social Theory*, op. cit.

35. Wright, op. cit., p. 62.

36. ibid., p. 78.

37. cf. Alfred Sohn-Rethel, *Intellectual and Manual Labour* (London: Macmillan 1978), who develops virtually a whole epistemology around the separation of manual and non-manual labour.

38. Nicos Poulantzas, *Political Power and Social Classes* (London: New Left Books 1973). I drew upon certain of the sections of the French edition of the book (first published in 1968), without analysing its arguments in any detail.

39. 'From the start structural class determination involves economic, political and ideological class struggle, and these struggles are all expressed in the form of class positions in the conjuncture' (*Classes in Contemporary Capitalism*, op. cit., p. 16).

40. ibid., pp. 230ff.

41. Wright, op. cit., p. 55.

42. For a discussion of these, see Wright, op. cit., pp. 46–50.

43. *Central Problems in Social Theory*, op. cit., pp. 100–1 and *passim*.

44. Marx himself dismissed as 'idiocy' Bakunin's suggestion that the controllers of 'collectively owned' property in a socialist society could create a new form of class domination.

45. cf., however my *Politics and Sociology in the Thought of Max Weber* (London: Macmillan 1972), pp. 44–9.

46. Max Weber, *Economy and Society* (New York: Bedmeister Press 1968), vol. 3, p. 998.

47. cf. my *Capitalism and Modern Social Theory* (Cambridge: Cambridge University Press 1971), pp. 224–42.

48. Georges Friedmann, *Industrial Society* (Glencoe: Free Press 1955); cf. also *La travail en mièttes*.

49. Harry Braverman, *Labor and Monopoly Capital* (New York: Monthly Review Press 1974).

50. A partly overlapping viewpoint is sketched in Stephen A. Marglin, 'What do bosses do?', in André Gorz, *The Division of Labour* (London: Harvester 1976).

51. The distinction between the social and technical division of labour is not as unambiguous as Braverman claims, nor is the technical division of labour peculiar to capitalism; Marx's critique of the division of labour (e.g., between the sexes, or town and country) is not confined to the technical division of labour.

52. Braverman seems to consider that Sweezy's and Baran's *Monopoly Capital* has said more or less all there is to say about this. See his comments in Braverman, op. cit., pp. 251–6; Sweezy's preface to Braverman's book also appears to take the same view.

53. Braverman, op. cit., p. 27.

54. cf. Russell Jacoby's review of *Labor and Monopoly Capital*, Telos **29**, 1976; and Gavin Mackenzie, 'The political economy of the American working class', *British Journal of Sociology* **28**, 1977.

55. See Bryan Palmer, 'Class, conception and conflict; the thrust for efficiency, managerial views of labour and the working class rebellion, 1903–22', *Review of Radical Political Economy* **7**, 1975; H. G. J. Aitken, *Taylorism at Watertown Arsenal* (Cambridge, Mass.: Harvard University Press 1960); Stanley Aronowitz, *False Promises* (New York: McGraw-Hill 1973), and S. Aronowitz, 'Marx, Braverman, and the logic of capital', *Insurgent Sociologist*, Winter, 1978–9; Andrew L. Friedman, *Industry and Labour* (London: Macmillan 1977).

56. Here I draw upon *Central Problems in Social Theory*, op. cit., pp. 147–50.

57. Michel Crozier, *The Bureaucratic Phenomenon* (London: Tavistock 1964).

58. cf. Aronowitz, *False Promises*, op. cit.

59. cf. Aronowitz, *False Promises*, op. cit., for a good discussion of various kinds of worker resistance to, and reappropriation of control over, their work situation.

60. Friedman, *Industry and Labour*, op. cit.

61. ibid., p. 7.

62. ibid., p. 137.

63. Poulantzas makes a similar point. 'A whole tradition of political theory',

he says, 'based on an ideological delimitation of the autonomy of the political from the economic (i.e., the theoretical tradition of the nineteenth century, which involves precisely the theme of the separation of civil society from the state) mistakes this autonomy for that specific non-intervention of the political in the economic which is characteristic of the form of liberal state and private capitalism'. On this view, the expanding intervention of the state dissolves the autonomy of the economic and political. But this is an error: 'The interventionist state, for example, exercises its intervention precisely by means of the particular forms assumed by its autonomy relative to the economic' (*Political Power and Social Classes*, op. cit., pp. 151–2).

64. Immanuel Wallerstein, *The Modern World-System* (New York: Academic Press 1974).

65. See, in particular, Robert Brenner, 'The origins of capitalist development: a critique of neo-Smithian Marxism', *New Left Review* **104**, July–August, 1977.

66. Wallerstein, op. cit., p. 348.

67. cf. 'Classical social theory and the origins of modern sociology', op. cit.

68. cf. Gianfranco Poggi, *The Development of the Modern State* (London: Hutchinson 1978), pp. 71ff.

69. See Boris Frankel, 'On the state of the state: Marxist theories of the state after Leninism', *Theory and Society* **7**, 1979, for an important discussion of this issue.

70. Here I follow the notion of contradiction formulated in *Central Problems in Social Theory*, op. cit., rather than that employed in *CSAS*, which I now regard as defective.

71. Claus Offe, *Strukturprobleme des kapitalistischen Staates* (Frankfurt: Suhrkamp 1972); *Industry and Inequality* (London: Edward Arnold 1976).

72. Offe, *Strukturprobleme des Kapitalistischen Staates*, op. cit., p. 47.

73. Claus Offe and Volker Ronge, 'Theses on the theory of the state', *New German Critique* **6**, 1975, p. 145.

74. In *The Cultural Contradictions of Capitalism* (London: Heinemann 1976), Bell seems less sanguine about the likely staying power of capitalism than Habermas does in *Legitimation Crisis* (Boston: Beacon 1975).

75. Alan Dawley, *Class and Community* (Cambridge, Mass.: Harvard University Press 1976), p. 236.

76. C. B. Macpherson, *The Real World of Democracy* (Oxford: Clarendon Press 1966), p. 9.

77. cf. 'Classical social theory and the origins of modern sociology', op. cit.

78. Serge Mallet, *Essays on the New Working Class* (St Louis: Telos Press 1975), p. 123.

79. A major contribution to discussion of the nature of the state socialist societies has recently appeared: Rudolf Bahro, *The Alternative in Eastern Europe* (London: New Left Books 1978). 'The abolition of private property in the means of production', Bahro argues, 'has in no way meant their immediate transformation into the property of the people. Rather, the whole society stands propertyless against the state machine' (p. 11). Controversial though some of Bahro's claims may be, this book must now be regarded as a focal point for the critical analysis of Marxism and of socialist thought and practice more generally.

WORKS CITED IN THE TEXT

Abegglen, James C., *The Japanese Factory* (Glencoe 1958)
Abegglen, James C., and Mannari, H., 'Leaders of modern Japan: social origins and mobility', *Economic Development and Cultural Change* **9**, 1960
Acton, H. B., *The Illusion of the Epoch* (London 1962)
Adorno, Theodor W., *Aufsätze zur Gesellschaftstheorie und Methodologie* (Frankfurt 1970)
Althusser, Louis, *For Marx* (London 1969)
Anderson, Perry, and Blackburn, Robin, *Towards Socialism* (London 1965)
Aron, Raymond, *Democracy and Totalitarianism* (London 1968)
——'La classe comme représentation et comme volonté', *Cahiers internationaux de sociologie* **38**, 1965
——*18 Lectures on Industrial Society* (London 1968)
——*La lutte des classes* (Paris 1964)
——*Progress and Disillusion* (New York 1968)
Atkinson, Dick, *Orthodox Consensus and Radical Alternative* (London 1971)
Azrael, Jeremy, *Managerial Power and Soviet Politics* (Cambridge, Mass. 1966)
Babeau, André, *Les conseils ouvriers en Pologne* (Paris 1960)
Baechler, Jean, 'Essai sur les origines du système capitaliste', *Archives européennes de sociologie,* **9**, 1968
Bain, George Sayers, *The Growth of White-Collar Unionism* (Oxford 1970)
Bain, Joe S., *Industrial Organisation* (New York 1968)
Banks, J. A., *Marxist Sociology in Action* (London 1970)
Bauman, Zygmunt, 'Economic growth, social structure, elite formation', *International Social Science Journal* **2**, 1964
——'Social dissent in East European politics', *Archives européennes de sociologie* **12**, 1971
Bell, Daniel, 'Labour in the post-industrial society', *Dissent*, Winter, 1972
——'Technocracy and politics', *Survey* **16**, 1971
——*The End of Ideology* (New York 1961)
——'Toward the Year 2000: Work in Progress', *Daedalus*, 1968
Belleville, Pierre, *Une nouvelle class ouvrière* (Paris 1963)
Bendix, Reinhard, *Embattled Reason, Essays on Social Knowledge* (New York 1970)
——*Higher Civil Servants in American Society* (Boulder 1949)

Bendix, Reinhard, *Nation-Building and Citizenship* (New York 1964)
——*Work and Authority in Industry* (New York 1956)
Bendix, Reinhard, and Seymour Martin Lipset, *Class, Status and Power* (London 1967)
Benoit, Odile, 'Statut dans l'entreprise et attitudes syndicales des ouvriers', *Sociologie du Travail*, 4, 1962
Bensman, Joseph, and Vidich, Arthur J., *The New American Society* (Chicago 1971)
Berg, Ivar, *The Business of America* (New York 1968)
Berle, Adolf A., and Means, Gardiner C., *The Modern Corporation and Private Property* (Chicago 1932)
Beskid, Lidia, 'Real wages in Poland during 1956–1967', *Eastern European Economics* 7, 1969
Birnbaum, Norman, 'The crisis of Marxist sociology', *Social Research* 2, 1968
Blau, Peter M., and Duncan, O. D., *The American Occupational Structure* (New York 1967)
Blauner, Robert, *Alienation and Freedom* (Chicago 1964)
Bloch, Marc, *Feudal Society* (London 1961)
Blumberg, Paul, *Industrial Democracy* (London 1968)
Bottomore, T. B., *Classes in Modern Society* (London 1966)
Bouvier-Ajam, Maurice, and Mury, Gilbert, *Les classes sociales en France* (Paris 1963)
Braun, Siegfried, and Fuhrmann, Jochen, *Angestelltenmentalität* (Neuwied 1970)
Brzezinski, Zbigniew, *Between Two Ages* (New York 1970)
——*Dilemmas of Change in Soviet Politics* (New York 1969)
Brzezinski, Zbigniew, and Huntington, Samuel P., *Political Power: USA/USSR* (New York 1964)
Burns, Robert K., 'The comparative economic position of manual and white-collar employees', *The Journal of Business* 27, 1954
Castles, Stephen, and Kosack, Godula, *Immigrant Workers and Class Structure in Western Europe* (London 1973)
Cohn-Bendit, Gabriel and Daniel, *Obsolete Communism, the Left-Wing Alternative* (London 1969)
Cole, Robert E., *Japanese Blue Collar* (Berkeley 1971)
Cox, Oliver C., *The Foundations of Capitalism* (London 1959)
Croner, Fritz, *Die Angestellten in der modernen Gesellschaft* (Cologne 1962)
Crozier, Michel, 'Classes sans conscience ou préfiguration de la société sans classes', *Archives européennes de sociologie* 1, 1960
——'L'ambiguité de la conscience de classe chez les employés et les petits fonctionnaires', *Cahiers internationaux de sociologie* 28, 1955
——*The World of the Office Worker* (Chicago 1971)
Currie, R., and Hartwell, R. M., 'The making of the English working class?', *Economic History Review* 18, 1965
Daheim, Hansjurgen, 'Die Vorstellungen vom Mittelstand', *Kölner Zeitschrift für Soziologie und Sozialpsychologie* 12, 1960
Dahrendorf, Ralf, *Class and Class Conflict in Industrial Society* (Stanford 1959)
——*Conflict After Class*, Noël Buxton lecture (Essex 1967)
——*Essays in the Theory of Society* (London 1968)
——*Marx in Perspektive: die Idee des Gerechten im Denken von Karl Marx* (Hanover 1953)
Delefortrie-Soubeyroux, N., *Les dirigeants de l'industrie française* (Paris 1961)

Dissent, Winter 1972, 'The World of the Blue-Collar Worker'

Djilas, Milovan, *The New Class, an Analysis of the Communist System* (New York 1957)

Dobieszewski, Adolf, *Wybrane problemy teorii i praktyki functionowania partii* (Warsaw 1971)

Dodge, Norman T., *Women in the Soviet Economy* (Baltimore 1966)

Doeringer, Peter B., and Piore, Michael J., *Internal Labour Markets and Manpower Analysis* (Lexington 1971)

Dollard, J. A., *Caste and Class in a Southern Town* (New Haven 1937)

Dolléans, Édouard, *Histoire du mouvement ouvrier* (Paris 1953)

Domhoff, G. William, *Who Rules America?* (New Jersey 1967)

Dore, R. P., *Aspects of Social Change in Modern Japan* (Princeton 1967)

——*City Life in Japan* (London 1958)

Dufty, N. F., *The Sociology of the Blue-Collar Worker* (Leiden 1969)

Durkheim, Émile, *Professional Ethics and Civic Morals* (London 1957)

——*Socialism* (New York 1962)

——*The Division of Labour in Society* (Glencoe 1964)

Duveau, Georges, *La vie ouvrière en France sous le Second Empire* (Paris 1946)

Ehrmann, Henry W., *Organised Business in France* (Princeton 1957)

Engels, Friedrich, *The Condition of the Working Class in England in 1844* (London 1968)

Faunce, William A., *Problems of an Industrial Society* (New York 1968)

Feiwel, George R., *New Currents in Soviet-Type Economies* (Scranton 1968)

Fischer, George, *The Revival of American Socialism* (New York 1971)

——*The Soviet System and Modern Society* (New York 1968)

Fischer-Galati, Stephen, 'East Central Europe: continuity and change', *Journal of International Affairs* **20**, 1966

Florence, P. Sargant, *Ownership, Control and Success of Large Companies* (London 1961)

Fogarty, M. P., 'The white-collar pay structure in Britain', *Economic Journal* **49**, 1959

Friedmann, Georges, *Industrial Society* (Glencoe 1955)

Friedrichs, Günther, *Computer und Angestellte* (Frankfurt 1971)

Friedrichs, Robert, *The Sociology of Sociology* (New York 1970)

Fromm, Erich, *Marx's Concept of Man* (New York 1963)

Geiger, Theodor, *Die Klassengesellschaft im Schmeltztiegel* (Cologne 1949)

——*Die soziale Schichtung des deutschen Volkes* (Stuttgart 1932)

Giddens, Anthony, *Capitalism and Modern Social Theory* (Cambridge 1971)

——'Durkheim's political sociology', *Sociological Review* **19**, 1971

——*Émile Durkheim: Selected Writings* (Cambridge 1972)

——'Elites in the British class structure', *Sociological Review* **20**, 1972

——'Four myths in the history of social thought', *Economy and Society* **1**, 1972

——*Politics and Sociology in the Thought of Max Weber* (London 1972)

Goldthorpe, John, 'Attitudes and behaviour of car assembly workers: a deviant case and a theoretical critique', *British Journal of Sociology* **17**, 1966

Goldthorpe, John, *et al.*, *The Affluent Worker in the Class Structure* (Cambridge 1969)

Gouldner, Alvin, *The Coming Crisis in Western Sociology* (London 1971)

Gramsci, Antonio, *The Modern Prince and Other Writings* (London 1957)

Graubard, R., *A New Europe?* (London 1965)

Gurvitch, Georges, *Industrialisation et technocratie* (Paris 1949)

——*Le concept de classes sociales de Marx à nos jours* (Paris 1954)

Gurvitch, Georges, *La vocation actuelle de la sociologie* (Paris 1950)

Guttsman, W. L., *The British Political Elite* (London 1963)

Habermas, Jürgen, *Antworten auf Herbert Marcuse* (Frankfurt 1968)

——*Theorie und Praxis* (Neuwied 1967)

Halbwachs, Maurice, *The Psychology of Social Class* (London 1958)

Hamilton, Richard, *Affluence and the French Worker in the Fourth Republic* (Princeton 1967)

——'The income difference between skilled and white-collar workers', *British Journal of Sociology* **14**, 1963

Herrnstadt, Rudolf, *Die Entdeckung der Klassen* (Berlin 1965)

HMSO, *Sick Pay Schemes* (London 1964)

Hörning, Karl N., *Der 'neue' Arbeiter* (Frankfurt 1971)

Horton, John, 'Order and conflict theories of social problems as competing ideologies', *American Journal of Sociology* **71**, 1965–6

——'The dehumanisation of anomie and alienation', *British Journal of Sociology* **15**, 1964

Hoselitz, Bert F., *The Role of Small Industry in the Process of Economic Growth* (The Hague 1968)

Hoselitz, Bert F., and Moore, Wilbert E., *Industrialisation and Society* (The Hague 1968)

(The) Industrial Society, *Status and Benefits in Industry* (London 1966)

Ingham, Geoffrey K., 'Plant size: political attitudes and behaviour', *Sociological Review* **17**, 1969

ILO, *Workers' Management in Yugoslavia* (Geneva 1962)

Jackson, J. A., *Social Stratification* (Cambridge 1968)

Jaffe, A. J., and Froomkin, Joseph, *Technology and Jobs* (New York 1968)

Janowitz, Morris, *The Professional Soldier* (New York 1960)

Johnson, Terence J., *Professions and Power* (London 1972)

Kalecki, M., *Essays in the Theory of Economic Fluctuations* (London 1939)

Kassalow, Everett M., *Trade Unions and Industrial Relations: an International Comparison* (New York 1969)

Keller, Suzanne, *Beyond the Ruling Class* (New York 1963)

Kelsall, R. K., *Higher Civil Servants in Britain* (London 1955)

Kerr, Clark, *Marshall, Marx and Modern Times* (Cambridge 1969)

Kerr, Clark, *et al.*, *Industrialism and Industrial Man* (London, 1960)

Kidron, Michael, *Western Capitalism Since the War* (London 1970)

Koch, C., and Senghaas, D., *Texte zur Technokratie-Diskussion* (Frankfurt 1970)

Kornhauser, Arthur, *et al.*, *Industrial Conflict* (New York 1954)

Kostin, L., *Wages in the USSR* (Moscow 1960)

Kubat, Daniel, 'Social Mobility in Czechoslovakia', *American Sociological Review* **28**, 1963

Kubota, Akira, *Higher Civil Servants in Postwar Japan* (Princeton 1969)

Kuper, Leo, *Living in Towns* (London 1953)

La documentation française, 'La courte expérience de conseils ouvriers en Pologne', no. 2453, 26 August 1958

Lane, David, *Politics and Society in the USSR* (London 1970)

——*The End of Inequality?* (London 1971)

Laslett, John H. M., *Labor and the Left* (New York 1970)

Lederer, Emil, *Die Privatangestellten in der modernen Wirtschaftsentwicklung* (Tübingen 1912)

Lederer, Emil, and Marschak, J., 'Der neue Mittelstand', *Grundriss der Sozialökonomik*, vol. 9, 1, 1926

Lefebvre, Henri, *Positions: contre les technocrates* (Paris 1967)

Leggett, John C., *Class, Race, and Labor* (New York 1968)

Lenin, V. I., *What is to be Done?* (Oxford 1963)

Lenski, Gerhard E., *Power and Privilege* (New York 1966)

Levine, Solomon B., *Industrial Relations in Postwar Japan* (Urbana 1958)

Lichtheim, George, *Marxism* (London 1964)

Lipset, Seymour Martin, *The First New Nation* (London 1964)

——*Political Man* (London 1969)

Lockwood, David, 'Some remarks on "The Social System" ', *British Journal of Sociology* 7, 1956

——'Sources of variation in working class images of society', *Sociological Review* 14, 1966

——*The Blackcoated Worker* (London 1958)

Lockwood, William W., *The State and Economic Enterprise in Japan* (Princeton 1965)

Luhmann, Niklaus, *Politische Planung* (Opladen 1971)

Lukács, Georg, *History and Class Consciousness* (London 1971)

Mackenzie, Gavin, 'The economic dimensions of embourgeoisement', *British Journal of Sociology* 18, 1967

Macpherson, C. B., 'Post-liberal democracy?', *Canadian Journal of Economics and Political Science* 30, 1964

——*The Political Theory of Possessive Individualism* (London 1964)

Maki, John M., *Government and Politics in Japan* (London 1962)

Mallet, Serge, *La nouvelle classe ouvrière* (Paris 1963)

Mandel, Ernest, *Marxist Economic Theory* (London 1968)

Mann, Michael, *Consciousness and Action among the Western Working Class* (London 1973)

——'The social cohesion of liberal democracy', *American Sociological Review* 35, 1970

March, James G., *Handbook of Organisations* (Chicago 1965)

Marchal, Jean, and Ducross, Bernard, *The Distribution of National Income* (London 1968)

Marris, R., *The Economic Theory of 'Managerial' Capitalism* (London 1964)

Marshall, T. H., *Class, Citizenship and Social Development* (New York 1964)

——'The welfare state: a sociological interpretation', *Archives européennes de sociologie* 2, 1961

Marx, Karl, *Capital* (vol. 1, Moscow 1958; vol. 3, Moscow 1959)

——*Grundrisse der Kritik der politischen Ökonomie* (Berlin 1953)

——*The Poverty of Philosophy* (London n.d.)

——*Theories of Surplus Value* (London 1969)

——*Werke* (Berlin 1962)

Marx, Karl, and Engels, Friedrich, *Selected Works* (London 1968)

——*The German Ideology* (London 1965)

Matthews, Mervyn, *Class and Society in Soviet Russia* (London 1972)

Meynaud, Jean, *Technocracy* (London 1968)

Michal, Jan M., *Central Planning in Czechoslovakia* (Stanford 1960)

Miliband, Ralph, *The State in Capitalist Society* (London 1969)

Miliband, Ralph, and Saville, John, *The Socialist Register, 1967* (London 1967)

——*The Socialist Register, 1971* (London 1971)

Milić, Vojin, 'General trends in social mobility in Yugoslavia', *Acta Sociologica* 9, 1965

Miller, S. M., 'Comparative social mobility', *Current Sociology* 1, 1960

Mills, C. Wright, *White Collar* (New York 1951)

Mommsen, Wolfgang J., *Max Weber und die deutsche Politik, 1890–1920* (Tübingen 1959)

Moore, Barrington, *The Social Origins of Dictatorship and Democracy* (London 1969)

Mumford, Enid, and Banks, Olive, *The Computer and the Clerk* (London 1967)

Mumford, Lewis, *The Myth of the Machine* (London 1967)

Nakane, Chie, *Japanese Society* (London 1970)

Nettl, J. P., 'Consensus or elite domination: the case of business', *Political Studies* **13**, 1965

Nicolaus, Martin, 'Proletariat and middle class in Marx: Hegelian choreography and the capitalist dialectic', *Studies on the Left* **7**, 1967

Nisbet, Robert, 'The decline and fall of the concept of social class', *Pacific Sociological Review* **2**, 1959

Nordlinger, Eric A., *The Working-Class Tories* (London 1967)

Osipov, G. V., *Industry and Labour in the USSR* (London 1966)

Ossowski, Stanislaw, *Class Structure in the Social Consciousness* (London 1963)

Page, Charles H., *Class and American Sociology* (New York 1969)

Parkin, Frank, *Class Inequality and Political Order* (London 1971)

——'Class stratification in socialist societies', *British Journal of Sociology* **20**, 1969

——'System contradiction and political transformation', *Archives européennes de sociologie* **13**, 1972

Parsons, Talcott, 'Equality and inequality in modern society, or social stratification revisited', *Sociological Inquiry* **40**, 1970

——'On the concept of political power', *Proceedings of the American Philosophical Society* **107**, 1963

Perlman, Selig, *A Theory of the Labor Movement* (New York 1928)

Phelps Brown, E. H., and Hart, P. E., 'The share of wages in the national income', *Economic Journal* **42**, 1952

Pirenne, Henri, 'The stages in the social history of capitalism', *American Historical Review* **19**, 1913–14

Popitz, Heinrich, *et al.*, *Das Gesellschaftsbild des Arbeiters* (Tübingen 1957)

Poulantzas, Nicos, *Pouvoir politique et classes sociales de l'état capitaliste* (Paris 1970)

Reissman, Leonard, and Halstead, Michael N., 'The subject is class', *Sociology and Social Research* **54**, 1970

Renner, Karl, *Wandlungen der modernen Gesellschaft* (Vienna 1953)

Reshetar, John S., *The Soviet Polity* (New York 1971)

Rex, John, *Key Problems in Sociological Theory* (London 1961)

Rhee, H. A., *Office Automation in Social Perspective* (Oxford 1968)

Ricardo, David, *Letters of David Ricardo to John Ramsey McCulloch* (New York 1895)

Rico, Leonard, *The Advance against Paperwork* (Ann Arbor 1967)

Robinson, Joan, *An Essay on Marxian Economics* (London 1966)

Routh, Guy, *Occupation and Pay in Great Britain, 1906–60* (Cambridge 1965)

Saint-Simon, Henri de, *La physiologie sociale* (Paris 1965)

Sartori, Giovanni, 'Technological forecasting and politics', *Survey* **16**, 1971

Schonfield, Andrew, *Modern Capitalism* (London 1969)

Schumpeter, Joseph, *Imperialism, Social Classes* (Cleveland 1961)

Scott, W. H., *Office Automation* (OECD 1965)

Seton-Watson, Hugh, *East European Revolution* (London 1955)

Sheldon, Eleanor, and Moore, Wilbert, *Indicators of Social Change* (New York 1968)

Shepard, Jon M., *Automation and Alienation* (Cambridge, Mass. 1971)

Shostak, Arthur B., and Gomberg, William, *Blue-Collar World* (Englewood Cliffs 1965)

Sombart, Werner, *Warum gibt es in den Vereinigten Staaten keinen Sozialismus?* (Tübingen 1906)

Sorokin, Pitrim A., 'Mutual convergence of the United States and the USSR to the mixed sociocultural type', *International Journal of Comparative Sociology* **1**, 1960

——*Russia and the United States* (London 1950)

Speier, Hans, *Social Order and the Risks of War* (Cambridge 1969)

Spulber, Nicolas, *The Economies of Communist Eastern Europe* (New York 1957)

Stammler, Otto, *Max Weber and Sociology Today* (Oxford 1971)

Strmiska, Zdenek, and Varakova, Blanka, 'La stratification sociale de la société socialiste', *Revue française de sociologie* **13**, 1972

Sturmthal, Adolf, *White-Collar Trade Unions* (Urbana 1966)

——*Workers' Councils* (Cambridge 1964)

Sweezy, Paul, *et al.*, *The Transition from Feudalism to Capitalism* (London 1954)

Szczepánski, J., *Empirical Sociology in Poland* (Warsaw 1966)

Taira, Koji, *Economic Development and the Labour Market in Japan* (New York 1970)

Tawney, R. H., *Religion and the Rise of Capitalism* (London 1948)

The Problems of Peace and Socialism **9**, 1970

Thompson, E. P., *The Making of the English Working Class* (London 1963)

Touraine, Alain, *La conscience ouvrière* (Paris 1966)

——*La société post-industrielle* (Paris 1969)

——*Sociologie de l'action* (Paris 1965)

——*The May Movement* (New York 1971)

Tropp, Asher, *The School Teachers* (London 1957)

Turner, Arthur N., and Lawrence, Paul R., *Industrial Jobs and the Worker* (Boston 1965)

Ullmann, Walter, *The Individual and Society in the Middle Ages* (Baltimore 1966)

US Department of Labor, *Adjustments to the Introduction of Office Automation,* Bulletin no. 1276 (Washington 1960)

——'Blue-Collar/White-Collar Pay Trends', *Monthly Labor Review* (June 1971)

Vogel, Ezra F., *Japan's New Middle Class* (Berkeley 1963)

Volkov, J., *Literaturnaya Gazieta*, no. 19 (Moscow June 1972)

Warner, W. L., *Social Class in America* (Chicago 1949)

Warner, W. L., and Lunt, P. S., *The Social Life of a Modern Community* (New Haven 1941)

Warren, Bill, 'Capitalist planning and the State', *New Left Review* **72**, 1972

Weber, Max, *Economy and Society* (New York 1968)

——*General Economic History* (New York 1961)

——*The Methodology of the Social Sciences* (Glencoe 1949)

Wedderburn, Dorothy, and Crompton, Rosemary, *Workers' Attitudes and Technology* (Cambridge 1972)

Weinstein, James, *The Decline of Socialism in America, 1912–25* (New York 1967)

Wesolowski, W., *Struktura i dynamika spoleczeństwa polskiego* (Warsaw 1970)

Wiatr, Jerzy J., *Studies in Polish Political System* (Warsaw 1967)

Wiles, P. J. D., and Markowski, Stefan, 'Income distribution under communism and capitalism', *Soviet Studies* **22**, 1970–1

Wiles, Peter, 'A comment on Bell', *Survey* **16**, 1971

Willener, Alfred, *Images de la société et classes sociales* (Berne 1957)

Wolfe, Bertram D., *An Ideology in Power* (New York 1969)

Woodward, Joan, *Industrial Organisation: Theory and Practice* (London 1965)

Wrangel, Georg von, *Wird der Ostblock kapitalistisch?* (Munich 1966)

Yoshino, M., *Japan's Managerial System* (Cambridge, Mass. 1968)

Zauberman, Alfred, *Industrial Progress in Poland, Czechoslovakia, and East Germany* (London 1964)

Zollschan, G. R., and Hirsch, W., *Explorations in Social Change* (London 1964)

INDEX

ACADEMIC SOCIOLOGY, 16-17, 18, 70
acquisition classes (*Erwerbsklassen*), 42, 43, 45, 47, 48, 75, 76, 79, 100, 101, 104
administrative workers, 96, 108, 128; *see also* white-collar workers
'advanced society', 147, 154-5; definition of, 142
'adventurers' capitalism', 139
affluence, 215-16, 220-1
agriculture, agricultural workers, 62, 95, 117, 155, 178, 211, 212, 226, 246; *see also* land-owning elite groups
alienation, 26, 46, 88, 94, 102, 129-30, 131, 136, 138, 204-5, 210, 214, 257, 277, 278
Althusser, Louis, 212
anarchism, anarcho-syndicalism, 208, 212, 213, 293
Ancient Rome, 26, 31, 44
aristocracy, *see* upper class
Aron, Raymond, 10, 98, 105; industrial society theories of, 59-63; and critique of, 69, 76-8
assembly-line, 203, 204, 205, 206
'authoritative allocation of work', 82, 133
authority, 206, 268; views of Dahrendorf, 57-9, 72-3, 78, 89, 100, 102, 105, 187, 188; of Aron, 63; of Ossowski, 64, 67-8; of Marx, 89-90; as source of class structuration, 108-9; 'new middle class' and, 182, 183, 185, 187-8; influence on working-class attitudes, 205; in

state socialist societies, 233-5, 268; capitalist and state socialist industrial authority compared, 268; *see also* power
autocratic power, 122, 123, 175
automation, 89, 90, 193, 194, 196

BALDWIN, STANLEY, 174
balkanisation, 191
Baltzell, Digby, 167
Baran, Paul A, 160, 172
Bauer, Bruno, 38
Bell, Daniel, 21, 255-9, 260, 263
Bendix, Reinhardt, 157, 181, 202
Berle, Adolf A., 159, 160
Bernstein, Eduard, 14, 178
Besitzklassen, see ownership classes
Birnbaum, Norman, 13
Bismarck, Count Otto von, 49, 125, 157
black/coloured workers, *see* 'underclass'
Blauner, Robert, 203-4
blue-collar labour, *see* manual workers
Böhm-Bawerk, E. von, 128
'Bonapartism', Marx's study of, 118, 125
Bottomore, T. B., 69
Boulding, Kenneth, 225
bourgeoisie, bourgeois society, 79, 164, 194; Marx's views, 30, 31, 32, 38, 39, 52, 83, 97, 98, 101, 216; German, 49-50; Aron's view, 62; conflict between proletariat and, 85, 92, 93, and between nobility, 92; class consciousness of, 77, 93; and conflicts within,